Organ Shortage: Ethics, Law and Pragmatism

Organ shortage is an ongoing problem in many countries. The needless death and suffering which have resulted necessitate an investigation into potential solutions. This examination of contemporary ethical means, both practical and policy-oriented, of reducing the shortfall in organs draws on the experiences of a range of countries. The authors focus on the resolution and negotiation of ethical conflict, examine systems approaches such as the 'Spanish Model' and the US Breakthrough Collaboratives, evaluate policy proposals relating to incentives, presumed consent and modifications regarding end-of-life care, and examine the greatly increased use of (non-heart-beating) donors suffering circulatory death, as well as living donors. The proposed strategies and solutions are capable not only of resolving the UK's own organ-shortage crisis, but of being implemented in other countries grappling with how to address the growing gap between supply and demand for organs.

Dr Anne-Maree Farrell is Senior Lecturer in Law at the Centre for Social Ethics and Policy and the Institute for Science Ethics and Innovation, School of Law, University of Manchester.

Professor David Price is Professor of Medical Law at Leicester De Montfort Law School, De Montfort University.

Dr Muireann Quigley is Lecturer in Bioethics at the Centre for Social Ethics and Policy and the Institute for Science Ethics and Innovation, School of Law, University of Manchester.

Cambridge Law, Medicine and Ethics

This series of books was founded by Cambridge University Press with Alexander McCall Smith as its first editor in 2003. It focuses on the law's complex and troubled relationship with medicine across both the developed and the developing world. In the past twenty years, we have seen in many countries increasing resort to the courts by dissatisfied patients and a growing use of the courts to attempt to resolve intractable ethical dilemmas. At the same time, legislatures across the world have struggled to address the questions posed by both the successes and the failures of modern medicine, while international organisations such as the WHO and UNESCO now regularly address issues of medical law.

It follows that we would expect ethical and policy questions to be integral to the analysis of the legal issues discussed in this series. The series responds to the high profile of medical law in universities, in legal and medical practice, as well as in public and political affairs. We seek to reflect the evidence that many major health-related policy debates in the UK, Europe and the international community over the past two decades have involved a strong medical law dimension. Organ retention, embryonic stem cell research, physician assisted suicide and the allocation of resources to fund healthcare are but a few examples among many. The emphasis of this series is thus on matters of public concern and/or practical significance. We look for books that could make a difference to the development of medical law and enhance the role of medico-legal debate in policy circles. That is not to say that we lack interest in the important theoretical dimensions of the subject, but we aim to ensure that theoretical debate is grounded in the realities of how the law does and should interact with medicine and healthcare.

General Editors
Professor Margaret Brazier,   *University of Manchester,*
Professor Graeme Laurie,   *University of Edinburgh*

Editorial Advisory Board
Professor Richard Ashcroft,   *Queen Mary, University of London,*
Professor Martin Bobrow,   *University of Cambridge,*
Dr Alexander Morgan Capron,   *Director, Ethics and Health, World Health Organization, Geneva,*
Professor Jim Childress,   *University of Virginia,*
Professor Ruth Chadwick,   *Cardiff Law School,*
Dame Ruth Deech,   *University of Oxford,*
Professor John Keown,   *Georgetown University, Washington, DC,*
Dr Kathy Liddell,   *University of Cambridge,*
Professor Alexander McCall Smith,   *University of Edinburgh,*
Professor Dr Mónica Navarro-Michel,   *University of Barcelona*
Marcus Radetzki, Marian Radetzki and Niklas Juth   *Genes and Insurance: Ethical, Legal and Economic Issues*

Organ Shortage

Ethics, Law and Pragmatism

Anne-Maree Farrell,

David Price

and

Muireann Quigley

CAMBRIDGE
UNIVERSITY PRESS

CAMBRIDGE UNIVERSITY PRESS
Cambridge, New York, Melbourne, Madrid, Cape Town,
Singapore, São Paulo, Delhi, Tokyo, Mexico City

Cambridge University Press
The Edinburgh Building, Cambridge CB2 8RU, UK

Published in the United States of America by Cambridge University Press,
New York

www.cambridge.org
Information on this title: www.cambridge.org/9780521198998

© Cambridge University Press 2011

First published 2011

Printed in the United Kingdom at the University Press, Cambridge

A catalogue record for this publication is available from the British Library

Library of Congress Cataloguing in Publication data
Organ shortage : ethics, law, and pragmatism / [edited by] Anne-Maree Farrell,
David Price, and Muireann Quigley.
    p.   cm. – (Cambridge law, medicine, and ethics) Includes bibliographical
references and index.
ISBN 978-0-521-19899-8
1. Organ donors – Supply and demand.   I. Farrell, Anne-Maree, 1964–
II. Price, David P. T.   III. Quigley, Muireann.   IV. Title.   V. Series.
RD129.5.O748   2011
362.19′795–dc22
                                                                    2010030513
ISBN 978-0-521-19899-8 Hardback

Contents

Figures

Tables

Contributors

MARGARET BRAZIER is Professor of Law at the Centre for Social Ethics and Policy and the Institute for Science Ethics and Innovation at the University of Manchester. She is a Fellow of the UK Academy of Medical Sciences and is currently Editor-in-Chief of the *Medical Law Review*. Her research expertise lies in the area of medical jurisprudence, particularly involving issues relating to consent and autonomy, reproductive medicine, the role of the criminal law in healthcare and the donation and use of body parts. Recent publications include: 'Respecting the living means respecting the dead too', *Oxford Journal of Legal Studies*, 28 (2008) and 'Human(s) (as) medicine(s)' in *First Do No Harm: Law and Ethics in Health Care* (2006).

JOHN COGGON is Research Fellow in the Institute for Science Ethics and Innovation at the University of Manchester. He is an International Associate Editor of the *Journal of Bioethical Inquiry* and a member of the ethics committee of the *British Medical Journal*. His research expertise lies broadly within the area of health law and ethics, with particular interests in legitimate decision-making, autonomy, best interests, end-of-life issues, analysis and application of theoretical constructs, public health law and ethics. Recent publications include: 'Doing what's best: organ donation and intensive care' in *Ethics and Law in Critical Care* (2010) and 'Best interests and potential organ donors', *British Medical Journal*, 336 (2008).

ANTONIA CRONIN is a Consultant Nephrologist at the NIHR Biomedical Research Centre, Guy's and St. Thomas' NHS Foundation Trust, and Honorary Clinical Research Consultant, MRC Centre for Transplantation, King's College London. She is also currently Chair of the Ethics Committee of the British Transplantation Society and Honorary Research Fellow, Institute for Science Ethics and Innovation, University of Manchester. Her research interests focus on ethico-legal issues involved in tissue and organ donation, clinical transplantation, and basic scientific inquiry in the field of transplant immunobiology. Recent publications include: 'Directed and conditional deceased organ donations: laws and misconceptions', *Medical Law Review*, 18 (2010); 'Editorial: Requested allocation of a deceased donor organ: laws and misconceptions', *Journal of Medical Ethics*, 36 (2010); and 'Directed organ donation: is the donor the owner?', *Journal of Clinical Ethics*, 3 (2008).

PHIL DYER is a Consultant Clinical Scientist at the Scottish National Blood Transfusion Service, Royal Infirmary of Edinburgh, and Honorary Professor in Transplantation Science, University of Manchester. He is a Fellow of the Royal College of Pathologists, and co-founded the British Society for Histocompatibility and Immunogenetics. Professor Dyer was President of the British Transplantation Society from 2002 to 2005. He has served on a number of committees, including the ethics committee of the Royal College of Pathologists, and was a member of the Human Tissue Working Group on the Human Tissue Act from 2004 to 2005. His research interests include organ and stem cell transplantation, the outcomes of clinical transplantation, pharmacoimmunogenetics, and organ allocation. He has published widely in the areas of organ and tissue transplantation.

ANNE-MAREE FARRELL is Senior Lecturer in Law at the Centre for Social Ethics and Policy and the Institute for Science Ethics and Innovation, University of Manchester. Dr Farrell's research expertise lies broadly within the area of health law, with a particular interest in governance and regulation of human material such as organs, tissue and blood at European and global levels. Recent publications include: 'Adding value? EU governance of organ donation and transplantation', *European Journal of Health Law*, 17 (2010) and 'Time for change: the need for a pragmatic approach to addressing organ shortage in the UK', *Clinical Ethics*, 3 (2008).

BOBBIE FARSIDES is Professor of Clinical and Biomedical Ethics at Brighton and Sussex Medical School, University of Sussex, and Visiting Professor at the Centre for Biomedicine and Social Science, King's College London. She is a Member of the UK Donation Ethics Committee, and was a Member of the UK Organ Donation Taskforce from 2008 to 2009 and Specialist Advisor to the House of Lords European Sub-Committee which conducted an inquiry into policy action on organ donation and transplantation at EU level. Her research interests are broadly focused on examining the experiences of healthcare practitioners and scientists operating in ethically contested areas of modern biomedicine. She was the lead author for the UK Organ Donation Taskforce's Ethics Sub-Group's Report: *The Potential Impact of an Opt Out System for Organ Donation in the UK* (2008).

ALEXANDRA K. GLAZIER is Vice-President and General Counsel of the New England Organ Bank, and Adjunct Professor of Law at Boston University. She is also a Member of the US Department of Health and Human Services Advisory Committee for Organ Transplantation and the Vice-Chair of the Ethics Committee, United Network for Organ Sharing (UNOS). Her research interests are focused on legal, policy and legislative issues related to organ donation and transplantation. Recent publications include: 'Regulatory face-off: what agency should oversee face transplantation?', *American Journal of Transplantation*, 8 (2008), and 'Organ donation and dual advocacy', *New England Journal of Medicine*, 358 (2008).

JOHN HARRIS is Lord Alliance Professor of Bioethics and Director of the Institute for Science, Ethics and Innovation, University of Manchester. He is a Fellow of the UK Academy of Medical Sciences, and a Member of both the UK Human Genetics Commission and the Ethics Committee of the British Medical Association. He was one of the founding Directors of the International Association of Bioethics and is currently Editor-in-Chief of the *Journal of Medical Ethics*. His research expertise and interests include ethics and policy dimensions of genetics, biotechnology, organ donation and transplantation, embryo experimentation, stem cells, genetic and other enhancement and disability issues. Recent publications include: 'Time to move to presumed consent for organ donation', *British Medical Journal*, 340 (2010) and 'Organ procurement – dead interests, living needs', *Journal of Medical Ethics*, 29 (2003).

MAIRI LEVITT is Head of the Department of Philosophy at Lancaster University. She has an academic and research background in social science and religious studies. Since 1993 she has been engaged in multi-disciplinary research on the ethical and social implications of genetics and medical technologies. Her research projects, in a variety of subject areas, have involved public engagement work with the general public, young people and stakeholders, and a critical perspective on the way health policy and information is communicated. Her most recent research has included children and the national DNA database, 'criminal genes' and public policy, and perspectives on the roles of nature and nurture in human development.

TRACY LONG-SUTEHALL is Senior Research Fellow in the School of Health Sciences, University of Southampton. Her research focuses on a range of issues concerning organ donation and transplantation, and currently involves examining the reasons why family members decline tissue donation, and how nurses facilitate end-of-life care in critical care settings. Recent publications include: 'What does a diagnosis of brain death mean to family members approached about organ donation: a review of the literature', *Progress in Transplantation*, 18 (2008), and 'Conflict rationalization: how family members cope with a diagnosis of brain stem death', *Social Science & Medicine*, 67 (2008).

SALLA LÖTJÖNEN is Senior Advisor, Legislative Affairs, Ministry of Justice, Helsinki, and Adjunct Lecturer in Medical and Biolaw at the University of Helsinki. Dr Lötjönen's research expertise is in the area of medical law, medical research, research ethics and family law. Relevant publications include: 'Biopankit' ('Biobanks') in *Bio-oikeus lääketieteessä* (*Biolaw in Medicine*) (2006) and 'Ihmisperäisten biologisten näytteiden käyttö lääketieteellisessä tutkimuksessa' ('The Use of Biological Samples in Medical Research'), *Lakimies* (2005).

SHEELAGH MCGUINNESS is Lecturer in Ethics and Law at the Centre for Professional Ethics, Keele University. Her research expertise lies in the inter-relationship between medical law, bioethics and public policy. She has particular research interests in human reproduction, religious beliefs and medical law, transgender medicine, organ donation, and research ethics. Recent publications include: 'Respecting the living means respecting the dead too', *Oxford Journal of Legal Studies*, 28 (2008).

PAUL MURPHY is Consultant in Neuroanaesthesia and Critical Care at The General Infirmary, Leeds. He is also National Clinical Lead for Organ Donation, NHS Blood and Transplant. His research interests focus on the epidemiology of deceased organ donation in the UK, ethico-legal issues involved in deceased organ donation and donation after cardiac death. Recent publications include: 'Controlled non-heart beating organ donation: neither the whole solution nor a step too far', *Anaesthesia*, 63 (2008), and 'Best interests and potential organ donors', *British Medical Journal*, 336 (2008).

MÓNICA NAVARRO-MICHEL is Reader in Law at the University of Barcelona. Dr Navarro-Michel's research expertise is in the area of medical law, with a particular focus on issues of consent, organ transplantation and assisted reproduction. Most of her research has been published in Spanish; recent English-language publications include 'The organs crisis and the Spanish model: theoretical versus pragmatic considerations', *Journal of Medical Ethics*, 34 (2008).

NILS H. PERSSON is Associate Professor and Senior Surgeon in the Department of Nephrology and Transplantation, Skåne University Hospital, Malmö. His research and professional expertise is in organ donation and kidney transplantation, with a particular focus on expanded/marginal donors and allocation strategies. Publications include articles on the potential for organ donation in Sweden in relation to ICU deaths, marginal donors and informed consent in kidney transplantation, and public perceptions of xenotransplantation.

DAVID PRICE is Professor of Medical Law at De Montfort University, Leicester. His research expertise lies within the areas of the use of human tissue for medical and scientific applications, physician-assisted dying and the withholding and withdrawal of life-sustaining medical treatment. He was a Member of the UK Organ Donation Taskforce from 2008 to 2009 and is currently a Member of the Nuffield Council on Bioethics Working Party on Human Bodies in Medicine and Research. Recent publications include *Human Tissue for Transplantation and Research: A Model Legal and Ethical Framework*, (Cambridge University Press, 2009) and he was Editor of *Organ and Tissue Transplantation* (2006) which includes a substantial Introduction by him.

MUIREANN QUIGLEY is Lecturer in Bioethics at the Centre for Social Ethics and Policy and the Institute for Science Ethics and Innovation at the University of Manchester. Her research focuses on the ethics of organ transplantation, reproduction and reproductive technologies, justice and responsibility in healthcare, and stem cells and rights (specifically property rights in the human body and its parts). Recent publications include: 'Best interests and potential organ donors', *British Medical Journal*, 336 (2008), and 'The organs crisis and the Spanish model: theoretical versus pragmatic considerations', *Journal of Medical Ethics*, 34 (2008).

GURCH RANDHAWA is Professor of Diversity in Public Health and Director of the Institute for Health Research, University of Bedfordshire. He was a member of the UK Department of Health's Organ Donation Taskforce from 2008 to 2009. As part of the work of the Taskforce, he was Chair of the Social and Cultural Working Group. He is currently Chair of the Department of Health's End of Life Care in Advanced Kidney Disease project. He is also Chair of the NHS Luton; Member of the UK Donation Ethics Committee; and a Non-Executive

Director of the Human Tissue Authority. Professor Randhawa's research expertise lies in the examination of diabetes, kidney disease, transplantation and end-of-life care amongst minority ethnic groups. Key publications in the area of organ donation and transplantation include: 'Faith leaders united in their support for organ donation – findings from the Organ Donation Taskforce's study of attitudes of UK faith and belief group leaders to an opt-out system', *Transplant International*, 23 (2010); and 'Utilising faith communities in the UK to promote the organ donation debate: the views of UK faith leaders', *Journal of Diversity in Health and Care*, 7 (2010).

DIEGO S. SILVA is a Doctoral Candidate at the Dalla Lana School of Public Health, University of Toronto, and a member of the Collaborative Program in Bioethics at the Joint Centre for Bioethics. His research interests focus on organ donation and transplantation, public health and mental health, and include the moral implications of policy and practice. Recent publications include: 'Incentives for organ donation: Israel's novel approach', *Lancet*, 375 (2010) and 'Of altruists and egoists: living anonymous donors' in *Organ Transplantation: Ethical, Legal and Psychosocial Aspects* (2008).

MAGI SQUE is Professor of Clinical Practice and Innovation at the School of Health and Wellbeing, Centre for Health and Social Care Improvement, University of Wolverhampton and The Royal Wolverhampton NHS Hospitals Trust. She currently acts as an advisor to the UK Department of Health on organ donation, and is a Member of its Research Commissioning Project Group. Her other research interests are focused on bereavement, life-limiting illness, social constructions and concepts of the dying and the dead body, the role of relatives and significant others in illness (particularly life-limiting trajectories), and the nature and quality of support given to them. She is currently International Chair of the European Platform's (ELPAT) Deceased Donation Working Group based at Erasmus University Medical Center. Recent publications include: *Organ and Tissue Donation: an Evidence Base for Practice* (2007) and 'Why relatives do not donate organs for transplants: "sacrifice" or "gift of life"?', *Journal of Advanced Nursing*, 61 (2008).

LINDA WRIGHT is Director of Bioethics at the University Health Network in Toronto. She is also Assistant Professor in the Department of Surgery and a member of the Joint Centre for Bioethics at the University of Toronto. Her research expertise lies in examining ethical issues that arise in the area of organ donation and transplantation, in particular those relating to living organ donors. Recent publications include: 'Incentives for organ donation: Israel's novel approach', *Lancet*, 375 (2010) and 'Living anonymous liver donation: case report and ethical justification, *American Journal of Transplantation*, 7 (2007).

Acknowledgements

This book has its origins in a five-part seminar series, *Transplantation and the Organ Deficit in the UK: Pragmatic Solutions to Ethical Controversy*, which was funded by the UK Economic and Social Research Council (ESRC) between 2006 and 2008 (RES-451-25-4341), and we gratefully acknowledge its support. The seminar series brought together a multi-disciplinary and international group of ethicists, lawyers, clinicians, scientists, sociologists and patient advocates who all had interests and expertise in the field of organ donation and transplantation. All participants in the seminar series were particularly interested in finding a principled and pragmatic way forward in order to address the problems created by the ongoing shortage of organs both in the UK and beyond. It proved to be a highly stimulating series of seminars, which challenged participants to examine alternative and creative ways in which this issue could be addressed. The seminar series coincided with a period of heightened policy activity and reform of organ donation and transplantation processes at both UK and EU levels, and several participants also consulted and/or advised on such processes. We would like to thank the participants in the seminar series, many of whom are contributors to this book, for their thought-provoking insights and lively exchange of ideas, as well as for the rapport that developed between us as a result.

We would also like to acknowledge the support we have received from Cambridge University Press in the preparation and completion of the book, in particular from Finola O'Sullivan, Brenda Burke, Richard Woodham and Jo Breeze – it has been much appreciated.

Anne-Maree Farrell would like to thank Ron, Tom and the Peek-Farrell family for their support and patience during the completion of this project. David Price wishes to offer his heartfelt thanks to Arlene. Muireann Quigley would like to thank Brian Willis, who always supports and believes in her.

The editors would like to especially thank Margot Brazier for her encouragement and support in relation to the seminar series, as well as in the preparation of this book.

Abbreviations

ABOi	ABO blood group incompatible
ACE	angiotensin converting enzyme
AIDS	acquired immune deficiency syndrome
AIT	antibody incompatible living donor renal transplantation
ATR	angiotensin receptor blockers
BBSRC	Biotechnology and Biological Sciences Research Council (UK)
BME	black and minority ethnic
CCDT	Canadian Council for Donation and Transplantation
DCD	donation after cardiac death
DMV	Department of Motor Vehicles (USA)
DSA	donor specific antibody
ECD	expanded criteria donor
ESRF	end-stage renal failure
EU	European Union
HIV	human immunodeficiency virus
HLA	human leukocyte antigen
HLAi	human leukocyte antigen incompatible
HLH	haemophagocytic lymphohistiocytosis
HTA	Human Tissue Authority (UK)
ICU	intensive care unit
KPD	kidney paired donation
LDT	living donor organ transplantation
MHC	major histocompatibility complex
NCCUSL	National Conference of Commissioners of Uniform State Laws (USA)
NDFC	National Donor Family Council (USA)
NHBD	non-heart-beating donors
NHS	National Health Service (UK)
NHSBT	National Health Service Blood and Transplant (UK)

NHSBT-ODT	National Health Service Blood and Transplant – Organ Donation and Transplantation Directorate (UK)
NICE	National Institute for Health and Clinical Excellence (UK)
NOTA	National Organ Transplant Act (USA)
NSF	National Service Framework (UK)
OMC	Open Method of Co-ordination (EU)
ONT	Organización Nacional de Trasplantes (Spain)
OPO	Organ Procurement Organization (USA)
PDA	Potential Donor Audit (UK)
PGD	pre-implantation genetic diagnosis
PMP	per million population
QOF	Quality and Outcomes Framework (UK)
RCIDT	Red/Consejo Iberoamericano de Donación y Trasplante (Latin America)
RRT	renal replacement therapy
UAGA	Uniform Anatomical Gift Act (USA)
UK	United Kingdom
USA	United States
WHO	World Health Organization

Table of cases

England and Wales

Felthouse v. Bindley (1862) CB(NS) 869
R v. Sussex Justices, ex parte McCarthy [1924] 1 KB 256
Cassidy v. Ministry of Health [1951] 2 KB 343
Barnett v. Chelsea & Kensington Hospital Management Committee [1969]
    1 QB 428
Collins v. Wilcock [1984] 1 WLR 1172, 1178 (CA)
Re F (mental patient: sterilisation) [1990] 2 AC 1
Re A (A Minor) [1992] 3 Med LR 303
Airedale NHS Trust v. Bland [1993] AC 789
Re Y (mental patient: bone marrow donation) [1997] 2 WLR 556
Capital & Counties plc v. Hampshire County Council [1997] QB 1004
Re A (medical sterilisation: male sterilisation) [2000] 1 FCR 193
Re S (adult patient: sterilisation) [2001] Fam 15
Kent v. Griffiths [2001] QB 36
R (on the application of N) v. M and others [2003] 1 WLR 562
Burke v. General Medical Council [2005] EWCA Civ 1003
Ahsan v. University Hospitals of Leicester NHS Trust [2007] PIQR P19

United States

Nicoletta v. Rochester Eye & Human Parts Bank, Inc., 519 NYS 2d 928
    (1987)
Kelly-Nevils v. Detroit Receiving Hosp., 526 NW 2d 15 (Mich. App. 1995)
Ramirez v. Health Partners of Southern Arizona, 972 P 2d 658 (Ariz. App.
    1999)
Schembre v. Mid America Transplant Ass'n, 135 SW 3d 527 (Mo. App.
    2004)
Carey v. New England Organ Bank, Inc., 843 NE 2d 1070 (Mass. 2006)
Montalto et al. v. Stoff et al., MA Sup. Ct. CA NO. 03-00557 (2007)

Table of legislation

Canada

The Constitution Act, 1867 30 & 31 Victoria, c. 3. (UK)
Human Tissue Gift Act, R.S.S. 1978
Criminal Code, R.S.C. 1985
Canada Health Act, R.S.C. 1985
Food and Drug Act, R.S.C. 1985
Human Tissue Gift Act, C.C.S.M. 1987
Human Tissue Act, R.S.N.W.T. 1988
Human Tissue Donation Act, R.S.P.E.I. 1988
Human Tissue Gift Act, R.S.N.S. 1989
Human Tissue Act, R.S.N.L. 1990
Trillium Gift of Life Network Act, R.S.O. 1990
Civil Code of Quebec, S.Q. 1991
Human Tissue Gift Act, R.S.B.C. 1996
Human Tissue Gift Act, R.S.A. 2000
Human Tissue Gift Act, R.S.Y. 2002
Human Tissue Gift Act, S.N.B. 2004

Council of Europe

Additional Protocol to the Convention on Human Rights and Biomedicine, on Transplantation of Organs and Tissues of Human Origin, Strasbourg, 24 January 2002

European Union

Directive 2002/98/EC of the European Parliament and of the Council of 27 January 2003 setting standards of quality and safety for the collection, testing, processing, storage and distribution of human blood and blood components and amending Directive 2001/83/EC (OJ L 33, 8 February 2003)

Directive 2004/23/EC of the European Parliament and of the Council of 31 March 2004 on setting standards of quality and safety for the donation, procurement, testing, processing, preservation, storage and distribution of human tissues and cells (OJ L 102, 7 April 2004)

Directive 2010/45/EU of the European Parliament and of the Council of 7 July 2010 on standards of quality and safety of human organs intended for transplantation (OJ L 207, 6 August 2010)

Italy

Law 91/1999, 1 April, on the retrieval and transplantation of organs and tissues (*Legge 91/1999, 1 Aprile, di disposizioni in materia di prelievi e di trapianti di organi e di tessuti*)

Nordic countries

Act relating to Transplantation, Hospital Autopsies and the Donation of Bodies (*Lov om transplantasjon, sykehusobduksjon og avgivelse av lik m.m.*), Nr. 6 of Statutes, 9 February 1973

Act on Transplantation (*Lag om transplantation m.m.*), Nr. 831 of Statutes, 8 June 1995

Regulations and General Guidelines by the Swedish National Board of Health and Welfare (*Socialstyrelsens föreskrifter och allmänna råd*) 1997:4, Removal of organs and tissue for organ transplantation and other medical purposes (*Organ-och vävnadstagning för transplantation eller för annat medicinskt ändamål*)

Governmental Bill to amend the Act on the Medical Use of Human Organs and Tissues Nr. 93 of 2000

Health Act (*Sundhedsloven*), Nr. 546 of Statutes, 24 June 2005, Part IV, Chapter 12

Governmental Bill to amend the Act on the Medical Use of Human Organs and Tissues Nr. 276 of 2009

Act on the Medical Use of Human Organs and Tissues (*Laki ihmisen elimien ja kudoksien lääketieteellisestä käytöstä*) Nr. 101 of Statutes, 2 February 2001 (as amended up until June 2010)

Spain

Law 30/1979, 27 October, on organ extraction and transplant (*Ley 30/1979, de 27 de octubre, sobre extracción y trasplante de órganos*)

Royal Decree 426/1980, 22 February, on organ extraction and transplant (*Real Decreto 426/1980, de 22 de febrero, sobre extracción y trasplantes de órganos*) (abolished by Royal Decree 2070/1999)

Law 29/1980, 21 June, on clinical autopsies (*Ley 29/1980, de 21 de junio, por la que se regulan las autopsias clínicas*)

Royal Decree 2230/1982, 18 June, on clinical autopsies (*Real Decreto 2230/1982, de 18 de junio, por el que se regulan las autopsias clínicas*)

Law 35/1988, 22 November, on human assisted reproduction techniques (*Ley 35/1988, de 22 de noviembre, de regulación de las técnicas de reproducción asistida humana*) (abolished by Law 14/2006)

Law 42/1988, 28 December, on donation and use of human embryos and foetuses, or their cells, tissues and organs (*Ley 42/1988, de 28 de diciembre, de donación y utilización de embriones y fetos humanos o de sus células, tejidos u órganos*) (abolished by Law 14/2007)

Royal Decree 2070/1999, 30 December, which regulates the activities of procurement and clinical use of human organs and territorial co-ordination in matters of organ and tissue donation and transplantation (*Real Decreto 2070/1999, de 30 de diciembre, por el que se regulan las actividades de obtención y utilización clínica de órganos humanos y la coordinación territorial en materia de donación y trasplante de órganos y tejidos*)

Civil Law of Criminal Procedure, 2000 (*Ley de Enjuiciamiento* Civil, 2000)

Law 41/2002, 14 November, on patients' autonomy, and rights and obligations with regard to information and documentation (*Ley 41/2002, de 14 de noviembre, básica reguladora de la autonomía del paciente y de derechos y obligaciones en materia de información y documentación básica*)

Royal Decree 1088/2005, 16 September, on the technical requirements and necessary conditions for blood donation and regulation of blood transfusion centres and services (*Real Decreto 1088/2005, de 16 de septiembre, por el que se establecen los requisitos técnicos y condiciones mínimas de la hemodonación y de los centros y servicios de transfusión*)

Law 14/2006, 26 May, on human assisted reproduction techniques (*Ley 14/2006, de 26 de mayo, reguladora de las técnicas de reproducción asistida humana*)

Royal Decree 1301/2006, 10 November, which establishes rules for quality and security for donation, obtaining, evaluating, processing, preserving, storing and distributing human cells and tissues, and rules on co-ordination and functioning for human use (*Real Decreto 1301/2006, de 10 de noviembre, por el que se establecen las normas de calidad y seguridad para la donación, la obtención, la evaluación, el procesamiento, la preservación, el almacenamiento y la distribución de células y tejidos humanos*

Part I

Setting the scene

1 A principled and pragmatic approach to organ shortage

Anne-Maree Farrell, David Price and Muireann Quigley

Ethical and legal issues concerning organ donation and transplantation have been the subject of much controversy and debate in many countries, especially over the last twenty years.[1] Technological developments in the field have opened up the possibility of transplanting an increasing number of human organs to those in need. The number of organs available for transplantation, however, has not kept pace with such developments. In the United Kingdom (UK) alone, the gap is widening between the number of persons on the national waiting list for organs and the number of available organs, with 7,980 persons on the active national waiting list as of the end of the financial year 2009–10 and approximately 1,000 people dying each year for want of a solid organ transplant.[2] Not only are transplant waiting times increasing in general (primarily for kidneys), but rates of development of end-stage organ failure and disease are continuing to increase, most notably amongst black and ethnic minority populations.

Whilst the number of solid organ transplants performed in the UK continues to rise, this masks two crucial and revealing trends. First, annually the number of living donors now exceeds the number of deceased donors with respect to kidneys, which itself generates accusations that too much reliance is being placed on living donors as sources for organs. The number of living donors has increased in the last decade from 338 in 1999–2000 to 1,032 in 2009–10, a more than 300 per cent rise.[3] Second, the volume of heart-beating, brain (stem) dead donors has steadily declined during this period, from 744 in 1999–2000 to 623 in 2009–10. This figure has, however, been more than compensated for by a large rise in the number of non-heart-beating donors (otherwise referred to as 'donors

---

[1] D. Price, *Human Tissue in Transplantation and Research: A Model Legal and Ethical Donation Framework* (Cambridge University Press, 2009); *Legal and Ethical Aspects of Organ Transplantation* (Cambridge University Press, 2000).

[2] NHS Blood and Transplant, www.uktransplant.org.uk/ukt/statistics/latest_statistics/latest_statistics.jsp.

[3] *Ibid.*

after cardiac/circulatory death') from 33 to 336 in the same period.[4] Although the number of such donors has historically been modest, they now account for more than a third of all deceased organ donors in the UK. Multi-organ retrieval is less common in the latter context (many are 'kidney-only' retrievals), and thoracic non-heart-beating donations are a relatively recent development, therefore heart-beating rather than non-heart-beating donors are generally still viewed as the optimal source of organs for transplant.[5] Indeed, some still consider organs from non-heart-beating donors to be 'marginal'.[6]

Numbers of heart-beating donors have reduced as a result of fewer younger people dying of severe head injury or catastrophic cerebrovascular events, such as road-traffic accidents. Changes in the diagnosis and management of severe brain injuries also now result in fewer critically ill patients fulfilling brain stem death testing criteria. The general decline in heart-beating donation represents a major problem with regard to addressing the problem of organ shortage. These trends are not just confined to the UK, but can be observed in most other countries with developed organ donation and transplantation systems. To a very significant extent, all such countries are in some form of crisis in terms of meeting the demand for organs, and those working in the field all largely share common concerns, anxieties and issues.

The organ-shortage crisis has recently led to the issue of organ donation assuming a prominent place on the political agenda at both national and European Union (EU) levels. The government in the UK established an Organ Donation Taskforce to examine a range of options to address the problem. In its first report, published in 2008, it set out a series of recommendations to address organ shortage in the UK, but within the existing legal and policy framework. In this report, the UK Organ Donation Taskforce stated that three key organisational issues needed to be addressed within the structure of the national health system if there was to be a significant increase in the rate of organ donation:

1. donor identification and referral;
2. donor co-ordination; and
3. organ retrieval arrangements.

Most importantly, there needed to be clear political leadership and commitment to addressing these issues in order to achieve the desired result.[7] A Clinical Director for Transplantation has now been appointed to, inter alia, implement the Taskforce's fourteen recommendations

---

[4] *Ibid.*   [5] See Chapter 9.   [6] See Chapter 7.
[7] Department of Health, *Organs for Transplants: A Report from the Organ Donation Taskforce* (London: Department of Health, 2008), pp. 3–19.

(principally relating to resourcing, systems and infrastructural factors),[8] which it is claimed will lead to a 50 per cent increase in organ donation within a five-year timespan.[9]

In addition, the previous Prime Minister, the Rt Hon. Gordon Brown, and the Chief Medical Officer for England both lent their support to calls for a presumed consent (opt-out) regime to replace the current opt-in arrangements in place in relation to organ donation.[10] This led to the Taskforce being reconvened and reconstituted to consider the issue. In late 2008, it advised that such a measure should not be considered at the present time, but should be revisited after five years if organ donation rates had not significantly improved by that time. Such calls for reform by senior government figures point to the severity of the crisis, notwithstanding the bitter legacy of organ retention scandals in the UK,[11] which led to consent becoming the centrepiece of a newly established legislative regime dealing with the use of human material, including organs.[12]

At EU level, the European Commission has recently recognised the importance and urgency of addressing ethical and legal issues concerning organ transplantation and shortage on a supranational basis. This led the Commission to publish an action plan setting out how it proposes to address the issue,[13] which was accompanied by a legislative proposal (Directive) to establish an EU-wide risk regulation regime in the field.[14] The Directive has now been adopted at EU level, and implementation is required by Member States by 27 August 2012.[15] In reviewing recent developments in EU organ donation and transplantation, the House of

---

[8] Department of Health, 'Government announces appointment of new national clinical director for transplant' (3 April 2008), http://nds/coi.gov.uk/Content/Detail.asp?ReleaseID=364434&NewsAreaID=2.

[9] Department of Health, *Organs for Transplants*, p. 3.

[10] Department of Health, *2006 Annual Report of the Chief Medical Officer: on the State of Public Health* (London: Department of Health, 2007), p. 33; the former Prime Minister, the Rt Hon. Gordon Brown, 'Organs can help us make a difference', *Daily Telegraph*, 14 January 2008.

[11] M. Brazier, 'Retained organs: ethics and humanity', *Legal Studies*, 22 (2002), 550–69.

[12] D. Price, 'The Human Tissue Act 2004', *Modern Law Review*, 68 (2005), 798–821. The new legislative regime for the UK is set out in two pieces of legislation, namely the Human Tissue Act 2004 and the Human Tissue (Scotland) Act 2006.

[13] Commission of the European Communities, *Action Plan on Organ Donation and Transplantation (2009–2015): Strengthened Cooperation between Member States* (COM (2008) 819/3, Brussels, 8 December 2008).

[14] *Ibid.*; Proposal for a Directive of the European Parliament and of the Council on standards of quality and safety of human organs intended for transplantation (COM(2008) 818 final, Brussels, 8 December 2008).

[15] Directive 2010/45/EU of the European Parliament and of the Council of 7 July 2010 on standards of quality and safety of human organs intended for transplantation (OJ L 207, 6 August 2010), in particular Article 31(1).

Lords EU Select Committee recognised the benefit to be gained from concerted cross-border action to address organ shortage of the type envisaged by the Commission, provided that such action did not become administratively burdensome in practice and did not inhibit the application of expert clinical judgement and informed patient choice.[16]

Various reasons have been offered to explain the shortage of organs. In terms of potential donors, public surveys and published academic research reveal a high level of public support for organ donation in general terms. When faced with the decision to donate a family member's organs, however, the reality has been somewhat different, with high rates of refusal. It has also been suggested that healthcare professionals involved in organ transplantation have failed to be sufficiently proactive in approaching potential donors and/or their families, and appropriate infrastructures and training in the field have been lacking in terms of promoting organ donation.[17] In the UK, consideration has been given recently to the identification of 'clinical triggers' that would immediately result in automatic notification of potential donors to transplantation agencies, as takes place in the United States (USA); however, such proposals have yet to be implemented. In addition, the 'gift relationship' which has been used to provide the ethical underpinning for the system of organ donation and transplantation has been criticised for failing to encourage sufficient numbers of individuals and their families to donate.[18]

Consideration has been given to a range of policy options to address supply and demand issues in organ transplantation, including:

1. the establishment of commercial market or monopsonistic schemes for organs;[19]

---

[16] House of Lords European Union Committee, *Increasing the Supply of Donor Organs within the European Union*, 17th Report of Session 2007–08, Volume 1: Report, HL Paper 123–I (London: The Stationery Office, 2008).

[17] T. Burroughs, B. Hong, D. Kappel and B. Freedman, 'The stability of family decisions to consent or refuse organ donation: would you do it again?', *Psychosomatic Medicine*, 60 (1998), 156–62; T. Long, M. Sque and S. Payne, 'Information sharing: its impact on donor and nondonor families' experience in the hospital', *Progress in Transplantation*, 16 (2006), 144–9; M. Sque, S. Payne and J. Macleod Clark, 'Gift of life or sacrifice? Key discourses to understanding organ donor families' decision-making', *Mortality*, 11 (2006), 117–32.

[18] M. Sque and S. Payne, 'Gift exchange theory: a critique in relation to organ transplantation', *Journal of Advanced Nursing*, 19 (1994), 45–51; L. Siminoff and K. Chillag, 'The fallacy of the "gift of life"', *The Hastings Center Report*, 29 (1999), 34–41; J. Childress, 'The failure to give: reducing barriers to organ donation', *Kennedy Institute of Ethics Journal*, 11 (2001), 1–16.

[19] L. Cohen, 'A futures market in cadaveric organs: would it work?', *Transplantation Proceedings*, 1 (1993), 60–1; C. Erin and J. Harris, 'A monopsonistic market – or how to buy and sell human organs, tissues and cells ethically' in I. Robinson (ed.), *Life and Death under High Technology Medicine* (Manchester University Press in association with the Fullbright Commission, London, 1994), pp. 134–53.

2. the expanded use and range of organs from living donors;[20]
3. the adoption of the 'Spanish model' to facilitate optimum institutional arrangements for organ donation;[21]
4. the implementation of presumed consent (opt-out) regimes for organ donation;[22]
5. the need for revised allocation criteria;[23] and
6. the implementation of supranational (regulatory) regimes to facilitate best practice and organ exchange.[24]

Given the current prominence of issues relating to organ donation and transplantation on the political agenda at both national and international levels, this book is both timely and innovative for a number of reasons. First, there is an urgent need for critical, informed and up-to-date analysis of such developments by those with the requisite academic and practical expertise. Second, there is a need to focus on strategies to increase organ donation that are likely to succeed in the short to medium term. The editors seek to move away from examining longstanding and unresolved ethical, religious and cultural conflict and controversy over issues in organ donation and transplantation, with the aim of identifying coherent and innovative solutions for addressing organ shortage. Such solutions should be principled yet pragmatic in approach, and capable of being implemented in a timely fashion in order to facilitate an increase in organ donation, primarily in the UK, but with potential application beyond this national context.

There are a number of reasons for focusing on the UK. First, it has a particularly low rate of deceased organ donation, when compared to many of its European neighbours.[25] There is a need to understand why

---

[20] A. Garwood-Gowers, *Living Donor Organ Transplantation: Key Legal and Ethical Issues* (Aldershot: Ashgate, 1999); M. Abecassis, M. Adams, P. Adams *et al.*, 'Consensus statement on the live organ donor', *Journal of the American Medical Association*, 284 (2000), 2919–26.

[21] J. Martínez, J. López, A. Martin *et al.*, 'Organ donation and family decision-making within the Spanish donation system', *Social Science and Medicine*, 53 (2001), 405–21.

[22] I. Kennedy, R. Sells, A. Daar *et al.*, 'The case for "presumed consent" in organ donation', *Lancet*, 351 (1998), 1650–2; J. Radcliffe-Richards, A. Daar, R. Guttmann *et al.*, 'The case for allowing kidney sales', *Lancet*, 351 (1998), 1950–2; R. Gimbel, M. Strosberg, S. Lehrman *et al.*, 'Presumed consent and other predictors of cadaveric organ donation in Europe', *Progress in Transplantation*, 13 (2003), 17–23.

[23] J. Childress, 'Putting patients first in organ allocation', *Cambridge Quarterly of Healthcare Ethics*, 10 (2001), 365–76.

[24] A. Farrell, 'Adding value? EU governance of organ donation and transplantation', *European Journal of Health Law*, 17 (2010), 51–79.

[25] Commission of the European Communities, Commission staff working document: accompanying document to the Communication from the Commission to the European Parliament and the Council: organ donation and transplantation: policy actions at EU level: summary of the Impact Assessment (SEC(2007) 705, Brussels, 30 May 2007).

this situation has developed, and whether a way forward can be found to redress it. Second, the UK is not alone in having to deal with a shortage of organs and, therefore, an examination of what may be done to address the issue is likely to have relevance beyond this national context. Third, the inspiration for this book derives from a seminar series funded by the UK's Economic and Social Research Council (ESRC) which ran for a period of eighteen months between October 2006 and March 2008. It brought together a diverse range of participants from various academic and practitioner backgrounds to examine the issue of organ shortage, with a particular focus on the UK context. The majority of the contributors to the book participated in the seminar series. Those contributors whose brief is to examine how the issue of organ shortage has been addressed elsewhere (e.g. in other European countries and in North America) will also focus on what can be learned from the approaches taken in their own national settings to inform UK policy-making on the issue.

The chapters in this book all examine ethical, legal and social concerns regarding the shortage of organs for transplantation. As a result, a diverse range of issues is examined within individual chapters. In Part I, the chapter by Margaret Brazier and John Harris sets the scene by reviewing long-running ethical and legal controversies in debates about organ donation and transplantation, where they have often sat on opposing sides. Notwithstanding their differences, however, they both agree on the end to be achieved – more organs need to be made available for transplantation. With this in mind, they propose a way forward towards ethical compromise in order to facilitate the achievement of this desired end, which may in turn enable others to develop realistic and pragmatic options for increasing the number of donated organs for transplantation.

Part II groups together a series of chapters which focus on issues which have not been fully addressed in UK government policy-making and initiatives in relation to increasing organ donation. In Chapter 3, Gurch Randhawa tackles an historically neglected issue in discussions on organ shortage, namely how it impacts upon particular ethnic or minority groups. He draws on a case study of South Asian and Afro-Caribbean groups in the UK, who suffer from a higher rate of renal failure than the Caucasian population and are disproportionately represented on UK organ transplant waiting lists, but who are also relatively less frequent organ donors. Indeed, rates of family refusal of donation amongst these populations are considerably higher than in the general population. Professor Randhawa emphasises the need to stimulate higher rates of organ donation amongst these populations at the same time as developing disease prevention strategies for avoiding organ failure. However, he also draws attention to the need for further research in many areas, exploring attitudes, treatment compliance, and referral, as well as socioeconomic and religious factors.

The next two chapters deal with the need for better education about organ donation and transplantation processes. These chapters show that we cannot draw and rely on the simplistic conclusion that more and better public education on its own is likely to be a panacea. Drawing on public engagement of science theories, Mairi Levitt argues in Chapter 4 that public education initiatives in the field of organ donation need to be integrated into a more complete account of why organ transplantation is needed. With this in mind, more attention needs to be paid to the context in which decision-making about donation will ultimately be made. In addition, she questions the supply-focused nature of current education initiatives which allow the public rather than the government to be blamed for any failure to meet the demand for organs. In Chapter 5, Magi Sque and Tracy Long-Sutehall examine the reasons behind the high rate of refusal on the part of families when asked to donate organs from deceased family members. They recognise that the families of potential donors are critical to the organ donation process, but argue that they need to be recognised as bereaved individuals above all else, and be properly supported by staff educated in dealing with bereaved persons. The authors discuss families' concerns about the donation process itself, as well as its consequences. They argue that, if the rate of organ donation is to increase, then there is an urgent need for better understanding of the social processes that are part of the organ donation process. Decision-making in the context of a bereaved family is multifaceted and multidimensional. Awareness of what is actually involved in the process should be made clear through suitable education mechanisms, so that if the issue of organ donation is raised at the bedside of a dying relative, it is neither foreign nor intimidating to the grieving family.

Part III examines some of the key issues around which ethical and medical conflict have arisen in the context of organ donation and transplantation, as well as strategies that could potentially be employed to address such conflict. In Chapter 6, Muireann Quigley provides an ethical perspective on the issue of incentivisation in organ donation. She considers general ethical issues surrounding the use of individual and institutional incentives to try and increase rates of organ donation. She argues that we need to accept that the essential purpose of incentives is to alter the decision-making process and to tip the balance in favour of donation. This, however, does not in itself render unethical the use of certain incentives. In accepting the need for incentives to act as encouragement to individuals or their families, she further argues that there is a need to let go of the idea that donations ought only to be motivated by altruistic ideals. This chapter briefly considers the creation of incentives, recently introduced in Israel, to donate by enhancing the likelihood of receipt of an organ in the event that one is needed. She warns that the widespread implementation of any incentive scheme, however, would need to be subject to ongoing empirical evaluation in order to determine whether or not it would actually achieve an increase in the supply of organs for transplantation, and whether it would result in any distorting or adverse effects. Following on from this contribution, Antonia Cronin observes in Chapter 7 that the shortage of organs means that it is not always possible to find the 'ideal' donor and, in light of this, examines the use of marginal donors in organ transplantation. Informed by her professional experience as a transplant clinician, she reviews the available empirical research on the use of such donors and assesses the outcomes resulting from the use of their organs in transplantation. She analyses the ethics involved in making decisions to use marginal donors and argues that what may have appeared at the outset to be a muddled compromise in addressing the problem of organ shortage has in fact legitimate utility in the absence of current real alternatives. In making such an argument, however, she points out that the resort to the use of marginal donors draws attention to the need for full consideration to be given to policy measures relating to organ donation which could substantially increase the supply of organs in the first place.

In Chapter 8, Phil Dyer and Sheelagh McGuinness examine the issue of organ allocation. An overview of the evolution of the allocation system in the UK and its current criteria is provided, as well as an analysis of its benefits and its shortcomings. The overview is informed by Phil Dyer's long-term involvement in transplantation medicine, both as a scientist and as a participant on relevant professional representative bodies. The authors provide an illuminating account of the medical and biological constraints within which such a system operates. They analyse critically the background assumptions implicit in the criteria used, arguing that allocation decisions cannot be made on purely medical or scientific grounds. For example, they argue that whilst justice is an important factor in allocation, benefit and utility must also be weighed in the balance to optimise each donation. In Chapter 9, John Coggon and Paul Murphy examine some of the difficult issues faced by intensive care clinicians when involved in decision-making about the care of patients who may potentially become organ donors. In this regard, Paul Murphy brings his extensive practical experience as a senior intensivist to bear on the subject matter examined. Specifically, the authors consider legal and ethical concerns regarding ante-mortem interventions that may facilitate posthumous organ donation. While they concede that greater ethical and legal clarity is needed in this area, they argue that where a patient's values support deceased donation, measures aimed at optimising the chances of successful organ transplantation will not contravene physicians' duties toward their patients. The authors show that a broad interpretation of the concept of best interests as understood in English common law, embracing as it does a plurality of values, supports this position.

Part IV focuses on best practices and current initiatives in organ donation and transplantation processes in a number of other Western countries. The overarching aim of this Part is to provide country case-study examples which could potentially be drawn upon and/or adapted for use in other countries to increase organ donation. In Chapter 10, Mónica Navarro-Michel examines the 'Spanish Model', which has enjoyed spectacular success in recent years in terms of increasing the rate of deceased organ donation both in Spain and in other countries which have adopted the model. She provides an overview of how the model works in practice, in conjunction with the legally mandated opt-out system for organ donation which operates in Spain. She considers whether the legal framework is a key factor in the substantial increase in the rate of organ donation in Spain, but goes on to argue that what was crucial to the success of the Spanish Model was the implementation of institutional and organisational reforms to the organ donation and transplantation system, rather than the law on its own. In order to illuminate which elements of the model can potentially lead to success, she examines the case studies of Italy (e.g. Tuscany), Australia and Latin America, which have adopted some of the key elements of the Spanish Model. She concludes by considering whether any, and if so which, aspects of the Spanish Model could usefully be transferred and implemented in the UK context.

In Chapter 11, Salla Lötjönen and Nils Persson examine kidney organ donation and transplantation processes in a discrete regional area – the Nordic countries – comprised of Denmark, Finland, Iceland, Norway and Sweden. Nils Persson's expertise and professional experience as a transplant surgeon inform the analysis. The authors trace the history of organ donation and transplantation processes and legislation in each of these countries. They argue that despite the organisational commitment towards a regional approach, and a generally homogenous population in the Nordic countries, national sociocultural, medical and legal differences prevail, resulting in differing rates of both living and deceased organ donation as between the countries. They analyse the reasons for these disparities, particularly in relation to the use of living organ donors, and assess the usefulness of a regionally based approach.

Chapters 12 and 13 focus on recent experiences in North America. In the first of these chapters, Linda Wright and Diego Silva provide an overview of the recent history of organ donation and transplantation in Canada. They examine the reasons for the wide variation among Canadian provinces in organs available from living and deceased donors. Against the background of rising demand for organs over the past decade, they identify initiatives that have been pursued, including the recent introduction of programmes that use cardio-circulatory criteria for the declaration of death, and the Organ Donation Collaborative, which has been used to share information and assist in the education of health-care workers. In addition, they examine programmes that have been instituted in three Canadian provinces to reimburse living organ donors for financial costs incurred through organ donation. The authors argue that the decentralised approach in Canada, while raising concerns about the unequal sharing of organs, has also facilitated the development of new initiatives aimed at increasing organ donation rates.

In Chapter 13, Alexandra Glazier discusses recent US initiatives to increase organ donation, most notably the introduction of the Organ Breakthrough Collaboratives, as well as reforms to the laws and systems governing organ donation. She observes that in the last 5 years, such initiatives have proved to be remarkably successful, resulting in a 30 per cent increase in the total number of organs donated for transplant, whereas the previous decade had only seen increases in the order of 1–2 per cent. She identifies the 'Breakthrough Collaborative' as spearheading this transformation, derived from process improvement principles. She discusses best practices which have emerged from this initiative and which she argues could be adapted for use in other national settings in order to increase organ donation. She argues that the Collaboratives are unique, as they were able to identify and implement methods for measurably improving organ donation rates without changing fundamental principles underlying the donation and transplantation system.

The three chapters in Part V focus on current reform initiatives, as well as likely future challenges in policy-making and regulation with respect to organ donation and transplantation, at both UK and supra-national levels. In Chapter 14, Bobbie Farsides reflects on her role as an adviser to a range of UK bodies examining policy reform in organ donation and transplantation, and analyses the ethicist's role in contemporary debates and policy formulation. She identifies the issues that have caused most ethical concern in the context of negotiating change in the field, and highlights the importance of taking into account the attitudes and beliefs of the healthcare professionals responsible for implementing such change with a view to increasing organ donation rates.

In Chapter 15, Anne-Maree Farrell examines emerging EU governance in organ donation and transplantation, in particular the European

Commission's Action Plan, as well as the legislation (Directive) which establishes an EU-wide risk-regulation regime in the field. She suggests that EU action in this sphere should be viewed as a positive development. While the Commission's Action Plan is ambitious in its scope, there is a need to prioritise the implementation of efficient and effective organisational structures for achieving the objective of increased organ availability at national level, particularly through deceased organ donation. With the adoption of a Directive in the field, she also suggests that there is a need on the part of the Commission to undertake ongoing evaluation with regard to the likely and actual transaction costs that may be involved in its implementation at national level, as well as being open to considering innovative and pragmatic ways to address organ shortage, notwithstanding ethical conflict. She argues that such implementation should not result in additional or unexpected administrative and regulatory burdens at national level, to the detriment of focusing on the main challenge of addressing organ shortage.

In the final chapter, Chapter 16, David Price picks up on a range of issues that have been examined in earlier chapters and reflects upon key issues in organ donation and transplantation that are likely to pose difficult ethical and legal challenges to policy-makers in the UK and other countries in the future. He argues that the plight of those patients on the waiting list requires us to make efforts which take us up to the ethical margins – but not beyond – in our attempt to provide them with organs for transplantation. First, he discusses the vexed issue of the use of organs from non-heart-beating donors and the ethical uncertainties and conflicts created by the increase in such donors. He then tackles controversy in the arena of living donors and provides counterarguments to accusations that living donors are being sacrificed in pursuit of a naked utilitarian ethic. Finally, he returns to the issue of deceased organ donation, considering whether the implementation of an opt-out system of donation would be suitable in the contemporary sociocultural UK context, and examines the nature and ethical underpinnings of presumed consent/opting out. He argues that regardless of the strategies and policies chosen to try and ameliorate organ shortage, open and full debate is needed across the community as a whole.

A number of themes can be identified as running through the chapters in this book. First, agreement on ethical issues in the field is unlikely and, if we are to see a measurable increase in organ donation, then there is a need for opposing parties to accept a principled compromise that allows for a primary focus on how best to achieve this desired end. This may require thinking in different ways about matters giving rise to ethical controversy. Second, there is a need to avoid a 'one size fits all' approach to solutions about how best to address organ shortage. There is a need therefore to think more carefully about the strategies employed, particularly with regard to encouraging donation within specific ethnic or minority communities, or how best to manage the emotional complexities of family bereavement in the context of a request for organ donation from a deceased relative. Third, there is a need to be creative in the design of policies in traditional areas of ethical concern, such as methods of donation, donor types and allocation criteria, as well as to be innovative in the implementation of preventative strategies which lessen the need for organ transplantation in the first place. The focus should be on what is most likely to redress organ shortage in a timely fashion and in a way that is principled but pragmatic in approach. Fourth, there is much to be learned in the UK from the experiences of other countries with regard to their efforts to increase organ donation. This is not to say that every local, regional or supranational initiative could or should be transferred without adaptation to the UK context. There are clearly sociocultural, economic and political issues that need to be taken account of, but a failure to engage in policy learning would no doubt be to miss a golden opportunity to draw on best practices developed in the field. Finally, while there is a clear need for reforms to be implemented in the UK given its current poor rate of deceased organ donation, there is also a need to be strategic about how this will be done in the face of finite financial, institutional and personnel resources. Ultimately, the success of any strategic policy initiatives to increase organ donation in the UK is likely to depend upon the ongoing political commitment of those at senior levels of government. Only time will tell whether this commitment will translate into meaningful action to redress what has become an ever-widening gap between the supply and demand of organs.

As a final point, it should be emphasised that in making the issue of organ shortage the central focus of this book, there is no suggestion that there is any automatic moral imperative to attempt to meet such shortages from human sources, however such shortages are framed or assessed. Not only is there a need to give proper attention to measures of disease prevention in the first place and to optimise outcomes from existing transplants performed, but there is also a need to explore proactively other ethically acceptable sources of organ supply, including the use of stem cell engineered materials and xenotransplant options. Notwithstanding such other ongoing activities, however, the suffering and death caused by end-stage organ failure is surely a source of moral obligation which provides a basis for action on the part of both governments and potential donors.

2   Does ethical controversy cost lives?

Margaret Brazier and John Harris

This chapter was originally conceived in 2006 as the opening address to the seminar series that gave birth to this book. Its purpose was to seek to demonstrate the need for all those involved in debates about the supply of organs for transplantation, to revisit any cherished preconceptions about ethical issues and at the same time focus on practical measures to increase the number of solid organs donated for transplant. The aim of this chapter is to underline both the need for, and the sheer difficulty of, attempting to reach agreement on what kinds of measures might properly be taken to increase the supply of organs when the debates have so often been sharply polarised. As will be apparent, our central focus is on measures that might be implemented in the United Kingdom (UK), but we hope that what we have to say is of some relevance to all jurisdictions.

Controversy about ethical and legal means of obtaining organs for transplant has raged since surgeons first demonstrated that major organs such as kidneys could successfully be transplanted. It is a controversy that embraces several different debates. To list but a few: are donors truly dead?[1] Should payments be allowed for live or deceased 'donations'?[2] Should 'presumed consent' be embodied in the law?[3] Or should all organs

We would like to acknowledge the support of the Wellcome Strategic Programme in *The Human Body, its Scope, Limits and Future,* conducted under the auspices of the Institute for Science Ethics and Innovation, School of Law, University of Manchester, UK, in relation to the preparation of this chapter.

[1] A debate that is still not wholly 'dead' itself. See C. Machado, 'A definition of human death should not be related to organ transplants', *Journal of Medical Ethics*, 29 (2003), 201–2.

[2] C. Erin and J. Harris, 'A monopsonistic market – or how to buy and sell human organs, tissues and cells ethically' in I. Robinson (ed.), *Life and Death under High Technology Medicine* (Manchester University Press in association with the Fullbright Commission, London, 1994), pp. 134–53; 'An ethical market in human organs', *Journal of Medical Ethics*, 29 (2003), 137–8; 'Janet Radcliffe-Richards on our modest proposal', *Journal of Medical Ethics*, 29 (2003), 141–2; J. Radcliffe-Richards, A. Daar, R. Guttmann *et al.*, 'The case for allowing kidney sales', *Lancet*, 351(1998), 1950–2.

[3] I. Kennedy, R. Sells, A. Daar *et al.*, 'The case for "presumed consent" in organ donation', *Lancet*, 351(1998), 1650–2.

from deceased individuals become the 'property of the state'?[4] Is elective ventilation an abuse of the dying, or a simple process which will save worthwhile lives?[5] Philosophers, lawyers and social scientists have had a field day generating literally thousands of books, as well as learned and less learned papers. Could their words be transformed into organs for transplant, the gap between supply and demand would narrow, and lives would be saved.

We have both engaged in these debates for longer than we care to remember, usually on opposing sides, sometimes in print,[6] but often in our almost daily encounters at work. Brazier has endorsed a policy of explicit consent for deceased donation and had profound misgivings about payments for organs from the living or the dead. Harris has long supported a regulated monopsonistic market in organs from the living and argued that organs from deceased individuals should become public property and be made automatically available for transplant. The academic engagement is fascinating. We have enjoyed ourselves. Yet in the UK and globally the number of solid organs available for transplant continues to fall short of the number required by sick and dying patients. No-one is 'winning' the ethical debate.

Means not ends are the problem

There is one feature of debates about the supply of organs for transplant that distinguishes them from many other debates in bioethics: virtually all participants are agreed on the ends. Transplantation is acknowledged as ethical medicine, and a sufficient supply of organs for transplant is a good to be fought for.[7] In other contexts where medical ethics are debated, it is often the outcome which is contested. Those who support the combination of Pre-Implantation Genetic Diagnosis (PGD) with tissue (HLA – Human Leukocyte Antigen) typing believe the creation of saviour siblings to be good, while those who oppose saviour siblings consider the saviour to be an unethical sacrifice. Those who oppose reproductive cloning devoutly pray there will never be such a clone, and those who support it

[4] J. Harris, 'The survival lottery', *Philosophy*, 50 (1975), 81–8; 'Organ procurement: dead interests, living needs: cadaver organs should be automatically available', *Journal of Medical Ethics*, 29 (2003), 130–5.

[5] J. McHale, 'Effective ventilation – pragmatic solution or ethical minefield', *Professional Negligence*, 11 (1995), 23–7.

[6] See for example J. Harris, 'Law and regulation of retained organs: the ethical issues', *Legal Studies*, 22 (2002), 527–49; M. Brazier, 'Retained organs: ethics and humanity', *Legal Studies*, 22 (2002), 550–69.

[7] However see B. Koenig, 'Dead donors and the "shortage" of human organs: are we missing the point?', *American Journal of Bioethics*, 3 (2003), 26–7.

will be happy to greet such a clone. By contrast, debates about the supply of organs for transplantation are not about ends, but *means*. Those who oppose markets in organs do not do so because they consider that people should not agree to provide organs to help others, or that transplant medicine is intrinsically wrong. Those who oppose presumed consent do not (for the most part) believe that agreeing to donate your own organs, or those of your deceased relative, is wrong. In Japan, agreed criteria for brain death across the world were rejected until recently,[8] and the effect that had on organ donation meant Japan tended to rely much more heavily on living donors. The end of saving or improving lives by transplants was not disputed, but harboured doubts concerning brain death criteria affected the means to attain that good end.

Debates about organ transplantation create an odd paradox, akin to a quarrel about map reading. Virtually all parties in the 'quarrel' agree that they should travel to city X; there is no easy route to X, as each possible route is beset by some danger. The travellers find it impossible to agree on the best, or the 'least bad', route, and each traveller refuses to compromise. Our metaphor is necessarily flawed. The physical journey to X is burdened by risks that can be objectively assessed; if A concedes to B's and C's judgements, she may necessarily have to confront a risk which she estimates to be higher than do B and C. The journey towards an agreed consensus on ethical means of organ procurement is beset by moral (not physical) dangers: A may be asked to concede some part of her own moral framework, to endorse a course of action about which she retains moral doubt; and B and C may be asked to accept moral constraints which they continue to consider to be poorly founded. If we genuinely wish to achieve our objective, then such compromise is a moral imperative – without it we will not achieve our ends. Another factor must be considered in any such attempt at compromise: the system for obtaining organs needs to command public trust. First, without such trust, legislatures in liberal democracies are unlikely to give legal force to radical proposals to obtain organs; and second, absent coercive measures of high order, radical measures may backfire.

We do have to consider when compromise can be ethical or indeed may be ethically required. Imagine evidence emerged that, as well as having low pain thresholds, redheads cost the NHS twice as much as non-redheads; so the government proposes not to treat redheads. Compromise should not be considered; compromise requires that no party in the debate is compelled to sacrifice core values. Alas this does

---

[8] D. Price, *Human Tissue in Transplantation and Research: A Model Legal and Ethical Donation Framework* (Cambridge University Press, 2009), p. 20.

not help us much, as beyond such obvious examples, we may struggle to agree what constitute core values, and then not all core values are plausibly of equal weight.

Harris utilises this scenario: his aunt is on life support but brain-dead; her organs will beyond doubt save at least one but probably more than one other life. It may be a core value of his and of his aunt that she be buried 'orgo intacta'; but Harris has to think about another core value of his and his aunt, namely that saving life is, in their moral system, as well as that of the potential recipients and their families, not simply a core value but one of the most important core values. Would a decent person be, should they be, prepared to sacrifice lesser core values of theirs to secure more important values of theirs which are also crucial to the survival of others? Now, as those who have read any of his work know, it is not a core value of Harris's to be buried with his organs intact, and of course his aunt is in no position to report on her core values. This is not least because she is non-existent, as well as dead. And here we hit an early obstacle in our search to agree a compromise. It is no more a core value of Brazier's than Harris's that she be buried 'orgo intacta'. However, before her own aunt's death (to use a similar scenario), had her aunt held to such a value Brazier would regard that value as at least worthy of respect and not to be dismissed as of no weight whatsoever; and Harris would agree that this view is worthy of respect (in the sense of showing respect for those who hold such a view, but not in the sense of allowing such a view to prevail). However Harris further demands that anyone suggesting that the wish to be buried with one's organs intact be respected at the cost of another's life must show how such a view could be worth the sacrifice of a life.[9]

But how do you weigh values? Harris offers another example of something that is one of his core values: he believes passionately in autonomy and his instincts are radically libertarian; he has championed many libertarian causes including the freedom of parents to adopt children with the same freedom people exercise when they are able to have children using unregulated sexual reproduction as their means. He has defended the freedom of people to clone themselves if they wish,[10] the freedom to choose the sex of their children[11] (and other traits),[12] and more mundanely, the freedom to indulge in sex, drugs and rock'n'roll.[13] However,

---

[9] S. McGuinness and M. Brazier, 'Respecting the living means respecting the dead too', *Oxford Journal of Legal Studies*, 28 (2008), 297–316.
[10] J. Harris, *On Cloning* (London: Routledge, 2004).
[11] J. Harris, 'Sex selection and regulated hatred', *Journal of Medical Ethics*, 31 (2005), 291–5.
[12] J. Harris, 'Rights and reproductive choice' in J. Harris and S. Holm (eds.), *The Future of Human Reproduction: Choice and Regulation* (Oxford University Press, 1998), pp. 5–37.
[13] See for example J. Harris, *The Value of Life* (London: Routledge & Kegan Paul, 1985).

he has also defended a system of mandatory availability of organs from deceased persons,[14] and even, in extremis, mandatory participation in scientific research.[15] What has led him to this reckless sacrifice of some of his core values? Why does he recommend the possibility of sometimes trampling on people's autonomous choices when it comes to scientific research and organs from deceased individuals? The answer is that although he believes in liberty, informed consent and autonomy of the individual, there are on occasion more important things at stake. One of his core values is that the lives of persons and the avoidance of the imposition of suffering on our fellows is supremely important. It is so important, indeed, that some of his own core values must give way, at least to some extent, when this is necessary to preserve that supreme value of saving lives and preventing human suffering. Acknowledging the importance to be accorded to saving life when one can do so is not something Brazier would dispute. The strong ethical imperative to help others and to love your neighbour leads her to agree that we all owe moral obligations to consider organ and tissue donation and participation in scientific research.[16] Harris's challenge to Brazier or his imaginary aunt is to show how their core values are plausibly as important as saving the life of a stranger.

Moral argument of the sort that can result in moral compromise is only possible for moral agents – people who take morality seriously and want not only to act for the best, but to act rightly. Such people have a powerful interest in reflective morality, in thinking through their moral position and in resolving inconsistencies and apparent or real conflicts between elements of their morality, including those elements they regard as core values. In just the same way as it is not usually possible for an agent to have everything they want, not least because not everything can be done at once, so also a moral agent has sometimes to choose between different moral priorities. In order to do so they must assess and perhaps re-evaluate these priorities in the light of their moral objectives and their sense of the sort of person they are or wish to become or to remain. Just as we have sometimes to choose between our own core values and priorities, we may also have to choose between our own core values and priorities, as well as the priorities and needs of others. There is a sense, of course, in which when we make a moral compromise we are not surrendering one of

[14] *Ibid.*
[15] J. Harris, 'Scientific research is a moral duty', *Journal of Medical Ethics*, 31 (2005), 242–8.
[16] M. Brazier, 'Do no harm – do patients have responsibilities too?', *Cambridge Law Journal*, 65 (2006), 397–422; 'Exploitation and enrichment: the paradox of medical experimentation', *Journal of Medical Ethics*, 34 (2008), 180–5

our values but modifying it or understanding it differently. So when Harris advocates the surrender of the right to refuse all participation in research, he can be thought either as compromising his autonomy, trading it off against another but different moral objective, or understanding the value of autonomy in a different or new way.

However, it is one thing for Harris and Brazier to make their own moral choices and elect on some occasions between their own core values, but it is quite another thing to dictate what others must do. Perhaps the essence of our disagreement is not what is morally right but what should be legally enforceable. Brazier would agree that a person should be prepared to donate their organs after death, but unlike Harris she would not wish to introduce laws to make them do so. In accepting that sometimes we must choose between core values, she is hesitant to claim that her choices must be the only right choices, especially in the face of strong evidence of the crucial value many place on the integrity of the corpse.[17] But it is here that we also need agreement on the nature of autonomy and, in particular, whether and how autonomy can survive death. Harris would argue that since autonomy does not survive death, there is no question of 'laws to make them' donate after death because you cannot violate the will of someone who lacks autonomy.

From debating ethics to decisions at the deathbed

Our debates take place in the calm of university halls far from the pain and grief of much actual decision-making in transplant medicine. Ethical controversy is just one factor in the struggle to achieve an adequate supply of organs for transplant. As much as there is a gap between supply and demand in relation to organs, there is also a gap between rhetoric and reality. In principle, it appears that most people will weigh their own needs and wishes against those of others and acknowledge an obligation to help others in need of organs. Surveys establish that a majority of people will, if asked, agree in the abstract both 1. that they would be ready to donate their own organs after death, and 2. to donate organs from their family members, if the latter had expressed no prior wishes themselves.[18] However, when families are approached after a relative's death, a much smaller number agree to donate organs.[19] Sometimes, relatives veto a donation when the deceased carried a donor card or was entered on a national or local organ donor register (other chapters explore this paradox much more fully).[20] In theory, explanations may include the possibility

---

[17] Brazier, 'Retained organs', 558–61.
[18] Price, *Human Tissue in Transplantation and Research*, p. 132.
[19] *Ibid.*, p. 144.   [20] See Chapter 5.

that those answering questions in surveys say what they think those asking want to hear; in addition, it may be argued that the recently bereaved may be too preoccupied or distressed to consider such moral choices adequately.

There are limitations on organs suitable for deceased donation, and immense problems surrounding communication with families in the wake of sudden traumatic bereavement. And there has been a cyclical climate of mistrust in the UK – as Mason and Laurie point out, the current legislation, the Human Tissue Act 2004, was 'born under the wrong star'.[21] The Act was prompted by revelations that pathologists and others had removed and retained organs and tissue after post-mortem examinations without consent from the deceased or their families for the purposes of research or education. In a number of cases organs had in the end been put to no use, simply stored in pots and cellars.[22]

We have seen how recognition that something is one of our core values is not the end of a moral argument, or a way of avoiding a struggle with our consciences (individual and collective). Instead, it is the beginning of such a process or struggle. We must not hide from the evidence that the shortage of donor organs and tissue for transplantation constitutes an acute emergency which demands a rethinking of our social policies, and possibly radical measures. The detailed statistics have been addressed in Chapter 1, but it is clear that donor organ shortage costs tens, probably hundreds, of thousands of lives per annum on a global basis.

Encouraging 'donors'

Advances in medicine, for example in stem cell research, offer prospects of other means of replacing failing organs, but not in the immediate future. The annual death toll of those who die for lack of organs sets limits to the time horizon within which we could wait for new methods of organ procurement to come on stream. We cannot simply accept the deaths of those today on the promise that others may survive tomorrow. In addition, the urgency of the need for organs for transplant now also impacts on how long we should wait for people to be comfortable with organ donation when the cost of waiting is numbered in lost and wasted lives. So what can be done?

Whenever something of value is in short supply, an obvious strategy is to attempt to increase 'production'. Artificial production of replacement

[21] J. Mason and G. Laurie, *Law and Medical Ethics*, 7th edn (Oxford University Press, 2005), p. 493.
[22] Brazier, 'Retained organs', 554.

organs is at least twenty to thirty years away. For the present, the pressing need is for more people to be donors. To ensure a sufficient supply of organs from deceased donors to meet demand, most of the population of most countries will need to be potential donors, so far more people need to be encouraged to become 'donors', whether they do so during their lives or after death. In other contexts, when it is desirable to persuade more people to engage in a particular activity, attempts are made to increase the attraction of that activity. When there is a drastic shortage of teachers of maths, potential maths teachers are subsidised during their teacher training, are promised that their student debt will be written off, and paid more than their colleagues teaching drama. *Inducements* are offered to the student contemplating teaching maths. So should inducements be offered to potential organ donors? And if so, what sorts of inducements could and should be on offer?

One argument might be this: deciding on whether to teach maths or drama is a morally neutral choice, and is likely to be driven by preference and aptitude. Nor are there values at stake if someone elects to teach drama rather than maths, choosing less money but more personal fulfilment. Society wants more maths teachers and so intervenes to influence potential teachers' choices. Donating an organ to save someone else's life, provided you are able to do so at an acceptable cost to yourself, is the moral thing to do – you ought to do it regardless of any inducement. Encouraging people to do what is right is not in itself morally problematic – there are many other contexts in which inducements to do something that you ought to do without any inducement are regarded as legitimate. One example is the provision of a reward for information leading to the arrest of a criminal: if Harris has information suggesting that it was Brazier who robbed a bank, as a good citizen he ought to give that information to the police without expectation of reward. If the police and a tabloid newspaper offer a £10,000 reward, is it unethical for him to accept the money? Is it unethical to offer the reward? We might see him as a better citizen if he acted without reward, but we would not consider that using inducements to attain the good end of the arrest of a thief was itself objectionable.

Money is just one form of inducement – Harris's reward may come in a different form: he may be awarded some sort of medal for good citizenship; in deciding that he will contact the police he may be influenced by his expectation that he will receive his medal. Or simply the publicity attached to his good act may offer sufficient inducement – the likely acclaim in the local paper for assisting in the capture of this evil lawyer may influence him. We should also note that any 'bad' motives will not in this context vitiate his 'good' act – if he turns Brazier in out of academic spite, informing the police remains the right thing to do. Inducements are part of the fabric of society, so why are they treated with some suspicion in the context of encouraging organ donation? Maybe the word 'inducements' itself conveys some negative message. Do we rename the process 'incentives' in order that it sounds less questionable?

Incentives and living organ donors

How should we approach the question of incentives for organ donors? The chapter by Quigley explores this issue much more fully; we simply seek to kick-start the debate. We begin by considering non-financial incentives. If any form of incentive is unacceptable, then it follows that financial reward must be ruled out and we can avoid the murky waters of the organ market debate altogether. Let us start with living donors: living donations are no longer the option of last resort and, despite continuing qualms about the growing numbers of such donations, they are central to any policy to increase organ supply. Moreover the evidence now shows that in many instances a living donation offers the best hope of a successful transplant and a longer shelf life for the transplanted organ.[23] Nor are living donors limited any longer to close relatives or the donation of kidneys. Developments in transplant medicine now allow greater scope for a person to donate a kidney, or a segment of liver, or lobe of a lung to someone to whom he or she is not genetically related.

In the UK, the Human Tissue Authority (HTA) has sanctioned two forms of living kidney donation between unrelated adults which inherently involve strong incentives to donate: paired and pooled donations.[24] Both involve relatives of patients with renal failure who are not tissue matches for their own sick relative. In paired donation, a kidney is removed from A and given to a stranger, B; a relative of B provides a kidney for A's sick wife or son. In pooled donations, a linked series of paired donations takes place: so A gives his kidney to B's son; B gives her kidney to C's husband; and C gives a kidney to A's wife. These 'exchange' donations will increase the supply of living donors. Are they in any sense exclusively altruistic? What greater incentive could there be to donate a kidney to a stranger than the guarantee that your son or daughter will receive a kidney as a *reward* for your donation? Are such *rewards* ethical? In a sense the new variants on living donation are little different from the case where A gives his kidney directly to his own wife or son; A acts because the

---

[23] Price, *Human Tissue in Transplantation and Research*, p. 200.
[24] Human Tissue Authority, Code of Practice: Donation of Organs Tissue and Cells for Transplantation, Code 2 (2006), paras 94–6.

benefit to his sick relative is the major factor motivating his donation. In addition, that benefit may be more direct than simply A being happier if his relative is well; he may also gain from having less caring to do and may even gain financially if his wife or son can start earning again.[25]

If benefit to a family member is a proper incentive, are there other analogous permissible incentives? Paired/pooled donations do not need to be confined to the nuclear family unit: Harris could give a kidney to X, if X's wife gave a kidney to Brazier. There could seem to be no valid objection and maybe a lesser risk of the 'donor' being subjected to family pressure. Other possibilities include the following:

1. Should living donors be guaranteed priority for transplant if their remaining kidney fails?
2. Should nominated relatives of a donor (relatives who are healthy at the time of the donation) be given priority should their kidneys fail?[26]
3. Are there other healthcare benefits (to the donor or their family) which could and should be made available to living donors?

We have previously speculated on such possibilities and now Israel has enacted a law that initiates a complex scheme of incentives of this kind to benefit both living donors who donate to a non-directed recipient (i.e. to a stranger), and their first-degree relatives.[27] As we shall examine later in this chapter, the Israeli law introduces analogous incentives to potential deceased donors and their families. Donation is perceived as a family enterprise and the 'reward' is shared by the family. What other sorts of incentive (if any) should be permitted? The analogy with rewards for information about crime might suggest some form of public recognition; should the Queen present organ donor medals? We doubt that a token of this kind would have much impact, but can see no ethical objection to such a formal recognition of good citizenship. What about more tangible rewards, such as hard cash, as it is cash payments that have traditionally provoked controversy?

In England and Wales, section 32 of the Human Tissue Act 2004 prohibiting commercial dealings in human material for transplantation makes any form of direct financial incentive illegal. Interestingly, the Act uses the language not of sale or profit, but of reward, so 'a person commits an offence if he (a) gives or receives a *reward* for the supply of, or for an offer to, supply any controlled material'; section 32 is entitled '*Trafficking*:

---

[25] The HTA announced on 8 March 2010 that it had approved the first three pair-pooled donations (see www.hta.gov.uk).
[26] This might be seen simply as a delayed form of pooled donation.
[27] J. Lavee, T. Ashkenazi and D. Steinberg, 'A new law for allocation of donor organs in Israel', *Lancet*, 375 (2010), 1131–3.

Prohibition of commercial dealings in human material for transplantation' (emphases added). The purpose of section 32 is stated to be to outlaw human trafficking, and therefore organs should not be bought and sold. We will ponder the notion of trafficking later in the chapter.

First, we reflect briefly on the word 'reward', defined in the *Concise Oxford Dictionary*[28] as:

- 'A thing given in recognition of service, effort or achievement.'
- 'A fair return for good or bad behaviour.'
- 'A sum offered for the detection of a criminal or the restoration of lost property.'
- 'Show one's appreciation of (an action or quality) by making a gift.'

Only the third of these definitions indicates any sort of commercial enterprise. Reward can be taken to connote a token of appreciation such as an organ donor medal, for example. If a reward could be perceived as a gift, could some form of financial recognition fit more easily into the enduring concept of a gift relationship? Can a reward of £15,000 for each donor be distinguished from a market? And would/should opponents of markets recognise such a distinction?

Opponents of markets usually build their case on three central arguments:

1. commodifying human body parts degrades our essential humanity; it is intrinsically wrong to sell your own body parts or those of deceased relatives;[29]
2. the prospect of financial gain will lure poor and vulnerable vendors into the market creating the risk of uninformed and less than wholly voluntary 'donations'; and
3. the market will endanger the safety of the product: vendors anxious to sell their organs will conceal evidence of ill health.[30]

Financial rewards for donating (selling) organs are widely condemned in national and international policy documents.[31] For Harris, any case against organ sales is weak to non-existent; he argues that reasons are seldom given and the grounds remain obscure. Perhaps it is the tendentious use of the word 'trafficking' as seen in the Human Tissue Act 2004 that creates alarm? Is the very word intended to evoke images of trafficking human beings as slaves or prostitutes? Why is selling organs trafficking but

---

[28] *The Concise Oxford Dictionary*, 10th edn (Oxford University Press, 2001).
[29] M. Radin, 'Market-inalienability', *Harvard Law Review*, 100 (1987), 1849–937; contra N. Duxbury, 'Do markets degrade?', *Modern Law Review*, 59 (1996), 331–53.
[30] R. Titmuss, *The Gift Relationship: from Human Blood to Social Policy* (London: Allen & Unwin, 1970).
[31] Price, *Human Tissue in Transplantation and Research*, pp. 17–18.

selling olives not? Consider again the above three arguments of the 'anti-marketeers':

1. *Commodifying human body parts degrades.* It is intrinsically wrong to sell your own body parts. However, it is seldom plausibly indicated how it degrades or what form the degradation takes. Alleging 'intrinsic wrongness' is handy but lazy, since it is assumed that the wrongfulness is obvious, and no arguments are given on the assumption that none are necessary.

2. *The prospect of financial gain will lure poor and vulnerable vendors into the market creating the risk of uninformed and less than wholly voluntary 'donations'.* However we have to ask whether donations of life-saving organs need to be fully voluntary. After all, we are talking of life-saving acts – we do not ask if firemen plunging into flames when they hear a cry are acting 'fully voluntarily'.

3. *The market will endanger the safety of the product: vendors anxious to sell their organs will conceal evidence of ill health.*[32] Screening and counselling will remove much of this danger and we must ask whether recipients are willing to run the remaining risks rather than die for want of the organs.

Brazier concedes that it has been amply shown that a traditional altruistic model will not guarantee safety in relation to contaminated blood products. Safety can no longer (in itself) be a ground for opposing markets.[33] However she remains deeply troubled by the concept and the practicalities of an organ market. Acknowledging that the human body has become a crucial source of materials that constitute therapies for others, she still perceives any move to equate human material with everyday chattels as diminishing the value we place on ourselves.[34] But if readers agree with her rather than Harris and rule out a market, does this also rule out any kind of cash reward, a reward short of a market? Would this serve any purpose?

Let us envisage a modest reward of £1,000. Unlike the £15,000 suggested previously, such a token sum is less likely to be conflated with a covert payment; it would not make either of us more ready to part with a kidney. At this sort of level (as a purely financial inducement), it might attract a few more 'donors' and those who might be so attracted by the money itself would be the poorest among us, the very people about whom opponents of markets are most concerned. Modest rewards might be seen

---

[32] This claim lies at the heart of Titmuss, *The Gift Relationship*.

[33] A. Farrell, 'Is the gift still good? Examining the politics and regulation of blood safety in the European Union', *Medical Law Review*, 14 (2006), 155–79.

[34] M. Brazier, 'Human(s) (as) medicine(s)' in S. MacLean (ed.), *First Do No Harm* (Aldershot: Ashgate, 2006), pp. 187–202.

as falling between two stools. Any payment will offend market opponents, while modest payments will make little difference to the level of supply. What we struggle to find is some means of acknowledging a signal service to society. Whether we like it or not, money or money's worth is the usual mode of recognising such service (medals and public recognition are often accompanied by some financial reward). If we are presented with a bunch of flowers by a grateful student, we do not see it as a fee for our services but rather as a concrete gesture of thanks.

Incentives and organ donation by deceased persons

We have noted that certain kinds of non-financial incentives are already allowed in relation to living donors. Could analogous inducements be identified to increase the number of potential deceased donors of organs? Incentives to living donors centre on the promise of benefit to the donor's close family, via paired or pooled donation. As we have previously noted, Israel has now given statutory force to extending such a policy to increase the number of deceased donations.[35] In brief, the new allocation rules are:

1. Registered donors of at least three years are promised priority if they themselves succumb to a disease where a transplant would be required.
2. First-degree relatives of registered donors and those whose relative donated an organ after his or her death are promised priority if ever in need of a transplant.

In effect, those who register as donors opt in to a framework where those prepared to *give* and their close family have the first call on available organs for transplant. Similar inducements could be extended to cases where the deceased had not directed that his or her organs be used for transplantation and the person highest in the hierarchy of 'qualified relationship' is asked to donate their relative's organs. If a husband agrees to donate his wife's organs for transplant, he (and their children) might obtain a greater priority if in need of an organ.[36]

Is such a scheme any more than a logical extension of paired and pooled donations? Are there problems with what might become a two-tier transplant system? Consider the following:

1. If a person has cultural, religious or purely personal objections to the use of their or their family's body parts after death, should they have a lower priority for, or be precluded from, receiving organs?
2. Should their objection affect the claims their close family members might have should they fall ill?

---

[35] Lavee *et al.*, 'A new law for allocation of donor organs in Israel'.
[36] On incentives generally, see Mason and Laurie, *Law and Medical Ethics*, pp. 503–4.

Yet then one must ask, should people's moral choices cost them nothing when these same choices cost others their very lives? Brazier argues that we should respect the convictions of those whose religious or cultural beliefs result in a decision that they could not donate organs and so go to the grave less than intact. That belief has consequences, however, one of which is that the believer cannot demand a sacrifice that he or she will not make himself or herself.

A comprehensive review of allocation policies may be one means of rethinking incentives. What other sorts of incentives to increase the supply of organs from deceased persons should be on the table? We dismissed the notion of donor medals for living donors fairly cavalierly (maybe too cavalierly). Mason and Laurie support the display of a 'permanent roll of donors in hospital entrance halls. Not only is this virtually free from ethical criticism but it is a form of recognition which, we believe, large numbers of bereaved relatives would positively endorse.'[37]

Such a roll of honour would be likely to achieve two ends: remembering and honouring family and friends after death is important to most people; and a public memorial testifying to the service rendered by the deceased in death may be of importance to the family, reinforcing their judgement that donation was the 'right thing to do'. Acknowledgement of the family's own 'gift' (or sacrifice) could also be beneficial – agreeing in the first five hours of bereavement to allow doctors to remove organs from a relative's body is easier to contemplate in the abstract than in reality.[38]

We discussed above some form of cash reward for donations by living organ donors. Much of the debate on markets centres on recruitment of living 'vendors'. Yet some of the objections to payment for living donors, such as those based on fears of economic coercion of and harm to the donor, do not apply to the family authorising a deceased donation. However, the notion of families putting their deceased relative's organs up for auction is widely perceived as distasteful. As one opponent put it bluntly:

A shift into any form of commercialism or its currently more fashionable cousin 'rewarded gifting' hold the potential of threatening the entire spiritual structure upon which organ transplantation is based at present.[39]

Harris has no intrinsic objection to paying families but sees it as pointless and irrational; a waste of money. For him, there are two well-established

---

[37] *Ibid.*   [38] See Chapter 5.
[39] F. Rapaport, 'Progress in organ procurement: the non-heart-beating cadaver donor and other issues in transplantation', *Transplantation Proceedings*, 23 (1991), 2699–701.

proposals for increasing the supply of organs from deceased persons: automatic availability and opting out. Both schemes involve no costs in obtaining the organs, since there is no-one who unequivocally owns the beneficial interest in the organs of deceased persons. There is no reason to compensate anyone. Harris stresses that we must keep our 'eyes on the prize'; the prize is increased supply and keeping the costs down for fear we will not have the resources to fund other essentials. Therefore, we should try these two proposals before even considering payment or other financial incentives for the supply of organs from deceased persons.

Brazier has not suddenly metamorphosed into a fan of markets in organs from deceased persons, but she struggles to see how a case against some form of reward to families can be made, if reward to living donors were to be allowed. She has no difficulty in maintaining an objection to conscription; for her, such a policy rides roughshod over the values of the living, for many of whom what happens to their corpse is a central part of the values by which they live. She is also fairly confident that no legislation endorsing automatic availability of organs will see the light of day in the UK in her lifetime.

So *pace* Harris what sort of incentives might be considered? A number of different proposals have been canvassed. All seek to find some tangible incentive short of an open market:

1. The NHS could meet the deceased's funeral expenses.[40] But does this smack of the spirit of the Anatomy Act 1832? That statute, which was designed to increase the number of bodies available for medical students to dissect, is still burned into the folk memory of many older British people, creating a fear that if you are too poor to pay for a 'proper' funeral you may end up being cut up.[41] Even today it might be seen as an inducement aimed at those too poor to pay for a decent funeral, or whose beneficiaries are too mean to expend money from their inheritance on a decent funeral. Or is that unfair? Is such a payment, which is common in many European countries, simply a gracious acknowledgement of the service rendered by the deceased and his or her family?

2. If some modest 'reward' is made available to living organ donors, could some similar reward be extended to deceased organ donation? But who would claim the 'reward'?

---

[40] Mason and Laurie, *Law and Medical Ethics*, p. 503.
[41] For a graphic account of the continuing fear of the dissecting table and lack of a proper funeral, see R. Richardson, *Death, Dissection and the Destitute*, 2nd edn (University of Chicago Press, 2000).

(a) Assume X gives directions that his organs should be donated after his death; at what point does the 'reward' become payable? When he signs on, or only if his organs are actually donated?

(b) Assume Y (X's partner) agrees to donate his organs; does she receive the 'reward' or does it fall into X's estate?

'Enforcing' donation

Where voluntary measures to increase the supply of a valuable product fail, consideration is usually given to other means of procurement. In the context of organ donation, the principal argument has been that in England and Wales a system of 'presumed consent' should operate; a system Harris endorses if his more radical proposal of automatic availability is not adopted. Consent would be presumed unless the deceased had expressly registered objections to organ donation when he or she was alive.[42] The Human Tissue Act 2004 expressly rejects such a system, requiring an explicit 'appropriate' consent to all donations for transplantation. Legislation in the UK to reverse this position is unlikely in the next decade; the UK Organ Donation Taskforce has expressly rejected a change in the law at the present time, considering that while such a system might deliver benefit, it also 'carries a significant risk of making the current situation worse'.[43] We do no more here than indicate that presumed consent is itself a misnomer and is in no sense a panacea for all the ills of an insufficient supply of organs for transplant.[44]

The very term 'presumed consent' suggests that any removal of organs is based on an assumption that, if he or she were able to do so, the person would agree to it; if we could talk to the recently deceased now silent forever they would answer 'yes, go ahead'. In English law generally, silence cannot be interpreted to mean agreement.[45] In the context of healthcare, certain actions and sets of circumstances are sufficient to presume consent. So if a patient complaining of a sore throat is invited to open their mouth as the doctor approaches with a scapula, their consent to the examination of their throat is presumed from their conduct. In everyday life, the law assumes consent to such physical contacts as are

---

[42] Special provision would have to be made in relation to minors, as, at least in relation to younger children, no consent could be presumed, nor would the child have had any opportunity to object.

[43] Organ Donation Taskforce, *The Potential Impact of an Opt Out System for Organ Donation in the UK: an Independent Report from the Organ Donation Taskforce* (London: Department of Health, 2008), para. 11.3.

[44] Price, *Human Tissue in Transplantation and Research*, p. 122.

[45] *Felthouse* v. *Bindley* (1862) 11 CB(NS) 869.

'generally acceptable in the ordinary conduct of everyday life'.[46] If Brazier taps Harris on the shoulder gently to attract his attention, without any direct knowledge that he abhors physical contact, she commits no battery. Neither precedent is helpful in the context of presumed consent and deceased organ donation: in the first example, some positive action on the part of the patient indicates consent; in the second, the triviality of the conduct in question is universally accepted. What is done does not matter much – there are no long-term consequences to the trivial contact. In the context of organ donation, while some would argue that the objections to removing organs are irrational, it cannot be argued that virtually no-one holds such objections.

Other justifications must thus be sought for moving away from explicit consent, justifications that acknowledge the force of objections, but find that those objections cannot outweigh the positive end of increasing the number of organs for transplant. For Harris, this is simple: the 'goods' that transplantation can deliver outweigh the harm to others involved in procuring them; if explicit consent fails to deliver those goods, other means of procurement become imperative. However this can be a difficult argument to analyse because of the very different perspectives participants in the debate hold on what might constitute harm (or goods). There cannot be a simple balancing exercise. Many orthodox Jews and Muslims place a high value on burial of the body intact. Religious leaders disagree about the legitimacy of organ donation, but many of the faithful hold to the view that their God commands such burial.[47] The grieving parent may perceive removal of his or her child's heart as a violation of that child; others will perceive such attitudes as wholly irrational, an imaginary harm. The logical consequence of accepting the latter view as grounds for abandoning explicit consent is not implementation of a fictitious 'presumed consent', but of conscription. If no harm ensued from removing organs from the deceased, and everyone acknowledged that this was so, then there is no rational objection to organ conscription, but probably no need for it either.

Harris would present opting out as an ethical compromise. He argues that the existence of any harm done by unconsented donation is disputed, as is any 'good' achieved by requirements for consent. Because that means it is impossible to 'weigh' the respective cases of those who do and do not ascribe intrinsic value to dead bodies, those who take the 'no (or little) value' stance *compromise* by allowing objection, but place the onus on the objectors. A view that you do not wish organs to be removed from your

---

[46] *Collins* v. *Wilcock* [1984] 1 WLR 1172, CA at 1178.
[47] Brazier, 'Retained organs', pp. 558–61; see also Chapter 3.

body after death remains one society will respect, but you must act to give it effect. Doing nothing results in the presumption that you either wish to donate organs after death, or are indifferent to the matter. Brazier and Harris both agree that such a system bears little resemblance to consent and so should not be so named, but defined as an 'opt-out' system. Given a change of nomenclature, Brazier's concerns about such a compromise focus strongly on the question: would it work so well that the inevitable fight to change the law would be worth the cost of renewed controversy in terms of delivering more available organs? Only extensive empirical research could establish how far it is (or is not) accurate to assume most people wish to be organ donors, or are indifferent to the question. What needs to be considered is the degree of strength of objection needed to make objections count at all. Let us consider some hypothetical examples, within an opt-out framework.

A young man dies of traumatic head injuries in a road accident three days after his eighteenth birthday. He had not registered an objection to organ donation. Few young people contemplate premature death on achieving their majority; any presumption that by failing to register an objection the deceased positively wished to be an organ donor must be *weak*. Any view on deceased donation requires contemplation of mortality. An opt-out system, if it is not to be automatic availability in disguise, will thus seek to ensure that citizens are aware of the presumption of organ donation and have ample opportunity to register their objections. Every person approaching eighteen years of age could be notified. However if this is contemplated, could such a system work equally well within a framework of explicit consent? This seems to be what has been achieved in the Netherlands through the Active Donor Registration Scheme.[48]

As Price so eloquently explains, the extent to which even in opt-out schemes families are still afforded a voice in the removal of organs from a relative who is not a registered objector varies widely: in 'strong' opt-out schemes such as the one in Austria, physicians simply take the organs in the absence of evidence of objection; in 'weak' schemes such as the one in Spain, relatives are still given an opportunity to object and veto donation in practice. How far an opt-out system will fill what Price phrases as the 'aching gap' is much debated.

At this point, Harris becomes a little irritated at what may be seen as niggling by Brazier. He asks whether we have lost sight of the reason why we want to increase supply of organs in the first place. It is because doing so is not just one of our core values; it is a vital interest, a prudential

---

[48] Price, *Human Tissue in Transplantation and Research*, pp. 81–5.

interest. We have a very strong obligation to protect the lives of others and ourselves, assuming all want to be saved. With this question, Harris in essence sums up the intractable nature of much of the debate. No-one could dispute the interest in preserving life. It seems nigh on immoral even to question him. But does that interest trump all others? For if it does, then is automatic availability (conscription) the answer? In response, Brazier argues that such an approach cannot be considered ethical in our diverse community.

Pragmatic solutions?

It may appear that we are not going to agree on much more than that 'something must be done'. That something has two parts: those like Brazier who have resisted many of the proposals to permit incentives that might increase the supply of organs must not close their minds to revisiting the arguments if there is no substantial improvement in rates of donation, and must be vigilant to ensure that any concerns they have about incentives are applied consistently; those like Harris who would applaud radical but unpopular solutions must nonetheless press as hard for pragmatic and smaller changes that might be viable without substantial changes in the law. The chapters that follow show that incremental change and measures to reduce the bitterness of some controversies may in fact deliver significant gains. Ethical debate conducted with restraint and mutual respect keeps the issues in the public domain and so may, we hope, save, not cost, lives.

Part II

Current issues affecting organ shortage

3 Organ donation and transplantation: meeting the needs of a multi-ethnic and multi-faith UK population

Gurch Randhawa

Inequalities exist in transplant services in the United Kingdom (UK), affecting minority ethnic groups in particular. The solutions to rectifying this situation are complex and require a holistic approach that considers both the short-term requirement to increase the number of organ donors from minority ethnic groups, and the longer-term focus to decrease the number of minority ethnic patients requiring a transplant, via preventative strategies. Focusing on disease prevention is important because the human and financial burden of not addressing these inequalities utilising a 'whole-systems' care pathway approach must be considered.

The previous UK government's seminal report, *Tackling Health Inequalities: 10 Years On*, published in 2009, reminded us not only that health gaps do still exist in the UK but are, in some cases, growing ever wider. The report stated: 'We recommend that the needs of minority ethnic groups are specifically considered in the development and implementation of policies aimed at reducing socioeconomic inequalities.'[1] This statement reflects the shift in the focus of policy during the last twenty years, in which there has been a growing interest in the health of minority ethnic populations in the UK. Throughout this period, the provision of transplant services for minority ethnic groups has become a particularly important area of debate. This is in part due to the realisation of high rates of end-stage renal failure (as a result of diabetic nephropathy) among South Asian and African-Caribbean populations and the disproportionately higher numbers of South Asians and African-Caribbeans represented on transplant waiting lists. It is of great significance that the recently established UK Organ Donation Taskforce made explicit recommendations to tackle the needs of the UK's multi-ethnic and multi-faith

---

[1] Department of Health, *Tackling Health Inequalities: 10 Years On* (London: Department of Health, 2009).

population. In the first of its reports, it stated: 'There is an urgent require-ment to identify and implement the most effective methods through which organ donation and the "gift of life" can be promoted to the general public, and specifically to the BME (black and minority ethnic) popula-tion. Research should be commissioned through Department of Health Research and Development funding.'[2] Its second report stated that: 'The Taskforce strongly recommends that the Programme Delivery Board builds on the foundations of the interviews with faith and belief groups ... to ensure that the valuable dialogue that was established is maintained.'[3]

Background

South Asians (those originating from the Indian subcontinent – India, Sri Lanka, Pakistan and Bangladesh) and African-Caribbean commun-ities have a high prevalence of Type 2 diabetes. It has been reported that 20 per cent of South Asians aged 40–49 have Type 2 diabetes, and by the age of 65 the proportion rises to a third.[4] A further complication is that diabetic nephropathy is the major cause of end-stage renal failure (ESRF) in South Asian and African-Caribbean patients receiving renal replacement therapy (RRT), either by dialysis or transplantation. When corrected for age and sex, it has been shown that there is a higher relative risk in terms of development of end-stage renal failure for South Asians and African-Caribbeans, than would be found amongst Whites, in England.[5] Published data shows that South Asians with diabetes are at 13 times the risk of developing ESRF compared to 'White' Caucasians.[6] Thus, not only are South Asians and African-Caribbeans more prone to diabetes than Whites, they are more likely to develop ESRF as a consequence.

[2] Department of Health, *Organs for Transplants: A Report from the Organ Donation Taskforce* (London: Department of Health, 2008), p. 48.

[3] Department of Health, *The Potential Impact of an Opt Out System for Organ Donation in the UK: an Independent Report from the Organ Donation Taskforce* (London: Department of Health, 2008), p. 30.

[4] V. Raleigh, 'Diabetes and hypertension in Britain's ethnic minorities: implications for the future of renal services', *British Medical Journal*, 314 (1997), 209–12.

[5] P. Roderick, V. Raleigh, L. Hallam and N. Mallick, 'The need and demand for renal replacement therapy amongst ethnic minorities in England', *Journal of Epidemiology and Community Health*, 50 (1996), 334–9.

[6] A. Burden, P. McNally, J. Feehally and J. Walls, 'Increased incidence of end-stage renal failure secondary to diabetes mellitus in Asian ethnic groups in the United Kingdom', *Diabetic Medicine*, 9 (1992), 641–5.

Importantly, the South Asian and African-Caribbean populations in the UK are relatively young compared to the White population. Since the prevalence of ESRF increases with age, this has major implications with regard to the future need for RRT and highlights the urgent need for preventative measures.[7] The incidence of ESRF has significant consequences for both local and national resources of the National Health Service (NHS). The National Renal Review has estimated an increase over the next decade of 80 per cent in the 20,000 or so patients receiving RRT and a doubling of the current cost of providing renal services, to around £600 million a year.[8]

Kidney transplantation is the preferred mode of RRT for patients with end-stage renal failure. As stated in Chapter 1, there are currently 7,980 people on the active transplant waiting list in the UK – the majority waiting for kidney transplants, but substantial numbers are also waiting for heart, lung, and liver transplants. However, a closer examination of the national waiting list reveals that some minority ethnic groups are more highly represented than others. For example, one in five people waiting for a transplant are from the African-Caribbean or South Asian communities (see Table 3.1).

14% of people waiting for a kidney transplant are South Asian and over 7% are African-Caribbean, even though they comprise only 4% and 2% respectively of the general population (Table 3.2).

South Asian people are also more likely to need a liver transplant. While 4% of the UK population are South Asian, Asian people comprise over 10% of the liver transplant list (see Table 3.3). This is because viral hepatitis – hepatitis B & C – that can lead to liver damage and liver failure, is more prevalent in the South Asian population.

Just 1% of people registered on the Organ Donor Register are South Asian and 0.3% of people registered are African-Caribbean; 1.2% of people who donate kidneys after their death are South Asian and 0.7% are African-Caribbean (see Table 3.4).

South Asian and African-Caribbean people wait on average twice as long as White people for a kidney transplant. White patients wait on average 722 days, Asian patients wait 1,496 days and Black people wait 1,389 days (see Table 3.5).

One in eight people who died waiting for a transplant in 2006 were of African-Caribbean or South Asian origin (see Table 3.6).

---

[7] G. Randhawa, 'The impending kidney transplant crisis for the Asian population in the UK', *Public Health*, 112 (1998), 265–8.
[8] Raleigh, 'Diabetes and hypertension'.

Table 3.1 Patients listed (active or suspended) for an organ transplant in the UK as at 31 December 2008, by ethnic origin and organ[9]

Ethnic origin	Organ awaited																Total	
	Kidney		Pancreas		Kidney/Pancreas		Heart		Lung		Heart/lung		Liver		Multi-organ			
	No.	%	No.	%	No.	%	No.	%	No.	%	No.	%	No.	%	No.	%	No.	%
White	6,802	74.7	77	92.8	346	93.3	90	90.9	222	96.1	10	83.3	277	82.7	24		7,848	76.5
Asian	1,360	14.9	2	2.4	18	4.9	5	5.1	2	0.9	2	16.7	37	11.0	0		1,426	13.9
Black	700	7.7	2	2.4	3	0.8	1	1	5	2.2	0	0	6	1.8	0		717	7.0
Chinese	97	1.1	0	0	1	0.3	1	1	0	0	0	0	2	0.6	0		101	1.0
Mixed	19	0.2	0	0	0	0	0	0	0	0	0	0	0	0	0		19	0.2
Other	125	1.4	2	2.4	3	0.8	2	2	2	0.9	0	0	11	3.3	0		145	1.4
Not received	6	0.1	0	0	0	0	0	0	0	0	0	0	2	0.6	0		8	0.1
Total	9,109		83		371		99		231		12		335		24		10,264	

[9] NHS Blood and Transplant, Transplant Activity in the UK 2008–2009 (2009), www.organdonation.nhs.uk/ukt/default.jsp.

Table 3.2 *Percentage of individuals registered (including suspended) on the list for a kidney (including kidney/pancreas) transplant in the UK as at 31 December 2008, by age decade and ethnic origin*[10]

Age (yrs)	Ethnic origin (%)							Total
	White	Asian	Black	Chinese	Mixed	Other	Not received	
0–9	0.5	0.9	0.4	0.0	5.3	0.0	0.0	0.6
10–19	1.2	2.3	1.4	1.0	5.3	0.0	0.0	1.4
20–29	6.2	7.4	4.4	4.1	10.5	7.8	0.0	6.3
30–39	11.7	13.1	16.6	9.2	21.1	18.0	16.7	12.3
40–49	22.7	20.8	34.3	17.4	21.1	28.1	66.7	23.3
50–59	25.0	31.1	23.0	40.8	21.1	25.0	0.0	25.9
60–69	24.6	19.4	15.7	21.4	10.5	15.6	16.7	23.0
70–79	7.9	4.9	4.0	6.1	5.3	5.5	0.0	7.1
80+	0.1	0.1	0.1	0.0	0.0	0.0	0.0	0.1
Total	*7,166*	*1,378*	*703*	*98*	*19*	*128*	*6*	*9,498*
Total %	*75.5*	*14.5*	*7.4*	*1.0*	*0.2*	*1.4*	*0.0*	
Population %	92.1	4.0	2.0	0.4	1.1	0.4		

Table 3.3 *Number registered on the list for a liver transplant in the UK as at 31 December 2008, by age decade and ethnic origin*[11]

Age (yrs)	Ethnic origin						Total
	White	Asian	Black	Chinese	Mixed	Other	
0–9	14	1	0	0	0	0	15
10–19	8	1	0	0	0	1	10
20–29	15	3	1	0	0	3	22
30–39	21	1	1	0	0	1	24
40–49	55	11	0	0	0	2	68
50–59	109	16	4	0	0	2	131
60–69	75	4	0	2	0	3	84
70–79	1	0	0	0	0	1	2
Total	*298*	*37*	*6*	*2*	*0*	*13*	*356*
Total %	*83.7*	*10.4*	*1.7*	*0.6*	*0.0*	*3.7*	
Population %	92.1	4.0	2.0	0.4	1.1	0.4	

The situation is clear: there is an urgent need to address the number of African-Caribbean and South Asian patients requiring a kidney transplant, otherwise the human and economic costs will be very severe. In

---

[10] *Ibid.* [11] *Ibid.*

Table 3.4 *Kidney donors in the UK, 2006–2008, by donor type and ethnic origin*[12]

Donor type	Ethnic origin						Total
	White	Asian	Black	Chinese	Mixed	Other	
Deceased	2,135	33	19	4	11	5	2,207
%	96.7	1.5	0.9	0.2	0.5	0.2	
Living	2,103	142	93	11	8	42	2,399
%	87.7	5.9	3.9	0.5	0.3	1.8	

Table 3.5 *Time actively registered on the list for a kidney transplant in the UK*[13]

Ethnic origin	Average wait median (days)
White	722
Asian	1,496
Black	1,389
Other	948

Table 3.6 *Patients dying in 2006 whilst listed for a transplant*[14]

Ethnic origin	Kidney	Pancreas	Kidney/ Pancreas	Heart	Lungs	Heart/Lungs	Liver	TOTAL	%
White	212	–	9	24	50	7	81	*383*	*85.5*
Asian	34	–	–	3	–	–	8	*45*	*10.0*
Black	10	–	–	1	–	–	1	*12*	*2.7*
Chinese	3	–	–	–	–	–	–	*3*	*0.7*
Mixed	1	–	–	–	–	1	–	*2*	*0.4*
Other	1	–	–	1	–	–	1	*3*	*0.7*
Total	*261*	–	*9*	*29*	*50*	*8*	*91*	*448*	

the short term, there needs to be a greater number of donors coming forward from these communities to increase the pool of suitable organs.[15] In the long term, there needs to be greater attention paid to preventative

[12] *Ibid.*   [13] *Ibid.* (based on registrations 1998–2000).

[14] NHS Blood and Transplant, *Transplant Activity in the UK 2006–2007* (2007), www. organdonation.nhs.uk/ukt/default.jsp.

[15] Randhawa, 'The impending kidney transplant crisis'; C. Exley, J. Sim, N. Reid et al., 'Attitudes and beliefs within the Sikh community regarding organ donation: a pilot study', *Social Science and Medicine*, 43 (1996), 23–8.

strategies to reduce the number of African-Caribbeans and South Asians requiring RRT. The latter can only be achieved if we begin to address the problem of poor access to health services for minority ethnic groups.[16]

Improving access to services

The UK Diabetes National Service Framework (NSF) highlights the importance of access to services, in particular to meet the needs of minority ethnic groups.[17] The Renal Services NSF also focuses on 'renal disease complicating diabetes' and emphasises inequalities experienced by minority ethnic groups.[18] However, there is evidence that knowledge of diabetes and its complications is poor among South Asians and African-Caribbeans.[19] Preliminary evidence also suggests that quality of healthcare for South Asians and African-Caribbeans is inadequate and compliance poor.[20] There is also a low uptake of hospital-based diabetes services, with growing evidence that South Asians are subsequently referred later for renal care, and are more likely to be lost to follow-up.[21] Late referral may reduce opportunities to implement measures to slow down progression of renal failure, or to prepare adequately for RRT, adding to morbidity and mortality.

The World Health Organization (WHO) study group on diabetes notes that resources should be directed to improving the quality of preventative care in primary care settings and to public health interventions for controlling diabetes. Education, early diagnosis and effective management of diabetes are important for safeguarding the health of susceptible populations and for long-term savings for the NHS.[22] Most encouragingly, recent studies from the United States and Finland have demonstrated that modest lifestyle changes can reduce the risk, by more than 58 per cent, of overt Type 2 diabetes developing in susceptible groups.[23]

---

[16] G. Randhawa, 'Developing culturally competent renal services in the United Kingdom: tackling inequalities in health', *Transplantation Proceedings*, 35 (2003), 21–3.

[17] Department of Health, *National Service Framework for Diabetes: Standards* (London: Department of Health, 2002).

[18] Department of Health, *National Service Framework for Renal Services* (London: Department of Health, 2004).

[19] J. Nazroo, *The Health of Britain's Ethnic Minorities* (London: Policy Studies Institute, 1997); M. Johnson, D. Owen and C. Blackburn, *Black and Minority Ethnic Groups in England: The Second Health and Lifestyles Survey* (London: Health Education Authority, 2000).

[20] Johnson *et al.*, *ibid.*; Raleigh, 'Diabetes and hypertension'.

[21] R. Jeffrey, G. Woodrow, J. Mahler, *et al.*, 'Indo-Asian experience of renal transplantation in Yorkshire: results of a 10 year survey', *Transplantation*, 73 (2002), 1652–7.

[22] Raleigh, 'Diabetes and hypertension'.

[23] Diabetes Prevention Program Research Group (DPPRG), 'Reduction in the incidence of type 2 diabetes with lifestyle intervention or Metformin', *New England Journal of Medicine*, 346 (2002), 393–403; J. Tuomilehto *et al.*, 'Prevention of type 2 diabetes mellitus by changes in lifestyle among subjects with impaired glucose tolerance', *New England Journal of Medicine*, 344 (2001), 1343–50.

Furthermore, various interventions, such as tight blood pressure control, effective use of angiotensin converting enzyme (ACE) inhibitors or angiotensin receptor (ATR) blockers, and tight blood sugar control can significantly delay the progression of diabetic nephropathy.[24]

'Reducing inequalities' is a theme cutting across a number of UK government health policy working groups – Diabetes NSF, Renal NSF, NSF for Children, and the UK Organ Donation Taskforce. It is essential that the Organ Donation Taskforce Delivery Board collaborates with the respective NSF Clinical Directors to ensure the best use of resources so that future rates of renal failure and heart failure are reduced among black and minority ethnic groups.

Improving transplantation rates

Although the transplant option may be medically and economically favourable, in reality there are unfortunately substantial constraints resulting from the severe lack of donors from the African-Caribbean and South Asian populations. This may be attributable to two main causes – a lack of awareness concerning organ donation and transplantation; and potentially low referral rates to the Intensive Care Unit.[25] It must be stressed that these factors are not unique to the African-Caribbean and South Asian populations, and have relevance to other members of the public in the UK. Furthermore, it is extremely important to recognise that the African-Caribbean and South Asian communities in the UK are

---

[24] UK Prospective Diabetes Study (UKPDS) Group, 'Intensive blood-glucose control with sulphonylureas or insulin compared with conventional treatment and risk of complications in patients with type 2 diabetes (UKPDS 33)', *Lancet*, 352 (1998), 837–53; T. Feest, E. Dunn and C. Burton, 'Can intensive treatment alter the progress of established diabetic nephropathy to end-stage renal failure?', *QJM*, 92 (1999), 275–82; B. Brenner, M. Cooper, D. de Zeeuw *et al.*, 'Effects of Losartan on renal and cardiovascular outcomes in patients with type 2 diabetes and nephropathy', *New England Journal of Medicine*, 345 (2001), 861–9; G. Cinotti and P. Zucchelli, 'Effect of Lisinopril on the progression of renal insufficiency in mild proteinuric non-diabetic nephropathies', *Nephrology Dialysis Transplantation*, 16 (2001), 961–6; E. Lewis, L. Hunsicker, W. Clarke *et al.*, 'Renoprotective effect of the angiotensin-receptor antagonist irbesartan in patients with nephropathy due to type 2 diabetes', *New England Journal of Medicine*, 345 (2001), 851–60; L. Lightstone, *Preventing Kidney Disease: The Ethnic Challenge* (Peterborough: National Kidney Research Fund, 2001).

[25] Exley *et al.*, 'Attitudes and beliefs'; A. Darr and G. Randhawa, 'Public opinion and perception of organ donation and transplantation among Asian communities: an exploratory study in Luton, UK', *International Journal of Health Promotion and Education*, 37 (1999), 68–74.

heterogeneous, and thus it is important to familiarise oneself with the demographics of the local population.[26]

Prompting awareness of the need for organ donors among the African-Caribbean and South Asian communities

Regrettably, very little research has been devoted to this area. The relatively few studies which have been carried out consistently show that whilst African-Caribbeans and South Asians are supportive of organ donation and transplantation, they are not aware of the specific needs of their community for organs.[27] These studies, however, do not identify what would motivate these communities to come forward as potential organ donors. Pertinently, Titmuss famously viewed the NHS, created in the post-World War II period, as a vehicle for institutionalising altruistic practices, notably the voluntary 'gift' of blood to strangers as represented by the transfusion service.[28] More recent advances in medical technology have made new forms of bodily tissue donation possible, including organs, gametes, eggs, stem cells and embryos. The limitation of Titmuss's analysis was an implicit assumption that all individuals would have a feeling of belonging to 'society' and would therefore wish to contribute to solving a 'societal problem'. Within the main South Asian religions, namely Hinduism, Sikhism and Islam, the concept of gifting to assist society is a highly valued virtue, 'Sewa', 'Sewa' and 'Zakat' respectively. This issue needs careful examination within the context of an increasingly diverse UK population, and research is required to identify what would make the 'gifting of organs' relevant to a multi-ethnic and multi-faith UK society.[29]

---

[26] Z. Khan and G. Randhawa, 'Informing the UK's South Asian communities on organ donation and transplantation', *European Dialysis and Transplant Nurses Journal*, 25 (1999), 12–14.

[27] Exley *et al.*, 'Attitudes and beliefs'; Darr and Randhawa, 'Public opinion and perception'; C. Hayward and A. Madill, 'The meanings of organ donation: Muslims of Pakistani origin and white English nationals living in North England', *Social Science and Medicine*, 57 (2003), 389–401; F. Alkhawari, G. Stimson and A. Warrens, 'Attitudes towards transplantation in UK Muslim Indo-Asians in West London', *American Journal of Transplantation*, 5 (2005), 1326–31; C. Davis and G. Randhawa, 'The influence of religion on organ donation among the Black Caribbean and Black African population – a pilot study in the UK', *Ethnicity & Disease*, 16 (2006), 281–5; M. Morgan, R. Hooper, M. Mayblin and R. Jones, 'Attitudes to kidney donation and registering as a donor among ethnic groups in the UK', *Journal of Public Health*, 28 (2006), 226–34.

[28] R. Titmuss, *The Gift Relationship: from Human Blood to Social Policy* (London: Allen and Unwin, 2003).

[29] The author has been commissioned by NHS Blood and Transplant to carry out a two-year national study examining this issue, the results of which will be published in 2011.

A growing amount of literature has shown that religion plays an important part in the decision to donate organs.[30] The religious beliefs of the major faiths of the UK's African-Caribbeans and South Asians – namely Islam, Hinduism, Sikhism, Buddhism and Christianity – have all been scrutinised in the literature. None of the religions object to organ donation in principle, although in some there are varying schools of thought. What is interesting, however, is that the position of one's religion is used by many people in informing their decision as to whether to donate or not.[31] This has also been highlighted in several studies conducted outside the UK.[32] Unfortunately, this issue has not been prominent in research carried out in the UK, but the findings of a pilot study to examine attitudes towards organ donation and transplantation among a cross-section of the UK's South Asian population have shed some light on the matter.[33] It was found that, far from being a barrier to organ donation, the respondents were more supportive of donation, and transplantation in general, when they were aware of the position of their religion with regard to these issues. This highlights the importance of education and raising awareness among the South Asian public.[34] There is a need to identify how best to encourage religious 'stakeholders' to engage with their local communities concerning the issue of organ donation and transplantation. It is encouraging to note that the Organ Donation Taskforce initiated some preliminary meetings with faith leaders in the UK and has recommended that this dialogue continues.

In recent years, the UK Department of Health and NHS Blood and Transplant (formerly known as UK Transplant) have produced a range of educational materials (including leaflets, posters and videos) in the main South Asian languages to increase awareness of transplant-related issues. Additionally, materials have been produced that set out the position of each religion regarding organ donation. However, current evidence shows that further thought is required with regard to the dissemination of this

---

[30] G. Randhawa, 'An exploratory study examining the influence of religion on attitudes towards organ donation among the Asian population in Luton, UK', *Nephrology Dialysis Transplantation*, 13 (1998), 1949–54; Hayward and Madill, 'The meanings of organ donation'; Alkhawari *et al.*, 'Attitudes towards transplantation'; Davis and Randhawa, 'The influence of religion'.

[31] Randhawa, 'An exploratory study'.

[32] C. Callender, 'The results of transplantation in blacks: just the tip of the iceberg', *Transplantation Proceedings*, 21 (1989), 3407–10; G. Kyriakides, M. Hadjigavriel, P. Hadjicostas *et al.*, 'Public awareness and attitudes toward transplantation in Cyprus', *Transplantation Proceedings*, 25 (1993), 2279; F. La Spina, L. Sedda, C. Pizzi *et al.*, 'Donor families' attitudes toward organ donation: the North Italy transplant program', *Transplantation Proceedings*, 25 (1993), 1699–1701.

[33] Randhawa, 'An exploratory study'.

[34] Exley *et al.*, 'Attitudes and beliefs'; Darr and Randhawa, 'Public opinion and perception'.

literature among African-Caribbean and South Asian populations[35] – care needs to be taken in specifying the target population, selecting the persons who will communicate the campaign appeal, designating the methodology of appeal delivery, and deciding upon the content of the appeal. There are indications from pilot work in the UK, as well as research outside it, involving minority ethnic groups, that appeals for African-Caribbean and South Asian donors may be more effectively communicated by employing a grassroots, community networking approach.[36] The UK Organ Donation Taskforce have placed great emphasis on achieving equity in organ donation and transplantation and have consequently recommended that there should be further consideration given to ensuring that organ donation is relevant to all of the UK's multi-ethnic and multi-faith population.

Low referral rates to the Intensive Care Unit (ICU)

The vast majority of organs are procured from ventilated patients in the ICU who have suffered some form of cerebrovascular accident.[37] Thus, an important point to consider is whether African-Caribbean and South Asian patients are reaching the ICU so that they may be considered as potential donors. It may be that the African-Caribbean and South Asian populations are simply not dying of the relevant causes or are not being referred to the ICU, rather than there being an unwillingness to become donors.[38]

Again, there is very little research in this area. Gore et al. carried out a comprehensive audit of all ICU deaths in the UK and suitability to become organ donors.[39] However, the main drawback to this study was that the ethnic group of each patient was not recorded. A pilot study in Coventry was carried out which sought to determine admission rates of South Asian and non-South Asian patients to ICUs;[40] the results

[35] Exley et al., 'Attitudes and beliefs'; Darr and Randhawa, 'Public opinion and perception'; Randhawa, 'An exploratory study'.

[36] Exley et al., 'Attitudes and beliefs'; Darr and Randhawa, 'Public opinion and perception'; Khan and Randhawa, 'Informing the UK's South Asian communities'.

[37] S. Gore, D. Cable and A. Holland, 'Organ donation from intensive care units in England and Wales: two year confidential audit of deaths in intensive care', British Medical Journal, 304 (1992), 349–55; G. Randhawa, 'Enhancing the health professional's role in requesting transplant organs', British Journal of Nursing, 6 (1997), 429–34.

[38] C. Exley, J. Sim, N. Reid et al., 'The admission of Asian patients to intensive therapy units and its implications for kidney donation: a preliminary report from Coventry, UK', Journal of Epidemiology and Community Health, 50 (1996), 447–50.

[39] Gore et al., 'Organ donation from intensive care units'.

[40] Exley et al., 'The admission of Asian patients'.

indicated that South Asians were less than half as likely to be admitted to an ICU than non-South Asians. These findings have serious implications, as they indicate that there are fewer instances where health professionals have opportunities of making requests for organs from South Asian families. Another important finding of this study was that the rates of referral from the ICU to the transplant unit were the same for South Asians and non-South Asians, as were subsequent donation rates.[41]

Thus, the results of this preliminary study suggest that lower rates of organ donation among the South Asian population are linked to the initial low admission rates to the ICU. Related to this, there is preliminary evidence emerging to suggest that the volume of brain-stem deaths is lower among minority ethnic groups. It is acknowledged that the recent work of the NHS Blood and Transplant-led national Potential Donor Audit has begun to address these issues. However, there is presently no firm evidence to support the view that access to ICUs is equitable across all ethnic groups. It is important therefore to identify whether Black and minority ethnic groups have the same likelihood of becoming potential organ donors as their White counterparts. The Potential Donor Audit has highlighted the fact that families and friends of African-Caribbean and South Asian potential donors are more likely to withhold consent for donation than is the case for White donors. Indeed, the refusal rate for non-White potential donors is 69 per cent, compared with 35 per cent for White potential donors. UK Transplant had previously commissioned research to identify why families refuse a request for organ donation. However, this research did not include non-White families, and there is a need to commission further research in order to understand why non-White families have a higher refusal rate than White families.

Looking to the future

It is clear that Black and minority ethnic groups are disproportionately affected by renal health problems both in terms of access to appropriate services, a higher prevalence of renal complications, a reduced likelihood of a transplant, and longer waiting times on the transplant waiting list. A major undertaking for researchers and clinicians in the UK will be to explore *access* to and the progression through the diabetes and 'renal disease complicating diabetes' care pathways, and to identify health beliefs and experiences associated with diabetes and diabetic renal complications among African-Caribbean and South Asian groups.

---

[41] *Ibid.*

A systematic exploration of these issues would provide a valuable resource for health professionals working with these groups and allow for the development of a culturally competent diabetic and renal service sensitive to the needs of minority ethnic groups.[42]

Specifically, important gaps include:

1. identification of cultural beliefs and practices relevant to diabetes and diabetic renal disease self-management, including attitudes to medication and attendance at GP surgeries, diabetic services and nephrology services (for routine monitoring);
2. examination of referral patterns to hospital-based diabetic services, and subsequent attendance;
3. exploration of referral patterns to nephrology services; and
4. exploration of the relevance of current renal complications education programmes for minority ethnic groups.

Kidney Research UK has recently launched the ABLE (A Better Life through Education and Empowerment) campaign which aims to redress some of the above issues by education and by raising personal awareness of kidney health issues among minority ethnic groups.[43] The author led a national pilot study (with colleagues from Imperial College and the University of Leicester) to explore the above issues, and the study was completed in September 2009.[44]

Concomitantly, there needs to be an increase in the supply of organs from the African-Caribbean and South Asian populations to alleviate the burden on current waiting lists and for those patients on dialysis. This process can only begin if the public are in an informed position to consider and debate the issues surrounding organ donation and transplantation. Central to attaining this goal is increased levels of health education and awareness of the specific problems within the African-Caribbean and South Asian populations. This is a difficult challenge, as many of these communities live within the most deprived (and hard-to-reach) communities in the UK. Not only should we engage the public with the discourse of 'disease prevention' as well as that of 'organ donation', but there is a need to identify whether the social class of a patient and/or their family influences *live* donation, as this may have implications for current reimbursement arrangements. This issue may have particular relevance to

---

[42] G. Randhawa, 'Increasing the donor supply from the UK's Asian population: the need for further research', *Transplantation Proceedings*, 32 (2000), 1561–2.

[43] N. Jain, A. Farooqi and J. Feehally, 'Raising awareness of chronic kidney disease among South Asians and primary care: the ABLE project', *Journal of Renal Care*, 34 (2008), 173–8.

[44] G. Randhawa, C. Jetha, B. Gill *et al.*, 'Understanding kidney disease and perceptions of kidney services among South Asians in West London: focus group study', *British Journal of Renal Medicine*, 15 (2010), 23–7.

Black and minority ethnic groups that experience the greatest levels of deprivation in the UK.

It has been suggested previously by commentators that religion acts as a prohibitor to organ donation among the South Asian population, but empirical research seems to suggest otherwise. The position of one's religion towards donation is used by individuals as a helpful guide in reaching their decision as to whether to donate or not.[45] The introduction of community-based information programmes needs to be evaluated to assess whether this impacts upon the number of African-Caribbeans and South Asians on the NHS Organ Donor Register. Indeed, all public organ-donor campaigns should be formally evaluated to identify which members of the public benefit from such campaigns, and which members are still not being reached. Moreover, research should be commissioned to identify how best to unravel public concerns that are 'cultural' as opposed to 'religious'.

Attention also needs to be given to the number of South Asian patients in ICUs who are eligible to become organ donors. The limited research conducted so far suggests that low rates of organ donation by South Asian people may be related to factors pertaining to low admission to ICUs rather than by those relating to the donation of organs.[46] There is a clear need for extensive research in this area. Preliminary evidence also suggests that the number of brain-stem deaths is lower among minority ethnic groups.[47] An audit of potential donors identifying ethnicity is urgently required to substantiate this, although it is recognised that the Potential Donor Audit is beginning to address this issue. Within the ICU also, there need to be clear guidelines as to how to approach individuals with requests for the donation of their loved one's organs, coupled with specific training and counselling relating to working with families from a range of ethnic and faith backgrounds.[48] Alongside these initiatives, efforts to promote living related kidney donation among Asian families need to be implemented, especially in the light of potentially lower admission rates to ICUs and lower deceased organ donation rates.

Conclusion

There has been substantial recognition of the need to improve organ donation rates among minority ethnic groups in the UK, as evidenced by the plethora of initiatives led by NHS Blood and Transplant, including:

[45] Randhawa, 'An exploratory study'.
[46] Exley *et al.*, 'The admission of Asian patients'.   [47] *Ibid.*
[48] Randhawa, 'Enhancing the health professional's role'.

1. running a multi-faith symposium in Bradford in 2000 aimed at the eight major faiths;
2. appointment of a project worker to look at organ donation and ethnicity in 2002 (leaflets and booklet led to another seminar in Birmingham involving 200 delegates);
3. UK Transplant taking over running in 2003 of all Black and Asian donor campaigns developed by the Department of Health;
4. using Black and Asian celebrities to highlight the importance of organ donation and transplantation;
5. developing training for donor transplant co-ordinators and clinicians in 2005 with a significant component of the training applied to cultural differences;
6. research commissioned by UK Transplant in 2006 into attitudes of ethnic minority groups to organ donation;
7. the development of a cultural guide for healthcare professionals as an aid for use in interviews when speaking to families with differing and diverse cultural backgrounds;
8. the launch in 2007 of the Can We Count on You? campaign, which was an organ donation campaign targeted at minority ethnic groups; and
9. the commissioning in 2009 of a two-year research study to explore how to make the gifting of organs relevant and meaningful to the UK's multi-ethnic and multi-faith population.

Many of these initiatives are recognised to be at the forefront in the worldwide development of culturally competent organ donation education materials. However, the success of these initiatives has been limited by the lack of a focused strategy that brings together the various strands of a multifaceted problem that would lead to a coherent implementation plan. It is hoped that the recent specific recommendations by the Organ Donation Taskforce focusing upon the needs of the UK's diverse population will enable the development of a clear action plan to achieve equity in organ donation and transplantation. It is further hoped that this chapter contributes to beginning and shaping the framework for such a process not only in the UK but for many other countries who have a multi-ethnic and multi-faith society.

Finally, it is worth noting that debates concerning organ donation and ethnicity are relatively new and are limited by the quality of data available, not just in the UK but also worldwide. In future, it is imperative that NHS Organ Donor Register data should include age, ethnicity, social class, gender and religion. The potential interaction of these variables should be analysed to inform future donor procurement strategies. It is only when these issues are addressed adequately that we will begin to see a transplant service that truly meets the needs of a multi-ethnic and multi-faith population within the UK.

4   Educating the public to encourage organ donation?

Mairi Levitt

The recent Organ Donation Taskforce Report published in the United Kingdom (UK) rejected an opt-out system but emphasised again the importance of educating the public, especially those groups with low rates of donation.[1] The call for more education often carries the assumption that increased knowledge will result in a specific (desired) action: more sex education to reduce unwanted pregnancies among young girls or more education on organ transplantation to increase donation rates. As shown by public engagement in science, however, it is too simple to assume that increased information will result in particular attitudes or behaviour. This chapter examines public education in the field of organ transplantation and how it relates to other public engagement activities, to public attitudes and to the usual focus of public health education on prevention, as well as treatment. The underlying question is why the need to find resources to meet the demand for organ transplants is not queried when other areas of healthcare, in a publicly funded system, are subject to various forms of rationing.

Engaging the public

Public engagement has become an expected part of research projects in the fields of science and technology, including those funded by the European Commission. The UK-government-funded Biotechnology and Biological Sciences Research Council (BBSRC) expects grant-holders to 'engage actively with the public at both the local and national levels about their research and its broader implications',[2] and the Medical Research Council (MRC) asks researchers to indicate, 'where appropriate', their plans for

---

[1] Department of Health, *Organs for Transplants – the Supplement Report* (London: Department of Health, 2008).
[2] Biotechnology and Biological Sciences Research Council (BBSRC), *Research Grants: The Guide* (BBSRC Research Innovation and Skills Directorate, October 2009) (www.bbsrc. ac.uk/funding/apply/grants_guide.pdf), para. 1.19.

'involving the public *actively* in *any of the stages* of your research' (author's emphasis).[3] One of the assessment criteria for all MRC grants is whether 'the arrangements for the promotion of the public understanding of science relating to this proposal [are] appropriate and sufficient'.[4] Some degree of public and patient involvement is also part of the process of developing healthcare policy both at national and local level.[5] This is a long way from the traditional view that the role of the scientific expert is to correct the public's deficit in knowledge and understanding by conveying 'the facts', preferably with attractive materials and interesting methods. The assumption was that an increase in public understanding would lead to a corresponding increase in public support for science and technology.[6]

The evidence is more mixed. In a study of the links between knowledge and positive attitudes, Evans and Durant found that there was a weak positive relationship between scientific understanding and attitude to science, but a stronger one between understanding and coherent and discriminating attitudes.[7] The public consultation on human cloning commissioned by the Wellcome Trust found that participants expressed more concerns about 'therapeutic cloning' when they had more information and time to consider.[8] The GM Nation Debate included focus group discussions with a sample of the general population, as well as meetings with those who chose to take part. It was found that with these general-public groups more information led to firmer views. They were more willing to accept some benefits but were more concerned about all of the risks.[9]

Where views are expressed that ignore scientific evidence and appear irrational, an understanding of the roots of these views might show that the provision of more scientific and medical information is unlikely to change anything. Dicksen gives the example of those in South Africa who deny that the Human Immunodeficiency Virus (HIV) causes the Acquired Immune Deficiency Syndrome (AIDS). He argues that former President Mbeki's reluctance to accept the science was not due to a lack

---

[3] Medical Research Council, *Applicant Handbook 2008–2009*, www.mrc.ac.uk/Utilities/ Documentrecord/index.htm?d=MRC001873, p. 18.

[4] *Ibid.*, p. 28.

[5] S. Waite and E. Nolte, 'Public involvement policies in health: exploring their conceptual basis', *Health Economics, Policy and Law*, 1 (2006), 149–62.

[6] D. Scheufele, 'Messages and heuristics: how audiences form attitudes about emerging technologies' in J. Turney (ed.), *Engaging Science: Thoughts, Deeds, Analysis and Action* (London: Wellcome Trust, 2006), pp. 20–5.

[7] G. Evans and J. Durant, 'The relationship between knowledge and attitudes in the public understanding of science in Britain', *Public Understanding of Science*, 4 (1995), 57–74.

[8] Wellcome Trust, *Public Perspectives on Human Cloning* (London: Wellcome Trust, 1998), p. 5.

[9] R. Heller, *GM Nation? The Findings of the Public Debate* (London: Department of Trade and Industry, 2003), p. 39.

of information on science or medicine but to an understandable mistrust of multinational pharmaceutical companies.[10] Here the relevant information would be on regulation and governance, but the reasons for a lack of trust have deep historical roots in colonialism, and *any* information alone would be unlikely to ensure trust. This example illustrates the complex relationship between knowledge and attitudes, and the importance of cultural and social context to the formation of attitudes.

The dominant rhetoric in the academic literature on public engagement no longer characterises 'the public' as a homogeneous mass, but recognises different forms of expertise that can contribute to the process of scientific research and its applications. So the old deficit model has, at least officially, given way to a view that diverse publics should be engaged with the consultation process and involved in dialogue rather than given information didactically.[11] Dialogue carries the expectation that both sides have something to say and can learn from each other. Furthermore, this dialogue should be at the early stages – upstream – so that publics have a role in the development of a technology and applications rather than a more limited one once the applications are developed.[12] Typically such dialogues reveal that publics may have different or broader concerns than those addressed by the experts. Rather than just asking about risks and benefits for users or consumers, publics ask questions like: Whose commercial or political interests are being served? Is this technology something we should be developing? What might be the long-term consequences for society, as well as for individuals?[13]

In the case of organ donation education, the technology is established and public engagement is undertaken to raise awareness of the need for organs. The twin aims are: to increase the numbers of individuals entering their names on the NHS Organ Donor Register, signing donor cards and telling their families their wishes; and increasing the percentage agreeing to the removal of organs when approached as next of kin of a potential donor. The 'urgent requirement' according to the recent Organ Donation Taskforce report is 'to identify and implement the most effective methods through which organ donation and the "gift of life" can be promoted to the

---

[10] D. Dicksen, 'Science and its public: the need for a "third way"', *Social Studies of Science*, 30 (2000), 917–23, 919.

[11] The deficit model assumed that negative attitudes towards science and technology were due to a lack of scientific knowledge. The role of scientists was therefore to inform the public in a one-way communication.

[12] J. Wilsden and R. Willis, *See-Through Science: Why Public Engagement Needs to Move Upstream* (London: Demos, 2004).

[13] A. Irwin, 'Beyond the toolkit: bringing engagement into practice' in Turney (ed.), *Engaging Science*, pp. 50–5.

general public, and specifically to the BME [black and minority ethnic] population'.[14] Organ donation undoubtedly saves lives without directly causing death or suffering to others, so a straightforward aim to promote it seems to be justified. When asked, the public say they support organ donation and transplantation, although, as discussed below, their actions are not always commensurate with the answers given in attitude surveys.

Public attitudes to organ donation and transplantation

There is very little opposition to organ donation in surveys in Britain, with over 90 per cent in favour in some surveys.[15] However, fewer than 30 per cent are on the NHS Organ Donor Register and 40 per cent of the relatives of potential donors refuse consent, a figure that rises to 75 per cent in the case of minority ethnic groups.[16] For the purposes of organ donation campaigns it is useful to be able to point to overwhelming public support, but given the gap between support and even the minimal action of signing a donor card, it seems to be a 'passive affirmation'.[17] The discrepancy probably indicates that when asked if you are in favour of organ donation, this is not the sort of question you can readily answer 'no' to, not only because it seems unfeeling to those who need a transplant, but also because you or someone you know might need an organ in the future. Even fewer people object, in a hypothetical question, to *receiving* a donated organ.

When more specific questions are asked, however, the *attitude/action* gap may narrow. Questions on organ donation were included in a Eurobarometer survey of a representative sample from each of the twenty-five European Union (EU) Member States which was conducted in 2006. The UK came out above average for EU Member States on all the questions:

1. for willingness to donate after death, the UK was ranked tenth;
2. for agreeing to donation on behalf of a close family member, the UK was ranked eighth;
3. in support of donor cards, the UK was ranked joint third at 89 per cent; and
4. for having a donor card, the UK was ranked fourth.

---

[14] Department of Health, *Organs for Transplants: a Report from the Organ Donation Taskforce* (London: Department of Health, 2008), Recommendation 13.

[15] *Ibid.*, p. 5.

[16] *Ibid.*, p. 18; K. Barber, S. Falvey, C. Hamilton *et al.*, 'Potential for organ donation in the United Kingdom: audit of intensive care records', *British Medical Journal*, 332 (2006), 1124–7.

[17] L. Baines, J. Joseph and R. Jindal, 'A public forum to promote organ donation amongst Asians: the Scottish initiative', *Transplant International*, 15 (2002), 124–31, 130.

Positive responses on all these issues were related to whether respondents had discussed organ donation with their families, and the UK was also above average for this, being ranked seventh.[18]

The attitudes expressed by UK respondents in the Eurobarometer survey matched the reality. In other words, there was no attitude/action gap: 63 per cent of the survey respondents were willing to agree to donation for a relative – in practice the actual figure agreeing is currently around 60 per cent; and 26 per cent of respondents claimed to have signed a donor card – the current figure is around 25 per cent. Nevertheless, the rate of deceased organ donation in the UK is lower than the EU average, at 14.7 donors per million population (pmp).[19] Interestingly, Spain, which is the Member State with the highest rate of deceased organ donation, had less favourable attitudes towards organ donation than the UK in the Eurobarometer survey. Lower percentages of respondents in Spain agreed that they were willing to donate after death themselves and fewer were willing to agree on behalf of a close relative. The much higher deceased organ donation rate in Spain might indicate that there would be more discussion within families about organ donation, but the figures were only marginally higher at 45 per cent for Spain, as compared with 43 per cent in the UK.[20]

Many commentators on the Spanish situation have focused on the importance of the organisational structure as an explanation for the high donation rates.[21] Given the Eurobarometer findings on representative samples from Spain and UK, it seems that the attitude/action gap might be greater in Spain than in the UK, but in the opposite direction – i.e. less favourable attitudes but high donation rates. This could mean that the concentration on attitudes is misplaced or that these questions do not capture what is important about attitudes in terms of increasing rates of organ donation. A simple tick box (Yes, No, Don't Know), or response using a one-dimensional attitude scale measuring agreement or disagreement, does not tackle the complexity of people's attitudes. More in-depth investigation may reveal concerns and uncertainties.

In an Australian study, Maloney and Walker examined the normal stance of pro-donation and found that it was nearly always qualified. In

---

[18] Eurobarometer, *Europeans and Organ Donation* (Report, Special Eurobarometer 272D) (Brussels: European Commission, 2007), pp. 8, 12, 16, 18.

[19] Council of Europe, *Transplant Newsletter: International Figures on Organ Donation and Transplantation – 2008*, 14(1) (2009).

[20] *Ibid.*, pp. 5, 12, 18.

[21] Department of Health, *Organs for Transplants*, p. 43. See also M. Quigley, M. Brazier, R. Chadwick *et al.*, 'The organs crisis and the Spanish model: theoretical versus pragmatic considerations', *Journal of Medical Ethics*, 34 (2008), 223–4.

focus group discussions, most participants talked about organ donation and transplantation positively using a discourse of altruism and sacrifice on the part of relatives and the 'gift of life'.[22] The majority then went on to express qualifications and concerns, however, using the medical-mechanistic discourse in which the body is made up of parts, like a machine, that can be removed; the donor supplies a spare part and the recipient waits to receive it. Participants could, and did, use both these competing frameworks. Maloney and Walker suggest that the first discourse, the gift of life, is the 'normative dimension', explaining the majority support for organ donation.[23] When qualifying their pro-donation views, participants used an alternative understanding to express fears about brain death, mutilation of the donor's body and mistrust of the medical profession's role in organ transplantation. Even healthcare professionals who usually enjoy a high degree of public trust may be viewed differently when they are not caring for the relative but hoping to harvest his or her organs: 'there was an implicit connotation that one had to be on one's guard against the medical profession because their hidden agenda was always the acquisition of organs'.[24] Differing views on these issues were not found to be dependent on differences in knowledge; in her research on relatives' attitudes to organ donation, quoted in the Scottish Transplant Group Report, Haddow found that 'if the family felt donation was not a good thing then positive messages from health professionals were regarded as self-serving'.[25]

Reports on ways of tackling the 'organ shortage' put a great emphasis on public education. Here the deficit model referred to earlier is operating, i.e. the assumption is that a more informed public will be more positive themselves about donation or when making a decision on it for a close relative. The public do need information to make informed choices and it is not suggested that public engagement should be content free. In the next section of the chapter, I will examine two recent education packages on organ donation and transplantation produced by the NHS and the Scottish Transplant Group, with materials for teachers and pupils, in order to ascertain what sort of information is provided and the kind of discussion that is encouraged.

---

[22] G. Maloney and I. Walker, 'Talking about transplants: social representations and the dialectical, dilemmatic nature of organ donation and transplantation', *British Journal of Social Psychology*, 41 (2002), 299–320.
[23] *Ibid.*, 312.   [24] *Ibid.*, 310.
[25] Scottish Transplant Group, *An Organ Donation Strategy for Scotland: Scottish Transplant Group Report* (June 2002), www.sedh.scot.nhs.uk/publications/odss/odss.pdf, p. 44.

Educating the public about organ donation and transplantation

The aims of NHS Blood and Transplant's 'educational resource' for schools are to:

Enable young people to see how they can make a difference to people's lives; raise awareness about donation and the ethics surrounding this area; help young people decide whether donation is something they want to do; give a scientific grounding in how blood, organ and bone marrow donation works.[26]

The focus on young people is explained by the assertion that 'many adults find this a difficult subject to discuss, but children of school age seem to have less difficulty in doing so'.[27] The conclusion is that school-based programmes 'would mean that young people could discuss with their peers or their parents topics such as the benefits of organ donation'.[28] Certainly young people are used to discussing current issues in, for example, Personal, Social Health and Economic Education (PSHE)[29] and Religious Education, but the attitudes expressed by teenagers are in fact less supportive of donation than those of adults.[30] On the other hand, discussion with others could enable people to express their concerns and examine them with those who have different attitudes.

The Scottish Transplant Group recently produced a teaching pack which clearly had high expectations, given its overarching claim that it 'has the potential to bring about, albeit over time, a fundamental shift in public attitudes towards organ donation'.[31] It is further stated that the Group is 'convinced' that the proportion of relatives withholding consent to transplant could be reduced and so numbers of organs available be increased 'if the public were aware of the general issues ... and did not have to think about them for the first time while in the throes of imminent bereavement'.[32] From this statement, it is clear that the point of providing information is so that it would result in consent; however, it is not clear that ignorance of the general issues is a barrier to relatives giving consent. The topics given prominence in the Scottish Transplant Group's educational materials are presumably the issues on which it is thought there is a deficit of knowledge. These general issues are: the need for transplants;

---

[26] NHS Blood and Transplant, *Give and Let Live*, www.giveandletlive.co.uk/en.
[27] Scottish Transplant Group, *An Organ Donation Strategy for Scotland*, p. 42.   [28] *Ibid.*
[29] Personal Social Health and Economic Education Association, www.pshe-association.org.uk.
[30] M. Sanner, 'People's attitudes and reactions to organ donation', *Mortality*, 11 (2006), 133–50, 135; National Assembly for Wales, *Inquiry into Presumed Consent for Organ Donation* (Health, Wellbeing and Local Government Committee, July 2008), www.assemblywales.org/cr-ld7192-e.pdf.
[31] Scottish Transplant Group, *An Organ Donation Strategy for Scotland*, p. 42.   [32] *Ibid.*

which organs can be donated; the gap between supply and demand; that transplants can save lives; and that most people and religions support donation after death. These are not the issues found to be of concern to those asked to agree to donation after the death of a close relative. Studies have identified different concerns, including: the nature of death; disfigurement of the body; scepticism towards the medical profession and their motives; difficulties in letting go of the deceased relative; and the need to recognise the family's sacrifice.[33]

Organ donation education, whether in schools or for the general public, employs the discourse of 'the gift of life' and the urgent need for organs. For example, NHS Blood and Transplant states on its website under the heading 'How to become a donor':

Transplants are one of the most miraculous achievements of modern medicine. But they depend entirely on the generosity of donors and their families who are willing to make this life-saving gift to others.[34]

In National Transplant Week a widely used press release from the same source stated that:

There is a desperate need for more donors. Last year more than 400 people died while waiting for a transplant. One in ten people waiting for a heart transplant will die and many others will lose their lives before they even get on to the waiting list.[35]

As propaganda aimed at encouraging voluntary donation this could be very effective, if putting one's name on the register or signing a donor card, or children going home from a class telling parents they would like to donate if anything happens to them, was enough to secure donation if the time came. However, when the decision has to be made years later on behalf of someone else in hospital after an illness or accident, the focus of attention will naturally be on the dying family member and what will be done to him or her – the sacrifice rather than the gift of life.[36] What Maloney and Walker refer to as the 'medical-mechanistic' discourse is reserved for information aimed at potential recipients of organs from deceased donors, such as hearts. In the Frequently Asked Questions (FAQ) section of the UK website for the To Transplant and Beyond

---

[33] Maloney and Walker, 'Talking about transplants'; M. Sque, S. Payne and J. MacLeod Clark, 'Gift of life or sacrifice? Key discourses to understanding organ donor families' decision-making', *Mortality*, 11 (2006), 117–32.

[34] NHS Blood and Transplant, *How to Become a Donor*, www.uktransplant.org.uk.

[35] NHS Press release at www.nuh.nhs.uk/newsdesk/%20pressreleases/2008/07_July/080708.htm.

[36] Sque *et al.*, 'Gift of life or sacrifice', 130.

charity, potential transplantees are told: 'it is important to remember that the heart is no more than a pump and that a transplant does not change your personality or behaviour'.[37]

Most educational programmes do acknowledge the concerns found in research with relatives, but answer them with a complete certainty that is inappropriate to their nature. For example, a lack of trust in the role of the medical profession is recognised in the FAQ section of the NHS website on organ donation; however, there is an attempt to simply close down the concern rather than discuss it more fully:

Q: Will they just let you die if they know you want to be a donor?
A: No. The doctors looking after a patient have to make every possible effort to save the patient's life. That is their first duty. If, despite their efforts, the patient dies, organ and tissue donation can then be considered and a completely different team of donation and transplant specialists would be called in.[38]

The answer provided above implies that the doctors attempting to save the patient's life will not be considering or raising the issue of organ donation, but the UK Organ Donation Taskforce report, having made a similar point, suggests the following approach:

There has to be an acceptance by all staff responsible for the care of potential donors that organ donation is a normal part of end-of-life care and that the option of donation must be explored in all suitable circumstances. Thus the early (and appropriate) identification of potential donors, and their referral to the donor co-ordinator network, should be the norm.[39]

Similarly, one of the recommendations of the Scottish Transplant Group report reads:

All ICU (Intensive Care Unit) staff should be made aware of the importance of making every reasonable effort to maximise donation rates from appropriate patients.[40]

There are good reasons to engage ICU staff in this way, as opportunities for donation may be missed by a reluctance of ICU staff to broach the possibility. However, the state-funded NHS materials reassure people that donation is considered only when, despite the efforts of staff, the patient dies. This is at odds with official government reports, however,

---

[37] NHS Blood and Transplant, *To Transplant and Beyond*, www.heart-transplant.co.uk/faqs. html.
[38] NHS Blood and Transplant, *How to Become a Donor*, www.uktransplant.org.uk.
[39] Department of Health, *Organs for Transplants*, p. 22.
[40] Scottish Transplant Group, *An Organ Donation Strategy for Scotland*, p. 35.

which ask staff caring for ICU patients to make 'every reasonable effort' (as in the quote above) to increase the number of organ donations.

Case studies on 'the ethics of donation'

Case studies are a well-used educational tool in medical ethics for high-lighting difficult decisions and initiating debate. The NHS Blood and Transplant website 'teachers' zone' provides materials for use in different curriculum subjects. In the teachers' materials for religious education, there are two newspaper stories said to be designed 'to stimulate debate about the ethics of donation'. The first is about a Jehovah's Witness who refused a blood transfusion and died following the birth of her twins, and the other is about the courts overruling parents who wanted to rely on their religious faith to protect their child, rather than agree to a bone marrow transplant. Neither seems to be about the ethics of donation, but rather about the ethics of receiving a donation. The Jehovah's Witnesses are a small sect with about 130,000 members in the UK whose stance on blood donation is probably the only thing most people know about them. The story of the refusal of a bone marrow transplant was taken from an article published in the UK newspaper, *The Daily Telegraph*, in 2007. The choice of this article only seemed likely to stimulate debate about the strangeness of religious beliefs, as there was a 50 per cent chance of the child living a normal life after the operation and only a 10 per cent chance that the child would die as a result of it.[41]

The only two case studies in the Religious Education section on the NHS Blood and Transplant website reflect the views of small minorities in the UK and do not engage with the ethics of *donation* as claimed. Issues that engage with the ethics of donation and are debated within more mainstream religions with large numbers of adherents in the UK include brain stem death and treatment of the body after death, both particularly controversial within Judaism and Islam. As discussed previously, these issues have been shown to concern the public and to be barriers to donation. Both issues would no doubt stimulate discussion among young people, but neither would necessarily unite them in a pro-donation

---

[41] NHS Blood and Transplant, *Give and Let Live*, www.giveandletlive.co.uk/docs/other/Religious%20education%20news%20stories.pdf. In the original newspaper article, it was stated that there was also 'a 30 per cent prospect that the treatment will not be successful and she will still die from her underlying HLH, and a 10 per cent prospect that, although she survives, she may have some significant impairment' (*Daily Telegraph*, 19 July 2007). Please note that 'HLH' is haemophagocytic lymphohistiocytosis.

stance, unlike two stories about refusing a blood or organ donation when it provided the only chance of life.

Building roads to cope with the increasing amount of traffic

It is clear from the content of the websites discussed previously that organ donation education has a narrow focus that does not engage in sufficient depth with the context in which organ donation takes place. The message is that there is an organ shortage that can be solved if more people sign the NHS Organ Donor Register and/or carry donor cards, and discuss their views with relatives; therefore ultimately more organs would be available for transplantation. This is an unusual message in government-sponsored public education because the focus is on meeting ever-increasing demand, with only a brief reference to why demand is increasing and typically no consideration of whether demand could be controlled or reduced. Public campaigns usually focus on prevention as well as cure and do not simply accept increasing demand as a given. The answer to rising levels of traffic is no longer simply to build more roads but to consider ways of controlling the demand through individual, organisational and government action. The focus on increasing supply would be understandable if there was no potential for reducing demand and if increasing supply and maintaining it at higher levels would indeed solve the organ shortage. However, neither of these is the case. The traffic example is a good analogy because if there is an increase in the availability of organs (or more roads), then demand will increase further. The criteria for getting on the waiting list could be less stringent if more organs were available and, if more transplants were performed, then the demand for re-transplants (where these are medically possible) would increase.

It is not easy to change behaviour through health education, but where there is scope for reducing demand it might be expected that it would be part of every educational programme. The UK Organ Donation Taskforce report has made only one recommendation in relation to the need for organ donation education and this was in the form of a question rather than a definite statement. In the Supplement to the report, the Taskforce asks in Recommendation 7: 'should we engage the public with the discourse of "disease prevention" as well as organ donation?'.[42] The unwillingness of scientists to admit to uncertainties, especially when discussing risk, has been recognised as a barrier to public trust and respect on issues ranging

---

[42] Department of Health, *Organs for Transplants – The Supplement Report*, p. 156.

from genetically modified food to climate change. In organ donation education, there seems to be the assumption that a clear message, with no extraneous, complicating factors, will be the most effective one.

A more complete picture

Transplantation may be needed because of inherited conditions and disease outside individual control, but individual lifestyle can also be a contributory or even a causal factor. The NHS-sponsored website, 'Your health, your choices', acknowledges the influence of lifestyle when discussing the causes of kidney disease, in the context of individual responsibility for health:

> Some causes are inherited and some people are born with an abnormality that affects their kidneys. But kidney disease is mostly caused by other long-term conditions. A healthy lifestyle will help to reduce the risk of developing these conditions.[43]

In the United States (US), diabetes is the single leading cause of kidney failure, accounting for about 44 per cent of the people who start treatment for kidney failure each year, and about 38 per cent of all those being treated for kidney failure. Type 2 diabetes is linked to the rise in obesity throughout the Western world. Obesity experts have shown that modest lifestyle changes can reduce the risk of Type 2 diabetes by over 58 per cent. Other reasons for transplantation that are potentially reducible are alcoholism, attempted suicide and drug abuse. The second most common indication for liver transplants in the US and Europe is alcohol-related damage. In 2007–08, nearly a quarter of liver transplants in the UK were needed because of organ damage related to alcohol intake (151 out of 623). This is an increase of 60 per cent over the last ten years and has contributed to the increase in the liver transplant waiting list.[44]

Public education on multi-factorial conditions like heart disease and cancer combines lifestyle advice with information on early-warning signs and treatments. The message on transplantation aimed particularly at young people tends to be more simplistic and focuses primarily on increasing the supply of organs. Certainly, transplants do save lives, and are often the only option; however, organ transplant is not a simple cure: organs may fail and all recipients experience side effects of varying severity.

---

[43] NHS, 'Your health, your choices', www.nhs.uk.
[44] Official figures provided by the Hon. Ann Keen, UK Minister for Health, in response to a parliamentary question from Don Foster (Member of Parliament) and widely reported in the press: see, for example, J. Doward and D. Campbell, 'Transplant row over organs for drinkers' (*Observer*, 15 February 2009).

Misleading information

A particularly striking example of the encouragement of unrealistic expectations of an organ transplant as a cure is found in the 'Give and Let Live' educational resource from the NHS in which the underlying assumption appears to be that a kidney lasts for 60 years:

NHS Blood and Transplant educational resource

Q: If a 20 year old has a kidney transplant and lives to 80, roughly how much money would the NHS save?

A: Cost of dialysis: 60 years × £23,000 = £1,380,000. Cost of transplant: (60 years × £6,500) + £42,000 = £432,000. Saving: £948,000 – roughly one million pounds.[45]

Kidney transplant recipients have the best prognosis for solid organ transplantation, but a transplant is not a solution for life for younger people. According to figures published by the National Kidney Federation, the average lifespan of a transplanted kidney ranges from ten years for a deceased donor kidney to twelve years for a living-related transplant. Kidneys can last over thirty years, and such a case was a newsworthy item in Canada,[46] but an economic argument might be expected to use figures that are the current expected or average, or a little higher to allow for future improvements. Even if the twenty-year-old in the example referred to in the above quotation needed three transplants, there would still be a considerable saving, quite apart from the humanitarian argument in favour of transplantation. Why use an imaginary and rarely, if ever, achieved length of time in an 'educational resource'?

A different sort of education?

Educational initiatives should be integrated into a more complete account of the need for organ transplantation with attention paid to the context in which decisions will ultimately be made. Information on how organs work and why people need transplants would then be part of the healthy lifestyle messages that schools already incorporate into different areas of the curriculum. This should encourage the conversations at home about transplantation that seem to be an important factor in willingness to donate. It is probably not possible to reduce demand in terms of absolute numbers – demand is going to increase with the epidemic of obesity and diabetes and the increase in the numbers of older people in high-risk groups.

[45] NHS Blood and Transplant, *Give and Let Live*, www.giveandletlive.co.uk.
[46] BC Transplant, '33 years and still counting', *Transplant Times*, Winter 2003, www.transplant.bc.ca/winter2003_times.htm.

Therefore, education must be education for prevention *and* for increased organ donation, acknowledging that preventative measures reduce risk overall but this does not mean that any one individual can avoid the need for an organ transplant. Of course, attention would have to be paid, as it is in other areas of health education, to avoiding blame or stigmatisation of individuals or groups. Currently, information and educational materials for adults and children have not proved to be effective in translating positive attitudes into increased organ donation, although short-term effects have been found when there have been special campaigns or high-profile cases in the media. The expectations of public education in raising donation levels are probably unrealistic. Attitudes in the UK are favourable, so perhaps it is the deeper concerns that need to be addressed, and not glossed over as in the examples cited and discussed in this chapter.

Conclusion

It seems to be taken for granted throughout Europe and the USA that organ shortage must be met and the gap between supply and demand must be closed.[47] In other areas of healthcare, whatever the system, there is discussion of resourcing and the public is encouraged to accept that the ever-increasing demands for healthcare cannot all be met, even with increased funding. Prioritising and rationing are inevitable and the public are invited to join in the debate.

Organ donation education stands out both for concentrating on supply, not on demand, and for assuming that demand must be met. The difference between organ transplantation and other fields is, of course, that the public have a direct and essential role in the treatment of organ failure and can be blamed for the gap between demand and supply. If organ failure could be treated by artificial organs or xenotransplantation, with a limitless supply, the focus would turn from supply to resourcing, from the public to health-system funding. In this situation education about transplantation would no doubt change from general promotion of the benefits to more specific examination of the demand for organs. In the current situation, where the focus is on supply rather than demand, the suggestion is that effective education would need to have a broader focus. On the one hand, donation might be increased by acknowledging and engaging with people's uncertainties and concerns about organ donation and transplantation.

---

[47] S. Schicktanz and M. Schweda, '"One man's trash is another man's treasure": exploring economic and moral subtexts of the "organ shortage" problem in public views on organ donation', *Journal of Medical Ethics*, 35 (2009), 473–6.

On the other, education could not be said to be effective, however, unless it addressed the reasons for an ever-increasing demand for organs. In the foreseeable future, the focus can remain on the public's failure to supply enough organs, and they, rather than government or insurance schemes, can be blamed for the organ 'gap'.

5   Bereavement, decision-making and the family in organ donation

Magi Sque and Tracy Long-Sutehall

Bereaved families are the critical link in actualising donation from potential organ donors as they are normally asked to facilitate, or make a decision about donation, on behalf of their deceased relative.[1] Whilst the merging of legislation and transplant ideology promotes organ donation as a social good,[2] most countries sustain high refusal rates by bereaved relatives, influenced in part by the circumstances of loss and bereavement, which are emotionally provocative and culturally challenging. So how do families conceptualise organ donation? What does the evidence suggest impacts families' experiences that might be helpful in eliciting positive decisions about donation but also decisions that remain right for family members? Drawing upon contemporary studies, this chapter discusses the social context of the death of the organ donor: how bereavement in this circumstance may be understood; families' concerns about the perceived death of an organ donor and what might be done to the body as a result of the donation operation; their beliefs, fantasies and feelings when viewing the body after the organs have been removed; the importance they place on restructuring the donor's life in the post-death relationship with recipients; and their distress if they were denied the knowledge that the organ had achieved a wholeness and purpose in another body. The authors suggest that the social processes integral to the donation event remain poorly understood by the public and that the function of public education should be to enhance awareness of organ donation to the extent that when an approach about organ donation is made in a hospital, the idea is neither new nor intimidating to the bereaved family; it simply reminds them of the potential impact of their decision on the lives of waiting recipients, their families and communities.

---

[1] This chapter discusses organ donation from donors who have been certified dead by neurological criteria referred to as 'brain stem death' in the UK.
[2] L. Sharpe, *Strange Harvest: Organ Transplants, Denatured Bodies, and the Transformed Self* (Berkeley: University of California Press, 2006).

Organ donation and post-mortem consent in social context

Walter observes that how a society organises itself for death depends on the characteristic form of death.[3] Traditionally, death was characterised by infectious disease, which was sudden, affected both children and adults, and was rooted in a community setting, supported by a dense network of social interaction. Death in modern Western society is no longer a community affair but is more often sequestered in institutions. The relatively hidden, private experience of death means that when individuals die, it is likely that they are isolated from family and friends, and subjected to professional control and expertise. With death most frequently occurring in hospital and palliative care settings, it is possible for individuals to die and be disposed of without relatives having any direct contact with the dead person. Iserson claims post-death activities have long been enveloped by a 'mystical shroud'.[4] What happens to corpses is for the most part unspoken and, sometimes, considered unspeakable. He believes that such behaviour is the sole deterrent for many people when contemplating organ donation.[5]

Furthermore, Kellehear emphasises the social expectations and social constructions of death held in societies that adhere to Western values as being influential in donation decision-making.[6] Kellehear states that social viewpoints with regard to dying, the determination of death and 'dying as a social relationship' are vital to understanding the levels of disagreement regarding organ donation and have been largely ignored in favour of biomedical, bioethical and legal perspectives.[7] In her thesis, Ben-David is clear that social perceptions of the body, which relate to both personal 'self' and organic manifestation, play a major role in understanding families' decision-making with regard to organ donation.[8]

Social expectations of death and social perceptions of how the body should be treated after death have recently gained intense public scrutiny in the United Kingdom (UK). The Harold Shipman affair[9] and the organ-

---

[3] T. Walter, *The Revival of Death* (London: Routledge, 1994).

[4] K. Iserson, *Death to Dust: What Happens to Dead Bodies?* (Tucson: Galen Press Ltd, 1994), p. 1.

[5] *Ibid.*

[6] A. Kellehear, 'Dying as a social relationship: a sociological review of debates on the determination of death', *Social Science & Medicine*, 66 (2008), 1533–44.

[7] *Ibid.*, 1534.

[8] O. Ben-David, *Organ Donation and Transplantation: Body Organs as an Exchangeable Socio-Cultural Resource* (Westport: Praeger, 2005).

[9] The Shipman Inquiry, www.the-shipman-inquiry.org.uk.

retention crisis[10] have impinged heavily upon the care of the dying, the dead and the bereaved and have led to a need to rebuild the trust that the British public is prepared to invest in the health system. Specifically, the inadequacy of consent for the retention of organs following post-mortem within a number of National Health Service (NHS) Trusts came to public attention during an investigation into the care of children receiving complex cardiac surgery at Bristol Royal Infirmary.[11] Subsequent inquiries indicated that organs, particularly hearts, were routinely removed post-mortem and retained for the purposes of research and teaching at a number of NHS Trusts, without the explicit consent of the next of kin.[12]

There was widespread concern about the quality of information given to families about post-mortem examinations and that relatives had not been specifically informed that this procedure would entail retention of organs and tissues for detailed laboratory investigations.[13] All these inquiries showed that at the time there were weaknesses in the arrangements and protocols for post-mortem consent, and that services for advising and supporting bereaved families were fragmented and inadequate.

The Human Tissue Act 2004 (the Act) arose out of concerns raised by the organ-retention scandals that the current law governing post-mortem use and storage of organs was not as clear and consistent as it might be. Whilst the Act was welcomed, as it promoted the principle of informed consent, its implementation raises specific challenges for healthcare professionals and bereaved individuals regarding the need to work in partnership. These challenges include the fact that the Act provides for individual parents to give or withhold consent regarding what happens to their child's body or body parts after death. Whose decision will healthcare professionals honour if there is conflict between parents about what is to happen to their child's body post-mortem? Section 3(6)(c) of the Act requires that in the case of an adult 'appropriate consent' rests with 'a person who stood in a qualifying relationship to him

[10] M. Sque, T. Long, S. Payne et al., 'The UK post mortem organ retention crisis: a qualitative study of its impact on parents', Journal of the Royal Society of Medicine, 101 (2008), 71–7.
[11] Department of Health, The Report of the Bristol Royal Infirmary Inquiry (London: Department of Health, 2001).
[12] M. Redfern, The Royal Liverpool Children's Inquiry Report (London: The Stationery Office, 2001); The Retained Organs Commission, External Review of Birmingham Children's Hospital NHS Trust: Report on Organ Retention (London: Department of Health, 2002); The Retained Organs Commission, Investigation into Organ Retention at Central Manchester and Manchester Children's University Hospitals (London: Department of Health, 2002); Department of Health, The Isaacs Report: the Investigation of Events that Followed the Death of Cyril Mark Isaacs (London: Department of Health, 2003).
[13] M. McDermott, 'Obtaining consent for autopsy', British Medical Journal, 327 (2003), 804–6.

immediately before he died'. In circumstances where prior to their death the donor neither gave an appropriate consent nor appointed a nominated representative to provide such consent, there are a number of criteria listed under section 27(4) of the Act defining qualifying relationships; but what difficulties could bereaved individuals encounter as they face the responsibility of making decisions on behalf of the deceased? The Act also opened the way for healthcare professionals to implement post-mortem procedures on the body, such as cannulation to augment organ preservation, prior to agreement of family members. Clinical guidelines have also been developed to assist the non-heart-beating organ donation programme, to increase the number of organs for donation.[14]

All the above initiatives create new educational needs for healthcare professionals and the public; public perception and acceptance also warrant investigation from a number of perspectives. A fundamental and neglected issue for organ and tissue donation and organ retention is the necessity of helping the bereaved make decisions they will not regret later and which have the potential to impact their bereavement.[15] There appears to be a need for education of the public and healthcare professionals, who are themselves part of contemporary society, in this field of bereavement care.

The bereavement of organ-donor families

Organ donation is a well-established, successful and often the only available therapeutic option for individuals with severe or end-stage organ failure. The bereaved family of a potential organ donor is a crucial link in the chain of organ donation procedures, as it is normal practice in most countries to discuss organ donation with them and seek their lack of objection or explicit consent to donation. Family agreement remains vital even in countries where the law allows donation to take place if the deceased person is known not to have registered an objection or expressed a wish not to be a donor during their lifetime.[16]

---

[14] T. Long and M. Sque, 'An update on initiatives to increase organ donation: a UK perspective', *British Journal of Transplantation*, 2 (2007), 10–15.

[15] M. Sque, T. Long and S. Payne, *Organ and Tissue Donation: Exploring the Needs of Families* (final report of a three-year study commissioned by the British Organ Donor Society, funded by the Community Fund (University of Southampton, 2003).

[16] B. Neades, 'Healthcare professionals' experiences in applying presumed consent legislation in organ donation in three European countries: a phenomenological study' in W. Weimar, M. Bos and J. Busschbach (eds.), *Organ Transplantation: Ethical, Legal and*

Studies indicate that bereaved families attribute importance to being asked to consider donation.[17] It has therefore been suggested that in situations of donor suitability, donation should be discussed with the family as part of high-quality, end-of-life and bereavement care.[18] It could even be considered unethical not to provide the bereaved family with the opportunity for a choice which could have positive outcomes for their bereavement and post-death relationship with the deceased. These findings should reassure healthcare professionals who are reported to have concerns about intruding in the family's moment of grief and are reluctant to approach families to discuss organ and tissue donation.[19] Including organ donation as an element of the Liverpool Care Pathway, which has been recognised as a clinical 'gold standard' tool for the care of the dying in the UK,[20] has acted as an important trigger and been associated with a substantial increase in donor rates in one intensive care unit in the North West of England.[21] Whilst it may be helpful for donation to be perceived as a 'usual' rather than an 'unusual' part of end-of-life and bereavement care, it should always be seen as something special and never taken for granted, lest the social role of the donating family and donor becomes relegated to the mere provision of spare parts.[22]

In view of these concerns, it is critical for healthcare professionals to be able to distinguish grief reactions from any reactions a family may have to donation, especially in light of the importance of focusing on the family's bereavement issues before any approach is made about organ donation.[23] Payne offered three discourses on bereavement – intra-psychic, interactional and social – to explain the reactions of families with whom donation is discussed.[24]

Psychosocial Aspects (Lengerich: Pabst Science Publishers, 2008), pp. 150–4; K. Barber, S. Falvey, C. Hamilton *et al.*, 'Potential for organ donation in the United Kingdom: audit of intensive care records', *British Medical Journal*, 332 (2006), 1124–7.

[17] Sque, Long and Payne, *Organ and Tissue Donation*; Sque, Long and Payne *et al.*, 'The UK post mortem organ retention crisis'.

[18] Department of Health, *Organs for Transplants: a Report from the Organ Donation Taskforce* (London: Department of Health, 2008).

[19] M. Sque, S. Payne and I. Vlachonikolis, 'Cadaveric donor transplantation: nurses' attitudes, knowledge and behaviour', *Social Science & Medicine*, 50 (2000), 541–52.

[20] J. Ellershaw and S. Wilkinson, *Care of the Dying: a Pathway to Excellence* (Oxford University Press, 2003).

[21] M. Clancy, 'Translating the success of organ breakthrough collaboratives from the USA to the UK', *British Journal of Transplantation*, 2 (2008), 3–7.

[22] A. Mongoven, 'Sharing our body and blood: organ donation and feminist critiques of sacrifice', *Journal of Medicine and Philosophy*, 28 (2003), 89–114.

[23] T. Shafer, D. Wagner, J. Chessare *et al.*, 'Organ Donation Breakthrough Collaborative: increasing organ donation through system redesign', *Critical Care Nurse*, 26 (2006), 23–49.

[24] S. Payne, 'Contemporary views of bereavement and the experience of grief' in M. Sque and S. Payne (eds.), *Organ and Tissue Donation: an Evidence Base for Practice* (Maidenhead: Open University Press, 2007), pp. 21–39.

Intra-psychic perspectives focus on cognition and how people think, and especially on how they feel and experience emotion.[25] They provide a framework for explaining differing emotions experienced by individuals at the time of death, including shock, numbness, anger and distress – emotions that underpin why people may find it difficult to make decisions relating to donation. Intra-psychic perspectives offer explanations as to why the loss of a particular relationship is more disruptive than losses of others, e.g. due to the intensity of the relationship shared. This perspective indicates that people have little control over their basic response to the threat of loss and that it may be difficult for them to be reassured by communication from healthcare professionals. However Sque *et al.* have shown that if healthcare professionals took time to develop rapport with families and indicated that they understood how grief could impact on family members' decision-making, then this was perceived positively by families as an indication that healthcare professionals cared about their critically injured relative and themselves.[26]

Interactional perspectives place importance on how individuals interact with others and the way they construe a situation. These approaches are helpful as they recognise individual diversity and that humans are interactional beings.[27] Interactional approaches provide explanations as to why individuals differ in their experience of, and reaction to, the loss of an important person and the request for donation. They further suggest that bereavement responses are mediated by the coping resources available to the bereaved individual. For example, individuals with supportive networks or strong beliefs in their own mastery may be better able to respond to the challenges of a sudden loss and a request for organ donation. Such individuals, whose coping is predominantly problem-focused, may value a lot of information about the process and procedures of donation, the chance to witness neurological testing and involvement in decision-making. Individuals whose coping is predominantly emotion-focused

[25] S. Freud, *Mourning and Melancholia* (London: The Hogarth Press, 1917); J. Bowlby, *Attachment and Loss* (Vol. 1: *Attachment*) (London: The Hogarth Press, 1969); E. Kubler-Ross, *On Death and Dying* (New York: Macmillan, 1969); J. Bowlby, *Attachment and Loss* (Vol. 2: *Separation*) (London: The Hogarth Press, 1973); J. Bowlby, *Attachment and Loss* (Vol. 3: *Loss: Sadness and Depression*) (London: The Hogarth Press, 1980); J. Worden, *Grief Counselling and Grief Therapy: a Handbook for the Mental Health Practitioner*, 3rd edn (New York: Springer Publishing, 2002).

[26] Sque, Long and Payne, *Organ and Tissue Donation*.

[27] R. Lazarus and S. Folkman, *Stress, Appraisal and Coping* (New York: Springer-Verlag, 1984); S. Folkman, 'Positive psychological states and coping with severe stress', *Social Science & Medicine*, 45 (1997), 1207–21; M. Stroebe and H. Schut, 'The dual process model of coping with bereavement: rationale and description', *Death Studies*, 23 (1999), 197–224.

may value empathetic healthcare professionals who acknowledge their distress and give them an opportunity to express their emotion and grief. However, this approach also reminds us that individuals may oscillate between emotion and problem-focused coping;[28] therefore it is important that healthcare professionals realise that individual family members may react to difficult communication about organ donation in different ways during the decision-making process, and may respond in apparently contradictory ways depending upon their current coping mode.

Social perspectives assume that bereavement is a social process in which an individual's position in society is changed, impacting their sense of self as a part of and shaped by the society and the culture in which they live, as well as acknowledging that this impinges on how people think and on their interactions.[29] Structural aspects such as age, gender and social status, both for the deceased and the bereaved, are recognised as important in constructing social responses to a death, such as the loss of a child or husband. They suggest that families may need time to engage in conversation to construct a biography of the deceased.[30] These biographies may also be influential in helping to make donation decisions, for example by describing the deceased person as someone who would like to help others, and attributing altruism and achievement to them. It is necessary to recognise the importance of allowing families to tell their story and talk about the critically ill or deceased person, often repeatedly. This helps to construct the identity of the person when healthcare professionals may have little knowledge about his or her social roles, attributes and beliefs. Some families may gain benefit in deriving a meaning for the death in permitting organ donation but this should not be assumed for all.[31] Some families may wish to obtain mementos of the deceased, such as a lock of hair, a photograph or piece of jewellery to help create a lasting sense of presence and a focus for a relationship that is transformed by death.[32]

Bereavement is an inevitable part of life and the pain of grief a consequence of forming significant relationships; it is the price we pay for love. We suggest that by placing the family's death experience at the centre of end-of-life care planning, a framework of bereavement support can be

---

[28] Strobe and Schut, 'The dual process model'.
[29] C. Seale, *Constructing Death: the Sociology of Dying and Bereavement* (Cambridge University Press, 1998); Kellehear, 'Dying as a social relationship'.
[30] T. Walter, 'A new model of grief: bereavement and biography', *Mortality*, 1 (1996), 1–29.
[31] T. Bellali and D. Papadatou, 'Parental grief following the brain death of a child: does consent or refusal to organ donation affect their grief?', *Death Studies*, 30 (2006), 883–917.
[32] D. Klass, P. Silverman and S. Nickman, *Continuing Bonds: New Understandings of Grief* (Bristol: Taylor & Francis, 1996).

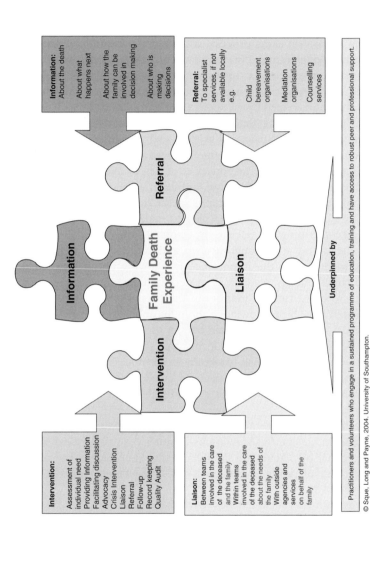

Information:
About the death

About what happens next

About how the family can be involved in decision making

About who is making decisions

Referral:
To specialist services, if not available locally e.g.

Child bereavement organisations

Mediation organisations

Counselling services

Intervention:
Assessment of individual need
Providing Information
Facilitating discussion
Advocacy
Crisis Intervention
Liaison
Referral
Follow-up
Record keeping
Quality Audit

Liaison:
Between teams involved in the care of the deceased and the family
Within teams involved in the care of the deceased about the needs of the family
With outside agencies and services on behalf of the family

Information

Family Death Experience

Referral

Intervention

Liaison

Underpinned by

Practitioners and volunteers who engage in a sustained programme of education, training and have access to robust peer and professional support.

© Sque, Long and Payne. 2004. University of Southampton.

Figure 5.1 Interlocking Model of Bereavement Services

initiated, which moves easily from bedside to community, supported by practitioners and volunteers who engage in a sustained programme of education. Such a framework is illustrated in the Interlocking Model of Bereavement Services shown in Figure 5.1.[33] Healthcare professionals will face losses in their own lives, as well as being exposed to the vicarious grief of families. They too need support and the opportunity to acknowledge their own grief.

How do family members conceptualise organ donation?

It is against the previously described psychosocial backdrop that the request for organ donation is most likely to arise, usually as a result of sudden, unexpected and untimely death that provokes a highly charged emotional environment. Evidence suggests that such bereavement is often more difficult than that which is anticipated.[34] Family members generally have little time to adjust to the loss before they are approached about organ donation and they may struggle with the enormity of the events that are unfolding around them. In addition, due to the low numbers of people who die in circumstances that facilitate donation, potential donor families are unlikely to have any role models for their behaviour.

To answer the question posed above, data from two qualitative interview studies carried out with families approached about organ donation, and an exploration of correspondence exchanged between organ donor families and recipients, will be presented with the aim of providing insights into families' representations of the experience of being approached and asked to consider donating organs of their recently deceased relative. The data discussed represent work carried out between 1996 and 2008.

The first dataset (1) comprised transcripts of individual, tape-recorded, qualitative, cross-sectional interviews carried out with 24 relatives of 16 organ donors in the UK, who agreed to donation.[35] These data were originally collected to explore family members' experiences of the donation process. Interviews examined their emotional reactions to the death of a relative and donation of their organs, their perceptions of the decision-making process and the benefits and concerns that organ donation

---

[33] M. Sque, T. Long and S. Payne, *From Understanding to Implementation: Meeting the Needs of Families and Individuals Affected by Post-Mortem Organ Retention* (final report of a study funded by the Department of Health and The Retained Organs Commission) (University of Southampton, 2004).

[34] D. Yates, G. Ellison and S. McGuiness, 'Care of the suddenly bereaved', *British Medical Journal*, 301 (1990), 29–31.

[35] M. Sque and S. Payne, 'Dissonant loss: the experience of donor relatives', *Social Science & Medicine*, 43 (1996), 1359–70.

generated for them. The second dataset (2) was derived from an investigation carried out in 4 United States (US) organ procurement organisations (OPOs) and the National Donor Family Council (NDFC).[36] The OPO dataset, from 333 donors, spanning a 7-year period, comprised 554 letters written by members of donor families to transplant recipients and 744 letters written by recipients to donor families. The NDFC dataset comprised 93 letters written to the NDFC by donor families. The study sought to explore the bereavement of donor families by establishing the role and importance of corresponding with transplant recipients and the nature and pattern of the correspondence. Letters were analysed for their pattern of interaction and thematically for content.

The third dataset (3) comprised transcripts of individual, tape-recorded, qualitative, cross-sectional interviews carried out with 26 relatives of 23 deceased individuals in the UK, who chose to decline donation.[37] These data were collected to explore the hospital experiences and end-of-life decision-making of relatives who chose to decline donation. Ethical approval was gained and ethical principles and mechanisms were followed for each of the studies. The studies cover a spectrum of families' experiences through cross-sectional investigations, providing a large sample of data to be explored, drawing on two types of data: interview responses and correspondence. The UK and the USA broadly share similar systems of involving families in decision-making with regard to organ donation. The datasets therefore provided the potential to explore cross-cultural similarities and differences. The limitations of drawing on relatively small, non-representative samples are acknowledged. The authors are also cognisant of the retrospective nature of the data, which could have afforded participants time for reflection, and which could have been influenced by the audience with whom the family was engaged, i.e. a researcher, recipient or the NFDC.

The findings were grouped and discussed under two broad themes: recognising death; and the fractured, fragmented body and organ transfer. Evidence of literal, symbolic or metaphorical representations related to the above discourses is presented as exemplar quotes from transcripts. Exemplars from the datasets are identified with a code, starting with 1, 2 or 3 followed by the interview or correspondence code.

---

[36] M. Sque, *'A Story to Tell'*: *Post Bereavement Correspondence between Organ Donor Families, Recipients, their OPOs and the National Donor Family Council – An American Investigation* (a report of a study funded by The General Nursing Council of England and Wales Trust) (University of Surrey, 2000).

[37] M. Sque, T. Long, S. Payne and D. Allardyce, 'Why relatives do not donate organs for transplants: "sacrifice" or "gift of life"?', *Journal of Advanced Nursing*, 61 (2008), 134–44.

Recognising death

Traditionally death was defined by the cessation of respiratory function and the heartbeat.[38] Death certified by neurological criteria (brain stem death) came as a natural consequence of technological advance, when it became possible to sustain a functioning body, but not the brain, artificially by ventilating machinery. The ability to diagnose death by neurological criteria meant that transplantation of organs became a viable medical treatment. However this new diagnosis of death introduced a concept of death that is unrepresentative of social expectations regarding the determination of death. The dead body is perceived by modern society to be still, pale and cold.[39] Therefore, family members faced with a death certified by neurological criteria have to reconstruct a new image of death to allow them to accept 'neurological (brain stem) death', as death.

Studies support the difficulty that both families[40] and healthcare professionals[41] have in accepting the death of an organ donor, confirmed by neurological criteria, in contrast to their social expectations of death. Long et al. have suggested that acceptance is facilitated by family members and healthcare professionals engaging in a process of practical and psychological activities aimed at rationalising real or potential conflict raised as a result of a death certified by neurological criteria.[42] Clearly the families of organ donors can be exposed to two representations of death: that of the 'functioning body' supported by the ventilator; and that of the body after the donation operation when it is congruent with the socially accepted still, pale, cold body. Here, a father who witnessed neurological (brain stem) testing and donated his son's organs describes these representations and what they meant to him and his family:

---

[38] P. Mollaret and M. Goulon, 'Le coma depasse', *Revue Neurologique*, 101 (1959), 3–15.

[39] Iserson, *Death to Dust*.

[40] Sque and Payne, 'Dissonant loss'; Sque, Long and Payne, *Organ and Tissue Donation*; T. Bellali and D. Papadatou, 'The decision-making process of parents regarding organ donation of their brain dead child: a Greek study', *Social Science & Medicine*, 64 (2007), 439–50; A. Kesselring, M. Kainz and A. Kiss, 'Traumatic memories of relatives regarding brain death, request for organ donation and interactions with professionals in the ICU', *American Journal of Transplantation*, 7 (2007), 211–17; Sque, Long, Payne et al., 'Why relatives do not donate organs for transplants'; T. Long, M. Sque and J. Addington-Hall, 'What does the diagnosis of brain death mean to families approached about organ donation: a review of the literature', *Progress in Transplantation*, 18 (2008), 118–25.

[41] Sque, Payne and Vlachonikolis, 'Cadaveric donor transplantation'; B. Kent, 'Protection behaviour: a phenomenon affecting organ and tissue donation in the 21st century?', *International Journal of Nursing Studies*, 41 (2004), 273–84; T. Long, M. Sque and J. Addington-Hall, 'Conflict rationalisation: how family members cope with a diagnosis of brain stem death', *Social Science & Medicine*, 67 (2008), 253–61.

[42] Long, Sque and Addington-Hall, 'Conflict rationalisation'.

A was still looking comfortable, rosy and warm, looking very much as if he was still alive [in the ICU], so it was very difficult for the other members of the family to understand that he was dead but I knew beyond any doubt that he was. The following day we went to the Chapel of Rest and we went in and saw A there . . . There we saw a body freezing cold, we saw death itself, which was a contrast. It was a stark contrast to what we had seen, or what I had seen in the brain stem situation. He was cold, motionless it was a shock . . . it underlined to us what the machine was actually doing for him, that [it was] the oxygen going in, that made him look alive. (1.16)

Seeing the body in the funeral directors' Chapel of Rest was also helpful in acting as closure for other relatives who had only seen the deceased while they were on ventilatory support:

My daughter did [went to the Chapel of Rest] and she found it quite helpful cause she said it was closure for her, she said, 'It finished it for me, I realised, you know, that wasn't my Dad that was a dead person kind of thing, it wasn't real to me that he died in the hospital. Because, I suppose, of the ventilation, I mean he did still look absolutely pink and healthy really.' (3.008.708–712)

There was difficulty for many families in equating death with the appearance of the deceased while on the ventilator, and this often worked toward them declining donation. A family's reluctance to switch off the ventilator, influenced by the normal appearance of the deceased and the short, sudden trajectory of the transition from health to death, is described by a mother:

I couldn't believe it because he looked like he was asleep and he didn't look like there was anything wrong with him at all apart from perhaps he was on a life support machine, but all his colouring, because he's got red hair and he always had plenty of colour, all was there he didn't look ill at all, so you just can't accept it you can't take that in. (3.015.50–56)

She describes the 'torment' that this picture of a 'living person' conveyed and the difficulty it caused in making the decision to switch off the ventilator, 'And then you are thinking if that is the case then we killed him' (3.015.288–289).

Family members needed time to 'accept' the death. The corpse is essentially a representation of the person who existed and bereavement researchers suggest that family members may wish to have the opportunity to spend time with the deceased.[43] This may be helpful to them in

---

[43] B. Raphael, *The Anatomy of Bereavement* (London: Routledge, 1985); B. Wright, *Sudden Death: a Research Base for Practice*, 2nd edn (New York: Churchill Livingstone, 1996); S. Li, C. Chan and D. Lee, 'Helpfulness of nursing actions to suddenly bereaved family members in an accident and emergency setting in Hong Kong', *Journal of Advanced Nursing*, 40 (2002), 170–80.

recognising the death and provides them with the opportunity to say goodbye and begin closure.

The importance families attached to the moment the heart stopped beating appears to fit with a personal view of death founded on societal expectations of a still, cold, pale body rather than death based on neurological criteria. Therefore being present at the physical end of life, marked by the cessation of heartbeat, was significant. A father recounts:

We felt we wanted or needed him to die in our arms, as the ventilator turned off, and felt that this would help us in the many years to come, to know we had done the best for us emotionally. (3.023. letter)

Whilst there may be debate about the appearance of a dead body, characteristics that are socially agreed are that a dead body does not breathe, is cold and motionless.[44] The diagnosis of 'brain stem death' was in conflict with the body in question, as the diagnosis did not agree with the expected appearance of a dead body. The term 'brain stem death' may itself suggest that death certified by testing is inclusive to the brain and exclusive of the body. This choice of language may undermine the acceptance of the irreversibility of the brain injury sustained and may support the view that the relative could recover with intensive rehabilitation. The fact that the family member continued to see a functioning body appeared to be a source of emotional and cognitive conflict, which could only be resolved when the body was concordant with the appearance of a dead body as seen in the mortuary, Chapel of Rest or funeral home.[45] The live-looking body promotes an 'illusion of lingering life' and undermines the recognition of death.[46]

The fractured, fragmented body and organ transfer

Featherstone suggests that consumer culture has made the modern individual's confrontation with death especially difficult, with additional value placed on the living, acting body, and higher expectations of health and longevity.[47] Death is thought to be the body's most polluted form, the antithesis of beauty, something worthy only of shame, denial and

[44] Long, Sque and Addington-Hall, 'What does the diagnosis of brain death mean to families'.

[45] Long, Sque and Addington-Hall, 'Conflict rationalisation'.

[46] M. Sanner, 'A comparison of public attitudes toward autopsy, organ donation and anatomic dissection', *Journal of the American Medical Association*, 271 (1994), 284–8; 'People's attitudes and reactions to organ donation', *Mortality*, 11 (2006), 133–50.

[47] M. Featherstone, 'The body in consumer culture' in M. Featherstone, M. Hepworth and B. Turner (eds.), *The Body: Social Process and Cultural Theory* (London: Sage Publications, 1991), pp. 170–96.

disguise.[48] Death, after all, is about decay, the shattering of aesthetic harmony and human failure.[49] Deaths outside the older age ranges are relatively rare occurrences, and thus make premature death, often the case in organ donation, that much harder for society to accept. How individuals look in death is also important to many in an appearance-oriented world. The emphasis on the body beautiful in life requires the deceased to be made to conform to a socially presentable and acceptable image. Richardson suggests that popular culture maintains distaste for the deliberate mutilation or destruction of the corpse.[50]

Study participants did appear to be concerned about the wholeness and integrity of the dead body, as this was the most frequently reported reason for declining donation.[51] They appeared reluctant to relinquish their guardianship and ability to protect the dead body, expressing two main concerns about donation: mutilation of the body; and the possible suffering the relative might sustain as a result of the donation operation. It was important to participants that the donation operation was carried out with the utmost dignity and propriety, and they found the knowledge that the donation operation was a standard surgical procedure comforting. A mother explains what was important to her and her husband about the donation from their ten-week-old baby:

We spoke to the doctor, and we did say to him if you can guarantee us that 100% that it is not a messy or in any way horrible operation, you know, whatever you do to a transplant, we'd be more than happy to oblige ... they say they do it so neat, especially for babies and small children you can't even see the stitches, they do it so neat and tidy, that was such a lot of reassurance. (1.08)

An important finding from the data reviewed was how important it was for many donor families to receive particular and continuing information about recipients of donated organs:

Would like to be kept informed how recipients are doing ... comfort to us to know that part of J is still doing some good to different people. (1.11)

Families needed information about what kind of people recipients were, what sort of life they had been living, how the organ affected that life, and how well they were doing.

---

[48] J. Foltyn, 'Dead beauty: the preservation, memorialisation and destruction of beauty in death', in G. Howarth and P. Jupp (eds.), *Contemporary Issues in the Sociology of Death, Dying and Disposal* (London: Macmillan, 1995), pp. 72–83.

[49] *Ibid.*

[50] R. Richardson, *Death, Dissection and the Destitute*, 2nd edn (University of Chicago Press, 2000).

[51] Sque, Long, Payne *et al.*, 'Why relatives do not donate organs for transplants'.

In some ways it would be nice to know more specifically what happened to P's organs. They gave a general scenario, but the problem in this case, it was that this person was doing O.K. but if they gave a little description ... what people are like, [participant suggests] a P.E. teacher who had a heart problem is back teaching, in that sense I guess it would be nice if one had more information. (1.04)

Bartucci and Seller,[52] and Sque,[53] suggest that family members are comforted when they know that other people are leading new lives because of the donation.

The biographies of the donor and recipient appeared to be very important. The biography of the donor explained three main attributes: their physical appearance, personality and hobbies. What their death meant to the family was most often described and donation legitimised as something they would have wanted. The following extract written by the parents of a heart donor succinctly describes all of these concepts:

We had a beautiful son ... D was a healthy, happy, bright, sweet, loving 9-year old ... He loved animals and nature. He liked to cuddle up with his Mom and he liked to go fishing, bike riding and ball playing with his Dad. He was an exceptionally gentle and sensitive boy. He never hurt anyone's feelings. When big kids would be nasty to little kids, he would befriend the little guy. D was open and friendly. Where he went, he made friends. D is deeply missed by his family, his classmates, our entire community, and in truth, by anyone who ever met him. His sudden death struck us all like a fist through the heart and it shattered our world. We will never recover. D would have thought the notion of organ transplant cool. Sharing was something that came easily to him. (2.105)

Likewise, a police officer wrote about her daughter who donated a liver and both kidneys:

She truly was an 'Angel on Assignment' ... when her mission was over, Jesus called her home, she had performed her mission well. (2.32)

Donor families sometimes highlighted particular donor characteristics to the recipients; for example a mother of a nineteen-year-old donor described some of her son's characteristics as follows:

Just one more thing: if you should have a sudden impulse to take up computers, or for some reason want to listen to the Beatles or Eagles, just smile and go for it. (2.64)

Biographical information may have had the effect of reassuring the recipient that the donation was from a 'nice' person and that the organ was generously given. Information about the recipient may have reassured

[52] M. Bartucci and M. Seller, 'Donor family responses to kidney recipient letters of thanks', *Transplantation Proceedings*, 18 (1986), 401–4.
[53] Sque, *'A Story to Tell'*.

the donor family that the organ was genuinely needed, and that the transplant had made a significant improvement to the quality of life of the individual, thus serving to highlight the vital achievement of the donor. The importance of this achievement was particularly in evidence in the extracts from letters written to the NDFC, which tended to view the organ donor as a 'hero': 'C is a hero in every sense of the word' (2.39); 'The only one who could give life' (2.17); and 'Even in death he made a difference' (2.61).

The concept of the donor 'living on' also appeared important to donor families, as these extracts from letters written to the NDFC by a mother and a wife describe:

He will live on in all the lives he helped through organ and tissue transplantation. Our family found much comfort in knowing that his death was not in vain for others were given a second chance in life; because of being a total organ and tissue donor he will live on through the lives of many other people. (2.32)

This may sound strange, but for me I just couldn't bear for his heart to quit beating, he had such a big heart. I felt that as long as it was beating that a part of him was still alive. (2.02)

One of the most difficult things for donor families appeared to be not hearing from recipients of successful transplants, particularly heart donors. These extracts were written to the NDFC by two mothers, the first by one of them about her eleven-year-old son who died in a motor vehicle accident and became a multi-organ donor:

I want to be able to correspond with these people (recipients). It would be very joyful and fill a part of me. I have been waiting for so long. I have love for these people. It has been over two years now and I would very much like to hear from you. Please write. I don't know you but I have a bond with you that nobody could understand. (2.3c)

My son D was an organ donor. He was a very kind and giving young man. I know in my heart that I did what he would have done. I would love to hear from anybody that has a part of him; it has been two years and I am still waiting. I love you. B. (2.03)

It is recognised that death does not cause the immediate separation of the 'self' from the body and therefore emotional ties to the deceased persist.[54] These bonds, generally understood as denoting the presence of an ongoing inner relationship with the deceased person, may account for the continued interest in recipients that was part of donor families'

---

[54] Klass, Silverman and Nickman, *Continuing Bonds*.

grief experience.[55] Organ transplantation is dependent upon the death of the body. However, donor families are challenged by the knowledge that part of their relative is giving life to or contributing to the life of the recipient. One way of continuing the bond with the deceased may be through knowledge of the recipient and maintaining 'the connection' through correspondence.

Continuing bonds also sit well with the ascribed roles and construction of an identity for the donor as a 'hero' or an 'angel',[56] and the importance donor families placed on the concept of continuance of life through organ donation, which helped to give death meaning.[57] As Becker described the hero: '... since primitive and ancient times (the) hero was the man who could go into the spirit world, the world of the dead, and return alive'.[58] However, it is possible, because some American OPOs do use slogans about heroes on their donor cards and related publicity material, that the 'hero' image may already have been part of donor families' vocabulary. 'Angel' also reinforces the concept of the continuity of life, as well as images of perfection, purity, beauty and purpose. Angels in Christian belief are usually sent by God to carry out specific tasks on earth. The mother in this study wrote of her daughter being sent to carry out her 'assignment'.[59] It is possible that donor families found comfort in being closely associated with, and continuing, an internal relationship with a person of intrinsic good who could be described as a 'hero' or 'angel'. Seale has suggested that such an association may affirm the status and worth of the bereaved.[60]

Whilst there is no doubt that bonds with, and to, the deceased may be felt, there is no sound empirical claim that continuing bonds serve a generally adaptive function in coming to terms with bereavement. Research needs to differentiate further between the types of continued bonds, i.e. those that provide comfort, promote adjustment to loss or reflect severe grief reactions. There is also a need to define how bonds are continued or relinquished in bereavement generally, and within the special circumstances of organ donation.[61]

Walter also offers insights into the need for donor families' contact with recipients. He views the purpose of grief as a time during which the

---

[55] Sque and Payne, 'Dissonant loss'; Sque, 'A Story to Tell'; Sque, Long and Payne, Organ and Tissue Donation.
[56] Klass, Silverman and Nickman, Continuing Bonds.
[57] Ben-David, Organ Donation and Transplantation.
[58] E. Becker, The Denial of Death (London: The Free Press, 1973), pp. 11–12.
[59] Sque, 'A Story to Tell'.   [60] C. Seale, 'Heroic death', Sociology, 29 (1995), 597–613.
[61] M. Stroebe and H. Schut, 'To continue or relinquish bonds: a review of consequences for the bereaved', Death Studies, 29 (2005), 477–94.

survivor constructs a durable biography of the deceased, allowing the living to integrate the memory of the dead into their ongoing lives. The process hinges on talking about the dead person, and moving on with them in a new relationship.[62] So how does donor families' need for contact with the recipient fit with Walter's durable biography of the dead and the role of the organ recipient? Clearly we are dealing with an irreconcilable tension. For donor families the recipient becomes part of the donor's biography, which may help to explain the need of families to exchange biographies and keep in touch. It also provides support for the notions of kinship, love and the bonds that were felt to exist between them. The discourse of biography may help the restructuring of the donor's life in the process of adaptation and change in the post-death relationship of new connections. It suggests that the continued motivation for donor families in seeking information about recipients could be understood as possibly compatible with healthy mourning. Therefore, information about recipients could be viewed as contributing to the increased capacity of the donor relative to resolve grief conflict,[63] by playing some part in helping to complete the biography of the deceased.[64]

The interpersonal nature of grief and the importance of social support is highlighted by Walter's biographical grief concept, where the ability to talk about the deceased is crucial to the construction of their biography and the integration of that new relationship into the lives of the survivors. This may explain why some donor families sought help and social support by writing about their organ donation and grief experiences to the NDFC – an organisation of people they felt would understand their situation, particularly with regard to not receiving correspondence from organ recipients. Therefore it is possible that the deep regret felt by these families, when the desired communication was not forthcoming from recipients, meant they could not achieve closure by completing the biography of the donor. They were thus denied the opportunity of constructing a new relationship and integrating the deceased into their ongoing lives.

Sque and Payne have demonstrated that the reciprocity desired by donor families did not appear to be egotistically motivated but was directed at *the achievement of the donor*.[65] Donor families appeared to regard themselves merely as facilitators of their relatives' donations, which helps to explain the importance given to the attributes of the donor.[66] It appeared that if relatives perceived donors to have been generous, caring

---

[62] Walter, 'A new model of grief'.   [63] Sque and Payne, 'Dissonant loss'.
[64] Walter, 'A new model of grief'.   [65] Sque and Payne, 'Dissonant loss'.
[66] *Ibid.*; Sque, '*A Story to Tell*'.

people, then giving their organs was viewed as something they would have been proud to do. It is suggested that it was from the recipients' acknowledgement and appreciation of this achievement that donor families received *reciprocity on behalf of the deceased*, and thus, potentially, solace in their grief. Alternatively, donor families experienced the 'tyranny of the gift',[67] if they did not receive reciprocity in the achievement of the donor, were unable to know that the donor's gift was appreciated and valued, and did not receive thanks on behalf of the donor.[68] Finally, they were denied the knowledge that the organ had achieved a human wholeness and purpose in another body. Some recipients were also subject to 'the tyranny of the gift', through the psychological burden of their inability to reciprocate. Other recipients found it difficult to write and thank the donor family[69] – an action sometimes only achieved after several years, with the felt inadequacy they described to reciprocate a thing of equal value – life itself.

Conclusion

It needs to be recognised that families of potential organ donors are first and foremost bereaved families, and they need to be supported by staff educated to work with bereaved people. Organ donation depends upon a decision-making process that is fragile in nature, multifaceted, multidimensional, with consequences for the bereaved that may continue long after the donation. The authors suggest that by centring families' decision-making within the emotional, social and cultural perspectives discussed in this chapter, and the concepts that underpin society's expectations regarding the determination of death and care of the corpse, healthcare professionals will be better prepared to support bereaved families throughout the donation process, thereby reducing their reported concerns.

Families appear to need constant and ongoing assessment, to elicit the family dynamics and recognition of the main decision-makers. Individualised, ongoing assessment is crucial to fulfil the family's needs, evaluate their ability to process and use information, and ensure the decision is timely. The 'sacrifice' of an unscathed body could be an important barrier to actualising donation even in populations where there is a high level of awareness of the benefits of transplantation. The propriety of the donation operation needs to be stressed in public education and in discussions with the bereaved family concerned.

---

[67] M. Mauss, *The Gift: The Form and Reason for Exchange in Archaic Societies* (London: Routledge, 1990).
[68] Sque and Payne, 'Dissonant loss'.   [69] Sque, '*A Story to Tell*'.

Part III

Strategies for addressing organ shortage

6   Incentivising organ donation

Muireann Quigley

The number of people on the waiting list for organ transplants dramatically exceeds the number of organs available for transplantation. There is ongoing debate about how best to tackle this problem as the chapters in this book demonstrate. The optimal solution may be the implementation of medical and public-health measures which aim to reduce the number of individuals who find themselves in need of an organ transplant in the first place. In the meantime, however, we need to find a way to increase the numbers of organs available for transplantation. In order to do this, we have to motivate individuals to donate their organs either while alive or after their deaths. A way to achieve this may be to offer individuals or their families some kind of incentive to donate.

One suggestion that has been made for increasing the supply of organs for donation is to allow a market in organs. Proposals along these lines generally refer to markets in living organs or, more specifically, live kidney sales. However, I am not going to deal with the ethics of such a market here. The arguments relating to markets in this respect have been well-rehearsed elsewhere.[1] The fact also remains that the sale of organs is illegal in most countries.[2] However, as will be seen there is an increasing call for

---

[1] For example see C. Erin and J. Harris, 'A monopsonistic market – or how to buy and sell human organs, tissues and cells ethically' in I. Robinson (ed.), *The Social Consequences of Life and Death Under High Technology Medicine* (Manchester University Press in association with the Fullbright Commission, London, 1994), pp. 134–53; J. Taylor, *Stakes and Kidneys: why Markets in Human Body Parts are Morally Imperative* (Burlington: Ashgate Press, 2005); A. Matas, 'Design of a regulated system of compensation for living kidney donors', *Clinical Transplant*, 22 (2008), 378–84; M. Gill and R. Sade, 'Paying for kidneys: the case against prohibition', *Kennedy Institute of Ethics Journal*, 12 (2002), 17–45; J. Radcliffe-Richards, A. Daar, R. Guttmann *et al.*, 'The case for allowing kidney sales', *Lancet*, 352 (1998), 1950–2; S. Rothman and D. Rothman, 'The hidden cost of organ sale', *American Journal of Transplantation*, 6 (2006), 1524–8; D. Satz, 'Why should some things not be for sale?' in S. Cullenberg and P. Pattanaik (eds.), *Globalization, Culture, and the Limits of the Market* (Oxford University Press, 2004), pp. 10–37.

[2] The notable exception here is Iran. For more on the Iranian system, see A. Bagheri, 'Compensated kidney donation: an ethical review of the Iranian Model', *Kennedy Institute of Ethics Journal*, 16 (2006), 269–82.

both financial and non-financial incentive schemes to be used in order to encourage people to donate their organs for transplantation.

This chapter examines some general ethical issues surrounding the use of incentives. A variety of incentives aimed at increasing both deceased and living donation are alluded to, including rewards for signing up to the donor register, payment of funeral costs for families who consent to the donation of a deceased relative's organs, and compensation for time off work for living donors. Additionally, incentives that could be deployed at an institutional level are considered. These include remuneration for action taken by hospitals to create an institutional environment which is conducive to increasing organ donation rates. Rather than each of the incentives mentioned being dealt with specifically, however, themes are examined which are common to them, and the ethical considerations relevant across the board are considered.

To begin, the discussion focuses on the incentives or rewards that could be offered to individuals while alive, or their families once they are deceased, in order to encourage the donation of organs after death – for example, small and large financial rewards versus non-financial rewards. Then the discussion moves to the issue of rewards for live donors; the focus is specifically on the removal of current financial barriers that may discourage live donors from coming forward. Finally, the problem at the level of healthcare institutions and practitioners is examined.

Incentives, motivations and altruism

There are a number of different approaches that could be taken to offering incentives. Different approaches may be more or less appropriate depending on which level they are aimed at. For example, potential incentives, be they financial or non-financial, could be aimed at individual donors, the families of donors, or institutions (such as hospitals) which are responsible for the administration and day-to-day running of donation and trans-plantation programmes. Additionally, the ethical analysis on the matter can be divided into those incentives that could be deployed to increase the supply of deceased donor organs and those relevant to the living donor.

Before these specific types of incentives and the ethics surrounding them are looked at, I want to briefly examine how the notion of incentives in general fits with the concept of altruistic organ donation. This is being taken as the starting point for analysis because many discussions regarding organ donation take altruism as their foundation.[3] As will

---

[3] For example see F. Delmonico, R. Arnold, N. Scheper-Hughes *et al.*, 'Ethical incentives – not payment – for organ donation', *New England Journal of Medicine*, 346 (2002), 2002–5;

become apparent in the next section of the chapter, this is because even recent commentators who support the introduction of incentive schemes try to work the idea of altruism into their proposals.

In the past, when speaking about organ donation, there has been an evident commitment on the part of both commentators and policy-makers to a system that is voluntary and non-remunerated.[4] As such, discussions tended to invoke appeals to altruism; that is they contended that individuals who donate their organs should do so from a position of selflessness where no external reward is expected. The good act, the philanthropy of giving, is meant to be reward enough in itself. While there have always been those who advocated the use of incentives such as payment for organs,[5] in general the literature embraced arguments which rejected their use.[6] Yet there has been a noticeable change in the tone of recently published literature. Proposals for the use of various financial and non-financial incentives to help combat the shortfall in organs are gaining substantial ground.[7] It seems that different commentators and groups are now open to the use of financial and non-financial incentives as means to increase the number of organs available for transplantation.

Despite this, the ideal of altruism still pervades proposals for tackling the organs crisis even where financial incentives are being offered. For

R. Arnold, S. Bartlett, J. Bernat et al., 'Financial incentives for cadaveric organ donation: an ethical reappraisal', Transplantation, 73 (2002), 1361–7, 1363; J. Jasper, C. Nickerson, P. Ubel and D. Asch, 'Altruism, incentives, and organ donation: attitudes of the transplant community', Medical Care, 42 (2004), 378–86; J. Prottas, 'Encouraging altruism: public attitudes and the marketing of organ donation', Milbank Quarterly, 61 (1983), 278–306; R. Epstein, 'The human and economic dimensions of altruism: the case of organ transplantation', Journal of Legal Studies, 37 (2008), 459–501; D. Landry, 'Voluntary reciprocal altruism: a novel strategy to encourage deceased donation', Kidney International, 69 (2006), 957–9.

[4] For example R. Sells, 'Voluntarism and coercion in living organ donation' in G. Collins, J. Dubernard, W. Land and G. Persijn (eds.), Procurement, Preservation and Allocation of Vascularized Organs (Dordrecht: Kluwer Academic Publishers, 1997), pp. 295–300; Delmonico et al., 'Ethical incentives'; R. Chadwick, 'The market for bodily parts: Kant and duties to oneself', Journal of Applied Philosophy, 6 (1989), 129–39; R. Titmuss, The Gift Relationship: from Human Blood to Social Policy (London: Allen & Unwin, 1970).

[5] For example Radcliffe-Richards et al., 'Kidney sales'; and A. Daar, 'Rewarded gifting', Transplantation Proceedings, 24 (1992), 2207–11.

[6] See n. 3 above.

[7] For example, G. van Dijk and M. Hilhorst, Financial Incentives for Organ Donation: an Investigation of the Ethical Issues (Ethics and Health Monitoring Report 2007/3) (The Hague: Centre for Ethics and Health, 2007) (www.ceg.nl/data/download/ Orgaandonatie_huisstijl_eng_def.pdf); Arnold et al., 'Financial incentives'; R. Veatch, 'Why liberals should accept financial incentives for organ procurement', Kennedy Institute of Ethics Journal, 13 (2003), 19–36; G. Becker and J. Elías, 'Introducing incentives in the market for live and cadaveric organ donations', Journal of Economic Perspectives, 21 (2007), 3–24.

example, Arnold *et al.*, in an article aimed at reappraising financial incentives as applied to deceased organ donation, propose what they call an 'ethical methodology' for assessing proposed incentives.[8] This consists of nine criteria and includes the following regarding any incentive that could be offered:

1. it should preserve the concept of the organ as a donated gift;
2. it should not subvert or diminish the current standard of altruism; and
3. it should not be an excessive inducement that would undermine personal values and alter decision-making solely to receive the compensation.[9]

At first glance, these criteria appear to represent both a laudable and a practicable endeavour. They seem to recognise the dire situation of those in need of organs while at the same time upholding ethical principles which purportedly ought to form the basis of an ethical organ procurement system. However, if we explore this we can see that such a compromise and its underlying assumptions do not hold up to scrutiny. The criteria being advocated are fundamentally at odds with the function that incentive schemes need to fulfil if they are to be successfully pursued.

Let us start with the contention that the incentive offered should not 'undermine personal values and alter decision-making solely to receive the compensation'.[10] To begin with, it should be noted that the authors do not give further explanation for this particular criterion, but we can examine it in two parts. What might be meant by the assertion that the incentive should not undermine personal values is not immediately obvious. It could be interpreted as something like the following statement: if a person does not already hold as a value the belief that the act of donating an organ is a good thing then the incentive should not be at such a level as to change their mind. Or perhaps it could be interpreted as meaning that if a person thinks that financial or non-financial inducements to donate an organ are morally wrong, then the incentive should not be at such a level as to change their mind. Both of these versions are connected to the second part of the criterion, which is that the compensation offered should not be the only factor that alters an individual's decision-making regarding the use of their organs. This seems somewhat strange: if individuals (or their families after death) were sufficiently motivated to make available their organs by factors other than the proposed incentive, then this would negate the need to offer the incentive in the first place.

By having to offer incentives we are recognising, whether explicitly or implicitly, that we have not been successful with the measures we have taken thus far to try to provide organs for transplantation for all those in

---

[8] Arnold *et al.*, 'Financial incentives', 1363.   [9] *Ibid.*   [10] *Ibid.*

need of them. If initiatives, such as education campaigns, were working and enough people were voluntarily making their organs available without any reward or remuneration, then the need for debate on whether offering incentives is ethical would be redundant. Therefore, we cannot incorporate a requirement that incentives not influence decision-making into a framework for ethical incentives because it is exactly this alteration of an individual's decision-making that is the aim of offering incentives in the first place. The authors surely recognise this incompatibility in the wording of the criterion, since they use the word 'inducement'. By its very nature this means that a stimulus or encouragement is required in order to try to motivate people and to bring about the required behaviour from them.

The objections expressed above also have a bearing on one of the other criteria suggested; that is the notion that the incentive should 'not subvert or diminish the current standard of altruism'.[11] The authors elaborate on this, saying:

Altruism is considered to be an action that is motivated primarily or *solely* by concern for the needs of others, and is freely chosen rather than done out of duty, obligation, *persuasion* or exploitation.[12] [Emphases added.]

Again this comes across as somewhat odd, given that the aim of any incentive scheme is to encourage individuals or their families who would not otherwise have donated organs to actually do so. This is not to say that they would have been wholly against donating organs before the incentive was offered, but merely that the purpose of an incentive is to give them an extra reason for doing so which tips the balance in favour of donation. As such, whatever altruistic motivations there are, they can no longer be said to be the sole reason for donation, nor can the individual concerned be said not to have been persuaded, especially since the aim of the inducement or incentive is to help to persuade.

On an individual decision-making level, what does it mean to say that a person should not decide to donate solely based on the offer of compensation? It could mean that it is acceptable if one decides to donate mostly for the inherent good of the act and only a little because of the incentive. If so then it might not be acceptable if there was an equal split between the reasons one might have to donate or if the proportion of reasons were reversed. Yet it is not obvious that it matters whether the act of making one's organs available for transplantation is no longer to be considered a solely altruistic one. When we speak of altruism, one of our core concerns is with the motivations and intentions of actors. When we insist that

---

[11] *Ibid.*   [12] *Ibid.*, 1365.

individuals donate their organs based on the principle of altruism, what we are saying is that the donor must have virtuous or good motives. In addition, when we condemn the use of incentives, be they financial or non-financial, we are implying that a person who decides to donate because of these can never do so for a good or a virtuous reason. It is, however, simply not clear what constitutes a good or a virtuous reason. It is highly unlikely that in the face of a premature death or a lifetime on dialysis, for example, those most in need of the organs are concerned about the virtuous, or otherwise, motivations of their would-be donors. While we might like it to be accompanied by virtuous motivations and might think better of a person who acts out of these rather than for other reasons, if an action is good in itself, then lack of virtue in intent might be insufficient to render the act wholly unethical.

Individual incentives and deceased organ donation

Providing incentives to individuals in the context of deceased donation means offering them some form of reward for the promise that their organs will be available for donation upon their death. This could be taken as being synonymous with them actively joining an organ donor register or equivalent. Incentives which have been suggested include:

1. a small financial reward;[13]
2. non-financial rewards such as a free passport;[14]
3. a small gift such as an MP3 player, or vouchers for electronic or white goods;[15]
4. a tax break;[16] and
5. even a full-blown futures market in organs where the individual sells their organs prior to their death.[17]

A recent report from the Netherlands explored some options for the employment of ethical incentives.[18] The authors, Hilhorst and van Dijk, emphasise the value that a reward represents:

---

[13] van Dijk and Hilhorst, *Financial Incentives*, p. 17.   [14] *Ibid.*, p. 18.
[15] A. Farrell, *Transplantation and the Organ Deficit in the UK: Pragmatic Solutions to Ethical Controversy* (ESRC Seminar Series Final Report), p. 7, available at www.esrcsocietytoday. ac.uk.
[16] F. Parker, W. Winslade and C. Paine, 'Organ procurement and tax policy', *Houston Journal of Health Law & Policy*, 2 (2002), 173–85.
[17] See L. Cohen, 'Increasing the supply of transplant organs: the virtues of a futures market', *George Washington Law Review*, 58 (1989), 1–51; G. Crespi, 'Overcoming the legal obstacles to the creation of a futures market in bodily organs', *Ohio State Law Journal*, 55 (1994), 1–77.
[18] van Dijk and Hilhorst, *Financial Incentives*.

The message [that a reward] puts across is that society is very appreciative of people who register as donors and are willing to offer their organs after death ... Offering a reward also shows that donation serves an important social interest, that post-mortem donation is morally justified, and that the government is committed to reducing waiting times.[19]

Seen in this way, incentive schemes that take the form of offering a small reward, not only express the gratitude of society for what that individual is willing to contribute, but act as a way to reinforce and send a message about the type of behaviour that society endorses in its citizens. Given this positive view of such schemes, what ethical concerns might we have with them?

First, certain incentives or rewards might induce some individuals into making a choice regarding their organs that they otherwise would not have made. However, as discussed in the first section of this chapter, this is not of great moral concern here. In any case, such small incentives, be they monetary or non-monetary, are unlikely to be so attractive that individuals who are against organ donation could be convinced to change their minds. What they may do, however, is provide an impetus for individuals who either already agree with donation or are merely disinterested to actually sign up to the organ donor register.

Another concern might be whether the use of incentives leads to the commodification of organs in particular and the body more generally. When incentives, for example small financial rewards, small gifts such as MP3 players or vouchers, or even non-financial rewards such as a free passport, are offered, it could be argued that the donation actually becomes a form of exchange and that this thereby makes organs into tradeable objects or commodities. This, it could be argued, would place an inappropriate value on organs. However, in the post-mortem context it is questionable whether we would be giving these tokens in exchange for the organs themselves or merely for the promise elicited and, even if it were the former, it would need to be shown that placing such a value on organs is indeed 'inappropriate'.

Whether or not the proposed incentives would be seen as being given in exchange for the organs themselves, or for the promise that the organs could become available, might be influenced by the level of incentive being offered. If the reward offered is small, we might be disinclined to think that it guarantees that organs are received in return. A small token would seem more in line with a demonstration of society's appreciation because an individual has expressed their willingness to allow their organs to be used after their death.[20] In contrast to small rewards, a large sum of

---

[19] *Ibid.*, p. 16.   [20] *Ibid.*, p. 17.

money, or a gift with a large monetary value attached to it, might shift our thinking towards a framework where any breach of the agreement to make the organs available begins to look more serious. The larger the monetary value of the incentives offered, the more binding we might think the agreement becomes, shifting the focus from a mere appreciation for the good deed of joining the register to a requirement for the guaranteed availability of the organs themselves. In this way, if commodification means making the organs or the body into a tradeable object (when it ought not to be), then small tokens, at least, would not seem to do this. Even if we were to decide that giving small rewards did constitute an exchange such that organs became tradeable objects, then it remains to be seen wherein the inappropriateness of such exchanges lies. If a monetary value were to be placed on the organs it would almost certainly far exceed the value of the gift or rewards being discussed here. As such, if an exchange could be said to be taking place then it would not be a fair exchange. Put this way we might be committing ourselves to offering larger rewards since it would actually be inappropriate to offer such small rewards, given the immense value of an individual's organs both in terms of the value to the recipient and the value to the healthcare system; and, by extension, society more generally.

As mentioned at the start of this section of the chapter, providing incentives to individuals in the context of deceased donation means offering them some form of reward for the promise that their organs will be available for donation upon their death. There is, therefore, a pragmatic concern regarding this. With any scheme which elicits a promise from individuals that their organs be made available for transplantation after their deaths comes the possibility that they may either change their minds or that some circumstances might change. This means that the promised organs may in fact never become available. This would not necessarily be a new difficulty since we already encounter this problem in relation to the register where no incentive is offered to sign up to it. If a small incentive, be it financial or non-financial, were offered then this leaves open the prospect that some people would sign up to the current organs register solely to receive the money, gift, voucher or whatever it may be, and then might withdraw their willingness to donate at a later date or instruct their families to refuse donation in the event of their death.[21]

---

[21] It might be that this problem could be overcome by offering some kind of deferred payment scheme where a payment would be made to the family or to a charity. However, if the payment were to be made to the family then this is no longer an issue about incentivising individuals. See the section below on families and the use of incentives.

Without empirical evidence on the matter it is difficult to tell whether this would happen and to what extent, but I would suggest that we can assume most people would not engage in such behaviour. If that turned out to be the case then there would only be a minority of individuals who would sign up knowing that they intended to withdraw from the register at a later date. Either way, a follow-up assessment would need to be made to establish whether this had resulted in an overall increase in the numbers of organs for transplantation.

Other considerations

Another possibility is that those who agree to donate their organs after their deaths should be given priority on waiting lists should they themselves become in need of an organ. Until recently there was no system of organ donation which incorporated such a provision, but one has recently been passed into law in Israel.[22] This law is the first to establish a system whereby individuals can gain waiting list priority points by expressing their willingness to be donors themselves. In the context of deceased organ donation, an individual's willingness is to be indicated by their possession of an organ donor card. At first glance this seems appealing and would appear to satisfy some sort of principle of justice as well as ensuring a reward, should it be needed, for those who are themselves willing to donate. Hilhorst and van Dijk see such assurances as promoting reciprocity between society and the individual and argue that donation in this context represents a form of 'enlightened self-interest' which there can be little objection to on ethical grounds.[23] They do, however, question whether such a scheme would be effective since individuals who are most at risk of needing an organ might 'engage in strategic behaviour'.[24] They are concerned that people with particular health conditions, for example those who are HIV positive, would join the organ donor register in order to benefit from higher waiting list priority should the need arise.

As pointed out by Hilhorst and van Dijk, this may not lead to 'any concrete results' since their state of health would actually preclude them from donating.[25] Quite apart from the fact that any scheme which did not lead to an actual increase in the numbers of organs for transplantation would simply be a waste of time and resources, such a scheme would in fact contain a double injustice. Not only would there never be a possibility of increasing the pool of organs from the participation of such individuals, but they would end up as higher priority cases than others already on the

[22] Israeli Book of Laws, Organ Transplantation Law 5768–2008.
[23] van Dijk and Hilhorst, *Financial Incentives*, p. 19.   [24] *Ibid.*   [25] *Ibid.*

waiting list. The priority in such cases would not seem to be justified, since there was never going to be an overall benefit to the system gained by the expression of willingness to donate from the high-risk individual.

It might be argued that the way around this problem is to simply exclude those groups who are unlikely to ever contribute to the organs pool from being able to gain an advantage through the scheme. However, such a suggestion seems to present its own difficulty; namely, that those individuals most likely to need a transplant due to a foreseeable health state would be the ones systematically disadvantaged. They would be disadvantaged relative to others because they would not have the possibility of waiting list prioritisation that others without current adverse health states would have. Thus, whether those individuals in adverse health states were permitted to join such schemes or not, there would appear to be issues of justice that would need to be addressed.

Family, incentives and deceased donation

Despite the fact that individual autonomy is lauded as one of the central principles of organ donation programmes, it is often the case that when a person dies it is their family who makes the decision about whether or not to donate their organs.[26] For this reason, it might be possible to develop incentive schemes which are aimed at convincing the relatives to make the organs of the deceased available for transplantation. Some incentives which have been suggested include small or large cash rewards, tax benefits, and payment of funeral costs. The first issue that needs to be examined, whether we are talking of financial or non-financial incentives, is what the role of incentives is in this context. This is closely connected to potential concerns about the role of individual autonomy, given that respect for individual decision-making seems to have significant support in the area of organ donation.

In examining the ethics of a range of incentives for deceased organ donation in general, and speaking of paying funeral costs more specifically, Arnold *et al.* favour incentives that 'reflect society's attempt to thank the deceased individual for giving an organ'.[27] As discussed earlier, certain incentives may indeed work to convey gratitude to the particular individual whose organs are being donated, but this can only be the case when the incentive is given pre-mortem. While incentives might still be used to show society's appreciation for the donation, it is a fiction to

---

[26] For some figures from the UK, see *Potential Donor Audit Summary Report 2007–09*, www.organdonation.nhs.uk/ukt/statistics/potential_donor_audit/pdf/pda_summary_report_2007–2009.pdf.

[27] Arnold *et al.*, 'Financial incentives', 1365.

suggest that this appreciation is directed at the individual after their death. Rather it is both a way to motivate families into making the organs of their relatives available for donation, and a way for society to express its gratitude for them doing so.

When discussing the various incentives, the authors often talk in terms of a gift. They are not alone in using this terminology. Hilhorst and van Dijk use the word reward,[28] while Daar talks of 'rewarded gifting'.[29] Such terminology should not, however, be used to try to distract attention from the function and role of the incentive, or from the fact that incentives such as paying funeral costs are of financial benefit to the family. After all, the cost of a funeral can be significant. However, even if the family do gain a benefit in this manner it does not automatically mean that the incentive is unethical. If we are happy to vest decisions, such as whether to donate organs, in the relatives of the deceased, then it may be that a suitable incentive is called for. It is going to be a difficult time for them and they will be grieving, but paying funeral costs might give them one thing fewer to worry about. It does, however, call into question the purported primacy of individual autonomy in relation to deceased organ donation.

Where we have no unequivocal indication of the wishes of the deceased regarding organ donation, the decision of the family is significant. This is especially so in a system such as the one in the United Kingdom (UK) where, although the legal emphasis is on the 'appropriate consent' of the individual,[30] the family still hold a veto after death at a practical level. This means that if an individual wanted to donate after their death, and perhaps was on the organ donor register, healthcare professionals might still be loath to take that individual's organs against the wishes of the family. This even occurs in countries such as Spain which have officially adopted an opt-out system.[31] When examining the ethical issues around the use of incentives, we are probably worried about the opposite scenario: that is, where a particular individual did not want to donate but the incentive being offered means that the family go against their wishes.

It is far more likely, however, that the situation will arise where the wishes of the deceased are not known but the decision to donate is swayed by the incentives offered. If individual autonomy in this context is as important as some would maintain, then we are at risk of violating the deceased's autonomous wishes either way. If they did not want to donate

---

[28] van Dijk and Hilhorst, *Financial Incentives.*   [29] Daar, 'Rewarded gifting'.
[30] Sections 2 and 3, Human Tissue Act 2004.
[31] M. Quigley, M. Brazier, R. Chadwick *et al.*, 'The organs crisis and the Spanish model: theoretical versus pragmatic considerations', *Journal of Medical Ethics*, 34 (2008), 223–4, 223.

and the family agree to donation, then it is a violation. Equally, if they wanted to donate but the family disagree, then it is also a violation. It is unclear what ethical consequences we should then impute from the employment of incentive schemes in such cases. This is because while there is a risk that more families would donate in situations where the deceased had not wanted to, there is also the chance that more donations would occur from individuals who did want to. Which side of the argument one favours will depend on whether we think it is a greater wrong to take organs from those who did not want to make them available than it is to not take them from those who would have wished them to be used in this manner.

Limiting disincentives to donate

Whatever the ethics of offering various incentives, one obvious starting point is to try and remove existing disincentives to individuals and healthcare institutions becoming involved in the organ donation and transplantation process. While there might still be ethical concerns regarding how this is to be done, these are likely to be fewer than with the types of incentives already discussed.

Removing individual disincentives

Where an individual elects to become a living organ donor there are financial and non-financial costs involved. These costs include the time that the individual spends attending various medical consultations, having numerous tests prior to the organ retrieval surgery, the surgery itself, and then time spent recuperating post-surgery. Living organ donors also incur the cost of getting to and from the hospital, as well as the cost of any food and accommodation required if they are travelling far from home. In addition, they may incur loss of income due to days off work required for consultations, the surgery and the recuperation period afterwards. In countries such as the UK, there is unfortunately no legal requirement for employers to cover the cost of sick leave due to organ donation.[32] No matter how committed one might be to the ideal of altruism, this should not require that an individual who is giving so much already should end up financially worse off. It is also not obvious that employers should have to bear the financial costs if one of their employees decides to donate an organ.

---

[32] Although in the UK Primary Care Trusts are starting to accept some responsibility in this sphere. For an account of some of the problems facing living donors in this regard see M. Harris, 'The donor's tale', *Journal of Medical Ethics*, 34 (2008), 511–12.

It has already been argued that in the context of deceased organ donation there are some ethical and practical difficulties with offering waiting list priority as an incentive to donate. However, in the case of living organ donation, it would not lead to the same ineffectiveness or injustices previously discussed. This is because the individual will already have made the donation that qualifies them for such priority if the need arises and, as such, there is no danger of them benefiting from the system without actually contributing to it. In this respect it would seem to be a matter of justice and fairness that individuals who become living organ donors do in fact get waiting list priority.[33] To do so would remove a worry that donors may have about being left, for example, with only one kidney. They may be reassured that in the event that their remaining kidney fails, it is likely that they will get another one. For this reason, waiting list priority in these circumstances may prove to be a key motivating factor in encouraging people to donate. This would be especially so in cases of altruistic anonymous donation where the individual is donating to a stranger and, therefore, does not have family ties as a factor in their decision-making.

Whatever the objections might be to the various financial and non-financial incentives outlined above, it is certain that there are barriers to organ donation at individual and institutional levels that need to be addressed if any headway is to be made. Even if one disagrees with offering overt financial or material inducements to donate, it seems fair that disincentives be removed at least.

Institutional incentives

Encouraging individuals or their families to donate organs for transplantation is certainly a step in the right direction, but is ultimately fruitless if there is institutional apathy at the hospitals where organs are procured and the transplants carried out. One of the crucial factors in the success of the Spanish deceased organ donation programme is thought to be the fact that there is a system of hospital reimbursement in place.[34] The regional healthcare authorities in Spain are responsible for ensuring that those hospitals involved in donation and transplantation activities are adequately reimbursed for the cost incurred. During the most recent substantive review of organ donation and transplantation in the UK, the

---

[33] See Chapter 8 for further detail on the issue of justice and fairness in the context of organ donation and transplantation.

[34] R. Matesanz and B. Domínguez-Gil, 'Strategies to optimize deceased organ donation', *Transplantation Reviews*, 21 (2007), 177–88.

Organ Donation Taskforce included a recommendation in its first report that the additional costs of organ donation activities in hospitals should be covered.[35] While the Taskforce rejected the use of explicit financial incentives, it advocated the covering of costs by hospitals even where organ retrieval does not take place. The reason for this was the recognition that the costs of running the system are incurred even where a potential donor's organs become unsuitable for transplantation.[36]

Other options

Another potential strategy for trying to increase the number of people that sign up to the organ donor register is to make greater use of the systems already in place in the primary care sector. Primary care practitioners, such as general practitioners or family doctors, could take on a greater role in encouraging their patients to join the register. In most primary care practices in the UK, for example, when a new patient joins they have to fill in an initial assessment form and then attend a consultation. Consideration could be given to adding questions about organ donation to this form. In addition, the appointment with the practice nurse would provide an opportunity to discuss any queries or concerns. Incentives could be put in place through, for example, the Quality and Outcomes Framework (QOF).[37] The QOF is a system whereby primary care practices can gain points if they achieve certain targets. These points then translate into a financial reward for these practices. For this reason the framework acts as a motivator for practices to be results-driven. Gaining the QOF points could be reliant not simply on numbers signed up to the organ donor register but on the condition that primary care practitioners undergo appropriate training and that patients are given appropriate information during consultations. Implementing this approach as standard practice could be viewed as superior to current methods, such as the internet, which are used by individuals to join the register. Having the opportunity to discuss the decision with a trained primary care practitioner may lead to more informed choices on the part of the person signing up to the register.

Conclusion

In this chapter some overarching ethical issues regarding various types of incentives that might be used to encourage individuals to donate their

[35] Organ Donation Taskforce, *Organs for Transplants: a Report from the Organ Donation Taskforce* (London: Department of Health, 2008), p. 41.
[36] *Ibid.*   [37] For more information, see www.qof.ic.nhs.uk.

organs, either while living or after their deaths, have been examined. It has been argued that in accepting the need for incentives to act as encouragement to individuals or their families we have to let go of the notion that donations ought only to be motivated by altruistic ideals. We should accept that the purpose of incentives is to alter the decision-making process and to tip the balance in favour of donation. This, however, does not render the use of certain incentives unethical.

It may be that offering incentives to those hospitals which positively pursue and implement an organ donation programme is deemed less ethically problematic than the kinds of incentives aimed at the individual or familial level. In any event, measures should be taken to remove disincentives to donation at every level. This may be in the form of the reimbursement of costs for individuals and for those hospitals which carry out transplantation activities. Whether or not such incentive schemes would actually lead to an increase in the number of organs available for transplantation remains an empirical question. Any such scheme which did not lead to an actual increase in the numbers of organs for transplantation would simply be a waste of time and resources. As a consequence, any incentive schemes, whether aimed at the individual, families or institutions, need to be carefully evaluated following their introduction in order to determine their practical effectiveness.

7 Making the margins mainstream: strategies to maximise the donor pool

Antonia Cronin

In 1955, Hume and colleagues published a report of the first blood group incompatible renal transplant.[1] The recipient had early rejection on day seven. In the fifty years since, experimental immunobiology has been able to explain why: naturally occurring antibodies (part of the body's natural defence against infection) attack and damage the transplanted graft.[2] Recently, techniques have become available to remove these, and other, circulating antibodies. These techniques, along with the development of newer and more powerful immunosuppression (anti-rejection) treatment regimes, have made organ transplants that were previously thought to be impossible, because of the presence of a prohibitive incompatible circulating antibody, a reality.

Of course, if the supply of compatible organs available for clinical transplantation was surplus to demand, it might never have been necessary for science to understand and explain how best to overcome these immunological barriers. Likewise, it would have been difficult for clinicians to justify performing experimental transplants on people when less problematic treatment (transplant) solutions were available to them. However, demand for organs has long outstripped supply and the number of individuals in need of a transplant is on the rise. So, in the knowledge that transplantation is the optimal treatment for almost all those in need of an organ, identifying and developing ways in which organs can be made available for transplantation has become a major priority. Antibody incompatible transplantation is just one example.

Organ shortage makes it likely that it will not always be possible to find an 'ideal' donor. However, by using 'expanded criteria' and 'marginal' donors and accepting organs from those who might previously have been

---

[1] D. Hume and J. Merrill, 'Experiences with renal homotransplantation in the human: report of nine cases', *Journal of Clinical Investigation*, 34 (1955), 327–82.

[2] Immunology is a broad branch of biomedical science that covers the study of all aspects of the immune system in all organisms. Transplantation immunology (or immunobiology) refers to the immunological study of events that occur after an allograft, or xenograft, is removed from a donor and then transplanted into a recipient.

considered unsuitable donors, meaningful expansion of both the deceased and living donor pool has been made possible. The term 'marginal donor' in living donation is analogous with the term 'expanded criteria donor' in deceased donation. Confusingly, both terms have come to be used interchangeably. Overall however, they refer to organs from donors (living or deceased) who do not meet standard donor criteria. Their acceptance and use has come to the fore along with a heightened awareness of the ever-increasing shortfall of organs available for transplantation.[3]

This chapter examines strategies that have been put in place in order to maximise the donor pool. It explores the legitimacy of using both 'expanded criteria' and 'marginal' donors, and performing high-risk antibody incompatible living donor transplants in order to help overcome the shortfall in organs available for transplantation.[4] Published empirical evidence is reviewed and outcomes assessed. It is argued that while these strategies may at first appear to be a straightforward solution to the problem of organ shortage, their implementation is not without ethical controversy and may even be a counterintuitive solution to the problem of organ shortage. However, in the absence of real alternatives, and in the knowledge that the outcome of what I collectively term 'marginal transplants' are considerably better than the alternatives available, namely treatment with dialysis or death on the transplant waiting list, it is conceded that continuing to support their use is legitimate.

Standard and expanded criteria donors

The use of expanded criteria donor (ECD) organs is probably the single most important way in which the deceased donor organ pool has increased in size over the last decade. The terms 'standard' and 'expanded criteria' donor have evolved alongside this development in response to the uncomfortable reality that although all deceased donor organs are placed equally on the national allocation scheme (a scheme which is committed to impartial equitable allocation), the plain fact is that some deceased

---

[3] In this chapter, the term 'expanded criteria' donors is intended to refer principally to deceased donors who do not meet standard deceased donor criteria, and the term 'marginal donors' is intended to refer principally to living donors who do not meet standard living donor criteria. However, in the discussion below regarding the legitimacy of using donors who do not meet standard donor criteria, they will be referred to collectively as 'marginal donors'.

[4] In discussion of expanded criteria donor and marginal donor transplants, or high-risk and antibody incompatible living donor transplants, these will be referred to collectively as 'marginal transplants'.

donor organs are better than others. Although some have given their support to using 'the kidneys that nobody wanted', it is generally acknowledged that the graft and patient outcomes achieved using ECD organs are not as good as those achieved using standard criteria donor organs.[5]

Traditionally, a standard deceased donor has met the following criteria: donor age of between 10 and 39 years; death did not result from a cerebral vascular accident (a stroke); there was no history of hypertension (high blood pressure); and there was a terminal serum creatinine of less than 132 µmol/L (normal range 80–120 µmol/L).[6] An ECD kidney is a kidney donated for transplantation from any brain-dead donor, or donor after brain stem death, over the age of 60 years; or from a donor over the age of 50 years with two of the following: a history of hypertension, a terminal serum creatinine greater than 132 µmol/L, or death resulting from a cerebral vascular accident. This definition applies to the allocation of deceased donor kidneys.[7] Definitions vary and may include other factors, such as the presence of infection, for example Hepatitis B, or a history of cancer.[8]

Non-heart-beating (NHB) organ donors, or donors after cardiac death (DCD), are often included in this expanded group of deceased donors.[9] Non-heart-beating donation (NHBD) raises a number of concerns, for some not least ambiguity as to the timing and definition of death. For

---

[5] C. Lee, J. Scandling, G. Shen *et al.*, 'The kidneys that nobody wanted: support for the utilisation of expanded criteria donors', *Transplantation*, 62 (1996), 1832–41; J. Pascual, J. Zamora and J. Pirsch, 'A systematic review of kidney transplantation from expanded criteria donors', *American Journal of Kidney Disease*, 52 (2008), 553–8; A. Ojo, 'Expanded criteria donors: process and outcomes', *Seminars in Dialysis*, 18 (2005), 463–8.

[6] United Network of Organ Sharing (UNOS) definition – see www.unos.org. The terminal serum creatinine means serum creatinine measurement at time of death. The serum creatinine is a marker which reflects overall kidney function.

[7] *Ibid.*

[8] S. Munoz, 'Use of hepatitis B core antibody-positive donors for liver transplantation', *Liver Transplantation*, 8 (2002), S82–7; C. Lo, S. Fan, C. Liu *et al.*, 'Safety and outcome of hepatitis B core antibody-positive donors in right-lobe living-donor liver transplantation', *Liver Transplantation*, 9 (2003), 827–32; A. Punnett, L. McCarthy, P. Dirks *et al.*, 'Patients with primary brain tumours as organ donors: case report and review of the literature', *Paediatric Blood Cancer*, 43 (2004), 73–7; H. Kauffmann, W. Cherikh, M. McBride *et al.*, 'Deceased donors with a past history of malignancy: an organ procurement and transplantation network/united network for organ sharing update', *Transplantation*, 84 (2007), 272–4; J. Buell, T. Beebe, J. Trofe *et al.*, 'Donor transmitted malignancies', *Annals of Transplantation*, 9 (2004), 53–6.

[9] Non-heart-beating donors fulfil the criteria for cardiac death. Non-heart-beating donors are also referred to as donors after cardiac death (DCD). This is in contrast to heart-beating donors who fulfil the criteria for death by brain stem criteria. Heart-beating donors are also referred to as donors after brain stem death (DBD). See C. Moers, H. Leuvenink and R. Ploeg, 'Non-heart-beating organ donation: overview and future perspectives', *Transplant International*, 20 (2007), 567–75.

example, Bell has argued that if a patient cannot be considered unequivocally dead, conducting invasive organ procurement procedures, for instance those aimed at reducing warm ischaemic time, may be failing to act in the patient's best interests, and more than this, comes perilously close to euthanasia.[10] Moreover he claims NHBD risks jeopardising professional and public confidence in the broader transplant programme.[11] Concerns regarding cumulative jeopardising of public confidence on this matter have been publicly aired in the United Kingdom (UK).[12] Despite these concerns, NHBD is increasingly regarded as a valuable source of organs for clinical transplantation. Consensus opinion guidance regarding the optimum management of NHBD has since been published by the UK Intensive Care Society.[13] In November 2009, the UK Department of Health published its view of the legal position in relation to the action that can be lawfully taken prior to death to support NHBD. The intention is that those working in this area will be able to use it to draw up more detailed guidance to support clinical practice.[14]

In 2000 Balpuri *et al.* highlighted that the long-term outcomes of transplanted kidneys retrieved from NHB donors are inferior to those retrieved from heart-beating donors.[15] Since that time, techniques to improve organ preservation and reduce warm ischaemic time have improved, and some centres have reported encouraging long-term NHB donor transplant graft outcome data.[16] However, NHB donor organs do appear to have a greater incidence of early adverse events.[17] In 2008–09, the number of UK NHB kidney donors increased to 275 from 195 in 2007–08. In the same time

---

[10] D. Bell, 'Non-heart-beating organ donation: old procurement strategy – new ethical problems', *Journal of Medical Ethics*, 29 (2003), 176–81. In surgery, the warm ischaemic time is the time a tissue, organ or body part remains at body temperature after its blood supply has been reduced or cut off but before it is cooled or reconnected to a blood supply. For a detailed examination of ethical and legal issues involved in non-heart-beating donation, see Chapter 9.

[11] *Ibid.*

[12] BBC, *Panorama*, 'Transplants: are donors really dead?', BBC2, 13 October 1980.

[13] S. Ridley, S. Bonner, K. Bray *et al.*, 'Intensive Care Society's Working Group on Organ and Tissue Donation, UK guidance for non-heart-beating donation', *British Journal of Anaesthesia*, 95 (2005), 592–5.

[14] www.dh.gov.uk/en/Publicationsandstatistics/Publications/PublicationsPolicyAndGuidance/DH_108825.

[15] S. Balpuri, P. Buckley, C. Snowdon *et al.*, 'The trouble with kidneys derived from the non heart-beating donor: a single centre 10 year experience', *Transplantation*, 69 (2000), 842–6.

[16] A. Barlow, M. Metcalfe, Y. Johari *et al.*, 'Case-matched comparison of long term results of non-heart-beating and heart-beating donor recipient transplants', *British Journal of Surgery*, 96 (2009), 685–91; M. Rela and W. Jassem, 'Transplantation from non-heart-beating donors', *Transplantation Proceedings*, 39 (2007), 726–7.

[17] C. Kokkinos, D. Antcliffe, T. Nanidis *et al.*, 'Outcome of kidney transplantation from non heart-beating versus heart-beating cadaveric donors', *Transplantation*, 83 (2007), 1193–9.

period the number of transplants from such donors increased by 41 per cent to 474.[18] Estimates vary, but some centres report that ECDs make up some 20 per cent of their total deceased donor pool. Ojo *et al.* report that ECD kidneys now account for 20 per cent of all deceased donor kidneys in the United States (USA) with the fraction being as high as 35 per cent in some donation service areas.[19]

Marginal donors

There are various accounts of 'marginal donors'. In general terms, marginality means that for whatever reason these donors and their organs are unlikely to be optimal. The main conditions that may pre-exist in potential marginal donors, and are of concern, are high blood pressure (hypertension), advanced age, obesity, kidney stone disease (also known as nephrolithiasis), proteinuria and haematuria.[20] There is no consensus over the definition or use of marginal donors; however, there is general support for the view that long-term prospective cohort studies are needed in order to evaluate the long-term outcome of these donors.[21] The favourable long-term outcome, in terms of blood pressure, proteinuria and renal function, of living donors post-nephrectomy is often considered central to the argument for their continued legitimate use.[22] There is published evidence which supports the view that hypertensive living donors do not incur a greater risk of morbidity or mortality following

---

[18] Figures: NHS Blood and Transplant (NHSBT), Organ Donation and Transplantation Directorate, www.uktransplant.org.uk/ukt/statistics/transplant_activity_report/current_activity_reports/ukt/2008_09/tx_activity_report_2009_uk_pp12–20.pdf.

[19] A. Ojo, F. Luan, R. Sung and R. Merion, 'The use of expanded criteria donor organs for transplantation', *Transplantation Reviews*, 20 (2006), 41–8.

[20] Proteinuria refers to the presence of quantifiable serum protein in the urine. Haematuria refers to blood in the urine. Together or separately proteinuria and haematuria may reflect underlying kidney (glomerular) pathology. Their presence should prompt further evaluation.

[21] A. Young, L. Storsley, A. Garg *et al.*, 'Health outcomes for living kidney donors with isolated medical abnormalities: a systematic review', *American Journal of Transplantation*, 8 (2008), 1878–90; A. Garg, N. Muirhead, G. Knoll *et al.*, 'Proteinuria and reduced kidney function in living kidney donors: a systematic review, meta-analysis and meta-regression', *Kidney International*, 70 (2006), 1801–10.

[22] J. Najarian, B. Chavers, L. McHugh and A. Matas, 'Twenty years or more of follow-up of living kidney donors', *Lancet*, 340 (1992), 807–10; D. Goldfarb, S. Martin, W. Braun *et al.*, 'Renal outcome 25 years after donor nephrectomy', *Journal of Urology*, 166 (2001), 2043–7; D. Narkun-Burgess, C. Nolan, J. Norman *et al.*, 'Forty-five year follow-up after uninephrectomy', *Kidney International*, 43 (1993), 1110–15; B. Kasiske, J. Ma, T. Louis and S. Swan, 'Long-term effects of reduced renal mass in humans', *Kidney International*, 48 (1995), 814–19.

donation.[23] However, hypertension remains a leading cause for exclusion from living organ donation.[24] In a recent multi-centre review, Karpinski *et al.* estimated that up to 17 per cent of potential living kidney donors are rejected because of hypertension or proteinuria, and that up to 40 per cent of those rejected may have been acceptable for living donation.[25]

Some centres have expanded their pool of potential living donors by including potential donors older than 60 years of age. There is evidence to suggest that donor outcome values are comparable in this age group with younger age groups and that age should no longer be considered as a contra-indication for living organ donation.[26] However, donors above the age of 60 are a known risk factor for delayed graft function and reduced renal allograft survival in deceased donation. Although the data are not as striking in living donor transplantation, it is clear that allografts from elderly donors are inferior.[27] Foss *et al.* have argued that these allografts perform acceptably, and should therefore certainly be considered for older transplant recipients, particularly in light of recent evidence which suggests that at least half of kidney transplant candidates who are older than 60 will die before receiving a deceased donor transplant.[28]

[23] S. Textor, S. Taler, N. Driscoll *et al.*, 'Blood pressure and renal function after kidney donation from hypertensive living donors', *Transplantation*, 78 (2004), 276–82; I. Fehrman-Ekholm, F. Duner, B. Brink *et al.*, 'No evidence of accelerated loss of kidney function in living kidney donors: results from a cross-sectional follow-up', *Transplantation*, 72 (2001), 444–9.

[24] I. Fehrman-Ekholm, H. Gabel and G. Magnusson, 'Reasons for not accepting living kidney donors', *Transplantation*, 10 (1996), 695–9; N. Boudville, G. Prasad, G. Knoll *et al.*, 'Meta-analysis: risk for hypertension in living kidney donors', *Annals of Internal Medicine*, 145 (2006), 185–96. A meta-analysis of 48 studies that enrolled 5,149 donors, with only 6 reports being controlled, reviewed the specific risk of increased blood pressure over time after kidney donation. The study documented that kidney donors may have a 5-mm Hg increase in blood pressure within 5 to 10 years after donation over that anticipated with normal ageing.

[25] M. Karpinski, G. Knoll, A. Cohn *et al.*, 'The impact of accepting living kidney donors with mild hypertension or proteinuria on transplantation rates', *American Journal of Kidney Disease*, 47 (2006), 317–23.

[26] M. Neipp, S. Jackobs, M. Jaeger *et al.*, 'Living kidney donors >60 years of age: is it acceptable for the donor and the recipient?', *Transplant International*, 19 (2006), 213–7; S. Textor, S. Taler, T. Larson *et al.*, 'Blood pressure evaluation among older living kidney donors', *Journal of the American Society of Nephrology*, 14 (2003), 2159–67.

[27] M. Giessing, T. Slowinski, S. Deger *et al.*, '20 year experience with elderly donors in living renal transplants', *Transplant Proceedings*, 35 (2003), 2855–7; L. Berardinelli, C. Beretta, M. Raiteri and M. Carini, 'Early and long term results using older kidneys from cadaver and living donors', *Clinical Transplantation*, (2001), 157–66; L. Resende, J. Guerra, A. Santana *et al.*, 'Impact of donor age on renal allograft function and survival', *Transplantation Proceedings*, 41 (2009), 794–6.

[28] A. Foss, K. Heldal, H. Scott *et al.*, 'Kidneys from deceased donors more than 75 years perform acceptably after transplantation', *Transplantation*, 87 (2009), 1437–41; J. Schol, T. Srinivas, A. Sehgal and H. Meier-Kriesche, 'Half of kidney transplant candidates who are older than 60 years now placed on the waiting list will die before receiving a deceased-donor transplant', *Clinical Journal of the American Society of Nephrology*, 4 (2009), 1239–45.

Opinions vary regarding the use of donors with kidney stones although there is a consensus view that potential donors with multiple stones and renal impairment should be excluded. Others who do not meet these criteria merit further assessment and evaluation prior to proceeding with donation. Evidence-based guidelines are lacking for these donors; however the general trend is to accept them.[29] Obesity is an independent risk factor for cardiovascular and renal disease.[30] This, together with the knowledge that obese kidney donors may subsequently develop long-term renal dysfunction and cardiovascular disease, makes a clear case for urging a cautious approach in the use of obese living kidney donors.[31]

Antibody incompatible living donor transplantation

Antibody incompatible living donor renal transplantation (AIT) refers to ABO blood group incompatible transplants (ABOi) and human leucocyte antigen (HLA)[32] incompatible transplants (HLAi). AIT is widely practised, but there remain uncertainties about long-term graft and patient outcome. Exceptionally, renal transplants which are both ABO and HLA incompatible are performed.

ABO blood group incompatible (ABOi) transplants

In humans (and some primates) the most important blood group system is the ABO system. An individual's blood type will depend on the antigens and antibodies present on red blood cells. ABO compatibility refers to which blood groups can be exchanged without incurring an adverse antibody-mediated reaction. ABOi kidney transplants were first reported by Hume *et al.* in the 1950s, Murray in 1960 and Starzl in 1964.[33] Although

---

[29] J. Ennis, M. Kocherginsky, L. Schumm *et al.*, 'Trends in kidney donation among kidney stone formers: a survey of US centres', *American Journal of Nephrology*, 30 (2009), 12–18.

[30] C. Hsu, C. McCulloch, C. Iribarren *et al.*, 'Body mass index and risk for end-stage renal disease', *Annals of Internal Medicine*, 144 (2006), 21–8.

[31] M. Tavakol, F. Vincenti, H. Assadi *et al.*, 'Long-term renal function and cardiovascular disease in obese kidney donors', *Clinical Journal of the American Society of Nephrology*, 4 (2009), 1230–8.

[32] The Human Leukocyte Antigen (HLA) system is the name of the human major histocompatibility complex (MHC). This group of genes resides on chromosome 6 and encodes antigen-presenting proteins. The proteins encoded by the HLAs are the proteins on the outer part of body cells that are (effectively) unique to that person. The immune system uses the HLAs to differentiate self cells from non-self (foreign) cells. HLA antibodies are typically not naturally occurring, and with few exceptions are formed as a result of an immune challenge of foreign material containing non-self HLAs via for example blood transfusion, pregnancy or organ or tissue transplant.

[33] Hume and Merrill, 'Experiences with renal homotransplantation in the human: report of nine cases'; J. Murray, J. Merrill, G. Dammin *et al.*, 'Study on transplantation immunity

long-term graft survival was observed in some cases, experience indicated that hyperacute rejection, occurring within minutes of the transplant, could take place and so progress was halted. In the early 1980s, Alexandre *et al.* initiated an ABOi kidney transplant programme using immunosuppression protocols that entailed removing antibodies pre-transplant. This prevented the antibody-mediated hyperacute rejection seen earlier.[34] It is now accepted that removal of anti-ABO antibodies (anti-ABO Abs) is mandatory to prevent hyperacute rejection, because pre-existing antibodies against blood group A/B antigens cause antibody-mediated rejection.

HLA antibody incompatible (HLAi) transplants

Sensitisation to HLA molecules results from previous exposure to allogeneic tissue, for instance through pregnancy, blood transfusion or previous transplants. In general, the greater the antigenic exposure the more highly sensitised an individual is likely to be. In some centres it has been estimated that up to 30 per cent of patients waiting on the transplant list are sensitised.[35] Highly sensitised potential transplant recipients who are HLA incompatible with their prospective living donor may be so because they have developed a donor specific antibody (DSA).[36] Currently in the UK there are two options available to highly sensitised ABOi and HLAi potential transplant recipients: desensitisation protocols and paired/pooled donor exchange. Determining which option is the best for an individual patient will depend on the breadth and strength of a potential recipient's ABO and HLA reactivity, donor and recipient blood types, and an overall risk assessment of antibody-mediated rejection.

Desensitisation protocols

Desensitisation protocols remove the offending (incompatible) antibody. Recent advances in immunosuppression protocols have made this possible, although these protocols are costly and not without risk. It is now relatively straightforward to overcome immunological barriers, such as

after total body irradiation, clinical and experimental investigation', *Surgery*, 48 (1960), 272–84; T. Starzl, T. Marchioro, J. Holmes *et al.*, 'Renal homografts in patients with major donor-recipient blood group incompatibilities', *Surgery*, 55 (1964), 195–200.

[34] G. Alexandre, J. Squifflet, M. De Bruyere *et al.*, 'ABO-incompatible related and unrelated living donor renal allografts', *Transplantation Proceedings*, 18 (1986), 452–5.

[35] A. Gupta, V. Iveson, M. Varagunam *et al.*, 'Pre-transplant donor specific antibodies in cytotoxic negative crossmatch kidney transplants: are they relevant?', *Transplantation*, 85 (2008), 1081–2.

[36] A donor-specific antibody is an antibody directed against the HLA antigens of the donor.

ABO blood group incompatibility and high recipient sensitivity. In general, the higher the ABO/HLA antibody titre, however, the more difficult it will be to reduce the titre of the antibody or remove it altogether. Patients with a high antibody titre pre-transplant are at a greater risk of antibody-mediated rejection. Short- and medium-term outcomes for AIT kidney transplant recipients seem to be comparable to compatible transplants, according to recent reports.[37] What remains unclear are the long-term effects and risks associated with using such heavy immunosuppression protocols. Long-term outcome data is eagerly awaited.

Paired and pooled donor exchange

Paired donor exchange programmes bypass rather than cross incompatible immunological barriers. In a paired exchange an incompatible living organ donor and recipient 'pair' can swap organs with another 'pair' in the same situation. If more than two donors and two recipients are involved in the swap it is called 'pooled donation'. The main advantage of a donor exchange programme is that an uncomplicated ABO/HLA compatible transplant is performed using standard immunosuppression treatment, with excellent results.[38] Expensive, time-consuming immunosuppressive protocols are avoided. Paired exchange transplants can be performed electively, and if done in a timely fashion may reduce or obviate the need for pre-transplant dialysis.

Some have argued that the main disadvantage of this system is conflict between the donor's and the recipient's families: relations can be particularly strained if there are significant discrepancies in post-donation and transplantation outcome. In order to minimise significantly different outcomes between the pairs, Delmonico has suggested that factors such as socioeconomic status, gender, age, any relationship, body weight and donor kidney function should be considered in addition to HLA match.[39] Others have identified that incompatible kidney donors are more willing to participate in donor exchange programmes as compared

---

[37] K. Tannabe, T. Tokumoto, H. Ishida *et al.*, 'Excellent outcome of ABO-incompatible living kidney transplantation under pre-transplantation immunosuppression with tacrolimus, mycophenolate mofetil and steroids', *Transplant Proceedings*, 36 (2004), 2175–7; R. Higgins, R. Johnson, S. Fuggle *et al.*, 'UK Registry of Antibody Incompatible Renal Transplantation, 2001–2009', Oral Abstract, British Transplantation Society Annual Congress, London, March 2010. The abstract reported three-year follow-up outcome data.

[38] R. Montgomery, A. Zachary, L. Ratner *et al.*, 'Clinical results from transplanting incompatible live kidney donor/recipient pairs using kidney paired donation', *Journal of the American Medical Association*, 294 (2005), 1691–3.

[39] F. Delmonico, 'Exchanging kidneys – advances in living-donor transplantation', *New England Journal of Medicine*, 350 (2004), 1812–14.

to list donation, where the recipient receives the next deceased donor kidney or non-directed donation.[40]

Why make the margins mainstream?

It is not clear against what, if any, baseline we should evaluate the claim that marginal transplants are better than no transplants at all. The global problem of organ shortage is oft quoted as good reason to support the continued use of marginal (donor) transplants, as though it were a relevant baseline. But is it? Arguably, the most important problems with the use of expanded criteria and marginal donors are the subsequent inferior graft outcome and patient survival statistics.[41] Matching an inferior donor organ with a high-risk recipient creates the greatest chance of a worst outcome, and when this fact is coupled with inevitable consideration of efficient use of resources it seems counterintuitive to encourage such transplants at all.[42] Worse still, it is self-defeating if all that is achieved is reinstatement onto the transplant waiting list of patients who are now immunologically sensitised and more difficult to successfully transplant. The corollary, however, is that the outcomes of marginal transplants are considerably better than the alternatives available, namely treatment with dialysis or death on the waiting list.[43]

Doing something, so it seems, is better than doing nothing, even if it means compromising the outcome of something that we know has the potential to be a 'gold standard' treatment. It is as though making the margins mainstream is legitimate because it is mutually advantageous to clinician and patient: it satisfies both the clinician's duty of care and the patient's entitlement to a life-saving (transplant) treatment.[44] Moreover,

---

[40] A. Waterman, E. Schenk, A. Barrett *et al.*, 'Incompatible kidney donor candidates' willingness to participate in donor-exchange and non-directed donation', *American Journal of Transplantation*, 6 (2006), 1631–8.

[41] A. Collini, C. De Bartolomeis, G. Ruggieri *et al.*, 'Long-term outcome of renal transplantation from marginal donors', *Transplantation Proceedings*, 38 (2006), 3398–9; Pascual, Zamora and Pirsch, 'A systematic review of kidney transplantation from expanded criteria donors'; Ojo, 'Expanded criteria donors: process and outcomes'.

[42] P. Kuo, A. Lu and L. Johnson, 'Expanded criteria donors/high risk recipients is not always cheaper than haemodialysis', *Transplantation*, 72 (2001), 554–5.

[43] United States Renal Data System, '2006 Annual Data Report', *American Journal of Kidney Disease*, 114 (2007), 2806–14. The mortality of dialysis patients is comparable to, or worse than, that seen in many cancers. Reports vary, but approximately 50 per cent of this increased mortality is due to cardiovascular disease. J. Mittler, A. Pascher, P. Neuhaus and J. Pratschke, 'The utility of extended criteria donor organs in severely ill liver transplant recipients', *Transplantation*, 86 (2008), 895–6.

[44] At common law doctors have a duty to provide a good standard of care. See Stuart-Smith LJ, *Capital & Counties plc* v. *Hampshire County Council* [1997] QB 1004 at 1035, referring to *Cassidy* v. *Ministry of Health* [1951] 2 KB 343 and *Barnett* v. *Chelsea & Kensington Hospital Management Committee* [1969] 1 QB 428.

implementing strategies to maximise the donor pool and transplanting high-risk recipients comfortably satisfies society's responsibility to make possible the best achievable outcome from the goods and services that are available. It even sits well with the Marxist concept 'from each according to his ability to each according to his need (or needs)'.[45] As such these strategies appear to go some way to providing pragmatic solutions to ethical controversy.

But however comfortable this may seem, it fails to take account of the fact that these downstream strategies, which are not without risk, are, or may be, a direct result of our failure to implement what some have argued are morally acceptable upstream solutions to the problem of organ shortage, for example Harris's scheme for the automatic availability of deceased donor organs.[46] If sufficient 'good' organs were available for transplantation it would not be necessary to use 'less good' organs, navigate our way across complex immunological barriers, incur greater risk and accept inferior outcomes. Crucially, what this point highlights is that in our quest as moral agents *qua* moral agents to avoid wrongdoing and to refrain from doing the things that can be said to be wrong, we inadvertently perform a different act, with foreseen bad consequences. This prompts an important theoretical question: what exactly is it that determines whether our upstream omission is morally more or less harmful than our consequent actions?

Harm

The idea of non-maleficence sits at the very core of organ donation. The principle 'first, do no harm', makes it difficult to explain the legitimacy of using a living donor organ from donor B, Lucy say, in order to benefit recipient A, her loved one, Tony. Living donor kidney donation, for example, is associated with a mortality risk of 1 in 3,000.[47] Living donor liver donation carries a far greater mortality risk of up to 1 in 100.[48] In its first report, the UK Organ Donation Taskforce suggested that nothing demonstrates the critical shortage of deceased donors more clearly than

---

[45] K. Marx, *Critique of the Gotha Program* (Rockville: Wildside Press, 2008).

[46] J. Harris, 'Organ procurement: dead interests, living needs: cadaver organs should be automatically available', *Journal of Medical Ethics*, 29 (2003), 130–4.

[47] E. Johnson, M. Remucal, K. Gillingham *et al.*, 'Complications and risks of living donor nephrectomy', *Transplantation*, 64 (1997), 1124–8.

[48] Estimates vary. See for example R. Ghobrial, C. Freise, J. Trotter *et al.*, 'Donor morbidity after living donation for liver transplantation', *Gastroenterology*, 135 (2008), 468–76.

the acceptance – by patients, clinicians and commissioners – of such risk to the life of a fit, healthy person.[49] This 'acceptance' is made all the more difficult when we consider that Lucy, donor B (a marginal living donor, say), incurs a considerably greater risk to herself for what may be little, if any, benefit to Tony, recipient A.

The more tangible way of making sense of this is to consider that Lucy also benefits, insofar as she sees her loved one, Tony, reaping the benefit of her donation; or perhaps her altogether good, altruistic, act benefiting society. Lucy has, after all, consented to donation. As Wertheimer argues:

> We do not need to be moral rocket scientists to know that it is wrong for A to gain from an action that unjustifiably hurts or coerces B ... In contrast, it is more difficult to explain when and why it might be wrong for A to gain from an action that benefits B and to which B voluntarily consents.[50]

Although the overarching sentiment of Wertheimer's assertion that we should all know that it is wrong for A to gain from an action that unjustifiably hurts or coerces B is clear, it is not clear that his assertion is in fact correct. Limited resources may quite easily result in such a state of affairs. Suppose for instance that funding for drug treatment A is available for, and allocated to, patient population A, but the resultant effect is that there are insufficient funds to provide drug treatment B for patient population B. While we might agree that there is no justice in our not treating patient population B, we ought to at least concede that commissioners and organisations such as the UK's National Institute for Health and Clinical Excellence (NICE)[51] in part depend on just such exploitative benefiting. If, however, we took Wertheimer's analysis a step further, it would become more difficult still to explain when, and why, it might be wrong for A to gain from an action that may harm, or even kill, B, from which B nonetheless may benefit and to which B voluntarily consents. On this analysis, living organ donation, so it seems, is tantamount to a set of circumstances in which we consider that the possibility of harming, hurting, even killing, one in order to benefit another, is legitimate; and moreover, remains legitimate even when this (un)justifiable possibility becomes more likely, and little, if any, benefit is achieved.

---

[49] Organ Donation Taskforce, *Organs for Transplants: a Report from the Organ Donation Taskforce* (London: Department of Health, 2008). It is interesting and noteworthy that the report does not appear to acknowledge the acceptance of the living donors themselves.
[50] A. Wertheimer, *Exploitation* (Princeton University Press, 1999), pp. 12–15.
[51] The National Institute for Health and Clinical Excellence (NICE) is the independent UK organisation responsible for providing national guidance on the promotion of good health and the prevention and treatment of ill health (www.nice.org.uk).

Harm as a comparative concept

Wilkinson argues that harm is a comparative concept. Judgements about harm, he says, compare someone's relative levels of welfare in two actual or possible situations. When these two comparators are actual, he says, we are looking at a welfare differential over time. For example, he suggests, 'we might say that someone has been harmed by an event, meaning that she is worse off *after* the event (and because of it) than she was *before* it'. But, he continues, 'more often than not, statements about harm involve comparing the actual world with a *merely possible* world. So, we might for instance say that someone is harmed by X (an event, say) if she would have been better off if X had not happened.'[52] Wilkinson's example of harm as a comparative concept can be usefully applied when thinking about living donor organ donation and marginal transplants. We might for instance say that Lucy, donor B, has been harmed by organ donation, meaning that she is worse off after the donation, and because of it, than she was before it. Likewise, it is straightforward to consider that Lucy is harmed by organ donation if she would have been better off if the donation had not happened.

Demonstrating that living organ donation is, or may be, harmful provides a powerful argument against it. Other things being equal, inflicting harm on persons is wrong. The difficulty, however, with importing this kind of justification into the context of living donor organ donation and transplantation is that it does not take account of other morally relevant reasons, in particular individual autonomy, which may have contributed to an individual's decision, and motivation, to donate. Nor does it adequately capture the real, or actual, circumstances in which an individual may be prepared to volunteer to incur, or risk, harm to themselves in order to benefit, or rescue, another and consider the overall benefit mutually advantageous regardless of the harm which may or may not be caused to self. In fact, if we were to apply Feinberg's concept of 'harm to interests', which he defines as 'a thwarting, setting back, or defeating of an interest', we might even consider that a greater harm would be incurred by Lucy were her donation not to be allowed to take place.[53] Circumstances vary. One person's success may be another's failure. What this makes clear is that it seems unlikely that any account of harm, comparative or

---

[52] S. Wilkinson, *Bodies for Sale: Ethics and Exploitation in the Human Body Trade* (London: Routledge, 2003), pp. 60–1. Wilkinson's discussion of harm in this book, which has as its focus the sale of body parts, is detailed and explores the connection between exploitation and harm.

[53] J. Feinberg, *Harm to Others: the Moral Limits of the Criminal Law* (New York: Oxford University Press, 1984).

otherwise, could provide us with a satisfactorily robust, reliable tool with which to predict an individual's consideration of the possible harm which may be done as against the possible benefit which may be achieved through their donation.

Matters differ when we apply Wilkinson's comparative model to marginal transplants. Consider for example Petra, who is a dialysis patient, and is also a potential kidney transplant recipient waiting on the transplant list. We might suppose that Petra is worse off because X, a gold-standard kidney transplant from Dominic, a young, fit and healthy donor, did not take place. Even if Petra receives a marginal transplant from an elderly, hypertensive, non-heart-beating donor, we might, in the same vein, consider that Petra would have been worse off if the marginal transplant had not happened. Both of these examples straightforwardly express harm to Petra as a comparative concept. Applying this account comparing relative levels of welfare to only two actual or possible situations, however, leaves matters too simple and may lead to counterintuitive results. For example, even though Petra is better off if the marginal transplant from the elderly non-heart-beating donor happens, she would have been even better off if the gold-standard kidney transplant from Dominic, the young, fit and healthy donor, had happened. So, although Petra has in this instance benefited by having the marginal transplant, she has also been harmed by not having the gold-standard kidney transplant from Dominic. What this highlights, and what Wilkinson makes clear in his discussion, is that assessing harm claims is less straightforward than it first appears, because of the difficulties associated with selecting an appropriate welfare baseline (or, as in this case, outcome) as a comparator.

As we have seen, according to the empirical data available at least, Petra would have been worse off if either transplant had not taken place. Either transplant is a better therapeutic option for Petra than the alternatives available, namely treatment with dialysis or death on the waiting list. And so even though by having the marginal transplant from the elderly, deceased non-heart-beating donor, the best possible outcome has not been achieved, a better outcome has been reached, and less harm has occurred, than had no transplant taken place at all. One might argue that the logical conclusion from this analysis is that overall, marginal transplants are legitimate because patients benefit from them and they would be worse off if the marginal transplant had not happened – the harm caused by using marginal organs is less than the harm caused by not using them. This conclusion is, however, problematic for at least three reasons. First, we are likely to be settling for an inferior transplant outcome. Second, we incur greater risk than we need to. Third, if sufficient 'good' organs were available for transplantation it would not have been necessary for the marginal transplant to occur. It seems wildly counter-intuitive to incur greater risk and reap less benefit, and it would be difficult to justify such a state of affairs if it were possible to demonstrate that alternative morally acceptable methods for overcoming organ shortage were available but had not been put in place.

If it is true that Petra is worse off, or has been harmed, because a marginal transplant rather than a gold-standard kidney transplant has happened and that Lucy, donor B, has been harmed by organ donation, meaning that she is worse off after the donation, and because of it, than she was before it, we must seriously consider whether this harm has been caused, at least in part, by our collective failure – our omission – to supply sufficient 'good' organs for transplant by alternative means.

Harmful omission

'The idea that if we are able to change things, to elect not to do so is also to determine what will happen in the world, is very old indeed.'[54] In his discussion of such a state of affairs, Harris claims that '[i]n such cases, many men have found it natural not only to blame those who could have prevented the harm, but did not do so, but also to think of such men as having brought the harm about, as being its cause'.[55] Whether our failure to supply sufficient 'good' organs for transplant amounts to omissive harm merits consideration and should be afforded considerable importance, particularly given the broad acceptance of Mill's 'harm principle', according to which 'the only purpose for which power can rightfully be exercised over any member of a civilised community against his will is to prevent harm to others'.[56]

Taken to its logical extreme this principle might even, as Harris has argued, provide us with legitimacy to kill one in order to save two and so on.[57] Many, probably most, would not endorse the Harris position nor consider this consequence of his account tenable. It is doubtful whether the availability of organs for transplantation was the particular application that Mill had in mind when writing his seminal work. However, if we accept the view that living organ donation is tantamount to a set of circumstances in which we consider that the possibility of harming, hurting, even killing, one in order to benefit another is legitimate, and, moreover, remains legitimate even when this (un)justifiable possibility

---

[54] J. Harris, 'The Marxist conception of violence', *Philosophy and Public Affairs*, 3 (1974), 192–220.
[55] *Ibid.*   [56] J. Mill, *On Liberty* (London: Penguin Books, 1985).
[57] J. Harris, 'The survival lottery', *Philosophy*, 50 (1975), 81–8.

becomes more likely and little, if any, benefit is achieved – as would appear to be the case in living donor marginal transplantation – we must concede that we run perilously close to endorsing a state of affairs that, from a utilitarian standpoint at least, makes the Harris position look attractive. Deciphering whether an act is the result of an exertion of power or altruistic volition is not always straightforward and may be notoriously difficult.[58] What this example demonstrates is how apparently appropriate solutions, responsive to the matter of organ shortage, inadvertently can and do amount to harmful, and possibly wrongful, action(s) with foreseen, bad consequences. The moral intuition of clinicians is that action is better than no action (omission) in these circumstances. If no transplant takes place the potential recipient is likely to die. However, any appeal to intuition here is a double-edged sword. If the avoidance of wrongdoing is the principle task of a moral agent, surely we should all support the strategy that avoids as much wrongdoing as possible.

More than 10,000 people in the UK currently need a transplant. Of these, 1,000 each year – 3 per day – will die waiting because there are not enough organs available. Importantly, of the 9,767 people currently listed for a kidney transplant in the UK, 2,006 have had a previous kidney graft. This means that of the people currently listed waiting for a kidney transplant, 20.7 per cent have had a previously failed kidney transplant.[59] Although there are likely to be several factors contributing to this, we must be prepared to at least consider whether this figure is in part because of reinstatement onto the transplant waiting list of patients whose previous transplant organ was 'marginal' and has failed prematurely.

Of course, not everyone will be a suitable organ donor upon their death. All sorts of reasons, not least malignancy, may preclude their potential to donate. However, as highlighted by the figures in Chapter 1, there is a shameful disparity between the number of deceased donor organs that ought to be available for clinical transplantation and the number of organs that are in fact transplanted. If we invoked Mill's 'harm principle' and entered everyone into the deceased organ donation scheme we would be faced with an organ surplus. What then? One could argue that there was good reason to put a stop to living donor transplantation altogether.

Of course, deceased donor organ donation is a matter more complex than a simple linear algebraic formula would have us believe. Death holds a powerfully important symbolic place in many people's lives. For some, so much so that death is inextricably linked with and gives meaning to the

---

[58] See for example A. Wertheimer, *Coercion* (Princeton University Press, 1987).
[59] NHS Blood and Transplant (NHSBT), www.nhsbt.nhs.uk.

value of their life.[60] Indeed, some would argue that respecting the living means respecting the dead too.[61] Whether the interests of one who is dead can be harmed is a contentious issue. If it were possible to demonstrate the truth of the assertion that one or more of a person's interests are in a worse condition than they would have been if it were not for their organs being donated after their death, matters would be straightforward. However, when they are dead they are no longer able to think critically about preferences, desires or wishes and so it is not clear that they are (or ever would be) able to support such a claim. Powerful though the arguments are in favour of the compulsory use – mandating – of organs posthumously, they are unlikely ever to receive unanimous support. However, if we are to rely on the figures highlighted in Chapter 1, it would appear that the mandating of organ retrieval after death need not even be invoked in order to overcome the problem of organ shortage. The mantra 'making organ donation usual not unusual' might well suffice.[62] Time will tell.

Faced with a hypothetical world in which deceased donor organs were available to all those in need of one, Lucy, donor B, might not need to volunteer to incur harm. Indeed, if systems were in place which meant that it was not necessary for Lucy to donate, it seems less likely that she would in fact donate. Systems notwithstanding, if in this hypothetical world Lucy's autonomous wish would still be to donate, her decision should be respected and not shrugged off. Placed, as we are, in the actual world, one in which the enterprise of transplantation is apparently frustrated by organ deficit, an individual's autonomous decision to donate and risk the possibility of incurring harm is a wonderful example of altruism which at the same time provides a pragmatic solution to ethical controversy.

Conclusion

In this chapter, strategies that have been implemented in order to maximise the donor pool, thereby increasing the number of organs available for lifesaving transplants, have been examined. These strategies include using extended criteria donors, marginal donors, and performing antibody incompatible living donor transplants. This group of transplants has been collectively referred to as 'marginal transplants' in this discussion. Marginal transplants appear to have gone some way to providing a

---

[60] See O. Hanfling, *Life and Meaning: a Reader* (Oxford: Basil Blackwell, 1987); and more generally, R. Lee and D. Morgan (eds.), *Death Rites: Law and Ethics at the End of Life* (London: Routledge, 1996).

[61] S. McGuinness and M. Brazier, 'Respecting the living means respecting the dead too', *Oxford Journal of Legal Studies*, 28 (2008), 297–316.

[62] Organ Donation Taskforce, *Organs for Transplants*, section 1.23, p. 9.

pragmatic solution to an apparent organ deficit. Moreover, this perceived deficit, coupled with the knowledge that outcomes from marginal transplants are considerably better than the alternatives available – namely treatment with dialysis, or death on the transplant waiting list – provide powerful reasons to support the continued implementation of such transplants. However, it is clear from this examination that their provision is not without ethical controversy, due not least to reported inferior graft outcome and patient survival statistics, as well as the risks undertaken.

As has been argued throughout this chapter, one difficulty with the continued unfettered use of marginal transplants is the realisation that if sufficient 'good' organs were available it would not be necessary to use 'less good' organs, navigate our way across complex immunological barriers, incur greater risk and accept inferior outcomes. While this does not straightforwardly provide the basis for a ringing endorsement of a scheme which confiscates deceased (or living) donor organs and makes them automatically available for clinical transplantation, it does highlight that in our quest as moral *qua* moral agents, to avoid wrongdoing and to refrain from doing the things that can be said to be wrong we inadvertently perform a different act, with foreseen bad consequences. Indeed, one might even conclude from the author's inquiry that, under the auspices of pragmatism, we have forsaken the outstanding success of the enterprise of clinical transplantation.

This realisation does not in any way threaten an autonomous individual's decision to donate and risk the possibility of incurring harm in so doing, nor yet any living donor transplant programme. It should, however, prompt us to consider carefully the principles and processes which underpin the provision of deceased donor organs for transplantation. Indeed, continuing to allow organ deficit to frame the legitimacy of innovative strategies to make good use of the organs available for transplantation is arguably unnecessary and may even be illusory. This difficulty and realisation notwithstanding, in the absence of real alternatives and in the knowledge that marginal transplants are better than no transplants at all, continuing to support their use is legitimate.

8   The allocation of organs: the need for fairness and transparency

Phil Dyer and Sheelagh McGuinness

Whilst every opportunity must be taken to increase organ donation within accepted legal, moral and ethical guidelines, it is equally important that no effort is spared to avoid wastage. This process demands the highest standards, if public and professional confidence is to be maintained. Donated organs should be placed where they are most likely to improve quality of life and to be of lasting benefit.[1]

This chapter considers the evolution of the organ allocation system in the United Kingdom (UK). As it has evolved, the system has incorporated many of the conflicts which can arise. These include (but are by no means limited to) conflicts over biological incompatibility between a donor and a recipient, legal issues, ethical principles, competing claims between individuals and between individuals and society, the objectives of healthcare regulators, and financial resources. The system of donation for thoracic organs and livers is not discussed in this chapter. Nor is there examination of the criteria for gaining access to the transplant list, an area which itself raises many issues worthy of consideration.[2] This chapter will instead focus on the allocation of kidneys to those on kidney transplant lists. There are certain background conditions against which any analysis of the organ allocation system must take place. These are: 1. biological compatibility is important to avoid immediate failure; and 2. demand for organs currently outstrips available supply of organs.

With these conditions in mind, this chapter provides a description of the organ allocation algorithm which exists in the UK. In the latter half of the chapter there is an analysis of the impact of certain 'trigger events' on the evolution of the organ allocation process. There is also analysis of

---

[1] British Transplantation Society, *Standards for Solid Organ Transplantation in the United Kingdom*, www.bts.demo.eibs.co.uk/transplantation/standards-and-guidelines.
[2] M. Volk, A. Lok, S. Pelletier *et al.*, 'Impact of the model for end-stage liver disease allocation policy on the use of high-risk organs for liver transplantation', *Gastroenterology*, 135 (2008), 1568–74; A. Klassen, A. Hall, B. Saksvig *et al.*, 'Relationship between patients' perceptions of disadvantage and discrimination and listing for kidney transplantation', *American Journal of Public Health*, 92 (2002), 811–17.

the importance placed on concepts such as 'fairness', 'justice' and 'equity' within the organ allocation algorithm. This examination takes account of the politico-legal framework within which the system exists.

Instituting an organ donation and allocation system raises a profound diversity of issues, which relate to ethics and public acceptability, and not merely to scientific viability. As David Price puts it:

It has been observed that what is truly distinctive about transplantation is not technology or cost, but ethics, emphasising the unique and virtually utter dependence upon the participation of the public for its continued viability as a therapeutic option at all ... In short, the fundamental nature of transplantation in clinical, physiological and biological terms is entirely matched by its significance in legal, ethical, theological and cultural terms.[3]

In this chapter the organ allocation system is introduced and presented against the background of scientific, ethical and public constraints. The benefits and shortcomings of the current kidney allocation system are considered and the chapter concludes with some challenges which future developments will have to overcome.

Biological compatibility is imperative to avoid immediate failure

To begin, the first background condition – biological compatibility – will be explored. This discussion relates to the notion of efficiency within the allocation system, as there is no point allocating organs in a way which is not likely to realise the value of those organs. In a North American study, Ubel and Loewenstein framed preferences in terms of allocation of organs as a trade-off between equity (equal access) and efficiency (health outcomes).[4]

ABO compatibility

In 1910, Landsteiner revolutionised blood transfusion when he demonstrated the existence of distinct blood groups.[5] This discovery led to the classification of the commonly occurring ABO blood groups; ABO-A, -B, -AB and -O. It was subsequently discovered that all individuals

[3] D. Price, *Legal and Ethical Aspects of Organ Transplantation* (Cambridge University Press, 2000), p. 2.

[4] P. Ubel and G. Loewenstein, 'Distributing scarce livers: the moral reasoning of the general public', *Social Science & Medicine*, 42 (1996), 1049–55.

[5] S. Lederer, *Flesh and Blood: Organ Transplantation and Blood Transfusion in Twentieth-Century America* (Oxford University Press, 2008), p. 143.

become immunised to non-self blood groups, probably by exposure to ABO-like sugars in the diet.[6] These classifications were by no means universally accepted at the time of discovery as they challenged accepted norms about blood relatedness. Lederer notes that: '[It] was not straight-forward that a mother would not be a compatible donor for her own child. Nor was it easy to accept that some brothers and sisters could be compatible blood donors and others not.'[7]

In the pioneering days of organ (kidney) transplantation in the 1950s, some transplants were carried out ignoring the established 'rules' of blood transfusion – that the donor ABO blood group must be compatible with that of the recipient. These early organ transplants were undertaken with little understanding of immunological processes in very sick recipients who were close to death and receiving poor-quality donor organs. With time and evidence of some improvement in transplant outcome, surgeons came to recognise that ABO blood group incompatibility might be the cause of some immediate failures. There has never been a controlled trial of ABO compatible versus incompatible organ transplantation, so no evidence base exists to support this hypothesis, other than case reports of ABO incompatible transplants performed in error.[8] These few reports largely support a very poor outcome for ABO incompatible transplants.[9] It must be noted that there has been recent progress in transplanting successfully with ABO incompatibility, but this requires specialised, careful intervention which is costly and not without risk.[10]

HLA

HLA (Human Leukocyte Antigens, 'tissue types') are proteins found on the surface of all nucleated body cells, so they are absent from red blood cells. When an individual is infected with a pathogen such as a virus or bacterium, the HLA molecules present the pathogen to the immune system so that, following activation of many cellular processes, the infected cell can be destroyed to minimise disease. Unfortunately, this process also leads to destruction of a transplanted organ through two routes. First, if a transplant recipient has been exposed to non-self HLA proteins at the time of a pregnancy, following a blood transfusion (which contains HLA positive white blood cells), or following a previous transplant, then

---

[6] *Ibid.*, Chapter 5.   [7] *Ibid.*, p. 147.
[8] N. Banner, M. Rose, D. Cummins *et al.*, 'Management of an ABO-incompatible lung transplant', *American Journal of Transplantation*, 4 (2004), 1192–6.
[9] K. Tanabe, K. Takahashi, K. Sonda *et al.*, 'Long-term results of ABO-incompatible living kidney transplantation: a single-center experience', *Transplantation*, 65 (1998), 224–8.
[10] See Chapter 7.

antibodies in the recipient directed to non-self HLA types in the donor may be present and may lead to rapid destruction of the transplanted organ by immune mechanisms. Second, there is good evidence that patients who receive a crossmatch negative but HLA antigen mismatched organ transplant do, in time, become immunised to the mismatched HLA antigens.[11] This process then contributes to gradual transplant failure. This evidence encourages transplantation when the difference between donor and recipient HLA types is zero or minimal. There is debate as to whether avoiding HLA mismatches is of cost-benefit. While practice in the United States (USA) ignores HLA matching, emphasis is placed on avoiding HLA mismatches in Europe and elsewhere.

The development of the organ allocation system in the UK

The NHS Blood and Transplant – Organ Donation and Transplantation Directorate (NHSBT-ODT)[12] is a Department of Health Authority which became a division of the NHS Blood and Transplant Authority in 2005.[13] Its origins are to be found in 1972 in the National Organ Matching and Distribution Service, subsequently rebranded as the 'UK Transplant Service', 'UK Transplant Support Service Authority' and 'UK Transplant'.[14] During its thirty-five-year existence, NHSBT-ODT has enhanced its role as the central body overseeing allocation of deceased donor organs throughout the UK. Currently NHSBT-ODT supports Organ Specific Advisory Groups comprising medical, surgical, immunological and co-ordinator NHS staff together with patient representatives who guide allocation polices and review their functioning.[15]

In 1989, the transplant community supported the NHSBT-ODT in its introduction of the 'Beneficial Matching' allocation algorithm for kidneys donated after brain death.[16] At the time, donation after cardiac

---

[11] J. Worthington, A. McEwen, L. McWilliam *et al.*, 'Association between C4d staining in renal transplant biopsies, production of donor-specific HLA antibodies, and graft outcome', *Transplantation*, 83 (2007), 398–403.

[12] The title NHSBT-ODT is used throughout this chapter as shorthand to refer to the various stages in the evolution of this body.

[13] www.organdonation.nhs.uk/ukt/about_us/about_us.jsp.   [14] *Ibid.*

[15] www.uktransplant.org.uk/ukt/statistics/statistics.jsp.

[16] W. Gilks, B. Bradley, S. Gore and P. Klouda, 'Substantial benefits of tissue matching in renal transplantation', *Transplantation*, 43 (1987), 669–74; W. Gilks, S. Gore and B. Bradley, 'Predicting match grade and waiting time to kidney transplantation', *Transplantation*, 51 (1991), 618–24.

death (DCD) was rare.[17] In essence, one kidney from each donor was offered to the national recipient pool for patients with no HLA mismatch, or just one mismatched HLA-A or -B antigen, with the donor HLA type. The remaining kidney could be used in the local centre and was allocated according to local policy, if any existed. In 1997, this sharing scheme was extended, adding in 'favourable' matches who were recipients with one mismatch for both HLA-A and -B antigens. In July 1998 recipients with no HLA mismatch were given priority over other 'favourable' matched recipients and a points scoring system was introduced for the first time to discriminate when more than one recipient competed for a donated kidney. The following criteria were used to allocate points to potential recipients:

- prioritise younger recipients;
- minimise donor and recipient age difference;
- prioritise recipients who had waited longer;
- prioritise 'difficult to match' patients (usually those with antibodies to HLA antigens or those with rare HLA types); and
- prioritise recipients at the donor centre.

From July 2000 onwards, the second kidney from any donor was prioritised for any potential paediatric recipient in the national recipient pool.[18] In April 2006, a full revision of the national allocation system was introduced.[19] The revision followed reports received from working groups established by the UK Transplant Kidney and Pancreas Advisory Group in March 2003.[20] The working groups addressed equity of access to kidney transplantation and allocation processes. The Allocation Working Group took on this challenge, and because of overall improvements in transplant outcome, which was the end-point used in all analyses, found that HLA mismatching had become less influential allowing a relaxation in HLA matching criteria. This relaxation was facilitated by improvements

---

[17] 'Non-heart-beating donation (NHBD)' versus 'donation after cardiac death (DCD)' and 'heart-beating donation (HBD)' versus 'donation after brain death (DBD)': approximately two years ago, the transplant community was made aware that the terms NHBD and DBD were confusing to non-medical communities: in essence, the word 'death' was not included. To avoid confusion the terms DBD and DCD were introduced, and importantly the word 'death' is included in these new terms. The change has been slow to catch on but all the leading transplant journals now require authors to use DBD/DCD. Regrettably, the UK Department of Health has issued documents recently using the outdated terms.

[18] UK Transplant Guidelines, *Donor Organ Sharing Scheme: Operating Principles for Cardiothoracic Transplant Units in the UK and Republic of Ireland*, 3.2 (www.organdonation. nhs.uk).

[19] www.uktransplant.org.uk/ukt/default.jsp.

[20] www.organdonation.nhs.uk/ukt/about_us/business_plan/previous_business_plans/bus_plan_2002–2003.pdf.

in immunosuppressant drugs.[21] Furthermore, the importance of minimising the time during which a donated kidney was stored out of the body in melting ice became evident, in particular after twenty hours of storage. Whilst exchange of kidneys between centres could influence storage time, constraints at the transplanting centre could also be influential. Finally, the level of definition of HLA types was revised, allowing a reduction in the number of possible mismatches. Importantly, none of these modifications adversely influenced transplant outcomes in the simulations performed on historic data. The new allocation scheme was predicted to:

- allow improved access by ethnic minorities to kidneys for transplant;
- reduce waiting time for those waiting the longest;
- minimise kidney storage;
- minimise HLA mismatches when important;
- give priority for children (under eighteen years of age) and young adults; and
- match the expected longevity of the transplanted kidney to that of the patient.

These recommendations by the UK Transplant Kidney and Pancreas Advisory Group were approved by the NHSBT-ODT Board and were implemented on 3 April 2006.[22]

Kidneys donated by deceased donors after brain death

In the early days of organ transplantation, kidneys transplanted from non-heart-beating donors had reduced outcomes, but because of the shortfall in availability of organs for transplantation, kidneys are now retrieved and transplanted from such donors. Recent analyses show that these kidneys do not function well in the very short term, but their outcomes are acceptable over time. This has encouraged a significant increase in this type of transplant activity.

Kidneys donated by living donors

Until the early 1990s, kidneys were transplanted only from close genetic relatives to ensure minimal HLA mismatching. As experience has been gained and outcomes have improved, this restriction has been relaxed. Living donors can be directed: 'I will donate my kidney to my brother/wife/friend'; or organs offered through non-directed altruistic donation:

---

[21] C. Geddes, R. Rodger, C. Smith and A. Ganai, 'Kidney transplants: more of them, better allocated', *British Medical Journal*, 332 (2006), 1105–6.
[22] *Ibid.*

'I want to donate one of my kidneys to any patient in need'. Altruistic donation in the UK is allowed under the Human Tissue Act 2004. NHSBT-ODT has been designated by the Human Tissue Authority, the body responsible for supervising the provisions of the Act, to oversee allocation of kidneys from altruistic donors, and the allocation process will essentially follow that for deceased donor kidneys. The donor may choose to travel to the recipient centre or may donate at their local centre.

The impact of 'trigger events' on the organ allocation system

Organ donation is an area which is undoubtedly highly sensitive to public feeling, and it is clear that public feeling is highly malleable.[23] Ubel suggests that the public wishes that everyone should have the opportunity to receive scarce resources, even if this is not the maximal approach in terms of efficiency and life-year maximisation.[24] In this section, the discussion focuses on the ways in which different 'trigger events' can impact on public perception of organ donation and thus the organ allocation process. Amongst other things, our current system of regulation is the result of various 'isolated' scandals, public outcry and legislative response to this outcry. It could be further argued that the unhappy history of measures which are aimed at increasing the amount of organs available for supply through legislative measures has created a residual heightened sensitivity about organ removal and retrieval which underpins current reluctance to legislate the area with a heavier hand.[25]

What follows is a discussion of two events, one past and one present, which have the capacity to be significant shapers of the organ allocation algorithm. In the late 1980s, a scandal erupted in England following the removal of kidneys from Turkish persons, for payment. This case resulted in kidney specialist Dr Raymond Crockett being struck off the medical register for buying kidneys from four individuals and selling them to private patients awaiting organs. Two other surgeons who were involved were also sanctioned.[26] The case resulted in the Human Organs Transplant Act

---

[23] P. Ubel, 'How stable are people's preferences for giving priority to severely ill patients?', *Social Science & Medicine*, 49 (1999), 895–903; A. Tong, K. Howard, S. Jan *et al.*, 'Community preferences for allocation of solid organs for transplantation: a systematic review', *Transplantation*, 89 (2010), 796–805.

[24] Ubel and Loewenstein, 'Distributing scarce livers', 1049–55.

[25] R. Richardson, *Death, Dissection and the Destitute*, 2nd edn (University of Chicago Press, 2000); 'Human dissection and organ transplantation in historical context' in M. Sque and S. Payne (eds.), *Organ and Tissue Donation: an Evidence Base for Practice* (Berkshire: Open University Press, 2007), pp. 4–20.

[26] BBC News, 'GMC hears "organs for sale" case', www.news.bbc.co.uk/1/hi/health/937204.stm.

1989, which imposed restrictions, for the first time, on transplant activity in the UK and required a central register of all transplant activity. The Crockett scandal entrenched the view that commercialisation of organ procurement was something which was unsavoury and to be avoided. Scandals like this have marred the history of organ transplantation in the UK, and the response to them may often be disproportionate to the threat posed; as Cronin and Price argue, we should be wary of allowing a few bad apples to spoil the whole of the transplant system.[27]

More recently, a case reached the public eye when a kidney patient's close relative died and donated their organs, but the related patient was not allocated a kidney.[28] Laura Ashworth died after suffering an asthma attack. At the time of Laura's death, her mother was on the waiting list for a kidney transplant. Despite requests from the family, none of Laura's kidneys could be donated to her mother. Following a review, it was established that the patient, although having kidney disease, was not on the active transplant list and was not suitable to be a recipient. In the wake of this case, a review of directed donation was carried out by the Human Tissue Authority, and the conclusion reached was that in certain rare circumstances directed deceased donation of this sort should be allowed.[29]

Cases like these undoubtedly damage public perception of the organ allocation system, and it is important to redress this negative fallout:

Donor organs are a scarce resource. Because of the extreme shortfall in donor organs, difficult decisions need to be made in determining who receives those scarce resources. The lack of transparency in the allocation criteria has fostered community scepticism regarding the fairness of the organ allocation process. However, there is growing recognition that a better understanding of community attitudes and preferences for these issues is required 'to ensure that clinicians and policy makers are in step with community values'. However, as our findings demonstrate, there is a lack of research examining community preferences and a wide variability in the studies identified.[30]

Given the close relationship between the media and organ donation, the impact which negative publicity can have on the whole system is obvious.[31]

---

[27] A. Cronin and D. Price, 'Directed organ donation: is the donor the owner?', *Clinical Ethics*, 3 (2008), 127–31.

[28] BBC News, 'Mother denied daughter's organs', www.news.bbc.co.uk/1/hi/england/bradford/7344205.stm.

[29] See Department of Health, *Requested Allocation of a Deceased Donor Organ*, March 2010, www.dh.gov.uk/prod_consum_dh/groups/dh_digitalassets/@dh/@en/@ps/documents/digitalasset/dh_114803.pdf.

[30] Tong *et al.*, 'Community preferences for allocation'.

[31] See examples in R. Matesanz and B. Miranda, 'Organ donation – the role of the media and of public opinion', *Nephrology Dialysis Transplantation*, 11 (1996), 2127–8.

The allocation of organs raises a number of interesting questions about how we understand the ethics of resource allocation. Organ allocation is reliant on positive public perception;[32] indeed there is some evidence to suggest that perception of the fairness of an allocation system can affect not just whether an individual is willing to donate an organ but also whether or not a patient wishes to undergo a transplant.[33] Organ donation rates are dependent on the goodwill and involvement of donors and their families – if there are no organs to donate, then there are no allocation problems. This creates a tension between public perception of what system of allocation is most justifiable, and the most ethically straightforward allocation system.[34] While the allocation process is framed in terms of concepts such as justice and fairness, there is often a gap between these concepts and public perceptions about how organs should be allocated. Should the surviving mother of an organ donor receive an organ before others who are ahead of her on the waiting list, even though this may contradict some of the basic principles which underpin the system? Is the prioritisation of children justifiable even though it may contravene the law as being discriminatory on the basis of age? No-one can explain why it is 'children first', but everyone seems to support this – especially patients. The following section will consider some of the ethical values which underpin the system.

Ethical principles which underpin organ allocation

Robert Veatch describes organs as being 'inherently scarce'. By this he means that not only is this an area of medical care where money is limited but organs themselves are in short supply.[35] Veatch thinks that this contributes to why we should understand allocation decisions as not simply medical decisions but rather as an inherently moral matter.[36] The decision to allocate an organ to one person by definition condemns others to death. Allocation decisions are thus life or death choices and

---

[32] There is also evidence to suggest that the attitudes of clinicians are sensitive to media portrayal of organ donation: see Matesanz and Miranda, 'Organ donation'.

[33] Klassen *et al.*, 'Relationship between patient's perceptions', 816.

[34] M. Schweda and S. Schicktanz, 'Public ideas and values concerning the commercialization of organ donation in four European countries', *Social Science & Medicine*, 68 (2009), 1129–36.

[35] R. Veatch, *Transplantation Ethics* (Washington, DC: Georgetown University Press, 2000), p. 277. Koch describes this as 'absolute scarcity': see T. Koch, 'Normative and prescriptive criteria: the efficacy of organ transplantation allocation protocols', *Theoretical Medicine*, 17 (1996), 75–93.

[36] Veatch, *Transplantation Ethics*, p. 279.

it is this that makes allocation questions moral questions. This section considers some of the ethical principles which are important in any allocation system. The sensitivity of public attitudes to allocation demands that ethical criteria are seen to apply to how organs are allocated[37] – it is not enough that justice is done; it must manifestly be seen to be done.[38] Given the high profile that organ donation has in the public consciousness, the principles underpinning the organ allocation process are not alone in being important; so too is transparency in the criteria for how organs are allocated.

Justice as a principle in healthcare can be understood in many ways. In terms of organ allocation, criteria which involve considerations of justice are issues such as medical need and length of time on the waiting list. Powers and Faden identify four eras of justice in healthcare.[39] The first era questioned whether there is a right to healthcare – the focus of this era was the inequalities that might arise due to ill health; this era ended with near universal consensus that individuals be entitled to a bare minimum standard of healthcare – what this standard was to be was subject to variation and lacked specification. The second era questioned how scarce resource budgets should be allocated and how healthcare services should be prioritised; the focus of this era was on cost-effectiveness analysis and how health resources should be distributed in order to maximise 'the bang per buck'. The third era emerged in the early 1990s and questioned how arguments about cost-effectiveness could be fairly balanced by the egalitarian concerns put forward in the first era. It is this stage which has now been reached with respect to the ethics of organ allocation. Proceduralism is an approach which was popularised by Daniels and Sabin in *Setting Limits Fairly*:[40]

When we lack consensus on principles that tell us what is fair, or even when we have general principles but are burdened by reasonable disagreements about how they apply, we may nevertheless find a process or procedure that most can accept as fair to those who are affected by such decisions. That fair process then determines for us what counts as a fair outcome.[41]

In the absence of a clear consensus as to how organs should be donated, the process through which they are allocated becomes pivotal in meeting standards of acceptability. The reasons which justify the procedures and

---

[37] Koch, 'Normative and prescriptive criteria'.
[38] *R* v. *Sussex Justices, ex parte McCarthy* [1924] 1 KB 256, per Lord Chief Justice Hewart.
[39] M. Powers and R. Faden, 'Inequalities in health, inequalities in health care: four generations of discussion about justice and cost-effectiveness analysis', *Kennedy Institute of Ethics Journal*, 10 (2000), 109–27.
[40] N. Daniels and J. Sabin, *Setting Limits Fairly* (Oxford University Press, 2002). [41] *Ibid.*

decisions made are important and must be accessible to all; they must be 'publicly justifiable' reasons. This approach is not without its critics. The previously mentioned sensitivity and malleability of public opinion on organ donation can impact on the deliberative justifications for different allocation decisions. Powers and Faden suggest that this approach does not negate 'the hard work to be done by substantive views of justice in determining which inequalities matter most in any given context'.[42] The weight which is placed on the algorithm by which organs are allocated shows that a proceduralist approach to justice has been endorsed. Consider the following statement by the British Transplantation Society:

Each Transplant Centre should have a written policy which defines its allocation process in a form which can be presented to patients and to society in general. There must be demonstrable equity of access to donor organs irrespective of gender, race or district of residence.[43]

This quote also highlights that equity of access is another vital feature of any system which regulates the donation of scarce resources. Systems are now in place which ensure equity of access, for example, with regard to the young and those from ethnic minorities. These systems came about as a result of reports from a number of working groups which addressed equality of access to donated kidneys, resulting in the current allocation system in the UK. The Equity of Access Working Group found that median time waited for a transplant varied according to: centre (1–4 years); recipient ABO group (-A less than 1 year, -B 3 years); ethnicity (white European Caucasians less than 2 years, South Asians 3 years, Black community 4 years); and recipients' HLA type frequency. These findings were considered unacceptable and the Group demanded a full revision of the existing allocation scheme in order to redress the inequity.

Another important principle is the view that scarce resources should be optimised – that is, used in a way which maximises the benefits of these resources. Maximisation is but one consideration, in addition to the importance of the notions of justice and fairness. There seem to be good arguments for why maximisation should not always take precedence over other principles, but may rather be traded off against them.[44] Veatch suggests that any organ allocation must conform to principles of efficiency and equity, and efforts to balance both these principles should be taken into account.[45] The biological criteria which have been discussed in this

---

[42] Powers and Faden, 'Inequalities in health, inequalities in health care', 116.
[43] British Transplantation Society, *Standards for Solid Organ Transplantation in the United Kingdom*.
[44] Ubel and Loewenstein, 'Distributing scarce livers', 1049–55.
[45] Veatch, *Transplantation Ethics*, p. 288.

chapter show how efforts are made to maximise the benefit which can be derived from organs.

An issue which is subject to much controversy is the question of whether it is legitimate to direct donations of both living organ donation and deceased organ donation, as mentioned previously. The British Transplantation Society's Standards for Solid Organ Transplantation emphasise the importance of the principle of non-directedness which underpins current donation practices for organs donated by the deceased.[46] The explanation for this is that to allow directed donation of organs from the deceased would be to open the door to the possibility of discrimination; this may be due to the few controversial cases where organs have been donated on the proviso they are given to a recipient of a particular ethnicity.[47] Many suggest that this principle of non-directedness is not suitable for all cases and, as a general policy, it fails to distinguish between 'vicious' and 'non-vicious' directions.[48] How such distinctions would cash out is unclear. We could, for instance, allow an individual to direct that their organs be made available primarily for the benefit of family members or other individuals with whom they have a significant relationship. There is also another way to understand the non-directedness of allocating organs: it can be understood in much the same way that we understand social systems of general healthcare; Singer describes a driver of such a system in the following terms: 'When it comes to vital things like medical care we are all in it together, and your money cannot buy you anything that I am not equally entitled to.'[49] When we allow for directed donation, we allow capital to become a driver in the organ allocation process – 'social capital'. This is a criticism which has been levelled by Giles at the directed nature of living donation.[50]

By having a system which means that those with social capital are more likely to gain, we could exacerbate inequalities by allowing the system to facilitate a solution whereby those without social capital, often already vulnerable individuals, are less likely to receive an organ. This criticism is

---

[46] British Transplantation Society, *Standards for Solid Organ Transplantation in the United Kingdom*.

[47] Department of Health, *An Investigation into Conditional Organ Donation* (London: Department of Health, 2000) (www.dh.gov.uk/en/Publicationsandstatistics/Publications/PublicationsPolicyAndGuidance/DH_4002934).

[48] J. Harris, *The Value of Life* (London: Routledge & Kegan Paul, 1985), pp. 71–3; M. Quigley, 'Directed deceased organ donation: the problem with algorithmic ethics', www.ccels.cf.ac.uk/archives/issues/2008/quigley.pdf (2008).

[49] BBC News, 'Racist organ donation condemned', www.news.bbc.co.uk/1/hi/health/652132.stm.

[50] S. Giles, 'An antidote to the emerging two tier organ donation policy in Canada: the Public Cadaveric Organ Donation Program', *Journal of Medical Ethics*, 31 (2005), 188–91.

most effective when discussing directed deceased organ donation; living-related organ donation does not generally diminish the donor pool and cause anyone to be less likely to receive an organ. The point, however, retains some force against living organ donation because although it does not take away from what others can access, it does allow some to use their social capital in order to access resources that are simply not available to others. It is interesting to note that this reliance on social capital is not seen as a drawback of the current living organ donor systems but rather as something that speaks in its favour. It is intended as a way in which 'respect be accorded to bonds of kinship in directing donations'.[51]

Cronin and Price have noted that directed donation should be distinguished from conditional donation and that not all conditions will be the same, suggesting that a blanket prohibition fails to distinguish between those conditions which are acceptable, and those which are not.[52] They argue that certain conditions or directions may in fact uphold principles, like community and kinship, which are integral to the operation of the transplant system. Organ donation has been characterised as a complex reciprocal interaction; such an interaction relies on foundational concepts such as kinship and community.[53] It could be argued that it is a mistake to view social capital in the organ allocation system as akin to monetary capital.[54] Rather than ignore or overrule the importance of concepts like kinship and reciprocity, we should instead focus on ways in which these concepts can be shared more widely.

Conclusion

This chapter has discussed the evolution of the organ allocation system, and explained the medical and biological constraints within which such a system must operate. It then continued by considering the various trigger events which have impacted on the organ allocation system; the discussion highlighted the symbiotic relationship between public perceptions of organ transplant and the transplant system; trigger events act as important markers in how the system has evolved and provide a depth of understanding to the process. The final section of the chapter considered some of the ethical principles which underpin the current allocation system. This section illustrated the fact that allocation decisions cannot be made

---

[51] 'Written evidence to the Select Committee on the European Union's Inquiry into the EU Commission's Communication on organ donation and transplantation: policy actions at EU level', www.hta.gov.uk/_db/_documents/2007–10–30_Evidence_to_HoL_select_committee_inquiry_on_organ_donation.doc.
[52] Cronin and Price, 'Directed organ donation', 130.
[53] Schweda and Schicktanz, 'Public ideas and values', 1129–36.   [54] *Ibid.*

on purely medical or scientific grounds – the criteria used involve some aspects of moral deliberation; like any area of healthcare where resources are scarce, morally justifiable reasons which are acceptable to society generally must be used to underpin any allocation algorithm.

In a time of severe shortage of organs, utility should prevail. Some moderation of the utility approach is justified though, especially for those waiting longest. Interestingly, those who have waited longest enter a clinically high-risk group thus shifting them further in the utility stakes. NHS resources are also an important factor. As dialysis is ten times the cost of transplantation we ought to pursue transplantation for all. At present, this indicates a huge expansion of living organ donation since deceased organ donation rates are static. We have liberalised donation by the living and recent experience is that altruistic donation is going to be more frequent than predicted. The US approach to a kidney failure patient is said to be 'go away and come back with your living donor', and this might have to be adopted throughout the UK, although it is rather abrupt. Disappointingly, the paired/pooled exchange programme has not so far delivered the numbers of transplants anticipated. We also need to address a national (rather than local) allocation system for organs donated after cardiac death (DCD). This is now a possibility since DCD organs are more frequently available and their outcomes are better than predicted.

Organ donation relies on public goodwill, and any system of allocation must take account of public perceptions and attitudes to organ donation. These attitudes may be difficult to decipher and at times contradictory, but they still have an important part to play in any allocation system. Without sufficient community engagement, distrust and scepticism will increase, often as a result of negative public trigger events.[55] However, as there is a lack of stability in public attitudes towards donation and allocation it would be unrealistic to suggest that such attitudes should be decisive. Given the sensitivity of the whole system to such attitudes, however, they should at least be taken into account, as there seem to be good arguments for community interest in how organs – an absolutely scarce resource – are allocated.[56]

---

[55] Tong et al., 'Community preferences for allocation'; Matesanz and Miranda, 'Organ donation', 2127–8.

[56] J. Childress, 'Ethics and the allocation of organs for transplantation', Kennedy Institute of Ethics Journal, 6 (1996), 397–401.

9 Ante-mortem issues affecting deceased donation: an ethico-legal perspective

John Coggon and Paul Murphy

Whilst living donation makes an increasing contribution to rates of organ transplantation in the United Kingdom (UK), its obvious clinical limitations, along with lack of progress with stem cell research or xenotransplantation, mean that transplantation overall continues to rely heavily on the retrieval of organs from people who have died. Deceased donation is associated with a unique constellation of clinical, ethical and legal challenges that represent real obstacles to achieving any increase in the number of deceased organ donors. For instance, whilst the distinction between life and death appears self-evident, the moment of transition from one state to the other remains a matter of some debate.[1] Furthermore, even if we have interests that survive our deaths,[2] our nature – and thus what constitutes, for example, harm – changes radically post-mortem.[3] While we live, our rights in medical law stem from our interests and their protection. Presumptively, individuals are best placed to judge their interests: hence requirements of consent and the right of patients to choose between interventions or ultimately to refuse any intervention. Although matters become more complicated for patients without decision-making capacity, the law maintains that:

1. interests should be protected;
2. a plurality of values underpin interests, so benefit and harm do not hold static or universal senses; and

---

[1] S. Youngner, R. Arnold and R. Schapiro (eds.), *The Definition of Death: Contemporary Controversies* (Baltimore: Johns Hopkins University Press, 1999); C. Machado and D. Shewmon (eds.), *Brain Death and Disorders of Consciousness* (New York: Kluwer Academic, 2004); President's Council on Bioethics, *Controversies in the Determination of Death* (Washington, DC, 2008), www.bioethics.gov.

[2] M. Brazier, 'Retained organs: ethics and humanity', *Legal Studies*, 22 (2002), 550–69. Note also the effects on the living of a policy that seems not to respect the purported interests of the dead: S. McGuinness and M. Brazier, 'Respecting the living means respecting the dead too', *Oxford Journal of Legal Studies*, 28 (2008), 297–316.

[3] J. Harris, 'Law and regulation of retained organs: the ethical issues', *Legal Studies*, 22 (2002), 527–49.

3. default positions on benefit and harm may be ignored for patients lacking capacity where there is evidence that their values underpin a particular best interests judgement requiring this.

This chapter addresses the following central questions: if death is imminent, but a patient is still alive, how does this constrain how we may treat him or her, and understand his or her best interests? Can robust legal and ethical arguments support the institution of measures designed to increase the chances of successful organ retrieval after death – and thus with clear regard to the benefit of third parties – when the dying patient is still alive? The authors answer these questions by exploring clinical, legal and ethical issues, and conclude that 'best interests' – defensible morally, and properly understood legally – permits 'other-regarding' considerations. Thus we caution against unduly, and unethically, narrow interpretations that protect only the dying patient's clinical interests, and demonstrate that measures designed to ensure the best chances of successful deceased organ donation can legitimately be instituted whilst the potential donor is close to death, but nevertheless still living.[4]

Deceased donation in the UK

Whilst the number of patients on transplant waiting lists rises each year, deceased organ donation rates in the UK over the last decade have remained essentially static, and now fall well short of those reported from many parts of the developed world, particularly mainland Europe and the United States (USA). The Organ Donation Taskforce was assembled by the UK Department of Health to identify barriers to donation and transplantation, and to recommend solutions to them, driven by the conviction that there was no *a priori* reason that organ donation rates in the UK should be worse than those achieved elsewhere in the world.

Strategies to increase donor numbers have two broad strands: increasing the proportion of current potential donors who go on to donate, and exploring new models for donation. The 'standard' model for deceased organ donation is that which follows the diagnosis of brain stem death. The clinical advantages to organ retrieval from heart-beating brain stem dead donors are clear: the person is mechanically ventilated on an intensive care unit (ICU) and has a circulation that maintains the delivery of

---

[4] This chapter builds upon two earlier articles that have considered controlled NHBD: J. Coggon, M. Brazier, P. Murphy *et al.*, 'Best interests and potential organ donors', *British Medical Journal*, 336 (2008), 1346–7; and J. Coggon, 'Doing what's best: organ donation and intensive care' in C. Danbury, C. Newdick, C. Waldmann and A. Lawson (eds.), *Law and Ethics in Intensive Care* (Oxford University Press, 2010), pp. 213–31.

oxygenated blood and nutrients to transplantable organs. In the UK currently, approximately 50 per cent of all suitable potential heart-beating donors do not donate their organs, usually because families decline this option of end-of-life care. A newer model of donation is that which follows death that is diagnosed by traditional cardio-respiratory criteria. Whilst so-called non-heart-beating organ donation (NHBD) is widely regarded as a model of donation that presents the most challenging ethical and legal issues,[5] it is clear that demands to increase the 'conversion rates' of brain stem dead donors will generate similar concerns, with the common theme being this: what can be done to facilitate donation from patients who are dying but not yet dead? The Taskforce was well aware of these issues, and recommended that urgent attention be given to the resolution of out-standing legal, ethical and professional issues, in order to provide clini-cians with a clear and unambiguous framework of good practice.

The root of the problem facing clinical staff caring for patients who have the potential to donate their organs posthumously is an ostensible conflict of interests. To realise or maximise this potential, clinicians may need to consider issues relating to donation not after their patient has died, but while he or she is dying. To pursue donation in such circumstances requires some adjustment to the management of the patient's death. This apparent transition from an exclusive focus on his or her needs, to the broader societal benefits of transplantation, and specifically the benefit to a third party recipient, is seen by some to violate clinicians' duty of care to their patient, and is therefore rejected.[6] Clinicians articulate various anxieties: some fear their motivations may be misinterpreted and chal-lenged by grieving and distressed relatives; others believe their actions could be judged unlawful.[7] Without an established and professionally endorsed national ethico-legal framework for deceased organ donation, clinicians have been left in the invidious position of having to formulate their own solutions to such problems; solutions that may be unduly (but perhaps not unreasonably) cautious, and influenced by a decline in public confidence in the medical profession, particularly regarding its manage-ment of certain aspects of death. Thus, although the Alder Hey[8] and

[5] Though we should note that brain stem death also gives rise to ethical contention in this area: see M. Potts and D. Evans, 'Does it matter that organ donors are not dead? Ethical and policy implications', *Journal of Medical Ethics*, 31 (2005), 406–9.

[6] D. Gardiner and B. Riley, 'Non heart beating donation – solution or a step too far?', *Anaesthesia*, 62 (2007), 431–3.

[7] P. Murphy, A. Manara, D. Bell and M. Smith, 'Controlled non-heart beating organ donation: neither the whole solution nor a step too far', *Anaesthesia*, 63 (2008), 526–30.

[8] M. Redfern, *The Royal Liverpool Children's Inquiry Report* (London: The Stationery Office, 2001), www.rlcinquiry.org.uk.

Bristol[9] scandals did not concern transplantation, they, along with public outrage at Shipman,[10] may nevertheless persuade doctors to adopt conservative approaches to organ donation.

The core problem appears to be as follows. The doctor's duty is to his or her dying patient. To what extent, if at all, can care be adapted to maintain or improve the prospects of that individual donating organs after death, noting that in almost all circumstances the patient will lack mental capacity in the time leading up to death?[11] Is it possible to describe a legitimate, practical framework that unifies the care of dying patients and donation after death, a framework that views donation as a component of end-of-life care? Placing these issues into their clinical context helps to emphasise the reality that clinical staff face.

Increasing donation after brain stem death

Whilst there are occasions when families raise the issue of organ donation spontaneously, in most circumstances it only happens because clinical staff take steps to pursue it. Most commonly this simply means that the possibility is raised with the bereaved family, perhaps in collaboration with a donor transplant co-ordinator. Few would take issue with this since the matter is raised after (neurological) death has been diagnosed, although suggestions that clinical staff should receive specific training to make such approaches have attracted adverse criticism. The focus here, however, is on interventions that generate greater professional concern.

The revised UK Code for the diagnosis of brain stem death only allows the diagnosis to be made when a patient is physiologically stable,[12] and yet death of the brain stem commonly results in cardiac and respiratory failure. Considerable clinical interventions may be required to correct such instability, for example the administration of fluids and inotropes, insertion of central venous and arterial catheters, and adjustments to mechanical ventilation. Some clinical staff would argue that if the patient has no prospect of recovery, and the purpose of these new therapies is to diagnose brain stem death and thereby maintain the potential for organ donation,

---

[9] *Learning from Bristol: the Report of the Public Inquiry into Children's Heart Surgery at the Bristol Royal Infirmary 1984–1995* (Command Paper: CM 5207, 2001), www.bristol-inquiry.org.uk.

[10] The Shipman Inquiry (2005), www.the-shipman-inquiry.org.uk.

[11] There may be concerns relating to the quality of 'consent' implied by registration on the NHS Organ Donor Register. Although it does not afford *informed consent*, with best interests an absence of consent does not close the option of organ donation: far from it; see below, and Coggon, 'Doing what's best'.

[12] Academy of Medical Royal Colleges, *A Code of Practice for the Diagnosis and Confirmation of Death* (London: Academy of Medical Royal Colleges, 2008).

such actions are unethical and unlawful. Similar arguments might apply to the particular clinical environment in which the patient finds themself. For instance, consider a patient with grave and non-survivable brain injury who arrives in an emergency department. It is suspected that the patient is brain stem dead, but confirmation would necessitate admission to ICU and some hours' maintenance on a mechanical ventilator. Some clinicians would argue that it is unethical and unlawful to manage the patient in this fashion, since the purpose of admission to ICU would be to diagnose brain stem death and maintain the potential for heart-beating multi-organ donation rather than to offer any prospect of recovery. These anxieties are compounded should this also impact on the capacity of the ICU to treat other critically ill patients.[13]

Non-heart-beating organ donation (NHBD)

One apparent solution to the issues above would be to accept that the recognition of futility *does* restrict what should be done to facilitate donation after brain stem death, but that the potential for organ donation can continue to be explored in the form of NHBD.[14] However, this model presents the greatest ethical and legal challenges. Controlled NHBD refers to the retrieval of organs following death determined by reference to cardio-pulmonary criteria (cardiac death) resulting from the withdrawal of life-sustaining cardio-respiratory support. Patients typically have an acute brain injury of such severity that death is inevitable or, more commonly, recovery would be associated with intolerable functional disability. Patients are likely to be deeply unconscious, with the actions of the clinical staff being guided by assessment of best interests as required by the Mental Capacity Act 2005 (which applies in England and Wales).[15] The principal challenge to successful transplantation in

---

[13] Complex practical allocation issues are raised, which cannot be considered here. Despite occupying a valuable space on ICU, lives might be saved by the patient's admission: an organ donor saves or transforms the lives of an average of three and potentially as many as nine other people.

[14] For the purposes of this chapter, NHBD refers to deceased donation following withdrawal of cardio-respiratory therapies that are judged futile and not in the patient's best interests. This is frequently referred to as *controlled* non-heart-beating donation, and may be contrasted with *uncontrolled* donation from Departments of Emergency Medicine, which occurs after unexpected cardiac arrest.

[15] The English law on best interests is *not* reflected in Scottish Law: see the Adults with Incapacity (Scotland) Act 2000, Part 5. The 2000 Act permits the provision of treatment 'designed to safeguard or promote [the patient who lacks capacity's] physical or mental health' (section 47(4)). In this chapter the focus is on the accommodation of measures specifically within a best interests judgement, so the Scottish position is not considered further.

such circumstances is minimising the ischaemic damage to donor organs before they can be removed.[16] The concern for critical care staff, and those with broader responsibility for donation and transplantation programmes, is whether interventions to allow organ retrieval after cardiac death can be professionally, ethically and legally justified, mindful that any professional or public outcry will likely adversely affect all forms of organ donation activity, not just NHBD.

To minimise warm ischaemic damage, organs from non-heart-beating donors must be removed as soon as possible after death. Although precise timings are patient- and organ-specific, organs are unlikely to be transplantable unless they are retrieved within twenty minutes of irreversible cardio-respiratory arrest. To achieve this, certain aspects of the management of death must be changed:

- A surgical retrieval team must be immediately available in a nearby theatre before death and, by implication, before cardio-respiratory support is withdrawn. Since the retrieval team may have to travel some distance to the donating hospital, it will be necessary to delay, by some hours, withdrawal of therapies the very continuance of which has been judged (clinically) futile.
- It is necessary to transfer the patient from the place of death to the operating theatre within minutes of death being diagnosed. Alternatively the patient may be transferred from the usual place of death to somewhere closer to the operating theatre before treatment is withdrawn, should the distance or complexity of the journey from critical care to the operating theatre be too great. In any event, the time available for a family to spend with their loved one after death is strictly limited and a significant deviation from what would happen were donation not being considered.
- There must be professional confidence that death indicated by loss of cardio-respiratory function can be satisfactorily diagnosed within these timescales, and that these timescales are determined by the irreversibility of cardio-respiratory and neurological arrest rather than the ischaemic tolerances of donor organs.

Ischaemic injury is central to the conflict between those focused only on meeting the needs of a dying patient and those whose concerns are also directed towards the unmet demand for donor organs. Whilst the former

---

[16] Ischaemia is a restriction in the supply of blood to an organ or tissue that results in dysfunction and damage. Such injury can be lessened by cooling, and there is therefore an important clinical distinction between *warm* ischaemia, which occurs at normal body temperature, and *cold* ischaemia. Warm ischaemia is much more damaging and ceases when an organ is cold perfused and placed on ice. Much longer periods of cold ischaemia can be tolerated, these periods ending when an organ is transplanted and re-perfused.

tend towards a conservative approach, risking no apparent harm to their patient (or to their profession and themselves), the latter call for measures to limit ischaemia. Such measures represent areas of possible professional, ethical and legal uncertainty, and fall under three headings:

1. Minimisation of the time interval between onset of irreversible cardio-respiratory arrest and commencement of organ preservation/retrieval.
2. *Ante-mortem* interventions designed to limit organ ischaemia.
3. *Post-mortem* restoration of oxygenated bloodflow to retrievable organs.

Warm ischaemic injury can be reduced by beginning organ retrieval as soon as cardiac death is diagnosable. UK guidance indicates that this can be determined after five minutes of complete and continuous absence of mechanical cardiac function.[17] Regardless of the time interval necessary to diagnose death, to approximate the period of warm ischaemia to the time required to diagnose death would necessitate that the patient be moved to the operating theatre *ante-mortem*. Although some units take this approach, others believe it represents too great a disruption for family members who might wish to remain with their loved one in the familiar surroundings of ICU until death occurs.

The second approach is to permit *ante-mortem* interventions to limit the ischaemic injury that organs might subsequently suffer. The intervention that is least contentious clinically is taking new samples of blood before death to allow the earliest possible tissue typing and virological screening.[18] More contentiously, some protocols advocate the *ante-mortem* administration of drugs such as heparin or steroids, or even the insertion of cannulae into the femoral vessels to allow the very rapid cooling of the abdominal organs with preservation fluids once death is declared. Evidence for the clinical effectiveness of such interventions has yet to be presented.

The third approach is most contentious, and involves restoration of the supply of oxygenated blood to the retrievable organs by placing the patient onto some form of 'heart-lung bypass' device after death has been declared. To do so in a fashion that might restore the cerebral circulation risks restoration of some cerebral function and would receive overwhelming clinical condemnation. Although some teams have taken steps to isolate the cerebral circulation in such circumstances, anxieties over interventions such as this will likely persist.

---

[17] Academy of Medical Royal Colleges, *A Code of Practice*.
[18] This avoids the risk of exposing a patient who is subsequently identified as HIV or hepatitis C positive to a fruitless surgical procedure, and means that the time taken to identify a suitable recipient, and therefore the cold ischaemic time of the organs, is reduced.

The emphasis of this discussion now shifts to ethico-legal analysis, exploring clinicians' concerns regarding apparent conflicts of interest, the (moral) integrity of their profession, and their wider duties to members of society who are outside their immediate clinical concern, i.e. potential organ recipients. We begin by considering what constitutes 'best interests' under English law, and then move on to ethical appraisal.

The law and 'best interests'

Patients who lack mental capacity must be treated according to their best interests. Unfortunately, at times best interests can prove to be a deceptively illusive concept. There are various levels to this deception; most basically, there is a danger – notwithstanding clear and consistent judicial and statutory statement to the contrary[19] – that best interests is erroneously conflated with pure *clinical* interests: i.e. what serves a patient considered as a physiological entity that we should restore to species-typical functioning, or palliate where this is impossible. Alternatively, best interests may be wrongly interpreted to demand imputed brutal self-interest, requiring what would be desired by an atomised individual with complete indifference to others.[20] Finally, the articulation 'objective best interests' may be taken to relate to some objective values-base: although patients with capacity can act in accordance with their own values, decisions made for incapacitated patients must accord with an objective standard; 'subjective' values are only for the 'competent'. This view is also flawed. Properly understood, patients' objective best interests relate to things that are objectively demonstrated to be in their interests. This requires taking account of *their* subjective preferences and personal values that can be demonstrated objectively to have existed. If a decision is made for an incapacitated patient, it is right to consider the values that *they* in fact had. This does not mean that the values are held objectively to be true; rather, it is found to be objectively true that the values recommending a particular decision existed.[21] To highlight the falsehoods in narrow interpretations of best interests, consider the law and lawfully accepted

[19] *Re A (Medical Treatment: Male Sterilisation)* [2000] 1 FCR 193; *Re S (Adult Patient: Sterilisation)* [2001] Fam 15; *R (on the application of N)* v. *M and others* [2003] 1 WLR 562; *Ahsan* v. *University Hospitals of Leicester NHS Trust* [2007] PIQR P19.

[20] 'Wrongly' here refers to the legal position, though the point holds ethically too: see below, and the argument in J. Harris and S. Holm, 'Should we presume moral turpitude in our children? Small children and consent to medical research', *Theoretical Medicine and Bioethics*, 24 (2003), 121–9.

[21] See further J. Coggon, 'Best interests, public interest, and the power of the medical profession', *Health Care Analysis*, 16 (2008), 219–32.

practice, as supported by the UK Department of Health's new guidance on this issue.[22]

Best interests, having been developed in the English courts, is established under section 4 of the Mental Capacity Act 2005. Section 4(6) of the Act obliges decision-makers to consider:

so far as is reasonably ascertainable–
(a) the person's past and present wishes and feelings . . .
(b) the beliefs and values that would be likely to influence his decision if he had capacity, and
(c) the other factors that he would be likely to consider if he were able to do so.

So 'best interests' is not born simply of clinical considerations. Dame Elizabeth Butler-Sloss states that judging best interests is not simply a question of meeting the '*Bolam* test' for clinically sound intervention, but requires 'broader ethical, social, moral and welfare considerations'.[23] Furthermore, we should stress an important matter of principle: law and practice both permit interventions that confer *no* clinical benefit.[24] Equally, law and practice permit that non-clinical considerations bear on what treatment is provided, how care is administered, and even *where* it is given.[25] Patients' values are of great importance whether patients have decision-making capacity or not. It is wrong – unlawful – for a clinician to refer simply to clinical indications and ignore the patient's values, beliefs, wishes, feelings and other factors that would bear on the decision. Necessarily, therefore, if patients harbour altruistic values concerning deceased organ donation, it is proper to account for these, rather than presume selfishness or moral turpitude.[26] It can be appropriate to perform procedures that confer no clinical benefit on the patient, but which further another goal, for example slight prolongation of life to optimise the chances of successful organ donation and transplantation; and conducting blood tests to assess suitability for donation. English law does not demand the impossible, but asks that clinicians act on reasonably ascertainable information about patients' values and preferences. Clearly, harming a patient in order to retrieve his or her organs is wrong. Where there is good reason to believe that he or she supported donation,

[22] Department of Health, *Legal Issues Relevant to Non-heartbeating Organ Donation* (London: Department of Health, 2009), www.dh.gov.uk/en/Publicationsandstatistics/Publications/PublicationsPolicyAndGuidance/DH_108825.
[23] *Re S (Adult Patient: Sterilisation)* [2001] Fam 15, 28.
[24] *Re F (Mental Patient: Sterilisation)* [1990] 2 AC 1; *Re Y (Mental Patient: Bone Marrow Donation)* [1997] 2 WLR 556.
[25] *Ahsan* v. *University Hospitals of Leicester NHS Trust* [2007] PIQR P19.
[26] Harris and Holm, 'Should we presume moral turpitude in our children?'.

however, there is also good reason to believe that *his or her* interests are served by undergoing measures that maximise the chances of donating successfully. As such, measures that constitute a prima facie harm under English law, because they constitute a battery, can become permissible. To understand harm, we need to weigh up the patient's values and their implications for a best interests assessment, and to consider some question of proportionality. Modest interventions carrying no serious imposition on the patient, which further their chances of successfully becoming an organ donor, can clearly be permissible.

Is altruistic best interests ethical?

The legal arguments surrounding *ante-mortem* measures that may increase *post-mortem* donation are clear. The law accommodates modest life-prolongation and other interventions that improve the chances of successful organ donation when these are commensurate with a patient's values, and even where they are not *clinically* indicated as beneficial to him or her. Nevertheless, there may be ethical concerns, especially absent clear formal guidance:[27] the authors therefore welcome the UK Department of Health's position on this, and hope it will go some way to allaying the fears of clinicians.[28] As well as according with our interpretation of the legal situation, as described above, we consider the position to be morally defensible. To demonstrate why, let us dissect the ethical issues that practitioners find taxing. We discern three principal areas of ethical contention: conflict of interests; acting with a concern for others when the moral duty is to the patient alone; and instrumentalisation of dying patients. The three become intertwined, and are best dealt with together.

Is there a conflict of interests at play, and if so, is it problematic? We take it as given that doctors have a moral duty of care to their patients. They are in a position of power and trust, with special liberties justified by the good they serve individuals in society; furthermore, they have special expertise that commands (a qualified level of) deference. A doctor acting as a public servant provides care to patients because the public interest supports his or her so doing. Yet, it might be said, 'public interest' or 'social benefit' arguments cause the greatest atrocities at the heart of bioethical concern: does morality not *demand* that we protect vulnerable patients from abuses

---

[27] Organ Donation Taskforce, *Organs for Transplants: a Report from the Organ Donation Taskforce* (London: Department of Health, 2008). Recommendation 3 of the report describes the need urgently to address 'the outstanding legal, ethical and professional issues in order to ensure that all clinicians are supported and are able to work within a clear and unambiguous framework of good practice'.

[28] Department of Health, *Legal Issues Relevant to Non-heartbeating Organ Donation*.

that a crass utilitarian assessment tells us benefit society overall? The answer, of course, is yes. However we deny that all measures aimed at optimising successful organ donation represent crass utilitarianism. Rather, we consider it crucial to look at the nature of the most defensible ethical system that forms the principles on which practices are built. We live in a liberal society in the UK, where a plurality of values is (supposed to be) upheld and respected, but also where state-provided welfare measures – including a health service – are instituted to maximise or uphold the general good. Medical practice here is not founded upon purely private agreements between doctors and patients. Privacy and confidentiality are of great importance, amongst other things, in sustaining sound doctor/ patient relationships. Equally, it is in everyone's interest that doctors direct healthcare towards the benefit of their patients. However this does not foreclose doctors' consideration of the interests of others.

Foreclosing consideration of others can mean an unethical denial of respect for patients' own values. In a pluralist system, we defer to individuals' values, rather than presume them, or know but deny them. Even in a system of state-funded welfare, wherein viable medical options are limited by professional consideration of what may be inappropriate or futile,[29] we commit ourselves to respecting, insofar as is reasonably possible, people's diverse views and values. The ethical position that supports this 'agnostic liberalism'[30] is entrenched in at least three ideas: there is a plurality of goods, many of them mutually exclusive; making strong value claims is not generally the state's role, rather that is for individuals; and deciding the sort of life you want to live is important in itself, as it allows you to live as a moral agent, so individuals should be free to act as they wish provided this does no excessive harm to others. Although foundationally arguments in bioethics vary, respectful treatment of patients' values (morally important values, especially) is unequivocally important. We are not suggesting that doctors should ignore their patients' interests in order to maximise the good of others. Rather, where respect for patients' values supports it, clinicians should be confident of the ethical propriety of acting to optimise the chances of successful posthumous organ donation. If a dying patient's values are clearly commensurate with procedures that will not harm them, and will provide real chances of a significant good to others, instituting the procedures is ethically defensible. Far from representing crude utilitarianism, the position

---

[29] As found in law: *Burke* v. *GMC* [2005] EWCA Civ 1003. For an ethical appraisal of a system that limits patients' demands, see R. Huxtable, 'Whatever you want? Beyond the patient in medical law', *Health Care Analysis*, 16 (2008), 288–301.

[30] A term taken from J. Gray, *Isaiah Berlin* (Princeton University Press, 1996).

operates within a liberal system that equally offers rights of non-interference to patients who oppose organ donation. The ethical defensibility of the law's construction of best interests comes in its protection of liberal pluralism; it ensures that our values survive loss of mental capacity. Decision-making according to best interests properly understood is supportive of legitimate options that are truest to patients' conceptions of the good.

The apparent conflict of interests that the doctor faces is, if not illusory, nothing special. A (rational) *fear* that malpractice may occur provides good reason for supervision and proper organisation of organ donation and retrieval. But what seems to be a conflict of interests is not problematic. We are not arguing that 'it is in every patient's interests to donate posthumously'. Rather, it is in the interests of patients who have made clear that posthumous organ donation is their preference, to undergo modest but crucial ante-mortem interventions to maximise the chances of successful transplantation. The doctor considers the patient's interests; if these conflict with an altruistic outlook, that is the end of things. Equally, without good grounding for a declaration of clinical futility, contriving this judgement in order to retrieve patients' organs is unethical (and legally would constitute murder). But where death is inevitable, controlled measures can be performed prior to its occurrence if the conditions described above are met, and this is ethically and legally justifiable.

How then can we specifically address some of the real issues that trouble clinicians? As emphasised in the UK Department of Health's guidance, a patient's interests, and thus what may constitute harm, depend on factors peculiar to the patient.[31] This means that, following a proper best interests assessment, accounting for section 4(6) of the Mental Capacity Act 2005, various interventions may be permissible. For example, transfer to ICU, brief extension of clinical support, and blood sampling may all serve a patient's interests, once it is established that posthumous donation is something he or she valued. *Consent* to such things is not inferred, presumed or constructed. Rather, such interventions can be found to benefit the patient and properly indicated even in circumstances where consent cannot be obtained. Failure to serve the patient's interests in this way wrongly treats him or her as being opposed to organ donation. Without any indication of the patient's probable wishes, failing to optimise the chance of successful donation is perfectly reasonable. Equally, where it is known that the patient would refuse consent, the measures discussed here would be inappropriate. But where the patient would support donation,

---

[31] Department of Health, *Legal Issues Relevant to Non-heartbeating Organ Donation*.

doctors should not fear repercussions from law that is designed to accommodate a rich variety of values and interests.

Conclusion

Having raised important clinical factors regarding *ante-mortem* interventions that affect *posthumous* organ donation, the authors have explored professional, legal and ethical concerns that some might feel impinge on the propriety of measures carried out on living, albeit close to death, patients, when such measures are aimed at optimising the chances of successful organ transplantation to the benefit of third parties. Whilst such conduct appears to contradict the primary (moral, professional and legal) duties that a doctor owes the patient, this will not always be the case. Where a patient's values support deceased organ donation, his or her best interests allow modest non-therapeutic interventions that maximise the chances of realising these values. English law *demands* a broad approach to best interests: it is neither an exclusively clinical judgement, nor does it require that patients be treated as selfish, atomised actors. Where incorporation of a patient's values is commensurate with harmless measures directed to the ethically valuable good of saving others' lives, this should not be ignored. An ethical commitment to value pluralism means that such decisions cannot be imposed on likely opponents to organ donation; but for those with altruistic outlooks, who are known to favour *posthumous* donation, decision-making that accords with such views is mandated both at law and in ethical reason.

Part IV

Comparative perspectives

10 Institutional organisation and transplanting the 'Spanish Model'

Mónica Navarro-Michel

In the debate over how to address organ shortage, one of the suggestions that has been made is that presumed consent legislation would help to increase the number of organ donations. Since Spain has the highest rate of deceased organ donation in the world (34.4 organ donors per million population (pmp) in 2009),[1] it may be easy to assume that it is a direct consequence of its presumed consent legislation. It would be easy, but misleading. On the one hand, if presumed consent legislation held the key to organ procurement success, then all countries with similar legislation would be among the countries with the highest rates of organ donation and this is clearly not the case.[2] On the other hand, this assumption fails to take into account any of the factors that make the Spanish system so successful.

Spanish legislation which introduced presumed consent for deceased organ donation dates back to 1979.[3] However the rate of deceased organ donation only started to rise after the Spanish National Transplant Organisation (*Organización Nacional de Trasplantes*) (ONT) was created in 1989.[4] From an average rate of organ donation in Spain at 14.3 donors pmp in 1989, it rose to having the highest world rate in 1993 with 22.6 donors pmp, reaching 35.1 donors pmp in 2005.[5] Key features of the ONT which contributed to this success include a national network of specifically trained, part-time, dedicated and strongly motivated hospital physicians in direct charge of the whole process of donation.[6]

---

[1] Organización Nacional de Trasplantes (ONT), *Evolución de la Actividad de Donación y Trasplante en España* (2010), www.ont.es.

[2] Presumed consent legislation can be found in countries with the highest rates of deceased organ donation (Spain, Portugal, Belgium, France), as well as in some of the countries with the lowest rates (Bulgaria, Greece, Lithuania). A successful donor rate is also compatible with informed consent legislation, as is seen in the United States (USA).

[3] Law 30/1979, which deals with organ extraction and transplant.

[4] ONT was first regulated by Resolution 27 June 1980, but it was not until 1989 that it was finally established.

[5] ONT, *Memoria de Actividad de Donación* (2008), www.ont.es.

[6] R. Matesanz and B. Domínguez-Gil, 'Strategies to optimize deceased organ donation', *Transplantation Reviews*, 21 (2007), 177–88, 179.

This impressive evolution in Spain is the result of a set of measures, mostly of an organisational nature, which taken together are known as the 'Spanish Model' of organ donation (the Spanish Model).[7] They are the only set of initiatives that have proven to be effective in increasing deceased donor rates in a sustained way.[8] This chapter presents the key features of the Spanish Model. First, I provide an overview of the legislative framework and its legal principles, before moving on to present the organisational network of organ procurement. Finally, there is a brief examination of the experiences and outcomes of implementing the Spanish Model in other countries.

Law and organ transplantation in Spain

There are two pieces of legislation which are key to understanding the regulation of organ transplantation in Spain: Law 30/1979, which deals with organ extraction and transplant, and Royal Decree 2070/1999, which regulates the activities of procurement and clinical use of human organs and territorial co-ordination in matters of organ and tissue donation and transplantation.[9] Law 30/1979 has just seven articles and therefore most of the principles set out therein are very general. For more detail, we need to turn to the Decree. The Decree is more specific than the Law, focusing on organisational aspects and also dealing with particular problems not addressed by the Law, including diagnosis of death, for example. This legislation does not apply to blood and other blood derivatives,[10] human cells and tissues,[11] or reproductive cells and tissues.[12] Key aspects of the

---

[7] As summarised by Matesanz and Domínguez-Gil in 'Strategies to optimize', 181, they are the following: 1. Transplant co-ordination network. 2. Special profile of the three levels of transplant co-ordination. 3. Continuous audit on brain deaths and outcomes of donation at ICUs in transplant procurement hospitals. 4. Central office as an agency in support of all the processes of donation (besides organ sharing). 5. Great effort in training. 6. Hospitals must be reimbursed for the cost of procurement. 7. Close attention to the media. These principles were included in a document published by the Council of Europe, *Meeting Organ Shortage: Current Status and Strategies for Improvement of Organ Donation. A European Consensus Document* (1998).

[8] Matesanz and Domínguez-Gil, 'Strategies to optimize', 179.

[9] This Decree substitutes Royal Decree 426/1980.

[10] Regulated by Royal Decree 1088/2005, which established the technical requirements and necessary conditions for blood donation and regulates blood transfusion centres and services.

[11] Royal Decree 1301/2006, which established rules for quality and safety for donation; obtaining, evaluating, processing, preserving, storing and distributing human cells and tissues; and rules on co-ordination and functioning for human use. As regards donation and use of human embryos and foetuses, and their cells, tissues and organs, see Law 14/2007 on Biomedical Research, substituting Law 42/1988.

[12] Law 14/2006 on Human Assisted Reproduction. First regulation dates from Law 35/1988.

Law will now be examined before a more detailed examination of the Decree is focused on.

The basic principles are set out in Law 30/1979 and may be summarised as follows. Article 1 sets out the therapeutic purpose of transplantation. The use of the organ must be for transplantation to another person, with the purpose of substantially improving their lifespan or quality of life.[13] Even though the Law states that organs may be used for therapeutic or other scientific purposes in relation to deceased organ donation,[14] separate specific legislation has been passed which regulates clinical autopsies and donation for research.[15] Organ donation must be gratuitous, based on solidarity and altruism. Article 2 of Law 30/1979 states that 'no compensation will be made for organ donation . . . under no circumstances can the donor receive economic compensation, and the recipient will not be made to pay for the transplanted organ'. This is compatible with reimbursement of certain expenses, since Article 2 also mentions that 'measures will be taken to ensure that these procedures are not costly for the living donor or for the family of the deceased donor'. In the case of living organ donors, follow-up healthcare will be provided following surgery to facilitate their convalescence and recuperation.[16] As regards deceased organ donors, expenses include transportation and burial costs, as well as repatriation services, if any.[17] These payments are not considered to be financial incentives, for two reasons. First, payment is never raised as an issue with the family until consent has been obtained; the transplant co-ordinator in any case deals with all the paperwork related to the death, and the reimbursed costs are a way of showing appreciation to the family of the deceased. Second, payment is never made directly to the family, but to the service provider. The recipient does not have to pay for the transplanted organ.[18]

---

[13] As specified in Article 4.d), Law 30/1979, which deals with living organ donors.

[14] Article 5.2, Law 30/1979.

[15] Law 29/1980, 21 June, on Clinical Autopsies; and for further regulation, see Royal Decree 2230/1982. Deceased organ donation can be expressed in an advance directive, as stated by Article 11 of Law 41/2002 on patients' autonomy, and rights and obligations with regard to information and documentation.

[16] Article 9.7, Royal Decree 2070/1999.

[17] For instance, in Cataluña reimbursement covers 'ordinary expenses, of a necessary nature, and does not include luxury or sumptuary costs', as stated by Instruction 4/2002 issued by the *Servei Català de la Salut* (Catalan Healthcare Authority). In the Basque country, there is a monetary cap on the cost of the casket, as established in Resolution 29 May 2007 of the *Departamento de Sanidad del Gobierno Vasco* (Basque Health Department). It is interesting to note that in Cataluña, the aforementioned Instruction states that expenses are covered only when there is no other person who, or organisation which, may be responsible for payment, such as an insurance company.

[18] Article 8.4, Royal Decree 2070/1999.

Anonymity is assured for both the donor and the recipient.[19] The donor's family may not have access to the identity of the recipient, nor may the recipient or their family have access to the identity of the donor. Needless to say, this requirement does not apply when the recipient is a relative of the donor. Transplantation, as with any other medical intervention, requires the patient's informed consent.[20] The doctor in charge of the transplantation team must ensure that the recipient is fully aware of the nature of the intervention and of what a transplant involves, and that they know about the possible risks and foreseeable advantages, both physical and psychological, that may result from the transplant. The patient must also be informed that the necessary histocompatibility immunological tests have been performed as between the donor and recipient in an authorised laboratory. Informed consent must be provided in writing by the recipient, and if the recipient is a minor or lacks full mental capacity, then the consent must be signed by the parents or legal representatives. Organ retrieval must only be carried out in authorised healthcare institutions.[21] Finally, Law 30/1979 refers to what has become the most important feature of the Spanish Model, namely its organisational model: 'facilities should be provided to create organisations at national and regional level [note that it is not an obligation], and co-operation will be fostered at an international level to ensure timely circulation of deceased organs for transplantation in order to find the most suitable recipient'.[22]

Royal Decree 2070/1999 fleshes out the principles contained in Law 30/1979, as well as including two other important aspects of transplantation, namely education and promotion. It states that healthcare authorities must provide information to the general public about organ transplantation and the expected benefits for the patients who are in need of an organ.[23] As regards promotion and publicity, it states that awareness campaigns must be general, and must highlight the voluntary, altruistic and disinterested nature of organ donation and transplantation; publicity focusing on the need for any specific person to receive an organ is forbidden.[24] The law makes a distinction between living and deceased organ donors.[25] Since requirements for consent differ (informed consent for the former, presumed consent for the latter) and specific formalities exist for each, they are now examined separately.

---

[19] Although Article 4.d), Law 30/1979 only refers to the recipient's anonymity, and not that of the donor, Article 5 Royal Decree 2070/1999 mentions both.

[20] Article 6, Law 30/1979.   [21] Article 3, Law 30/1979.

[22] Article 7, Law 30/1979.   [23] Article 6, Royal Decree 2070/1999.

[24] Article 7, Royal Decree 2070/1999.   [25] Articles 4 and 5 of Law 30/1979, respectively.

Living organ donors

In Spain only 7 per cent of all renal transplants are from a living donor, compared to 37.1 per cent in the United Kingdom (UK).[26] Up until recently, the high rate of deceased organ donation in Spain has made it unnecessary to explore other ways to increase living organ donation. This may be changing, however, as it may be argued that Spain has reached the limit of its capacity with respect to deceased organ donors, given that this category of donors are increasingly older; deaths due to road accidents have decreased;[27] and there is a rising need for organs. In the past few years, the annual rate of deceased organ donation has not been increasing as quickly as in previous years, and this has also contributed to growing interest in the possibility of obtaining organs from living donors. The ONT recently issued a statement saying that it aims to increase the level of living organ donation to at least 15 per cent of all kidney transplants in the next few years.[28] One way to do this is through paired donations and the first transplant from paired donation was performed in Spain in June 2009.[29]

However, living organ donors still face a number of socioeconomic difficulties in relation to organ donation. One of the difficulties concerns employment legislation: since an organ donor is a healthy person, they are unable to obtain sick leave, so must choose between having the organ retrieval done during their holidays (hoping there will be no complications), or risk having difficulties at work (perhaps having to ask for unpaid leave). It has been suggested that living organ donors should legally be compared to pregnant women, who do not suffer a disease and are able to take maternity leave with full pay; the law should be amended in order to redress this problem. In addition, there may also be difficulties in obtaining an insurance policy, since insurance companies in Spain do not deem an organ donor to be eligible for insurance; again, access to insurance should not be a barrier for living organ donation, but the law should be reformed to introduce the necessary changes, perhaps making a distinction according to organ donated and policy type.

Legal requirements for living organ donation are contained in Article 4 of Law 30/1979 and Article 9 of Royal Decree 2070/1999. It

---

[26] Council of Europe, *Transplant Newsletter: International Figures on Organ Donation and Transplantation – 2008*, 14(1) (2009).

[27] Car accidents as the cause of death of organ donors amounted to 35 per cent in 1993, but this figure has diminished over time, from 24.9 per cent in 1998 to only 8.2 per cent in 2008. See ONT, *Memoria de Actividad*.

[28] Ministry of Health and Consumer Affairs – Press Release: *Symposium: Trasplante renal de donante vivo: nuevos retos*, 23 June 2008.

[29] *Diario médico*, 30 July 2009.

is necessary for the donor to consent; otherwise organ extraction would constitute a criminal act, a punishable injury (Article 156, Spanish Criminal Code), for which the healthcare professionals involved would also be disqualified from professional practice.[30] In order for a person to give their valid consent to organ donation, certain requirements must be met.

First, potential donors must be of legal age, and have full mental capacity. Organs may not be procured from persons who, due to mental deficiency or illness, or any other reason, lack capacity and therefore are not able to express their consent in a direct, free and conscious manner. Minors' consent will not be valid, and parents or legal guardians may not consent to the removal of their children's organs. This final requirement is clear and there should be no exceptions; however, it is interesting to note the case of Rocío, a seventeen-year-old mother who wanted to donate part of her kidney to her baby daughter, who was suffering from a disease which could lead to her death if it reached its acute state and no compatible donor was found. The situation involved a mother who wanted to be an organ donor for her baby but who was unable to give legal consent to organ extraction, although she would be able to do so in a few months' time when she reached full legal age. By this time, it may have been too late for her baby and this made it a very dramatic case. The grandmother of the sick baby applied to the courts to try and obtain judicial authorisation for organ donation in the case of her daughter; the Court of First Instance in Seville authorised the organ donation in a ruling given on 18 October 2007, and this decision received a great deal of media coverage at the time. Although it was perceived to be just and fair, it was nevertheless illegal in technical terms as it was contrary to existing law.[31] This was a troubling ruling in the sense that judges in Spain, like in other civil law countries, are not supposed to create law, but should instead interpret and apply existing law.[32]

---

[30] If organ retrieval amounts to the loss or maiming of a main organ, healthcare professionals could be sentenced to imprisonment for a period of between six and twelve years (Article 149, Spanish Criminal Code); if it affects some other organ, the prison sentence would be from three to six years (Article 150, Spanish Criminal Code). In both cases, the criminal court is also required to disqualify the professional from practice (Article 56, Spanish Criminal Code).

[31] Likewise, J. Ruiz Jiménez and L. Tejedor Muñoz, 'Notas sobre la responsabilidad en torno a las donaciones de órganos cuando el donante es un menor', *Revista Crítica Derecho Inmobiliario*, 705 (2008), 427–40, 39.

[32] For an alternative way in which this ruling could have been validly grounded under Spanish Law, see M. Navarro-Michel, 'Los derechos a la intimidad y propia imagen del menor de edad. Algunos supuestos conflictivos', *Revista de Derecho Privado*, 2 (2009), 47–74; in particular, see 69–70.

Second, consent must be informed and in writing. Potential donors must be made aware of the material risks of the intervention,[33] as well as the 'foreseeable consequences of the decision, both somatic and psychological, and the possible repercussions donation may have on their personal, family and professional life, as well as the expected benefits for the recipient'.[34] In practice, this is usually undertaken by the transplant co-ordinator, who will also enquire about the potential donor's decision to donate, their personal and professional situation and any other relevant information in order to determine whether the decision is made freely.[35]

Third, a medical evaluation is required to determine that donors are generally healthy persons and that their health will not be endangered by organ donation: the organ shall be compatible with the donor's life and their functional capacity must not be substantially diminished.[36] The examination will be made by a physician who is not involved in the transplantation process.[37] Spanish regulations do not require a genetic link between donor and recipient.

Fourth, the ethics committee of the hospital where the transplantation is to take place must issue a report approving organ retrieval in relation to the living donor.[38] Before it can consider a particular case, the committee will need to have access to the medical reports on both the potential donor and the potential recipient, their consent, and the transplant co-ordinator's report. Regulations are very imprecise about the exact nature of this report, whether it is binding or not, and what exactly the ethics committee is required to do, such as whether it should analyse the medical aspects of the transplantation (to ensure it has a good chance of success), or whether it should instead or in addition consider the legal and ethical aspects (valid consent without duress, be it of an economic, social or psychological nature). Since ethics committees do not generally issue binding reports, but rather operate in a consulting capacity, such a report would generally not be binding. Although some authors have criticised the need for this type of report, others consider it to be beneficial, since it ensures the process will be done with due respect to legal and ethical principles.[39]

---

[33] Article 9.3, Royal Decree 2070/1999.   [34] Article 4.b), Law 30/1979.
[35] M. Manyalich, D. Paredes and J. Vilardell, 'La donación de vivo para trasplantes' in R. Matesanz (ed.), *El Modelo Español de Coordinación y Trasplantes*, 2nd edn (Madrid: Aula Médica Ediciones, 2008), 181–5, 183.
[36] Article 9.1.b), Royal Decree 2070/1999.   [37] Article 9.3, Royal Decree 2070/1999.
[38] Requirement introduced by Article 9.2, Royal Decree 2070/1999.
[39] J. Terés, 'Transplantament hepàtic de donant viu a l'adult. Elements per una anàlisi ètica', *Annals de Medicina*, 87 (2004), 1–10.

Finally, certain legal formalities need to be complied with once all the previous requirements have been fulfilled.[40] Such formalities require that the potential living organ donor must give their consent anew before the judge in charge of the Civil Registry. The donor needs to be accompanied by three people who will also need to sign the organ donation consent document: the doctor who will carry out the organ extraction, the doctor who examined the potential donor and issued the medical report, and the person who authorises the operation (usually a representative from the authorised healthcare centre, or the transplant co-ordinator). Before the judge, doctors will, once again, provide the relevant information, and the document will be signed by all. If, at any time, any of the aforementioned persons has any doubts about the manner in which consent is given (ignorance, coercion, non-altruistic) they may oppose the organ donation. Otherwise, the judge will authorise it.

Once consent has been given before the judge, the operation to extract the organ may not take place until after twenty-four hours have elapsed, in order to give the donor a final chance to revoke their consent. Consent may be revoked up to the moment of organ extraction,[41] with no formalities needed and no adverse pecuniary consequences (there is no need to pay compensation or expenses to the healthcare centre and/or to the recipient).

Deceased organ donors

The vast majority of organs in Spain are provided by deceased donors. In this category, donation after cardiac death represents only 5 per cent of all such donation activity.[42] Article 5 of Law 30/1979 and Article 10 of Royal Decree 2070/1999 deal with the specific requirements necessary for deceased organ donors. In the following section, the discussion will focus in particular on death certification and management of the potential organ donor, as well as on presumed consent requirements. Diagnosis of death must be made before any organ extraction takes place, and can be based on either irreversible cessation of cardio-respiratory function or irreversible cessation of brain function.[43] Death after cardiac arrest must be certified by one physician, but a declaration of brain death must be signed off by three physicians, one of whom must be a neurologist or a

---

[40] Article 9.4, Royal Decree 2070/1999.   [41] Article 9.5, Royal Decree 2070/1999.
[42] R. Matesanz, 'El diagnóstico de la muerte encefálica en Latinoamérica', *Medicina Intensiva*, 33 (2009), 423–4.
[43] Royal Decree 426/1980 only refers to brain death, and the distinction between brain death and death following cardiac arrest was introduced on a legal basis through Royal Decree 2070/1999.

neurosurgeon, and the other the head of the unit where the patient is hospitalised. The physicians who are involved in the diagnosis of death cannot be involved in the organ extraction or the organ transplantation.[44]

Once a person is certified as dead after a cardiac arrest, the deceased's body is turned over to the team in charge of transplantation who may apply preservation techniques with judicial authorisation.[45] Because time is often of the essence in these situations, the law states that if a judge does not refuse authorisation within fifteen minutes of the request, then consent may be presumed.[46] Therefore, when the physician receives express judicial authorisation, or when there is a fifteen-minute lapse without a reply, they may then proceed to apply preservation techniques[47] (and extract samples for the court in the case of accidental death).[48]

In cases of violent death or where there is suspicion that death was caused by violent or unnatural means, an Examining Magistrate (*Juez de instrucción*) must begin an investigation during which an autopsy will be carried out.[49] This is contrary to the position in England, for example, where a coroner will usually be in charge of the inquiry. Organ retrieval is still possible, but the Examining Magistrate must authorise it.[50] If the cause of death seems unclear and organ retrieval could interfere with the autopsy and the criminal investigation, authorisation will be denied.[51]

Presumed consent legislation[52] makes every dead person a potential organ donor, if the deceased did not state otherwise.[53] However, regardless of the law on presumed consent, Spain operates under an

---

[44] Articles 10.3 and 10.4, Royal Decree 2070/1999.
[45] Article 10.5.a), Royal Decree 2070/1999.   [46] Annex I.3, Royal Decree 2070/1999.
[47] Preservation techniques for Maastricht Type I and II Organ Donors consist of cardiopulmonary bypass with external oxygenation, and femo-femoral bypass with extracorporeal membrane oxygenation; for a Maastricht Type IV Organ Donor, resuscitation measures are not withdrawn, and heparin is administered intravenously as well as renal perfusion with preservative solution. It must be highlighted that there is no programme in Spain for organ retrieval from Maastricht Type III Organ Donors, who are excluded from the ONT *Consensus Document on Organ Retrieval after Cardiac Arrest* (1995). It is commonly argued that their acceptance as potential donors could fracture society's trust in the Spanish organ procurement system, given strong ethical controversy; see F. Río-Gallegos, J. Escalante-Cobo, J. Núñez-Peña and E. Calvo-Manuel, 'Donación tras la muerte encefálica. Parada cardíaca en el mantenimiento del donante en muerte encefálica', *Medicina Intensiva*, 33 (2009), 327–35, 330.
[48] 20 cc of blood, a 20 cc urine sample and 20 cc of gastric fluids, as stated in Annex I, Royal Decree 2070/1999.
[49] Articles 340 and 343, *Ley de Enjuiciamiento Civil* (Law of Criminal Procedure).
[50] For details, see J. Rodríguez Lainz, 'Juzgado de guardia y trasplante de órganos', *Diario La Ley*, 6809 (2007), 1–20.
[51] Article 10.5, Royal Decree 2070/1999.
[52] Article 5.3, Law 30/1979; Article 10.1, Royal Decree 2070/1999.
[53] Article 5.3, Law 30/1979.

opt-in system in practice.[54] Once death has been certified, the transplant co-ordinator will hold an interview with the family to obtain their consent, which must be done in a sympathetic, timely and appropriate fashion.[55] Families are always approached, not merely as a way of understanding the deceased's wishes concerning organ donation (to ensure that the 'deceased did not expressly oppose organ donation after death'),[56] but also as a way of getting permission to proceed with donation, both in cases where the wishes of the deceased were unknown and where they were known.[57] Families' wishes are always respected, even when the deceased relative had a donor card authorising organ donation.[58] The rate of family refusals was 27.6 per cent in 1992; it reached an all-time low of 15.2 per cent in 2006, although it rose slightly to 17.8 per cent in 2008.[59]

Among the arguments that have been put forward to explain this deviation in practice from the presumed consent law (i.e. from presumed to informed consent) are the following. Originally, there was a fear of liability, since this law was passed with little social debate, and many physicians were unsure as to what might be the potential legal outcome in the event of a legal claim being lodged objecting to an approach taken based on presumed consent. Currently, the main reason for applying an opt-in system in practice is the need to build trust. If, regardless of what the law says,

---

[54] With the exception of cornea extractions, which 'may be done without delay and in the place of death'. Second additional disposition of Law 30/1979.

[55] For details on how the family interview is conducted, see P. Gómez, C. Santiago, A. Getino *et al.*, 'La entrevista familiar: enseñanza de las técnicas de comunicación', *Nefrología*, vol. XXI, Supp. 4 (2001), 57–64; P. Gómez and C. De Santiago, 'La entrevista familiar. Técnica y resultados' in R. Matesanz (ed.), *El Modelo Español de Coordinación y Trasplantes*, 2nd edn (Madrid: Aula Médica Ediciones, 2008), pp. 105–19.

[56] Article 10.1.a), Royal Decree 2070/1999.

[57] Some legal scholars have criticised the role of the family, whether it be as witnesses of the deceased's wishes (as intended by the law) or in exercising full authorisation in their own right; see J. Marco Molina, 'El régimen jurídico de la extracción y trasplante de órganos', *Diario La Ley*, 5 (2001), 1714–20, 1717; C. Romeo-Casabona, 'Los principios jurídicos aplicables a los trasplantes de órganos y tejidos' in C. Romeo-Casabona (ed.), *El Nuevo Régimen Jurídico de Los Trasplantes de Órganos y Tejidos* (Granada: Comares, 2005), pp. 1–81, p. 47; V. Angoitia Gorostiaga, 'El régimen reglamentario de la extracción y trasplante de órganos' in C. Romeo-Casabona (ed.), *El Nuevo Régimen Jurídico de Los Trasplantes de Órganos y Tejidos*, (Granada: Comares, 2005), p. 219.

[58] Surveys in Spain show that even though there is a generally positive attitude towards organ donation, less than 10 per cent of the population carry a donor card; see M. Frutos, 'Percepción social de la donación' in R. Matesanz (ed.), *El Modelo Español de Coordinación y Trasplantes*, 2nd edn (Madrid: Aula Médica Ediciones, 2008), pp. 161–73, p. 162.

[59] ONT, *Memoria de Actividad*. Reasons for family refusals have been analysed by M. Frutos, P. Ruiz, M. Requena and D. Daga, 'Family refusal in organ donation: analysis of three patterns', *Transplantation Proceedings*, 34 (2002), 2513–4; M. Frutos, M. Blanca, P. Ruiz *et al.*, 'Multifactorial snowball effect in the reduction of refusals for organ procurement', *Transplantation Proceedings*, 37 (2005), 3646–8.

physicians will not override the family's wishes, this sends a strong message of respect which, in turn, generates trust. In addition, it avoids conflict and bad publicity, which could also undermine trust in the organ procurement system.

Organisational network

The key to Spanish success rates on organ procurement lies in its organisational aspects, which are as follows.

Transplant co-ordination network

Transplantation procurement in Spain has been organised at three strongly co-ordinated levels: national, regional and local (in-hospital). Each of these levels has specific responsibilities within the process of organ procurement. The ONT[60] is an autonomous health authority attached to the Spanish Ministry of Health and Social Policy,[61] and it is responsible for organ promotion and in charge of co-ordination and support covering the whole process of organ procurement, allocation and transplantation. It manages waiting lists and transplant registries; organises transportation; compiles statistics; ensures public awareness and provides information to the general public; gives ongoing training and education for health professionals (which is specifically focused on each step of the process: donor detection, legal aspects, family approach, organisational aspects, management of resources, and communication); and manages media relations, seeking to promote a consistent, positive message, as well as dealing with adverse publicity.

At the regional level, there is one co-ordinator (CAT, which stands for *Co-ordinador Autonómico de Trasplantes*) for each of the seventeen Spanish autonomous communities. CAT works as a link between the in-hospital transplant co-ordinators at local level and the ONT, as well as with the other autonomous communities. Representatives meet regularly at a regional council, the *Comisión de Trasplantes del Consejo Interterritorial*, made up of national and regional executives, where all technical decisions regarding transplantation are reached by consensus. CAT is perhaps the

---

[60] For a brief period, the ONT became the *Centro Nacional de Trasplantes y Medicina Regenerativa*, according to amendments introduced by Law 45/2003. Law 14/2006 on human assisted reproduction techniques re-established its original name and functions, giving the government a period of six months to issue new regulations on the ONT; it finally did so with Royal Decree 1825/2009, which approves the statutes of the ONT.

[61] Article 1, Royal Decree 1825/2009.

less well-known level of co-ordination – in many respects, it has the same role as the ONT, but at a regional level.

Transplant co-ordinator

At the third level of the transplant co-ordination network, there are in-house transplant co-ordinators who play a key role in identifying potential donors, approaching the families and managing the whole process of transplantation. The transplant co-ordinator is considered by many as the key aspect of the Spanish Model.[62] So much so that the Council of Europe issued a Recommendation in 2005[63] which required that trans-plant co-ordinators be appointed in every hospital with an intensive care unit (ICU), and this was modelled on the role and functions of the Spanish transplant co-ordinator. Transplant co-ordinators are mainly physicians, and they receive support from nurses in hospitals where there is a large amount of donation activity, as required by regulations.[64] Although in the 1980s most co-ordinators were nephrologists, the major-ity are currently ICU specialists.[65] They are accountable to the medical director of the hospital, not the transplant team. By contrast, in most countries procurement activities tend to be the responsibility of services based outside the hospital, where they are generally run by healthcare professionals who are not physicians.

The fact that the transplant co-ordinator works inside the hospital allows for proper donor detection, which is vital, since it has been argued that organ shortage may be attributed not to the lack of potential donors, but to the failure to identify them and to obtain proper consent from families. In addition, the fact that the transplant co-ordinator is a doctor also means that they have the requisite medical knowledge, and this allows for meaningful discussion of the potential donor's situation with the doctors in charge of their care. Transplant co-ordinators are also in

---

[62] Cataluña was the first autonomous community with transplant co-ordinators who were in-hospital physicians. After the decentralisation of the Spanish healthcare service, and the enthusiasm that followed in the mid-1980s, young nephrologists established what was to become the regional co-ordination of organ donation and transplantation.

[63] Council of Europe, Recommendation 11 (2005) of the Committee of Ministers to Member States on the role and training of professionals responsible for organ donation (transplant donor co-ordinators) (adopted 15 June 2005).

[64] Circular 3/1997, issued by the *Dirección General de Atención Primaria y Especializada* of the *Instituto Nacional de la Salud* (Spanish National Healthcare Service), 10 April 1997. This regulation substitutes Order 7 March 1986, on appointment of transplant co-ordinators in Social Security hospitals and healthcare centres.

[65] Matesanz and Domínguez-Gil, 'Strategies to optimize', 182.

charge of monitoring the donation and procurement process in order to help identify and implement improvements. There is a continuous audit on brain deaths and outcomes of donation within ICUs.[66]

It is usually the case that the co-ordinator works on a part-time basis with respect to transplant co-ordination activities. This appears to be an important factor:[67] on the one hand, it allows small hospitals to have transplant co-ordinators, which would not be possible if they had to pay a doctor's full-time salary; on the other, it creates a structure which means that a flexible approach can be taken to doctors who become 'burned out' by transplant co-ordination activities. Given the stress and emotional demands of organ procurement, evidence shows that physicians who are 'burned out' have a negative impact on organ procurement rates, and replacement of the transplant co-ordinator usually restores such rates. Replacing transplant co-ordinators is much easier when those stepping down can return to their medical duties full-time, without needing a period of adjustment.

Small hospitals without transplantation facilities could become uninterested in identifying potential donors unless they were able to appoint such part-time transplant co-ordinators and were properly reimbursed for promoting organ donation activity. This is important since the number of hospitals integrated into the transplant procurement network seems to have a direct impact on the number of deceased organ donors. The number of small hospitals involved in the procurement of organs has increased in Spain, from fewer than twenty in 1988 to one hundred and fifty-six in 2007. The contribution these small hospitals make to organ donation and transplantation activity is considerable: 40 per cent of deceased organ donors in Spain are detected and referred by these small hospitals, representing a deceased donation rate of 14 donors pmp. Taking this into account, hospital reimbursement has become an important factor in promoting organ procurement. Without it, procurement activity would simply have become impossible for these small non-university, non-transplant hospitals.[68]

---

[66] The Quality Programme on Organ Donation is based on a continuous self-auditing of performance, where the internal audit is done by the transplant co-ordinator and the external audit by co-ordinators from other regions. This programme provides very useful information about the number of deaths, brain deaths and organ donors for every ICU, and identifies the reasons why potential donors do not become actual donors. The results show that it is mainly because of medical contra-indications to donate (27.1 per cent) and family refusals to donate.

[67] R. Matesanz, 'El modelo español de donación y trasplante de órganos: la ONT' in R. Matesanz (ed.), *El Modelo Español de Coordinación y Trasplantes*, 2nd edn (Madrid: Aula Médica Ediciones, 2008), pp. 11–26, p. 16.

[68] Matesanz and Domínguez-Gil, 'Strategies to optimize', 182.

Experiences in implementing the Spanish Model

Several countries, including Italy, Australia, Argentina and Uruguay, have implemented some of the key elements of the Spanish Model. The countries or regions that have implemented the most key elements of the model are likely to enjoy the greatest improvement in deceased organ donation rates, as improvements in such rates in both South Australia and Tuscany reveal.

In Italy, Law 91/1999[69] introduced presumed consent for deceased organ donors and an organisation at four levels (national, inter-regional, regional and local). After the introduction of the Law, the rate of deceased organ donors rose in Italy from 13.7 pmp in 1999 to 21.1 in 2004.[70] Before the Law was passed, some regional and inter-regional transplant agencies already existed, and the region that has had the highest increase in the rate of deceased organ donors in the shortest period of time is Tuscany. This region introduced an action plan in 1995 that instituted in-hospital transplant co-ordinators, allocated supplementary funds to regional donation and transplantation programmes, enforced educational programmes for healthcare professionals, and introduced mass campaigns for the public.[71] Tuscany doubled the rate of deceased organ donors in just 1 year, from 13.1 pmp in 1998 to 27.1 pmp in 1999, reaching 37.5 pmp in 2006 and 32.5 pmp in 2008.[72] Law 91/1999 had been only partially implemented, so the initial increase could not be ascribed to it. On 29 July 2003, the *Organizzazione Toscana Trapianti* (OTT) was created, in charge of monitoring and improving all transplantation activities. Success has been attributed mainly to the transplant co-ordinators.[73]

Australia does not have impressive figures for deceased organ donors, for example 12.1 pmp in 2008, though figures have increased from 9 to 11 pmp during the past 5 years.[74] The range between states, however, differs considerably. In 2008, such differences ranged from 8 pmp in

---

[69] Law 91/1999 on the retrieval and transplantation of organs and tissues.

[70] Organizzazione Toscana Trapianti (OTT), *Attività* (2008), www.sanita.toscana.it.

[71] F. Filipponi, P. De Simone and E. Rossi, 'The Tuscany model of a regional transplantation service authority: Organizzazione Toscana Trapianti', *Transplantation Proceedings*, 39 (2007), 2953–60, 2958.

[72] OTT, *Attività*.

[73] R. Pretagostini, P. De Simona, D. Peritore and R. Cortesini, 'The organizational model of interregional transplant agency – Organizzazione Centro-Sud Trapianti', *Transplantation Proceedings*, 37 (2005), 2417–8; F. Filipponi, P. De Simone and F. Mosca, 'Appraisal of the co-ordinator-based transplant organizational model', *Transplantation Proceedings*, 37 (2005), 2421–2 .

[74] ANZDATA, *The 32nd Annual Report* (2009), www.anzdata.org.au.

New South Wales to 27 pmp in South Australia.[75] This difference can be explained by the implementation in the latter state of key elements from the Spanish Model. In 1996, the South Australian Organ Donation Agency was established, which adopted elements of the Spanish Model, and this was soon followed by other states in Australia. The state agency which replicated the most elements of the Spanish model (that of South Australia) enjoyed the greatest improvement in deceased organ donation rates, as compared to the agency (in New South Wales, established in 1997) adopting the fewest elements of the model.[76] South Australia placed donation teams inside every hospital where donation could be available, including at least one member who was medically qualified, as opposed to New South Wales, where the transplant team is not empowered to manage donations beyond the identification of potential donors.[77] Other elements of the Spanish Model that were replicated in South Australia were the establishment of nationally consistent 'best medical practices' for identification, management and care of donors and their families, as well as state management of the relationship with the media, emphasising consistent messages to the public.[78]

Great efforts are currently being made to adapt the Spanish Model in a number of Latin American countries, through the Iberoamerican Network/Council of Donation and Transplantation (RCIDT, for *Red/ Consejo Iberoamericano de Donación y Trasplante*), which represents twenty-one Spanish- and Portuguese-speaking countries. Since its establishment in October 2005, the RCIDT has produced thirteen recommendations, two of the earlier ones concerning the need for a transplant donor co-ordinator in every ICU[79] and the need for creation of a National Transplant Organisation.[80] One of the most outstanding features of the project is the training in Spain of Latin American professionals to become transplant co-ordinators. The three countries with higher deceased organ donor rates (Uruguay, Cuba and Argentina, with 19.1 pmp, 16.6 pmp and 13.1 pmp in 2008, respectively)[81] have the highest number of

[75] *Ibid.*
[76] B. Lindsay, 'Translation of the Spanish model to Australia: pros and cons', *Nefrología*, vol. XXI, Supp. 4 (2001), 130–3, 132.
[77] Lindsay, 'Translation', 131.
[78] R. Matesanz, 'Factors influencing the adaptation of the Spanish Model of organ donation', *Transplant International*, 16 (2003), 736–41, 740.
[79] Recommendation Rec RCIDT 2005 (2) on the role and training of professionals responsible for organ donation (transplant donor co-ordinators).
[80] Recommendation Rec RCIDT 2005 (3) on the functions and responsibilities of a National Transplant Organisation.
[81] Council of Europe, *TRANSPLANT*.

transplant co-ordinators pmp,[82] and these rates have been attributed to the implementation of transplant co-ordinators.[83]

In Latin America, there are added difficulties to improving donation and transplantation activities, such as the lack of public-health financial coverage for the entire population in many countries.[84] A prerequisite of the Spanish Model is a national publicly funded healthcare system which provides full coverage to the population;[85] financial resources must be dedicated to transplantation, particularly in relation to hospital reimbursement for organ procurement and transplantation. However, that does not mean that organ procurement should be exclusive to rich countries. Spain is in the middle-to-low range of Western countries in terms of the percentage of its gross domestic product (GDP) dedicated to healthcare,[86] and yet it can afford an organ transplant system, as the national budget dedicated to transplantation is economically sound since it saves on the overall cost of dialysis.[87] The most important economic factor is reimbursement for organ procurement and transplantation. Other hurdles in Latin America for deceased organ donation are the lack of information and knowledge regarding the donation/transplantation process, and a lack of understanding of the concept of brain death by the general public.[88]

Transplanting the Spanish Model to the UK

In this chapter, it has been argued that efforts to increase deceased organ donation should focus on organisational arrangements, not on presumed consent legislation. Although it is too often taken for granted, there is no correlation between presumed consent legislation and higher rates of

[82] Red/Consejo Iberoamericano de Donación y Trasplante (RCIDT), *Trasplante Iberoamérica Newsletter* (2009), www.ont.es.

[83] R. Mizraji, S. Pérez and I. Alvarez, 'Activity of transplant coordination in Uruguay', *Transplantation Proceedings*, 39 (2007), 339–40; the authors found that the implementation of transplant co-ordinators and intensive care medical doctors has had a strong impact on these results.

[84] R. Mizraji, I. Alvarez, R. Palacios *et al.*, 'Organ Donation in Latin America', *Transplantation Proceedings*, 39 (2007), 333–5.

[85] At the other end of the spectrum in private healthcare, organ donation is hardly likely to be an attractive option, although this may not apply to organ transplantation.

[86] epp.eurostat.ec.europa.eu.

[87] For figures on Spanish expenditure on transplantation, see B. Miranda, J. Cañón and N. Cuende, 'The Spanish organizational structure for organ donation – up to date', *Chirurgische Gastroenterologie*, 18 (2002), 7–16.

[88] K. Sasso-Mendes, P. Curvo, R. Silveira and C. Galvao, 'Organ donation: acceptance and refusal among users of the public health system from Brasil', *Transplantation Proceedings*, 40 (2008), 660–2.

deceased organ donors.[89] Presumed consent legislation alone does not explain the variation in organ donation rates between different countries: not only because there are other measures that have a greater impact on the rise in such rates, but because presumed consent is a misnomer. Such jurisdictions comprise countries where presumed consent is applied rigidly (where doctors can remove organs from every adult who dies, unless they have previously registered to opt out, as in Austria) as well as countries where, in practice, informed consent is applied (where doctors remove organs from the deceased only after obtaining consent from the relatives, as in Spain). Changes in the law as regards presumed consent have been abandoned for the present in the UK since the Organ Donation Taskforce recommended that there be no change to the current opt-in regime[90] because, among other things, passing such legislation could backfire, and produce an increase in the already high rate of family refusals to donate the organs of their deceased relatives.[91]

Efforts should focus instead on the organisational arrangements put into place with regard to organ procurement that are most likely to bring about an increase in rates of organ donation;[92] these arrangements can be summarised in four principal developments: transplant co-ordinators; a central office for support; reimbursement; and close attention paid to the media. Pivotal among them is the in-house transplant co-ordinator, at the first level of organisation; the importance of this key figure has already been recognised in the international arena: in the Action Plan on Organ Donation and Transplantation (2009–2015) the European Commission identified the need for Member States to appoint transplant donor co-ordinators in every hospital where there is potential for organ donation, as Priority Action No. 1.[93] Transplant co-ordinators should be independent of transplantation teams and should be specially trained to

---

[89] G. Nowenstein, 'Organ procurement rates: does presumed consent legislation really make a difference?', *Law, Social Justice & Global Development Journal*, 1 (2004), 1–17.

[90] Organ Donation Taskforce, *The Potential Impact of an Opt Out System for Organ Donation in the UK: an Independent Report from the Organ Donation Taskforce* (London: Department of Health, 2008).

[91] As cited in the aforementioned report, the family refusal rate was 41.1 per cent in 2007, but is currently 38.1 per cent. Council of Europe, *Transplant Newsletter: International Figures on Organ Donation and Transplantation – 2007*, 13(1) (2008).

[92] M. Quigley, M. Brazier, R. Chadwick *et al.*, 'The organs crisis and the Spanish model: theoretical versus pragmatic considerations', *Journal of Medical Ethics*, 34 (2008), 223–4.

[93] Commission of the European Communities, Communication from the Commission: *Action Plan on Organ Donation and Transplantation (2009–2015): Strengthened Cooperation between Member States* (COM (2008) 819/3, Brussels, 8 December 2008). For an analysis of the Commission's Action Plan and the recently issued Organs Directive (2010/45/EU), see A. Farrell, 'Adding value? EU governance of organ donation and transplantation', *European Journal of Health Law*, 17 (2010), 51–79.

identify potential organ donors at an early stage, approach the family and manage the whole process of organ procurement.

The UK Organ Donation Taskforce made a number of recommendations in January 2008 that should help increase the rate of deceased organ donors, including the need to increase the number of donor transplant co-ordinators and introduce changes in their employment, training and working arrangements, to ensure a comprehensive, highly skilled, specialised and robust service.[94] If transplant co-ordinators are answerable to the transplant team, or are located outside the hospital, their ability to identify potential donors is limited or inefficient. Transplant co-ordinators should be involved early on so that efforts at all levels in hospitals can be co-ordinated to maximise the possibility of consent and donation. In addition, timely contact with potential donor families is important. A number of new strategies have already been implemented which are proving to be successful.[95]

The Organ Donation Taskforce also recommends a UK-wide Organ Donation Organisation to be established within the National Health Service (NHS).[96] First, a national organisation should fulfil two functions: it should provide overall support for the donation and transplantation process, but should not be concerned only with organ sharing. Second, it should have a clear objective of maximising the supply of donor organs, and be able to detect problems which could lead to a loss of donors and offer solutions. Such an organisation could develop protocols, audit the results and provide training programmes. This is relevant not only to ensure a safe and efficient donation/transplantation process, but to guarantee the fairness and transparency of organ allocation criteria and the equity of access of all recipients, thus ensuring the acceptability of the donation process. The organisation envisaged by the Organ Donation Taskforce intends to implement these changes.[97] Another key issue is appropriate reimbursement, which the Organ Donation Taskforce also appreciates is important, in order to eliminate disincentives to organ donation management.[98]

Could the Spanish Model be transplanted into the UK? If the right measures are adopted, a positive change in organ donation rates may be

---

[94] Organ Donation Taskforce, *Organs for Transplants: a Report from the Organ Donation Taskforce* (London: Department of Health, 2008), Recommendation 9.

[95] J. Griffiths, M. Verble, S. Falvey *et al.*, 'Culture change initiatives in the procurement of organs in the United Kingdom', *Transplantation Proceedings*, 41 (2009), 1459–62; the authors describe how prior to 2000, transplant co-ordinators were called in only after a patient had been identified as a potential donor and the family had been approached and had given consent to donation.

[96] Organ Donation Taskforce, *Organs for Transplants*, Recommendations 1 and 2.

[97] *Ibid.*, Recommendation 9.   [98] *Ibid.*, Recommendation 8.

achieved, and the Organ Donation Taskforce recommendations appear to adopt some aspects of the model. But changes should not be expected to happen swiftly: although there have been cases of a dramatic increase in deceased organ donation rates in as little as one year (e.g. Uruguay), it would be more reasonable to expect significant changes in a longer period (e.g. Tuscany), particularly if a more sustained increase is to be achieved.[99]

However, implementation of the Spanish Model may not be easily accomplished in the UK, since there are other factors not specifically related to the organ procurement system which may influence the adaptation of the model, such as the number of doctors and nurses available to work on organ procurement, as well as the number of acute beds and ICU facilities available at a given hospital.[100] Physicians in Spain have a low basic pay, when compared to those in other countries,[101] but significant pay rises may be linked to the achievement of particular objectives, such as organ procurement, and this makes the job of transplant co-ordinator an attractive one. Where there are low numbers of doctors with high incomes not linked to such an objective, then it may not be easy to attract transplant co-ordinators, or it may be too costly. The number of nurses also seems to be an important factor, not only because they are part of the transplant co-ordinator's team, but because they ensure that there is a sufficient number of available ICU beds. The number of ICUs is also important, given that the majority of potential deceased organ donors were originally patients in an ICU.[102]

Finally, a word on Spanish society. It is not more generous than other societies: the ONT undertook a survey within the general population on three different occasions (1993, 1999 and 2006) regarding the attitude of the Spanish towards organ donation, and it showed that the perception had not significantly changed during this period of time.[103] In spite of this lack of change in the general attitude towards organ donation, a progressive decline in the rates of refusals to donate has been observed (in 1993,

[99] After reaching an all-time high of 25.2 pmp in 2006, Uruguay's rate fell to 19.1 pmp in 2008. Council of Europe, *Transplant Newsletter 2007* (2008); Council of Europe, *Transplant Newsletter: International Figures on Organ Donation and Transplantation – 2004*, 10(1) (2005).

[100] R. Matesanz, 'Factors influencing the adaptation of the Spanish Model', 738.

[101] europa.eu.int/co/mm/eurostat.

[102] Identified by R. Matesanz as a problem in the implementation of the Spanish Model to the UK: 'La insólita traslación del "modelo español" de donación de órganos al Reino Unido', *Nefrología*, 21 (2001), 99–103, 101.

[103] Organización Nacional de Trasplantes (ONT), *Organ Shortage for Transplantation: Increasing Deceased Donation Activity Through the Spanish Model of Organization* (18 June 2007), www.ont.es.

the refusal rate was 27.5 per cent of families as opposed to 15.2 per cent in 2006).[104] Other studies have shown that public knowledge of and attitudes to organ donation do not differ in Spain as compared to other countries.[105] The factors that explain higher rates in organ donation are the efficiency of the transplant co-ordinator, and the way the family is approached (which has improved as a result of special training). It is also worth noting that when British people living in Spain are approached about donation in Spanish hospitals, the family refusal rate falls to 9 per cent, as opposed to 41.1 per cent in the UK.[106]

There is one important element missing in the UK Organ Donation Taskforce Recommendations, namely attention to the media. The Spanish ONT is responsible for the provision of accurate and positive information for the public and the media, a feature that has also been implemented by the Tuscan OTT. Organ transplantation is a part of medicine that is feasible only when the public participates and contributes by donating organs; in order to do so, the public must trust the healthcare system that makes it possible. Bad publicity about brain death, organ trafficking, fairness of access to organ transplantation, and retrieval without consent can all have an adverse effect on the public's predisposition to consent to organ donation.[107] Unfortunately, previous scandals in the UK may have broken that trust, and efforts must be made to rebuild it.

---

[104] ONT, *Memoria de Actividad*.
[105] H. Schauenburg and A. Hildebrandt, 'Public knowledge and attitudes on organ donation do not differ in Germany and Spain', *Transplantation Proceedings*, 38 (2006), 1218–20.
[106] Organ Donation Taskforce, *The Potential Impact of an Opt Out System*, p. 22.
[107] Council of Europe, *Organ Shortage*.

11 Kidney donation: lessons from the Nordic countries

Salla Lötjönen and Nils H. Persson

The first successful kidney transplant in the world was performed in Boston, United States (USA), in 1954. Only two years later, the first kidney transplant in the Nordic countries was performed in Norway. The technique spread quickly across the Nordic countries: the first successful kidney transplantation with long-term functionality was performed in Norway in 1963, closely followed by Denmark, Finland and Sweden in 1964.[1] Currently, the majority of organ donation (around 67 per cent) involves kidneys.[2] The Nordic countries have long shared historical, cultural and political traditions; in the aftermath of the Second World War, the Nordic Council was founded in 1952, and an agreement on Nordic co-operation was signed in 1962 which became known as the Helsinki Treaty. The Treaty provides a basis for co-operation at many levels, for example in the areas of law, education, social welfare, economy and transportation. The Nordic countries also have a longstanding tradition of working together on legislative issues, as well as being influenced by each other's laws and jurisprudence. This includes the area of legislating for organ procurement and transplantation.

Co-operation amongst the Nordic countries on organ transplantation commenced very early on. Scandiatransplant was founded in 1969 in order to pool Nordic resources and to find matches for rare tissue types. In the early years, drugs for immunosuppression were not very effective and therefore matching for tissue type (HLA, Human Leucocyte Antigen) was more important. More than 50 per cent of kidneys were shipped to another Nordic country. In 1982, a new immunosuppressant agent, Cyclosporin, was introduced, and as a consequence HLA matching

---

[1] A. Reisaeter, 'Kidney transplantation in Norway – an historical perspective', *Tidskrift for den Norske lægeforening*, 119 (1999), 3163–6. The first liver transplantation in the Nordic area was performed in Finland in 1982 and the first heart transplantation took place in Norway in 1983. Lung transplantation was initiated in the Nordic region in the late 1980s and early 1990s.
[2] Figure calculated on the basis of statistics from Scandiatransplant (2008), www.scandiatransplant.org.

became less important. Subsequently, kidney exchange between countries has typically occurred in situations where the patient is a perfect tissue match, especially where the patient carries HLA antibodies. Exchanges of kidneys between Nordic nations now constitute less than 5 per cent of all organs procured nationally. Coupled with the duty to reciprocate for organs received, the overall rate of international shipping amounts to around 10 per cent of organs annually; the great majority of organs available for transplantation are therefore used domestically. In Iceland, only transplantation from living donors is performed, a programme that started in 2003; Icelandic patients needing a transplant from a deceased organ donor are sent to Denmark for treatment. Therefore, this chapter focuses on Denmark, Finland, Norway and Sweden.

For deceased organ donors, most of the Nordic countries (apart from Denmark) have adopted policies based on the model of presumed consent. For living organ donors, full informed consent by the donor himself or herself is a necessity in all of the countries in question. However, there are slight variations in the permissibility of living donation in terms of the requirements of proximity between the donor and the recipient, and in the conditions for donations from a minor. Despite the general degree of harmonisation in Nordic laws on organ transplantation, however, there is variation in the statistics that cannot be explained by legal differences. For example, whereas the relative number of deceased organ donors (per million inhabitants) is lowest in Denmark (arguably due to its policy of requiring explicit informed consent), the average difference in availability of deceased organ donors between Denmark and the other Nordic countries such as Sweden (which has adopted the model of presumed consent) in the last fifteen years has been relatively small. There has also been a worrying decline in deceased organ donations in Finland over the last two years, which cannot be explained by any changes in the law. Another example is the statistics relating to living organ donations. The virtual absence of such donations in Finland stands in stark contrast to the situation in other Nordic countries. In addition, whereas neither Denmark nor Norway has specified the necessary proximity of the relationship between the donor and the recipient in law, the relative number of kidney donations from living donors is considerably higher in Norway than in Denmark.

Understanding the respective national legislative frameworks in the field is therefore not sufficient on its own to gain a full understanding as to the reasons for the variation in organ donation rates. It is suggested that the interpretation of legislation, the available resources, as well as the efficiency of recruitment policies, all have a strong impact on the extent to which either living or deceased organ donation has been favoured in a particular national context and on how successful such national measures have been. This chapter provides a comparative account of the interrelationship between legislation, statistics and performance policies in Denmark, Finland, Norway and Sweden.

Statistics of organ procurement in the Nordic countries

Based on the statistics for the period 1993–2008 collected by Scandiatransplant (see Figure 11.1),[3] historically Finland and Norway have taken the lead in the Nordic countries in organ transplantation from deceased donors. It is, however, interesting to follow recent trends in the statistics. Norway is still at the top in organ procurement from deceased donors, but Finnish donations have fallen rapidly in the last two years. In comparison, there has been a slow but steady increase of deceased donations in Sweden. The Danish situation has remained fairly constant throughout the period.

Kidney transplantation can also be performed with an organ donated by a living donor. In Figures 11.2 and 11.3, the development of living donations of kidneys is compared to the development of kidney donations performed from deceased organ donors.[4] These diagrams are based on absolute numbers, which do not take into account the relative variation in population between the countries.[5] Therefore, the Swedish columns seem

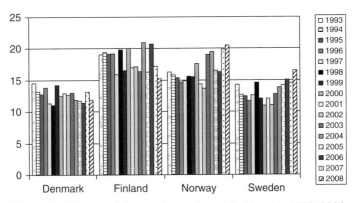

Figure 11.1 Deceased donors (per million inhabitants): 1993–2008

---

[3] The chart is modified from the original provided by Scandiatransplant. Original chart available at www.scandiatransplant.org/aar08_04/dias2008.html.
[4] The charts are modified from the originals provided by Scandiatransplant – see n. 3 above.
[5] As at the end of 2008, Denmark had 5.5 million, Finland 5.3 million, Norway 4.8 million and Sweden 9.2 million inhabitants.

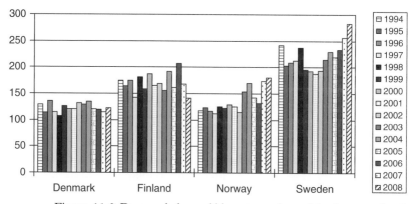

Figure 11.2 Deceased donor kidney transplants (absolute numbers):
1994–2008

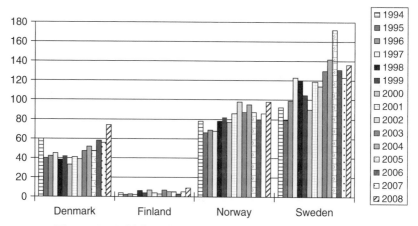

Figure 11.3 Living donor kidney transplants (absolute numbers):
1994–2008

higher than they actually are, although relatively speaking Sweden has
moved ahead of both Denmark and Finland in both living and deceased
organ donations in recent years. However, it is immediately apparent that
whereas Finland was (until recently) managing relatively well with
deceased donor kidney transplantation, the number of donations from
the living is negligible when compared to the other Nordic countries.
Based on the last two years, the overall trend in all countries other than
Finland appears to be an upward one, although one can see from the
columns that over time there has been quite a lot of variation and the
figures in the last two years may be just a passing anomaly.

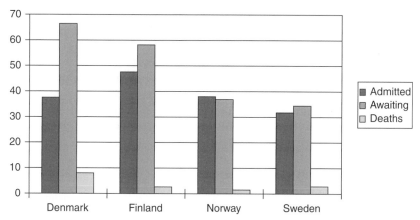

Figure 11.4 Patients admitted to the kidney waiting list, waiting for donation and deceased while waiting in 2008 (per million inhabitants)
* Figures calculated on the basis of statistics from Scandiatransplant (2008) at www.scandiatransplant.org.

Figure 11.4 deals with waiting lists. Organs are a scarce resource, and if the demand for them could be satisfied with the existing measures, there would be no need to alter the existing legislation or organ procurement practices. However, according to Scandiatransplant statistics, 93 patients died in 2008 in the Nordic countries while waiting for a kidney, and over 1,000 kidney patients alone are on the waiting list. It can be seen from Figure 11.4 that the most pressing need in 2008 was in Denmark, where the waiting list for a new kidney was longest and where there was the greatest number of deaths while waiting. In relative terms the second-longest waiting list was in Finland, but as can be seen from the columns, Finland also admitted the most patients onto the waiting list. In addition, the columns show that the criteria for accepting a patient onto the waiting list vary across the Nordic countries and, therefore, the statistics based on the waiting lists must be viewed with caution. What cannot be seen from Figure 11.4 is that Finland had the second-lowest average waiting time for kidney donation amongst the Nordic countries – 18 months – compared to 16 in Norway, 22 in Sweden and 37 in Denmark.[6]

Removal of organs from a deceased donor

Legislative approaches towards organ transplantation from a deceased donor are reasonably well-harmonised in the Nordic countries. The

---

[6] See population figures in n. 5 above.

Finnish, Norwegian and Swedish laws are all based on varying degrees of presumed consent. This means that if the deceased had not made known their opinion on organ transplantation while living, then consent is presumed to exist. However, the Nordic presumed consent regimes are weaker than explicit consent, in the sense that consent can be overridden by the objection of the relatives or other persons close to the deceased. Denmark is the only Nordic country where actual informed consent is required in order to remove organs or tissue from a deceased donor.

The Nordic model of presumed consent

Although the texts of the Finnish, Norwegian and Swedish legislation on organ transplantation are not identical, their main content is very similar. Each gives priority to the wishes of the deceased if made known while alive. Actual consent by the donor cannot be overridden by the objection of the relatives. However, removal of organs is also allowed without consent unless there is reason to believe that the deceased would have objected to the procedure or a close relative or other person close to the deceased objects. At a legal level, the only substantial difference between Finland, Norway and Sweden can be found in the level of obligation of medical staff to inform next of kin about the contemplated transplantation procedure.

In the Finnish Act on the Medical Use of Human Organs and Tissues (101/2001)[7] there is no mention of the extent to which 'near relatives' or other 'close persons' should be made aware of the death or the anticipated removal of organs from the deceased. However, in order for the healthcare staff to satisfy themselves as to the lack of objection amongst the near relatives (and other close persons), it is evident that they need to be in contact with the patient's next of kin. It is also debatable how close a relative needs to be in order for the duty to inform to apply. In the preparatory documents to the 2001 Act, it is stated that a 'near relative' means in most cases a spouse, children, parents and siblings, and 'other close persons' can refer to a cohabitee or other person living permanently with the patient.[8] In the Norwegian 1973 Act relating to Transplantation, Hospital Autopsies and the Donation of Bodies,[9] it is stated in section 2(3)

---

[7] Laki ihmisen elimien ja kudoksien lääketieteellisestä käytöstä, Nr. 101 of Statutes, 2 February 2001.

[8] Governmental Bill to amend the Act on the Medical Use of Human Organs and Tissues, Nr. 93 of 2000; detailed reasons given in relation to the interpretation of section 4.

[9] Lov om transplantasjon, sykehusobduksjon og avgivelse av lik m.m., Nr. 6 of Statutes, 9 February 1973.

that the deceased's next of kin shall 'as far as possible' be notified of the death before the operation takes place.

In the Swedish Act on Transplantation (831/1995),[10] section 4 forbids the performing of the transplant procedure before someone close to the deceased has been informed of the planned procedure and about his or her right to veto it. The person who is informed about the procedure shall, in addition, be given reasonable time to discuss the matter of donation with the rest of the family before making a decision. It has been especially pointed out in the related regulation that donation cannot be performed in a case where there are no relatives or if the relatives cannot be contacted within the 24 hours that are allowed for treatment after the declaration of death. The regulation also specifies what is meant by the notion of 'close persons'. First and foremost, it relates to the family and the near relatives, i.e. spouse or registered partner, cohabitation partner, children, parents, siblings, grandparents and spouse's children. A very close friend can also sometimes count as a 'close person'.[11] As can be concluded, the Swedish legislation places the strictest obligation on healthcare staff to inform relatives about their options, whereas the Finnish and Norwegian regulations leave a broader margin of discretion to such staff.

The consent model

According to section 53 of the Danish Health Act (546/2005),[12] the (explicit) consent need not be in writing, but only a written consent is considered sufficiently valid to be safe from the independent objections of the relatives. A specific registry has been established in order to clarify the status of the wishes of the Danes towards organ transplantation. However, if there is no information about the wish of the deceased prior to his or her death, the consent of the deceased may be replaced by the consent of the next of kin. If the deceased does not have any next of kin, the removal may not be performed. If the deceased is under eighteen years of age, the intervention may only be performed if the legal custodian has given consent to the intervention. According to the preparatory documentation of what now constitutes section 53 of the Health Act, the expression 'the deceased's next of kin' '. . . includes a spouse or cohabitee, direct descendants and, depending on the particular circumstances, siblings. Adopted

---

[10] Lag om transplantation m.m., Nr. 831 of Statutes, 8 June 1995.
[11] Regulations and General Guidelines by the Swedish National Board of Health and Welfare (Socialstyrelsens föreskrifter och allmänna råd) 1997:4, Removal of organs and tissue for organ transplantation and other medical purposes (Organ- och vävnadstagning för transplantation eller för annat medicinskt ändamål), Chapter 4.4.
[12] Sundhedsloven, Nr. 546 of Statutes, 24 June 2005, Part IV, Chapter 12.

children will generally, and foster-children will usually, be covered by the rule. According to circumstances – and more particularly when the deceased leaves no spouse, co-habitee or children – the provision may include relatives to whom the deceased was closely attached, or closely related by marriage.'[13]

In a recent study by the Danish Council of Ethics, the Council discussed whether there were sufficient reasons for suggesting a change in the Danish legislation to follow the presumed consent model adopted in other Nordic countries. A majority of the Council's members (nine) thought that the present regulation system for organ donation should be retained. They justified this position on the grounds that it is important to respect citizens' freedom to make decisions over their own bodies and their freedom to choose the values they emphasise when construing their view of life and the role death plays in it.[14] The informed consent model arguably also caters best for 'doubters' and those who do not wish to be organ donors. Almost as many members (seven), however, thought that presumed consent should be introduced for organ donation in Denmark. They argued that it would send a positive signal to society in support of organ donation, also making it easier for the relatives to make a decision if the deceased has not clearly indicated his or her objection on the matter. According to a survey conducted by the Danish National Board of Health in 2006, the majority of Danes (78 per cent) would be happy to donate an organ themselves. Switching to the presumed consent model would reflect that position.[15] Persons who object to organ donation would always opt out of the presumed consent regime by registering their objection or making it clear to their next of kin. However, the majority of the Danish Council of Ethics did not recommend such a change to the country's preferred regime of informed consent.

Removal of organs from a living donor

The grouping of the Nordic countries according to legislative schemes changes considerably when the question concerns removal of organs from living donors. The element featuring in all of the Nordic laws is that organ transplantation from a living donor requires informed consent from the donor. In Denmark, Finland and Norway, consent is required in writing for both regenerative and non-regenerative tissue, but in Sweden an oral consent is sufficient for removal of regenerative tissue. In all the countries,

---

[13] Danish Council of Ethics, *Organ Donation – Ethical Deliberations and Recommendations* (2008), Chapter 4.2.2., www.etikoglivet.dk/sw310.asp.
[14] *Ibid.*, Chapter 6.2.   [15] *Ibid.*, Chapter 2.3.

information on the nature, consequences and risks of the procedure must be given prior to asking for consent. In the Danish, Finnish and Norwegian legislation, it is specified that the information must be given by a physician. Greater legal variation takes place at two other levels: at the level of restrictions concerning organ transplantation from adult donors (eighteen or above) and at the level of restrictions concerning organ transplantation from children and other incapacitated donors. In this chapter, only non-regenerative organ transplantation is discussed.

Removal of organs from living adult donors

The two countries that in law most restrict the removal of organs from living donors are Finland and Sweden. Both have introduced conditions that require the donor and the recipient to be either related or otherwise in a close relationship with each other. In Finland, this requirement is non-negotiable, and in addition, permission from the National Supervisory Authority for Welfare and Health is required for the procedure to be allowed. In Sweden, however, although proximity between the donor and the recipient is required as a general rule (the donor should be a family relative or someone especially close to the recipient), organ transplantation may also be performed without a link to the recipient. This, however, requires 'particular reasons'. The Swedish interpretation of 'particular reasons' has been fairly liberal. Since the early 1990s, long-standing friends have been accepted as living donors, then later work colleagues, and from 2004 onwards, completely unrelated anonymous donors. Although no permission from a particular licensing body is required for living adult organ donations in Sweden, the development of such interpretation has been made openly, with the National Board of Health and Welfare, as well as the media, being kept informed along the way. No objections from the public have emerged. Apparently, as long as Swedish healthcare staff and the public are convinced that no financial incentives are involved, saving a human life has been seen to fulfil the 'particular reason' condition with respect to living adult organ donations.

The laws of Denmark and Norway do not recognise the proximity rule with regard to organ transplantation from an adult donor, although in practice, organ donation is conducted solely between relatives in Denmark.[16] In Norway they now also accept longstanding friends as donors in addition to relatives, but to our knowledge, neither country has implemented a policy comparable to that in Sweden.

[16] *Ibid.*, Chapter 2.2.1.

Removal of organs from incapacitated donors

Another level of legal variation between the Nordic countries can be found with regard to regulating organ donation from children (under eighteen) and persons who lack capacity to make health-related decisions. Whereas Denmark and Finland have ruled out the donation of non-regenerative organs and tissue from children and incapacitated adults altogether, both Sweden and Norway have left this door slightly ajar. The Swedish Act on Transplantation states that permission from the National Board of Health and Welfare is required in addition to consent by the legal guardian, if non-regenerative tissue is to be removed from an incapacitated person. The Act also requires that special reasons for such a procedure must exist. Similar conditions are included in the Norwegian legislation, for children between twelve and eighteen years of age. Norway has, however, altogether banned non-regenerative organ transplants from children under twelve years of age.

Discussion

It might be that differences in legislation can explain national disparities *only* where major differences are concerned, e.g. with regard to whether the country has adopted a legal framework based on informed consent or presumed consent. This is to be seen in the law and statistics of Denmark as compared to the other Nordic countries. However, although noticeable, the differences between Denmark and the other Nordic countries are surprisingly low in both numbers and scope. For example, the extensive duty to inform the relatives and other close persons as to the planned procedure with a specific veto right in Sweden brings the Swedish regime close to the Danish system with regard to informed consent. However, in the last couple of years, Swedish deceased organ donations have still risen above the Danish figures.

Interpretation of legislation and the policies developed to support the recruitment of organ donors play an important role in this field. This is best seen in the case of living organ donation. A good example of the varying impact of laws is the Swedish interpretation of the proximity rule in living adult donations, which has led to a more liberal end result than in countries where no proximity rule has been stated in the law. Restrictive legislation and restrictive policies can also work hand-in-hand. Finland is the only country in the Nordic region that requires permission from a licensing body prior to a living adult donation. This may be one reason why living donations are so low in Finland compared to other Nordic countries. A successful history of deceased organ donation and low average waiting times may be other reasons; with a substantial availability of organs from deceased donors, living donation was generally only used as a true 'last option' in cases of patients with rare tissue types. However, another plausible reason lies in the way relatives are informed about the need for an organ. In Finland, this has been left to the patient, whereas in Norway, for example, healthcare staff contact the relatives (with the patient's consent) and inform them of the need, benefits and risks involved in order to avoid the awkwardness of direct contact by the patient.

Information campaigns are nothing new in this area. Organ donation cards are widely available in all Nordic countries, although only Denmark and Sweden have a centralised registry. In Denmark, less than 11 per cent of the population has registered in the national registry, notwithstanding survey findings which found that 87 per cent of the population viewed organ donation positively and 78 per cent would even be willing to donate an organ themselves. However, if the wish of the deceased is not known and the relatives are faced with the decision-making, only half will give their consent to the procedure.[17] The popularity of organ donation is even higher in Finland, where according to the poll conducted for the Kidney and Liver Foundation in 2006, as many as 83 per cent of the population would be willing to donate an organ. According to the same poll, however, only 16 per cent of the population carries an organ donation card.[18] By 2009, 90 per cent of the population was willing to donate an organ when asked the same question.[19]

In most cases, restrictive legislation cannot be blamed for organ shortages in the Nordic region. Nordic co-operation as between healthcare professionals functions well and the population in general has a very positive view of organ donation. What then are the barriers to donation faced by the Nordic countries? Why are there not enough organs for all in need? It is difficult to gather hard evidence on issues such as resource allocation, the availability of intensive care beds for potential donors and whether potential donors are simply not followed up. However, these factors have a clear connection to organ procurement. Good results have been obtained from Norway and Sweden as a consequence of the clarification of responsibilities amongst healthcare staff, as well as from nominating transplantation co-ordinators outside the University hospitals.

---

[17] *Ibid.*, Chapter 2.2.
[18] S. Sarnesto, 'Uusin tutkimus: suomalaisilla on myönteinen asenne elinluovutukseen' (12 October 2006), www.musili.fi/fin/ajankohtaista/?nid=20&fs=m.
[19] Governmental Bill to amend the Act on the Medical Use of Human Organs and Tissues, Nr. 276 of 2009, Chapter 2.1.

The clearest barrier is the lack of communication between potential donors and their relatives. If the number of potential donors could be increased by 30 per cent simply by the carrying of donor cards, why shouldn't this be done? Another route is to abolish the relatives' right to veto the transplantation from the deceased, as has been done in Finland. In June 2010, the Finnish Parliament approved an amendment to the Finnish Act on the Medical Use of Human Organs and Tissues,[20] which means that the relatives of the deceased will no longer be given an independent right to object to the organ procurement, based simply on their own views. In addition, the wishes of minors and adults who lack capacity must be respected, if they had the capacity to form an opinion on the matter before death or before the onset of incapacity. The amendment places a duty on healthcare professionals to provide an explanation to close relatives or other persons close to the deceased as to what is involved in organ retrieval. In the case of the death of a competent adult, the purpose of contact would, however, mainly be to enquire about the wishes of the deceased. If it was known or there was reason to believe that the deceased had objected to his or her organs being used for organ transplantation, then the removal of organs would not be allowed.

Thus far, public discussion has mostly been in favour of this legislative amendment. The Constitutional Law Committee specifically emphasised the importance of recognising the self-determination of the deceased and called for an amendment to the original Governmental Bill in favour of the self-determination of minors.[21] One of the justifications for the proposal was the mismatch between public opinion on organ transplantation based on public polls, and the number of transplants that did not take place (leading to lives being lost) because of objections by relatives. The reasons for relatives' objections can be very different, but certainly one possible reason is that when the wish of the deceased is not known, it may feel as if the 'safer' option is to object rather than consent. After all, the body of the deceased will then be left intact until the funeral. At the moment of loss of a near relative, it is difficult to take into account the consequences that the decision may have upon persons who are unknown to us. In addition to the aim of increasing the number of organs available for organ transplantation, one of the advantages of this legislative amendment is that by changing the role of the relatives from decision-makers to information-providers, they will be saved from making hard and painful decisions in the most difficult of situations.

---

[20] Governmental Bill to amend the Act on the Medical Use of Human Organs and Tissues, Nr. 276 of 2009.
[21] Statement of the Constitutional Law Committee, Nr. 24 of 2010 (Finland).

Conclusion

What can the Nordic legal framework and experience in the area of organ transplantation offer the international community? The Nordic countries consist of a rather homogeneous population with a tradition of arriving at a consensus. In general, the population trust their healthcare staff more than their politicians, and hence it has been possible to draft legislation that has been rather broadly formulated and leaves a good deal of discretion to the healthcare professionals working in the field. This has resulted in the advantage of healthcare professionals being able to develop new strategies more quickly than the legislative process can, but this approach will only take matters so far. When considerable changes in the system are required, which must be supported with public funds, governmental involvement is essential.

One of the key concepts seems to be public trust. Developing better organ procurement strategies within the profession can only function if this is done openly and in close collaboration with the patient organisations and media. Organ transplantation in the Nordic countries is viewed amongst the population almost as a civic duty, and virtually no negative connotations are linked to the activity. With the exception perhaps of Denmark, all the Nordic countries have been relatively successful in managing organ donation as compared to international standards, albeit more so in some Nordic countries than in others. None of the Nordic countries have contemplated changing their organ procurement regime from presumed consent to informed consent. On the contrary, Finland has taken a step forward towards a more 'pure' presumed consent model by legislating that the relatives' opinions are no longer to be given legal significance. In addition, in Denmark the first attempt to switch from the informed consent model to a presumed consent model was lost by a very narrow majority vote in the Danish Council of Ethics. At least the majority of the Danish population seem to be ready for the switch, according to the polls – but are the politicians?

However, one must be careful not to give too much weight to the majority in the public-opinion polls. Although around 80 per cent of the Danish (and around 90 per cent of the Finnish) population is in favour of organ donation, a minority of 10–20 per cent is not an insignificant minority. Moving closer to a pure presumed consent regime needs to be supported with strengthened measures allowing individuals to opt out and ensuring mistakes are not made. Public popularity is based on trusting that the system works and that individuals are not harmed against their wishes. That trust has been gained through hard work, but it is easy to lose.

Being part of an international community is generally very rewarding, and the Nordic countries have been happy to co-operate within the Nordic region and to share the Nordic experience. In organ transplantation, being part of a global community is a double-edged sword. It is very useful to gain insights into other regimes and to learn about how organ transplantation has been organised and resourced in other countries, but there are many other key important factors in organ transplantation that make close collaboration problematic. Organ transplantation is closely connected to personal convictions, trust in healthcare professionals, resource allocation and varying degrees of solidarity. Optimal collaboration requires a homogenous population, similar levels of expertise between the participants, all participants being able to pay their dues and true reciprocity in organ exchange. This has been achieved amongst the Nordic countries via Scandiatransplant and professional collaboration. Hopefully, good co-operation will continue, and the example provided by the Nordic countries can also be used as a model in other regions.

12 Organ donation and transplantation: the Canadian experience

Linda Wright and Diego S. Silva

Canada has approximately thirty-three million inhabitants, spread over nine million square kilometres, and there are two official languages: French and English. There is a Canadian federal government as well as ten provincial and three territorial governments which are in charge of local affairs. Canada has many First Nations populations; it is multicultural and multi-lingual, particularly in large cities such as Vancouver, Montreal and Toronto, reflecting extensive immigration of peoples from many parts of the world. Universal access to publicly insured healthcare is funded from general taxation, in accordance with the Canada Health Act 1984.[1] This federal Act influences provincial healthcare insurance plans nationally by promising to pay out if the provinces and territories meet a number of requirements. The administration and delivery of healthcare is carried out by each province and territory, producing variation in services across the country.

Canada has an opt-in system of organ donation. In 2007, 2,153 transplants were performed in Canada,[2] and the country recorded a deceased organ donation rate of 14.7 per million population (pmp) in 2008.[3] There is a significant shortfall in the availability of organs for transplantation, with variation between the provinces. In 2008, 4,380 Canadians waited for a transplant, 2,083 received a transplant and 215 died waiting (see Table 12.1 below).

Organ transplantation is administered provincially, with limited national regulatory authority. The federal government's health agency, Health Canada, is empowered to require registration and to inspect Organ

The authors wish to thank Dr Peter Nickerson and Mr Kelley Ross for their comments on this manuscript.

1 Canada Health Act, RSC 1985, c. C-6.
2 Canadian Organ Replacement Registry, *Treatment of End-Stage Organ Failure in Canada 1999–2008 – Report of the Canadian Organ Replacement Register 2010* (Canadian Institute for Health Information, 2010).
3 Canadian Organ Replacement Registry, *Organ Donor Activity in Canada, 1999–2008* (Canadian Institute for Health Information, 2009).

Table 12.1 *Waiting times for transplants by Canadian province 2008*[4]

Jurisdiction	No. of transplants	No. of patients waiting	No. of patients who died waiting
Canada	2,083	4,380	215
Alberta	286	621	60
British Columbia	266	308	25
Manitoba	53	167	1
Nova Scotia (Atlantic Canada)	128	242	4
Ontario	836	1,739	81
Quebec	479	1,159	44
Saskatchewan	35	144	0

Procurement Organizations (OPOs) and living donor transplantation programmes. Currently this regulatory regime pertains to safety.[5] Many provinces have an OPO that maintains lists of patients waiting for transplantation and organises the procurement and delivery of organs from deceased donors. Organs from living donors are handled by individual hospitals in most places. However, in British Columbia, BC Transplant, whose funding is mainly from the provincial Ministry of Health, directs, delivers or contracts for all transplant services in that province.[6] In 2008, the government of Canada announced the merger of the Canadian Council for Donation and Transplantation (CCDT), an advisory body, with Canadian Blood Services, to provide national leadership for organ and tissue donation and transplantation. This was accompanied by an investment of $35 million CDN over five years to create an integrated national system to significantly improve organ donation and transplantation in Canada. The Canadian Society for Transplantation, a professional organisation, provides a national forum for voluntary collaboration and development of practice guidelines in transplantation.

Transplantation in Canada: a brief history

In 1958, the British Commonwealth's first successful kidney transplant, between identical twins, was performed at the Royal Victoria Hospital, Montreal, Quebec by Dr John Dossetor. The Toronto General Hospital performed the world's first single-lung transplant in 1983 and the first ever double-lung transplant in 1986. This hospital is now one of the most

---

[4] Canadian Organ Replacement Registry, Tables 1A, 2A and 2B (Canadian Institute for Health Information, 2009).
[5] Food and Drug Act, RSC 1985, c. F-27.   [6] BC Transplant, www.transplant.bc.ca.

active living donor liver transplant centres in the Western world. Today, Canada offers adult and paediatric organ transplantation of kidney, heart, lung, liver, pancreas and small intestines and has transplant centres in most provinces.

Canadian jurisdiction and transplant laws

Although Canada's territories are partially sovereign and often enact laws to govern many of the same issues as provinces, they are created by the federal government. The ten Canadian provinces, however, have their sovereignty and jurisdictional boundaries constitutionally entrenched. Canada's Constitution Act 1867 delineates enumerated legislative power for the federal government under section 91 and provincial governments under section 92.[7] It is generally understood that section 92(7) gives provinces the exclusive power to control all healthcare-related matters (with certain exceptions). This provincial power over matters of healthcare means that provinces control activities including the regulation of healthcare professionals, taxation for healthcare and the allocation of resources, and are responsible for legislating on matters of procedure and protocol including organ donation and transplantation. Therefore, each province has legislation on donation and transplantation; Canada's federal government has no jurisdictional authority over transplantation. An exception is the province of Quebec, which functions primarily under a civil law system (as opposed to the common law system in other provinces and at the federal level); its transplantation rules are found in the general Civil Code of Quebec.[8]

Despite Canada's constitutional division of powers, the federal government exerts control over the healthcare decisions of the provinces by way of 'transfer funds', i.e. the federal government can enact legislation whereby the provinces have access to federal money on the condition that certain criteria are followed as stipulated within a given federal Act. The Canada Health Act is the overarching federal legislation that grants the provinces financial capital on the condition that certain healthcare criteria are followed. Two important criteria are that healthcare must be publicly administered by the provinces, and universal in scope so all insured residents have access to all the insured health services provided by the province.[9]

Although each province has its own donation and transplantation law, there is significant overlap between the provinces. In terms of donation

---

[7] The Constitution Act, 1867 30 & 31 Victoria, c. 3 (UK).
[8] Civil Code of Quebec, SQ 1991, c. 64, a. 19, 42–5.
[9] Canada Health Act, RSC 1985, c. C-6.

post-mortem, adults can consent to donate organs and tissue, either in written form or verbally, for therapeutic or scientific purposes including medical education. An 'adult' is usually defined as someone nineteen years or older in most provinces,[10] with the exception of Ontario,[11] Manitoba[12] and Prince Edward Island[13] where an adult, for the purposes of donation, is anyone sixteen years or older, and in Quebec where an adult is any person fourteen years or older.[14] If a deceased individual's wishes for organ donation are unspecified, the next of kin are asked to give consent based on evidence of the deceased's wishes on organ donation. Minors and persons with cognitive disabilities can be donors if the family chooses to donate upon death. Some provinces require that after a patient dies either the physician who cared for the deceased person or a representative of the provincial transplant organisation offers the possibility of donation, if this is medically suitable, to the family of the deceased; however, neither Quebec[15] nor Alberta,[16] two of the provinces with the best deceased organ donation rates, have this criteria within their transplant legislation, which brings into question the effectiveness of such provisions. Selling organs is explicitly prohibited in all provinces. Recently, the Criminal Code has been amended to make the removal of organs or tissues for commercial purposes a criminal offence, even if the organs or tissues were removed with an individual's consent.[17]

Ethical issues in Canadian transplantation

The conceptual basis for organ donation and transplantation in Canada is that of Judaeo-Christian values and metaphysical beliefs. It embodies the Cartesian elements of mind-body dualism. The framework for organ donation is an opting-in system whereby organ donation is rooted in consent and volunteerism and is viewed as the expression of altruism.

---

[10] Human Tissues Act, RSNL 1990, c. H-15; Human Tissue Act, RSNWT 1988, c. H-6; Human Tissue Gift Act, RSA 2000, c. H15; Human Tissue Gift Act, RSBC 1996, c. 211; Human Tissue Gift Act, SNB 2004, c. H12.5; Human Tissue Gift Act, RSNS 1989, c. 215; Human Tissue Gift Act, RSS 1978, c. H-15; Human Tissue Gift Act, RSY 2002, c. 117.
[11] Trillium Gift of Life Network Act, RSO 1990, c. H.20.
[12] Human Tissue Gift Act, CCSM 1987, c. H180.
[13] Human Tissue Donation Act, RSPEI 1988, c. H-12.1.
[14] Civil Code of Quebec, SQ 1991, c. 64, a. 19, 42–5.   [15] *Ibid.*
[16] Human Tissue Gift Act, RSA 2000, c. H15.
[17] Criminal Code, RSC 1985, c. C-46, s. 279.01–279.04.

Organ donation from deceased donors

Transplantation rates vary across Canada. Persons in Alberta, for example, are 3.74 times more likely to receive a kidney transplant than persons living in Ontario, Canada's most populated province.[18] One reason for the differences between the provinces stems from there being no central authority on procurement and transplantation. A thorough understanding of Canada's transplantation rates is difficult to achieve because provinces and hospitals are not required to disclose how they procure and allocate organs. At a consensus conference in 2006, Canadian kidney transplant professionals established eligibility criteria for kidney transplantation; most kidney transplant programmes across Canada follow this algorithm, which balances (in descending order of priority):

1. the medical urgency for transplantation;
2. prioritisation of children;
3. near-perfect matches and sensitisation; and
4. how long a person has been waiting.[19]

The Canadian Cardiovascular Society has a nationally accepted standardised algorithm to guide listing criteria and indications for cardiac transplantation.[20]

For livers, certain behavioural criteria (e.g. alcoholism or drug addiction) prevent individuals from being placed on transplant waiting lists, while the severity of the liver disease as well as urgency are the primary criteria used to determine who receives a liver once an individual is placed on a waiting list.[21] It has been suggested that these criteria are standardised across Canadian liver transplant centres.[22] Lungs are allocated in a similar manner to livers, i.e. some behavioural factors (e.g. smoking) would operate to the detriment of an individual's opportunity of being placed on a transplant waiting list, while the main positive criteria for allocation is medical urgency. The main ethical principles used in allocating organs in Canada are medical utility and prioritising patients for whom an organ would be most beneficial, as determined by medical need (i.e. illness acuity), or normative advantages such as being a child.

---

[18] M. Tonelli, S. Klarenbach, B. Manns *et al.*, 'Residence location and likelihood of kidney transplantation', *Canadian Medical Association Journal*, 175 (2006), 478–82.

[19] Canadian Council for Donation and Transplantation (CCDT), 'Collaborative', www.ccdt.ca/collaborative/index.html.

[20] H. Haddad, D. Isaac, J. Legare *et al.*, 'Canadian Cardiovascular Society Consensus Conference update on cardiac transplantation 2008: Executive Summary', *Canadian Journal of Cardiology*, 25 (2009), 197–205.

[21] M. Mullen, N. Kohut, M. Sam *et al.*, 'Access to adult liver transplantation in Canada: a survey and ethical analysis', *Canadian Medical Association Journal*, 154 (1996), 337–42.

[22] S. Martin, 'Letter', *Canadian Medical Association Journal*, 176 (2007), 1128.

In keeping with a lack of central authority for organ transplantation, there is no national directive on sharing organs with foreign nationals, as seen in some other countries.[23] Each province is left to make its own policy, which may result in uneven practice across the country.

A second issue related to deceased donations is the extent to which there must be equitable access or rates of transplantation across Canada. The Canada Health Act, which is often invoked in conversations as representative of Canadians' healthcare values of 'equity and solidarity',[24] has among its criteria 'universality' and 'portability'. 'Universality' states that all insured medical services in a province must be available to all insured residents of that province. This principle is often extrapolated and combined with the criteria of 'portability', which states that Canadians should receive equal access to medical services while visiting or residing in other provinces. In terms of transplantation, some have questioned whether such vast differences in waiting times and transplantation rates amongst the provinces is morally acceptable.[25] And there are those who argue that, given Canadians espouse notions of solidarity and equality in terms of healthcare, and that these values are, in part, criteria within federal legislation, then there must be some equality and solidarity in sharing organs and resources for transplantation across Canada. This has led to some Canadians calling for a national organ registry or central-ised transplantation system.[26] A counterargument to this position is that provinces which increase their rates of organ donation, often through public campaigns with provincial resources, should be entitled to more organs for their residents. An additional challenge is how to address waitlisted individuals who move to other provinces. Some might argue that time accrued on a waiting list in one province should be portable to a new province of residence. It may be countered that this new resident has not given as many resources to the new province (e.g. taxes, community service) to merit bypassing other residents on the waiting list. The Canadian Kidney Transplant Organ Allocation Forum, organised by the CCDT in 2006, made two relevant recommendations. First, patients should be listed in one local or regional transplant list at a time. Second,

---

[23] United Network for Organ Sharing (UNOS), Policy 6.0, Transplantation of Non-Resident Aliens (2005).

[24] Health Canada, 'Canada's Healthcare System (Medicare)', www.hc-sc.gc.ca/hcs-sss/medi-assur/index-engphp.

[25] Tonelli *et al.*, 'Residence location'; Z. Zaltzman, 'Kidney transplantation in Canada: unequal access', *Canadian Medical Association Journal*, 175 (2006), 489–90.

[26] W. Kondro, 'Fragmented organ donation programs hinder progress', *Canadian Medical Association Journal*, 175 (2006), 1043–5.

patients should be able to maintain their accrued wait time since starting dialysis when they move from one jurisdiction to another.[27]

Several initiatives have been introduced to increase organ donation from deceased donors. Proclaiming death by cardio-circulatory criteria, also known as donation after cardiac death (DCD), was debated widely in Canada before being introduced gradually into several hospitals. The CCDT supports the conclusions and guiding values of DCD as articulated by the Canadian Critical Care Society, including respect for the life of all individuals, optimal end-of-life care, upholding patient autonomy, support for the family of dying patients, upholding public trust, and respect for healthcare professionals.[28]

A second initiative to increase organ donation is the Organ Donation Collaborative, which has been used to share information and assist in the education of healthcare workers in obtaining organs.[29] Much of the education has centred on teaching healthcare workers about the stages of the donation process, with the goal that greater knowledge will lead to better systematic results. The province of Quebec, which has seen an increase in the number of organs available for transplantation despite a stable rate of donation from deceased donors in the last decade, credits the introduction of these two initiatives as factors that have helped offset a decrease in the number of neurological deaths.[30]

Organ donation from living donors

The rates of organ donation by living persons vary across the country, with more use of such donors in areas where the deceased donor rate is low.[31] As the demand for organs has increased, the use of living donors has expanded, with more centres using living donors of kidneys and livers. A lung transplant from two living lung donors was performed in Winnipeg, Manitoba in December 1999, but most lung transplantation in Canada is from deceased donors.[32] Some living donor innovations have been developed or initiated in Vancouver, including the use of anonymous living

---

[27] CCDT, 'Collaborative'.
[28] S. Shemie, A. Baker, G. Knoll et al., 'Donation after cardiocirculatory death in Canada', Canadian Medical Association Journal, 175 (2006), S1–24.
[29] CCDT, 'Collaborative'.
[30] Quebec Transplant, www.quebec-transplant.qc.ca/QuebecTransplant_en/PDF/Press_release_January_9.pdf.
[31] V. McAlister and K. Badovinac, 'Transplantation in Canada: report of the Canadian Organ Replacement Register', Transplantation Proceedings, 35 (2003), 2428–30.
[32] J. Stewart, 'First Canadian live-donor lung transplants performed in Winnipeg', Canadian Medical Association Journal, 162 (2000), 1339.

kidney donors.[33] An anonymous living donor is a living donor who donates a kidney or liver lobe to a hospital for the transplant team to allocate as they see fit.

Another innovation is the kidney transplant exchange programme, where medically incompatible living donor volunteers may donate by exchanging a kidney with another mismatched pair. The two Toronto hospitals offering kidney transplantation to adults, Toronto General Hospital and St Michael's Hospital, established a joint paired exchange kidney transplant programme in 2006. In February 2009, Canadian Blood Services launched a national Living Donor Paired Exchange Registry, where all Canadian mismatched pairs can register their willingness to participate in a national kidney exchange programme. This programme is a Canadian first in addressing transplantation on a national basis and promotes fairness for patients by extending the programme to all parts of the country. An important procedural and implementational element is that British Columbia, Manitoba and Ontario have programmes to refund living organ donors' expenses incurred by donation, such as loss of income, travel, accommodation and childcare costs. Initiated by the British Columbia Transplant Society, in conjunction with the Kidney Foundation of Canada in July 2006, these programmes offer financial support to Canadian living organ donors who may face significant challenges in the costs of donating far from home. Some other provinces are considering similar programmes. The goal of these programmes is to make living donation revenue-neutral, addressing the injustice of living donors being financially penalised for donating an organ and removing the financial disincentive to living donation. Criticism that these steps may lead to paid donation is met by capping reimbursements at modest amounts ($5,500 CDN) paid only with proof of allowable, receipted expenses related to the donation.[34] The first Canadian four-way kidney transplant exchange, involving an anonymous donor, one recipient from the waiting list, and three living donor and recipient pairs, occurred simultaneously in four operating rooms, across three time zones, in Vancouver, British Columbia, Edmonton, Alberta and Toronto, Ontario on 24 June 2009.[35]

---

[33] A. Henderson, M. Landolt, M. McDonald *et al.*, 'The living anonymous kidney donor: lunatic or saint?', *American Journal of Transplantation*, 3 (2003), 203–13.

[34] Trillium Gift of Life, www.giftoflife.on.ca/assets/pdfs/PREPublicFAQsV1.pdf.

[35] M. Jimenez, 'A surgical marathon that spanned the country: unprecedented chain of kidney transplants traded vitally needed organs among three recipients in three different cities all at once', *Globe and Mail*, Toronto, 25 June 2009.

Public solicitations for organs have had a small impact on organ donation. Whilst no centre explicitly encourages this practice, the Toronto General Hospital will evaluate potential living donors and recipients who met in this way. The rationale is that how people connected is less relevant than the existing relationship between the parties, their expectations of the procedure and the fulfilment of informed consent. Some solicitations have been very public, including a 2006 front-page tabloid appeal for a liver segment for an infant, which elicited 900 telephone calls to the transplant centre and one eventual living donor. This case highlighted some ethical issues, including whether a public solicitation privileges recipients who are resourceful or have a more appealing story or appearance than others. One challenge is to determine if the donor expects money or goods from the recipient family. Solicited volunteers are evaluated very carefully and recipient families are made aware of any risks associated with a solicited donation. To achieve an informed-consent process, solicited potential living donors are informed that there may be others waiting for the same organ whose need is greater. No confidential information about any patient is disclosed. The donor is informed of their right to direct an organ to a particular individual, as in other living donor situations, and it is explained that anonymous non-directed donations are allocated to the recipient who is deemed the best match and in the greatest need.

Living donation presents additional moral challenges to Canadian transplant teams. The Toronto General Hospital houses a large multi-organ transplant programme, which includes living liver and kidney donor transplantation. As living organ donation has developed there, demands for innovative donation solutions have challenged staff as to how to respond to new situations. As a result, the Bioethics programme helped to develop Ethical Guidelines for the Evaluation of Living Organ Donors in 2003–04.[36] By embarking on a process to establish principles of practice, the centre attempted to achieve some standardisation of practice, based on clearly stated values and considered opinions. The Guidelines provide a process for the evaluation of living donors and recommend separate teams for recipients and donors, which is common in several centres where staffing levels permit, but is a challenge in smaller centres. The Guidelines also outline a process for dispute resolution when a team cannot agree on the acceptability of a donor.

---

[36] L. Wright, K. Faith, R. Richardson *et al.*, 'Ethical guidelines for the evaluation of living organ donors', *Canadian Journal of Surgery*, 47 (2004), 408–14.

Conclusion

The Canadian federal system of government accounts for the lack of central regulation in its system of organ donation and transplantation, differing from other countries such as the United Kingdom or the United States. Whilst this has led to uneven practice throughout the country, it has also facilitated some centres in initiating new practices to increase organ donation.

13   Systematic increases in organ donation: the United States experience

Alexandra K. Glazier

The demand for organ transplantation outstrips the supply of donated organs by a high margin in the United States (USA). As of December 2009, there were over 105,000 Americans awaiting an organ transplant and approximately 18 people per day dying whilst waiting.[1] This public-health crisis is being addressed in the USA on several fronts, including significant changes in the laws governing consent to donation, as well as in organ donation practices. As a result, organ donation in the USA has gone through a remarkable transformation: there was a 30 per cent increase in the total number of organs donated for transplant between 2004 and 2009, contrasting with the previous decade which experienced an average increase per year of only 1–2 per cent. Although a confluence of factors, including changes in the law and practice of donation, have contributed to this outcome, it is the federal-government-sponsored 'Breakthrough Collaborative' initiative which is credited with stimulating the change. This initiative, designed with a clear intent to increase organ donation for transplantation, is derived from process-improvement principles and has produced measurable results.

This chapter examines best practices which have emerged from the initiative, as well as developments in the law and process that have improved rates of organ donation in the USA. In particular, consideration is given to how these changes have led to an increase in the potential pool of donors through donation after cardiac death protocols, innovative living donor programmes and increased rates of consent through more effective opt-in donation laws. These changes can serve as a model for other countries seeking to boost organ donation without drastic changes in fundamental principles. The primary lesson exemplified by the USA is that a 'from the top' focus on donation and widespread adoption of identified best practices by those responsible for co-ordinating donation,

---

[1] United Network for Organ Sharing (UNOS), www.unos.org/data/about/viewDataReports. asp.

in collaboration with hospitals where the organ potential resides, can achieve measurable and sustainable results.

The United States organ donation system

In the USA, the organ donation system is organised through Organ Procurement Organizations (OPOs), which are non-profit organisations designated by the federal government to serve specific geographic regions. Federal law requires hospitals to refer all imminent deaths to the regionally assigned OPO.[2] In turn, the OPO assesses the referred patient's organ donation potential by screening for medical suitability. If the OPO determines there is organ donation potential, the OPO is responsible for obtaining or confirming donation consent and, after the potential donor is declared dead, co-ordinating the logistics for surgical recovery of the donated organs. The OPO is also accountable for allocating the donated organs for transplant to compatible recipients in accordance with United Network for Organ Sharing (UNOS) policies. In addition to developing and implementing organ-specific allocation policies, UNOS is the entity responsible for overseeing the country's transplantation system, including maintenance of the national transplantation 'wait list'.[3]

Consistent with the high premium placed on individual liberty within the USA, organ donation is an opt-in system. Individuals must affirmatively consent to donation or families may choose to do so at the time of an individual's death. Although a recent Gallup survey showed that over 95 per cent of the US public support organ donation, only 53 per cent of Americans have taken the step of granting permission for donation of organs or tissues on a driver's licence or organ donor card.[4] Given this disparity, recent improvements to the organ donation system and the donation laws, designed to increase the availability of organs for transplant, are firmly anchored in a realistic reflection of public attitudes within the USA.

The Organ Donation Breakthrough Collaborative

In 2003, the US Department of Health and Human Services embarked on a formal intervention to improve the organ donation and transplantation system. This concerted effort, named the Organ Donation Breakthrough Collaborative (Collaborative), used a technique developed by the

---

[2] 42 CFR §482.45.   [3] See www.unos.org.
[4] The Gallup Organization, *2005 National Survey of Organ and Tissue Donation Attitudes and Behavior*, www.organdonor.gov.

Institute for Healthcare Improvement to identify and share best practices. The concept behind the Collaborative method is to apply intense focus 'to facilitate break-through transformations' in organisational performance.[5] The method includes defining, documenting and sharing what already works, accelerating improvement and achieving results by building 'clinical leaders of change'.[6]

The first Collaborative was set up as six two-day learning sessions spread over a little less than a two-year period. Participants at the learning sessions included staff from ninety-five large hospitals and forty-two of the sixty OPOs.[7] The Collaborative drew upon representatives from the top-performing organisations with sustained high organ donation rates and employed the 'All Teach, All Learn' approach for participants to share effective change strategies.[8] A second Collaborative was run in 2004–05 building on the momentum created by the first Collaborative.

The goal of the Collaborative was to systematically increase the number of organs donated for transplantation by maximising donor potential. The Collaborative set out to achieve this objective in a way that would be 'clear, measurable, ambitious and achievable'.[9] The participating organisations were committed to achieving organ donation rates of 75 per cent or higher, which would result in saving thousands of lives.

Identifying and proliferating best practices

The first step in the Collaborative was to study the top-performing OPOs and identify common best practices. The Collaborative did this by looking intensely at six OPOs and eighteen affiliated hospitals through data collection, interviews and observations. From this study emerged fifteen best practices that ranged from focusing organisational mission and board membership on achieving increased organ donation rates, to identifying champions of organ donation within a hospital, to using data to promote decision-making. The Collaborative incorporated these identified best practices into the improvement model of Plan, Do, Study, Act (commonly referred to as PDSA) in order to leverage positive change.[10] The

---

[5] T. Shafer, D. Wagner, J. Chessare *et al.*, 'US Organ Donation Breakthrough Collaborative increases organ donation', *Critical Care Nursing Quarterly*, 31 (2008), 190–210.
[6] *Ibid.*
[7] '*Spreading the Gift of Life: Organ Donation Breakthrough Collaborative*', www.ihi.org.
[8] Shafer *et al.*, 'US Organ Donation Breakthrough Collaborative'.
[9] T. Shafer, D. Wagner, J. Chessare *et al.*, 'Increasing organ donation through system redesign', *Critical Care Nursing Quarterly*, 26 (2006), 44–8.
[10] See G. Langley, K. Nolan, T. Nolan *et al.*, 'Methods for improvement' in G. Langley, K. Nolan, C. Norman *et al.* (eds.), *The Improvement Guide: A Practical Approach to Enhancing Organizational Performance* (New York: Jossey-Bass, 1996), pp. 49–138.

premise was that by replicating the best practices, participating organisations would achieve dramatic increases in donation rates.

As part of this study, the Collaborative also identified critical information relating to the underlying organ donation potential in the USA. Based on the 2002 national data studied, the Collaborative calculated that 80 per cent of the organ donation potential existed in only 20 per cent of the total number of hospitals in the USA.[11] The practical implications were immediately apparent: the Collaborative's efforts had to focus on those hospitals with the significant underlying organ donation potential, in order to see effective improvement to organ donation rates. This conclusion allowed OPOs to appropriate triage resources to efficiently achieve the greatest improvements in donation rates.

The change package

The Collaborative sought to implement a 'change package' in each of the participating organisations. The change package consisted of four strategies for success:

1. unrelenting focus on change, improvement and results;
2. rapid early referral and linkage;
3. management of an integrated donation process; and
4. aggressive pursuit of every donation opportunity.[12]

The concept behind a focus on change, improvement and results is that successful organisations have a strong culture of accountability for outcomes. The Collaborative harnessed this concept and helped define its application in organ donation. OPOs and hospitals with significant donor potential must have shared accountability for increasing organ donation through a culture of excellence, which is created in part by measuring and disseminating process and outcomes data.[13] Developing a seamless integration with hospital staff and other stakeholders in the organ donation process (such as medical examiners whose pathology duties may come into conflict with organ donation if collaboration is not fostered) was also identified as critical to achieving a culture of excellence and breakthrough levels of organ donation performance.[14]

Rapid early referrals were recognised as the foundation for other best practices and as directly associated with increased donation rates. The Collaborative also identified early notification to the OPO of a potential donor as essential in order for the OPO to assess donation potential and to

---

[11] Institute for Healthcare Improvement, *Improvement Report: Organ Donation Breakthrough Collaborative*, www.ihi.org.
[12] *Ibid.*   [13] Shafer *et al.*, 'US Organ Donation Breakthrough Collaborative'.   [14] *Ibid.*

increase the OPO's time to interact with potential donor families.[15] The Collaborative recognised management of an integrated donation process as a key component of the change package, based on the finding that the high-performing OPOs and hospitals fostered joint accountability for donation rates by maintaining highly collaborative relationships at all levels.[16] This relationship-building begins with defining roles and responsibilities for the organ donation process and establishing joint expectations and goals. Another important piece of this strategy is maintaining a high degree of communication through after-action reviews of all potential and actual donation cases, to rapidly identify and communicate learning opportunities.

The fourth and final component of the change package, aggressive pursuit of every donation opportunity, is self-evident as an improvement strategy and yet, unless this expectation is explicitly built into the culture of OPOs and hospitals, is difficult to achieve. The Collaborative identified several components of this change concept including early deployment of OPO staff, reapproaches for consent and aggressive efforts for organ placement.[17] The pursuit of donation after cardiac death (DCD) was also identified as a critical component of this change strategy. Systematic efforts to expand DCD practices in the USA will be addressed more specifically later in this chapter.

The Collaborative implemented the concept of the change package in a stepped fashion. Those changes which were expected to achieve the most immediate improvements were called 'first-things-first changes', and participating organisations were encouraged to implement these before moving on to other components of the change package. As the Collaborative matured, other more complex change strategies were identified. These strategies, which cut across concepts, were called 'high-leveraged changes' and were developed through experience and data-driven observations.

Results achieved

The results from the Collaborative intervention were stunning – the number of organ donors in participating hospitals increased by over 14 per cent in the first year, which constituted a 70 per cent greater increase than experienced by non-participating hospitals.[18] These increases were sustained over time with a reported 22.5 per cent increase in organ donors from October 2003, when the Collaborative began, to September 2006.[19]

[15] *Ibid.*   [16] *Ibid.*   [17] *Ibid.*   [18] *Ibid.*   [19] *Ibid.*

Consequently, record numbers of organ transplants occurred within the USA during these time periods. Since 2006, the USA has sustained the gains in donation rates but has not been able to continue the sharp increase in them experienced during the active phase of the Collaborative.[20] The challenge remains within the organ donation and transplant community to continue the unrelenting focus on a culture of improvement without the infrastructure of the government-sponsored Collaborative.

Consent for organ and tissue donation: improvements to law and practice

Consent for organ and tissue donation in the USA is governed by individual state law, creating the possibility of significant variations from state to state. In 1968, the Uniform Anatomical Gift Act (UAGA) was promulgated in an attempt to provide national uniformity to the laws governing organ donation. As with all uniform laws in the USA, the UAGA was drafted by the National Conference of Commissioners of Uniform State Laws (NCCUSL), a non-profit association comprised of commissioners appointed by each state.[21] The first UAGA was subsequently adopted – with some variation – by all fifty states and the District of Columbia.[22] In 1987, NCCUSL amended the UAGA to remain current with significant legal changes that had occurred, especially federal legislation that nationalised the system of allocating organs for transplant in the USA. Although fewer than half of the states enacted the 1987 UAGA, many states have amended the UAGA over time to address specific changes and accommodate modern practices.

New legislation: a revised UAGA

In late 2006, NCCUSL drafted a revised version of the UAGA which was immediately enacted in twenty states in 2007 and passed in an additional twenty in 2008.[23] It is anticipated that all fifty states will have passed the revised UAGA by 2012. The 2006 UAGA is endorsed by ten prominent organisations within the USA, including the American Bar Association and the American Medical Association, and has received bipartisan

---

[20] http://optn.transplant.hrsa.gov/latestData/rptData.asp.
[21] See Uniform Law Commission, www.nccusl.org.
[22] *Ibid.* Table of Jurisdictions wherein Act has been adopted, Uniform Anatomical Gift Act (1968).
[23] See www.nccusl.org/Update/uniformact_factsheets/uniformacts-fs-uaga.asp.

political support as a rational measure to provide the public with easier and more efficient methods to 'say yes' to donation. The 2006 UAGA keeps many of the central legal underpinnings of organ and tissue donation in the USA, including basic gift law principles and the clear authority, which cannot be overruled by family, for an adult to consent to donation prior to death. There are, however, several significant improvements in the 2006 UAGA which have contributed to positive change in daily donation consent practices in those states where the legislation has been adopted.

Defining donor registries

The 2006 UAGA includes several new definitions that facilitate easier consent practices. Most notably, 'donor registries' are defined and specifically recognised.[24] Donor registries are electronic databases, available to OPOs on a twenty-four-hour basis, that provide a legally valid mechanism for individuals to consent to donation by making a binding anatomical gift prior to death. The successful implementation of donor registries in the USA as a strategy to increase consent will be discussed in more detail below.

Expanded list of those who can authorise donation

The 2006 UAGA also aids increased opportunities for organ donation by expanding the list of those who can authorise donation if a patient dies without having made an anatomical gift. The new law now includes: an agent appointed under a healthcare proxy; adult grandchildren; grandparents; and an adult who exhibited special care and concern for the deceased and who is familiar with his or her personal values.[25] The addition of these new categories of donation decision-makers, particularly healthcare proxy agents, is likely to make the donation process more consistent with hospital policies on healthcare decisions when a patient is not capable of providing consent. By expanding the list of those who can authorise donation, the law seeks to reduce the circumstances where a potential donor is identified but the donation cannot move forward because there is no legally recognised donation decision-maker.

---

[24] Uniform Anatomical Gift Act §2 (2006).
[25] Uniform Anatomical Gift Act §9(a) (2006).

Majority rule

Previous versions of the UAGA provided that one person in a 'class' could veto an anatomical gift made by another member of the class. This meant that in families where two of three siblings strongly favoured donation, a single dissenting veto disrupted the family consensus and the ability to move forward with donation. For many such families, the concept of a single-member veto runs counter to their sense of fairness and can cause discord among family members. Addressing this issue, the 2006 UAGA establishes that a majority of the members of a class who are reasonably available may make a gift, where there is more than one member of a class.[26] This legal change is expected to ease family consent discussions and increase the opportunity for donation.

Conflicting advance directives

The 2006 UAGA is not completely without controversy. Section 21 of the model Act attempts to address the tension that could exist in a case where there is both an advance directive instructing the withdrawal or withholding of life support, as well as consent for donation. The potential conflict arises from the need for maintenance of life support until the donated organs are recovered. The original 2006 UAGA stated that in such circumstances, ventilator support could be maintained in order to facilitate donation; this stance caused significant debate among bioethicists and others.[27] The concern raised was whether it was appropriate, as a matter of law and policy, to assume that donation trumps an individual's advanced directive regarding withdrawal of ventilator support. Ultimately, the Uniform Commissioners responded to the critique by revising the section to require that parties look toward the patient's intent to resolve any potential conflict between the decision to donate and such an advance directive.[28] If the patient's intent cannot be discerned or agreed upon, a conflict resolution procedure is outlined in the law. Although this is likely to arise only on rare occasions, the new law is intended to facilitate donation as consistent with other end-of-life directives. This provision is also understood to support systematic efforts to increase DCD opportunities.

---

[26] Uniform Anatomical Gift Act §9(b) (2006).

[27] R. Stein, 'States revising organ-donation law: critics fear measure may not go far enough to protect donors', *Washington Post*, 4 April 2007, A01.

[28] See www.anatomicalgiftact.org, Amended Section 21.

Full faith and credit from state to state

Because the laws governing organ and tissue donation in the USA are state rather than federal laws, jurisdictional issues can arise when an individual registered as a donor in one state dies in another (the law of the state in which the donation will be co-ordinated prevails). To address this issue, the 2006 UAGA clarifies that a donation which is valid where executed is valid in the state where the individual dies.[29] This provision is expected to improve organ donation rates in cross-state cases.

Establishing donor rights and registries

Another recent measure designed to improve organ donation rates in the USA is the proliferation of donor registries. Successful donor registries allow people to designate themselves as donors in a manner that is both legally recognised and readily available to the healthcare and procurement professionals who may perform the donation.

Changing consent practices

The UAGA has always authorised an adult to make a 'gift' of organs and tissues upon death without requiring further family consent or permitting family to override that gift. Despite strong law, fear of litigation or negative publicity has thwarted recognition of an individual's right to choose donation and driven the past practice in the USA of always obtaining family consent. There are, however, no reported cases in the USA of a family suing healthcare or donation professionals for recovering organs and tissues, over the family's objection, from an individual who, prior to his or her death, had made a valid donation under the law. Moreover, the UAGA provides legal immunity for those professionals who act in good faith in performing organ and tissue donations.[30] The courts have repeatedly upheld this liability protection.[31]

---

[29] Uniform Anatomical Gift Act §19 (2006).

[30] See section 18 of the 2006 UAGA: 'A person that acts in accordance with this chapter or with the applicable anatomical gift law of another state or attempts in good faith to do so is not liable for the act in a civil action, criminal prosecution or administrative proceeding.' Both the 1968 and the 1987 UAGAs have similar provisions.

[31] See *Carey* v. *New England Organ Bank, Inc.*, 843 NE 2d 1070 (Mass. 2006); *Schembre* v. *Mid America Transplant Ass'n*, 135 SW 3d 527 (Mo. App. 2004); *Ramirez* v. *Health Partners of Southern Arizona*, 972 P 2d 658 (Ariz. App. 1999); *Kelly-Nevils* v. *Detroit Receiving Hosp.*, 526 NW 2d 15 (Mich. App. 1995); and *Nicoletta* v. *Rochester Eye & Human Parts Bank, Inc.*, 519 NYS 2d 928 (1987).

Donor registries as an electronic donor card

Deferring to families may also have become standard practice because previous versions of the UAGA limited an individual's options to document a gift through either a donor card or will – but these items are rarely found within the critically short timeframe required for a donation to proceed. To advance donation, the law needed to expand the legally recognised ways in which a person could 'gift' organs and tissues. The concept behind donor registries is simple: people who designate themselves as donors are entered into an electronic database of individuals who have consented to organ and tissue donation upon death. The new UAGA (and the vast majority of state laws) now recognise inclusion in the donor registry as the legal equivalent of signing an electronic donor card. With legal consent for donation already secured, the need for family consent – the primary donation-rate limiting factor – is removed.

The vast majority of donor registries in the USA are established through each state's Department of Motor Vehicles (DMV), where individuals apply for and renew their driving licence. The DMV forms for licensure include a simple option for the individual to be added to the state Donor Registry. The DMVs then upload the lists of individuals who designated donation to a secure web-based registry. The advantage of establishing donor registries through the DMVs is that millions of people go through the process on an annual basis. This creates a large-scale captive audience to which the opportunity for donation is presented. The DMVs, however, only reach the segment of the populace that drives – approximately 67 per cent of the resident US population.[32] More importantly, the mission of increasing organ donation is not a priority or goal of the DMVs, which makes it difficult to ensure that positive donation messages are disseminated to the public at the point of potential donor registration.

To address these concerns, OPOs have begun partnering with DMVs to educate and train personnel on the critical importance of increasing organ donation. OPOs are also establishing independent web-based donor registries which provide an opportunity for direct donation sign-up over the internet. These donor registries must meet certain standards under the applicable UAGA. Some of the web-based registries are completely paperless, employing instant identity verification technology used by the banking industry. The advantage of these independent web-based donor registries is that they can provide far more information about organ donation at the point where donation decisions are being made than is possible through the DMVs. They also provide an available donor registry

---

[32] www-fars.nhtsa.dot.gov/Main/index.aspx.

opportunity at any time, rather than that limited to a driver's licence renewal cycle, which is usually every five years. The proliferation of web-based donor registries in the USA is expected to greatly increase the effectiveness of marketing and public education campaigns, which are now able to deliver a 'sign up now' message, rather than reminding the public to register as donors when they renew a licence. At the time of hospital referral, OPOs search all applicable donor registries to confirm whether the potential donor had authorised an anatomical gift. The OPO's identification of a potential organ donor (from a medical perspective) as a registered donor greatly facilitates successful organ donation by eliminating the family consent hurdle.

In 2007, Donate Life America, an independent non-profit organisation, launched a donor registry collaborative to identify best practices, and measure and improve donor designation rates nationwide. The collaborative pulled together strategic leaders from OPOs and DMVs in order to focus on how best to increase donor designation on a state-by-state basis. As of 28 August 2009, there were 83.7 million registered donors in the USA, representing 27.5 per cent of the US population.[33] This marked an approximate 21 per cent increase from 69.3 million in 2007.[34] The percentage of registered donors in the general population appears generally to reflect the number of actual recovered-organ donors identified through a donor registry. For the second quarter of 2009, for example, 28.1 per cent of actual recovered-organ donors were in a donor registry and 31.9 per cent of actual recovered-tissue donors.[35]

It is very difficult to measure what impact donor registries have had on actual organ donation rates thus far. There are several reasons for this. First, the rise of donor registries in the USA coincided with the Collaborative initiative. Second, with multiple changing variables it is difficult to identify a causative relationship between donor registration and increased donation rates: although the number of actual donors, where donation was authorised through a donor registry, can be measured, it is unclear whether these registered donors would have nonetheless become actual donors through family consent, if they had not registered. In other words, do donor registrations increase actual donation rates, or allow facilitation of donations that would have occurred regardless? For this reason, in order to see a dramatic impact on the rate of actual donors, it is expected that the donor registry rates as a percentage of population

---

[33] Data provided by Donate Life America as part of the Donor Designation Collaborative, presented 28 August 2009.
[34] *Ibid.*   [35] *Ibid.*

need to exceed the expected donation rate, which for 2008 hovered at around 66 per cent.[36]

Increasing organ donation after cardiac death

Donation after cardiac death (DCD), a subset of deceased donation, occurs when the donor's death has been declared on the basis of cardio-pulmonary criteria, rather than the neurological criteria used to declare brain death. DCD accounted for 9.8 per cent of all deceased donors in 2007.[37] It has the official support of the Institute of Medicine, which issued reports endorsing DCD practices in 1997 and again in 2000.[38] Nonetheless, DCD raises a number of ethical and procedural clinical concerns because it involves the voluntary withdrawal of life-sustaining measures from a patient who has suffered severe brain injury but is not dead, and the immediate recovery of donated organs after the patient is declared dead.

A basic tenet of organ donation is the 'dead donor rule': the donation of organs for transplantation may not cause the death of a donor.[39] A complicating factor in DCD is that there is a planned withdrawal of care with the expectation that the patient will die shortly thereafter. In order to ensure that the dead donor rule is adhered to in DCD cases, the patient or family must make the decision to withdraw or withhold life-sustaining treatment before there is a discussion regarding the potential for organ donation. This procedure is designed to protect the withdrawal of care decision from being inappropriately influenced by the organ donation decision.[40]

One of the main principles in DCD protocols is the careful avoidance of any real, perceived or potential conflict of interest that could occur between the physician who attends the potential donor at death (whose

---

[36] National 'crude donation rate' calculated as organ donors per one hundred eligible deaths. Data provided by SRTR at www.ustransplant.org.

[37] See www.ustransplant.org/annual_reports/current/201_don-non-hr-beat_dc.htm. See also R. Steinbrook, 'Organ donation after cardiac death', *Journal of the American Medical Association*, 357 (2007), 209–13.

[38] Institute of Medicine, *Non-Heart-Beating Organ Transplantation: Medical and Ethical Issues in Procurement* (Washington, DC: National Academy Press, 1998); Institute of Medicine, *Non-Heart-Beating Organ Transplantation: Practice and Protocols* (Washington, DC: National Academy Press, 2000).

[39] 'Report of a National Conference on Donation after Cardiac Death', *American Journal of Transplantation*, 6 (2006), 281–91, 281 (citing J. Robertson, 'The dead donor rule', *Hastings Center Report*, 29 (1999), 6–14).

[40] *Ibid.*, 282: 'The decision to withdraw or withhold treatment should be made on its own merit, with the patient's physician having established the futility of any further treatment, and not for the purpose of organ donation.'

primary responsibility is the dying patient), and the organ recovery and transplant teams (whose primary responsibilities are recovering organs and transplanting recipients). This potential conflict must be carefully managed to avoid any appearance that the donation in any way hastened or caused the donor's death. While this potential conflict exists in all organ donations, it is particularly visible in DCD cases because withdrawal of life-sustaining care, pronouncement of death, and recovery of organs all take place within a brief period of time.[41] Some minimally invasive measures to preserve the organs for transplant may even take place prior to withdrawal of care, before the potential donor is dead. The complex issues raised by the DCD process prompted UNOS to issue rules and standards regarding DCD. Laws governing death declarations and donation also provide applicable legal requirements.

Legal considerations regarding DCD in the USA

The Uniform Determination of Death Act was promulgated in 1980 and has been passed in one form or another in all fifty states and the District of Columbia.[42] The statutory language defines death as '(1) irreversible cessation of circulatory and respiratory functions, or (2) irreversible cessation of all functions of the entire brain, including the brain stem'.[43] In DCD cases, the potential donor is declared dead after a physician determines that there is an irreversible loss of circulatory and respiratory function. 'Irreversible' can be interpreted to mean that loss of circulatory and respiratory function is 'permanent' in cases of withdrawal of care (whether DCD cases or outside of donation) because there will be no attempt to resuscitate respiratory or circulatory function in that patient.[44]

To address the issue of a potential conflict, the 2006 UAGA draws a strict line between the physician who declares a potential donor dead and the physicians who participate in removing or transplanting the donor's organs: 'Neither the physician who attends the decedent at death nor the physician who determines the time of the decedent's death may participate in the procedures for removing or transplanting a part from the decedent.'[45] The concern that a physician would, acting in the interest of a potential transplant recipient, hasten or cause a potential donor's

---

[41] Institute of Medicine, *Practice and Protocols.* For example, heparin may be administered to prevent clotting, and in rare cases, catheters may be placed in large arteries and veins to facilitate the rapid infusion of organ-preservation solutions after death. See also n. 40 *ibid.*

[42] Uniform Anatomical Gift Act (1980), available at www.nccusl.org. [43] *Ibid.*

[44] J. Bernat, 'The whole-brain concept of death remains optimum public policy', *Journal of Law, Medicine and Ethics*, 34 (2006), 35–43. See also Chapter 16.

[45] Uniform Anatomical Gift Act §14(i) (2006).

death is perhaps the main concern in DCD, and one that is addressed by UNOS policy as well.

UNOS's 2007 policy requirements and model elements

In a clear effort to increase DCD activity as a strategy to maximise organ donation potential, UNOS policy requires that DCD protocols address the 'Model Elements for Controlled DCD Recovery Protocols' which became effective in 2007.[46] The model elements outline:

1. donor candidate selection;
2. consent by next of kin;
3. procedures for withdrawal of life-sustaining measures;
4. pronouncement of death;
5. organ recovery; and
6. financial considerations.

Under the UNOS model elements, a suitable DCD candidate is a patient who has a 'non-recoverable and irreversible neurological injury resulting in ventilator dependency but not fulfilling brain death criteria'.[47] Assessment of whether a patient is a suitable candidate is to be conducted in collaboration with the hospital's affiliated OPO and the patient's primary healthcare team.[48] An important consideration in the assessment is whether death is likely to occur after the withdrawal of life-sustaining measures within the short timeframe that allows organ donation to proceed.[49]

In addition to consent for organ donation, the UNOS model elements specifically require documented consent from next of kin for withdrawal of care and any pre-mortem procedures or drug administration intended to facilitate the DCD.[50] This is to ensure that there is a separate consent process for the withdrawal of care from that of the authorisation for donation. If the potential DCD donor is on a donor registry, the family or healthcare decision-maker would need to consent to the withdrawal of care, but legal authorisation for donation already exists. The result of these measures is that DCD activity has steadily increased from 391 DCD donors in 2004 (representing 5.5 per cent of all deceased donors in that year) to 793 DCD donors in 2007 (representing 9.8 per cent of all deceased donors in that year). This marks an increase of over 100 per cent

---

[46] Attachment III to Appendix B of the UNOS Bylaws, 23 March 2007.
[47] *Ibid.*, Part A.1.   [48] *Ibid.*, Part A.4.
[49] *Ibid.*, Part A.5. Evidence-based clinical judgement should be used to assess whether cardiac death will likely occur within a period of two hours after the withdrawal of life support. See 'Report of a National Conference', 282.
[50] Attachment III to Appendix B of the UNOS Bylaws, 23 March 2007, Part B.1.

in DCD activity over the 4-year period. It is expected that DCD experience will continue to increase as a significant strategy to increase overall organ donation rates in the USA.

Increasing living donation

Living donation has gained a significant place in the field of donation for transplant: 44 per cent of all organ transplants in the USA since 1988 have come from living donors.[51] With approximately 6,000 living donor transplants per year, there is an increased legal and regulatory focus on living organ donation and the innovative programmes that have emerged to maximise the benefits of this new trend to those awaiting transplant. Some legal concerns have been raised in the USA regarding the potential conflict of interest the transplant surgeon faces with respect to preserving the best interests of the living donor, while simultaneously fulfilling a legal fiduciary duty to the transplant recipient. A recent lawsuit highlights this potential conflict and liability that can result when the recipient transplant surgeon provides care to, or is involved in screening, the living donor.[52] The case involved a claim by the living donor against the recipient's transplant surgeon. The court held that a patient-physician relationship existed between the living donor and the recipient's transplant surgeon; accordingly, the plaintiff's malpractice claim that the defendant negligently induced the plaintiff to donate a kidney could proceed. In an effort to address some of the legal concerns surrounding living donation, new regulatory standards and guidelines have been developed.

New regulatory standards

In 2007, UNOS approved new guidelines on living organ donor consent.[53] The purpose of these guidelines is to protect living donors while supporting significant increases to living donation experienced in the USA. Two of the most important issues identified in the guidelines are a requirement that the donor is willing to donate free from inducement or coercion, and the need for a psychological evaluation of the potential donor by a mental health professional. The guidelines also suggest that the potential donor should be offered a general non-specific statement of unsuitability if he or she does not wish to proceed with donation

---

[51] Based on current OPTN data: see www.unos.org.
[52] *Montalto et al.* v. *Stoff et al.*, MA Sup. Ct CA NO. 03–00557 (2007).
[53] UNOS *Resource Document for Informed Consent of Living Donors*, 18 September 2007: see www.unos.org.

(e.g. provide the potential living donor with an acceptable excuse for his or her family and friends). In addition to these UNOS guidelines, the new regulations that apply to transplant centres also provide standards for living donor programmes, which include the requirement that the donor receive psychological screening, and that the programme establishes living donor selection criteria that are consistent with the general principles of medical ethics.[54]

Paired exchange programmes

Kidney paired donation (KPD) programmes have emerged as an innovative way to maximise living donor transplants in the USA. The idea behind KPD programmes is that biologically incompatible but willing donors can help their loved ones or friends receive a living donor kidney by matching one incompatible donor/recipient pair with another incompatible pair. The donors then exchange kidneys with a recipient of the other pair with whom they are compatible (see Figure 13.1).

Multiple incompatible pairs can also be matched for a 'chain' of paired exchanges. This has resulted in simultaneous exchanges involving up to sixteen patients and eight kidney transplants.[55] Paired donation benefits those awaiting kidney transplant by either removing patients from the waiting list or avoiding the need for patients to be listed in the first place. In this manner, all kidney transplant candidates benefit from KPD because it increases access to organs.

An identified legal concern has been whether exchange of kidneys in the USA violates the National Organ Transplant Act (NOTA). Originally enacted in 1984, NOTA contains a federal criminal prohibition

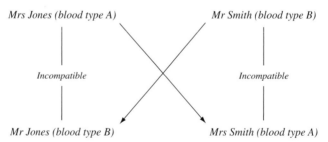

Figure 13.1 Example of kidney paired donation exchange

[54] 42 CFR §482.90(b).
[55] At www.hopkinsmedicine.org/Press_releases/2009/07_07_09.html.

precluding the provision or acquisition of organs 'for valuable consideration'.[56] The issue has been whether the exchange of donated kidneys from living donor pairs involves 'valuable consideration' in violation of NOTA. UNOS has maintained that KPD does not implicate NOTA because 'valuable consideration' is properly interpreted to mean a monetary transfer or sale transaction and not the emotional or psychological benefit which may be derived from paired donation.[57] Using the example above, UNOS and others have argued that the intent of NOTA's prohibition was not to prohibit the 'benefit' Mrs Jones experiences in knowing that by donating to Mrs Smith, Mr Jones would receive a kidney from Mr Smith. Rather, NOTA was concerned with prohibiting Mrs Jones from selling her kidney to Mrs Smith. In 2007, the US Attorney General's Office released an official opinion that KPD programmes were not in violation of NOTA.[58] These legal positions created an opportunity for federal legislation to clarify the Act.

On 21 December 2007, the 'Charlie W. Norwood Living Organ Donation Act' was signed into law, amending NOTA by specifically defining paired donations as outside of 'valuable consideration'. These recent legal developments are expected to pave the way for construction of a national KPD programme for living donors in the USA. Recently UNOS selected several KPD programmes to participate in a pilot programme. These plans have been on hold, however, pending resolution of lingering concerns as to whether KPD programmes adequately protect living organ donors.

Conclusion

Over the last ten years, the USA has experienced dramatic increases in organ donation and transplantation rates. The basis for this improvement is multi-factorial but is understood to be founded in the gains created by the Organ Donation Breakthrough Collaborative. To complement that effort, recent changes to the law governing consent to organ donation and the proliferation of effective donor registries hold out the promise of a continuing increase in donation rates. Further efforts to systematically improve donation rates in the USA, such as support for DCD and living donation programmes, have increased total organ donations but have also

---

[56] 42 USC §274e. Penalties for violations include up to US$50,000 in fines or five years in prison.
[57] UNOS *Position Statement: Intended Recipient Donations, Paired Donations and NOTA 301*, 2005: see www.unos.org/publications.
[58] *Memorandum for General Counsel, Department of Health and Human Services: Legality of Alternative Organ Donation Practices Under 42 USC § 274e*, 28 March 2007.

brought a host of ethical and legal concerns. These concerns have been managed primarily through clinical consensus which creates an accepted standard of care, as well as through legislative resolution. While ethical debate remains, the practices have forged ahead, creating sustained gains in organ donation.

The Collaborative approach differs significantly from initiatives introduced in other jurisdictions, which have included significant public policy or legal changes, such as moving to a system of presumed consent. In this regard, the US experience with the Collaborative is distinguishable, as it was able to identify and implement methods for measurably improving organ donation rates without changing fundamental principles underlying the donation and transplantation system. Accordingly, the Collaborative may be of value to other countries as a process model that can achieve system improvement and bring the stakeholders in the donation and transplant system together to achieve meaningful results.

Part V

Current reform and future challenges

14 Negotiating change: organ donation in the United Kingdom

Bobbie Farsides

An ethicist is someone who often finds themself pulled into other people's worlds, sometimes acquiring honorary status and membership, other times remaining very much an outsider. The ethicist serves as a friendly critic, a facilitator, the person who asks the difficult and sometimes inconvenient questions and attempts to resolve some of the challenging dilemmas that people face. In this chapter, I will reflect upon my role as an ethicist in various settings, and the ways in which resolving, or at least acknowledging, ethical issues has become crucial when developing effective strategies and organisational change. I shall also reflect upon how the processes I have been a part of have led me to think about the complex relationship between ethical reflection and public policy-making at a national level. As such this is a very personal piece, the conclusions of which other ethicists may well choose to challenge.

Local first steps

My first significant professional encounter relating to the complex issues around organ donation and transplantation came about because of the dedication of the in-house organ donation co-ordinator at my local hospital, who decided to grasp a particularly prickly nettle that was growing on our patch. A significant difference of opinion had emerged amongst local clinicians regarding the ethics of identifying and caring for people who could potentially go on to become non-heart-beating donors – that is, organ donors who do not become brain dead prior to cardiac death, and whose death is most likely to follow the withholding or withdrawal of medical treatment subsequent to a decision that further treatment is futile. The issues involved in this donation pathway are complex, and many would say unresolved, but in the face of significant scarcity of donor organs it was important to face the issues, and at least see what, if anything, could be done to facilitate such donations locally.

An excellent meeting ensued, well-attended by clinicians from the intensive care unit (ICU), emergency medicine and renal care. Frank

215

discussions took place, and a major outcome of the day was the demonstration that people with profoundly different views regarding ethically sensitive issues can have a sensible and productive discussion when the right environment is created. As a newcomer to some of the issues discussed, I was struck by the fact that there was clearly a lot of 'ethics work' that needed to be done in order to ensure that the professionals involved were comfortable to facilitate certain forms of organ donation. In common with others I had tended to focus on the idea of encouraging the public to donate more organs as the way to boost transplantation, on the assumption that more willing organ donors would, without further problem, lead to more transplants. This was a form of reductionism that I had not yet recognised as such. Willingness to donate is of course crucially important, but so too is willingness to 'retrieve'.

The impact of professional differences of opinion on donation and transplantation activity should not have surprised me given my longstanding research interest in the beliefs and moral attitudes of healthcare professionals operating in ethically contentious areas of medicine. In the course of our work my collaborators and I have discovered, for example, that some stem cell scientists have strong moral views regarding whence they should obtain human gametes and embryos for use in scientific research. This in turn means that for some a willingness to donate may not be enough to ensure that the individual stem cell scientist feels ethically comfortable in accepting the embryo; other factors may need to be taken into account.[1] In another project we discovered that clinicians in the field of ante-natal screening and testing can struggle with whether or not to give parents information about their unborn child, when the meaning of that information is unclear and the clinician cannot be sure how it will be utilised; the fear being that the woman concerned will make a choice the clinicians consider morally unjustified by the facts as known.[2]

How clinicians think and feel about the work they do is documented and analysed far less than the views of patients or service users in the increasingly consumerist National Health Service (NHS). Yet, in order to understand fully the obstacles to delivering a good service in any sphere it is important to understand the motivations and impediments

[1] A. Cribb, S. Wainwright, C. Williams *et al.*, 'Towards the applied: the construction of ethical positions in stem cell translational research', *Medicine, Health Care and Philosophy*, 11 (2008), 351–61.

[2] C. Williams, P. Alderson and B. Farsides, 'Dilemmas encountered by health care practitioners offering nuchal translucency screening: a qualitative case study', *Prenatal Diagnosis*, 22 (2002), 216–20; B. Farsides, P. Alderson and C. Williams, 'Aiming towards "moral equilibrium": health care professionals' views on working within the morally contested field of antenatal screening', *Journal of Medical Ethics*, 30 (2004), 505–9.

of those who carry out the labour required to make it happen. Either explicitly and consciously, or implicitly and subconsciously, the moral attitudes of healthcare professionals can shape the services they provide both locally and nationally. This can be true at both an individual and a professional level.

It is therefore extremely important to remember from the outset that in the context of organ donation and transplantation there is the potential for those involved to feel conflicted over a number of different complex moral issues relating to the recruitment and treatment of donors and the selection and treatment of recipients. Each of these issues can often present as a moral conflict of duties, be it between the patient as patient and as potential donor, or the potential donor and another potential recipient of care. Whatever the exact circumstance, the possibilities for discomfort are real and significant, and what one hears from clinicians working in ICU, emergency medicine or any other part of the hospital must remain with the ethicist if and when they go to work in different arenas.

Going national

Shortly after this local meeting I was invited to join the Department of Health's Organ Donation Taskforce, (the Taskforce), which had been established in December 2006. Its terms of reference were to identify barriers to organ donation and transplantation and recommend solutions within existing operational and legal frameworks; and to identify barriers to any part of the transplant process and recommend ways to overcome them in order to support and improve transplant rates.[3] When outlining the expertise of its 'wide-ranging' membership, the Taskforce's final report states that 'an academic ethicist joined the Taskforce after two meetings'.[4] This is an interestingly specific observation, the possible suggestion being that an ethicist had not initially been seen as a key member, but the business of the first two meetings revealed the need for one. I would argue that after two meetings it did indeed become clear that some of the obstacles the Taskforce needed to remove were to do with ethical uncertainty and disagreement, and a first step towards addressing them would be to acknowledge and clearly articulate them within the Taskforce. I think it was also clear that some of these disagreements or concerns were not raised from outside the transplant world, but rather were issues for

---

[3] Organ Donation Taskforce, *Organs for Transplants: a Report from the Organ Donation Taskforce* (London: Department of Health, 2008), p. 54.
[4] *Ibid.*, p. 20.

those whose everyday work was crucial to a successful system being developed. The Taskforce sets out the substance of this all-important second meeting early on in their final report, which states:

> The second topic discussed at the meeting concerned legal and ethical concerns. These were eloquently expressed by clinicians responsible for the care of patients who had the potential to become organ donors. They focused principally on the steps that could be taken to facilitate donation after death, particularly donation after cardiac death, and on the potential for an actual or perceived conflict of interests, together with concern about the ambiguity of the law relating to some of the procedures that are involved.[5]

It was against the background of these concerns that the work needed to be done, and looking forward the Taskforce acknowledged the need for ongoing engagement with ethical issues, Recommendation 3 of its final report stating:

> Urgent attention is required to resolve outstanding legal, ethical and professional issues in order to ensure that all clinicians are supported and are able to work within a clear and unambiguous framework of good practice. Additionally an independent UK-wide Donation Ethics Group should be established.[6]

Essentially, ethics was to become part of a structural and organisational solution to the problem of organ shortage. Alongside the practical and far-reaching changes proposed by the Taskforce (to be funded by the United Kingdom (UK) government) comes an explicit acknowledgement of the importance of offering ongoing support to clinicians facing ethical concerns which could in turn become the type of obstacle to donation the Taskforce was charged to remove.

The obstacles

In the absence of major advances in the development of artificial organs or stem cell and regenerative medicine, transplantation relies on the availability of good-quality organs from living or deceased donors. As in other areas of medicine such as assisted reproduction, this builds a vulnerability into the system – a supply factor that will not necessarily be responsive to, or well-matched with, demand. In the absence of a market-based system which balances supply and demand through manipulations in price, we are reliant upon the goodwill of those who donate their organs during life or after death. The British public regularly declare their support for organ donation in principle, with polls often quoting positive responses at around 90 per cent.[7] However, the

---

[5] *Ibid.*, p. 30.   [6] *Ibid.*, p. 33.   [7] *Ibid.*, p. 5.

important issue is whether these statements of support translate into actions which in any way boost the supply of organs available for transplant. Sadly this is not the case, and one of the first challenges facing the Taskforce was to understand the factors that might intervene to prevent positive attitudes regarding donation translating into successful transplants. In many respects closing the gap between donations made and transplants required will rely on the work of clinicians, psychologists, sociologists and cultural interpreters as opposed to ethicists. Ultimately the skill of educators and publicists, advertising executives and media commentators will also have an important part to play. Therefore, without wishing to minimise the importance of understanding why people find it difficult to donate or why they don't think it important enough to do so, I shall not discuss that issue here.

Research carried out by both the Taskforce and the UK House of Lords European Affairs Sub-Committee clearly demonstrated that moral objections to donation were unlikely to be accurately or legitimately based on religious objections.[8] Indeed the vast majority of religious groups were keen to define the decision to donate as an issue of individual conscience, and where an official line was stated it tended to be positive, emphasising the worth of altruistic gifting. Some religious groups were concerned at the definitions of death utilised in the context of donation, specifically brain stem death,[9] and the importance of this issue was acknowledged and addressed in recently published and updated UK guidance on the issue.[10]

Individuals will decide whether or not to donate their organs for transplant after their death on the basis of their own beliefs, attitudes and values. Given the almost universal agreement that it is a good thing to do, the ethicist does not need to engage in discussions of why people should be donating – the facts speak for themselves. On this occasion, the psychologist will be better placed to provide a relevant account of the gap between belief and action than the philosopher. What the ethicist can be involved with is discussions concerning what action can be taken in the face of a lack of altruistic donation, and of what action can be taken to ensure that a donation once made translates into a transplant. Both issues bear ethical scrutiny and some degree of ethical 'push'.

---

[8] House of Lords European Union Committee, *Increasing the Supply of Donor Organs within the European Union*, 17th Report of Session 2007–08, Volume 1: Report, HL Paper 123–I (London: The Stationery Office, 2008), pp. 66–71.

[9] *Ibid.*, p. 67.

[10] Academy of Medical Royal Colleges, *A Code of Practice for the Diagnosis and Confirmation of Death* (London: Academy of Medical Royal Colleges, 2008).

The ethicist's role

My colleague, Professor John Harris, who is also a contributor to this book, once said to a group of enthusiastic social scientists who wanted, as he saw it, to run yet another survey on what people did in an ethically challenging context: 'I'm a philosopher, I'm not interested in what people do, I'm interested in what they *ought* to do.' Clearly an ethicist can have an empirical interest in whether or not people do the right thing, indeed it would seem odd not to, but he or she could reasonably be *more* interested in establishing what the right thing to do is in a given set of circumstances. However, in the context of a public body charged with developing policy options this question might already have been resolved, and the issue becomes one of strategy, and later, implementation. Given that the Organ Donation Taskforce had been set up with the express purpose of increasing donation rates, the ethical question of whether this is what ought to be done should be assumed to have been resolved to the satisfaction of those now coming together to make it happen.

It is rare to have almost universal agreement that a goal is a good one to pursue, unless of course it is so generic as to be benignly meaningless without further qualification. We can say that we want the world to be a better place and people to be happier, but the interesting work then begins in terms of defining what that means in practice. It is easier perhaps to discuss the outcomes that individuals and societies wish to avoid, suffering and premature death being clear and obvious examples. In discussing organ donation, we feel confident in bringing these two forms of evaluation together and in saying that we can avoid tangible forms of suffering by providing someone with a new organ; can avoid or at least substantially postpone death; and can release people from a life that restricts their access to many forms of human flourishing. Organ transplantation is seen as one of the great advances of modern medicine and few if any would argue against the idea that a developed economy seeking to meet the healthcare needs of its citizens should support the practice culturally, economically and politically.

Having said this, transplantation is only one small element of the portfolio of healthcare interventions available to the cash-strapped NHS. It is crucial therefore that those of us immersed in addressing the challenge of increasing rates of organ donation and transplantation acknowledge and take true cognisance of the fact that others are pursuing equally worthwhile goals which transplantation-related activities could be seen to disrupt. In a broader sense, as a society we also need to be comfortable that the steps we take in the interest of increasing donation rates are consistent with our values as expressed in other and maybe wider contexts. Acknowledgement of these tensions becomes particularly important when developing guidance and policy that could have an impact on professional groups and individuals who do not see donation as their core activity, but whose work must be part of a successful system of donation.

Whatever the context, an ethicist looking at why people fail to do something they identify as a good thing can legitimately look at how this happens in terms of issues such as weakness of will or the problem of moral motivation. They can also question whether altruism is an appropriate driver if a good is not delivered to a sufficient degree by altruistic impulses. It is perhaps less appropriate for an ethicist alone to make claims about the specific beliefs and attitudes that might intrude to disrupt good intentions around donation – fear of death, concerns about bodily integrity, religious and cultural prohibitions. This is the work of psychologists, sociologists and social anthropologists, and happily there is a respectable body of empirical work that demonstrates the substantial issues that exist in this regard.

It is crucially important, however, having established that people ought to be doing something, for ethicists to look at available strategies which seek to encourage, or maybe even require, people to do that thing, thereby closing any gap between expressed approval and action. An ethicist needs to assess whether all routes are open to pursue a particular good, or whether the end, however worthy, does not in itself justify some available means of achieving it. It is also important, as suggested at the outset, to consider the pursuit of any particular goal in the context of other morally relevant goals with which it may not always be consistent. Thus, in broad-brush terms the job of the ethicist is to confirm the moral value of the goal in question; assess the ethical acceptability of the means proposed to reach that goal; address the tensions that might arise as a result of the need to pursue competing goals; and help to address ethical issues identified by those who will be required to 'do the work' – as donors and donor families, as members of the transplant community and as policy-makers.

An interesting example of how complicated this final task can become arose when, towards the end of the Taskforce's work, the Chief Medical Officer for England, Sir Liam Donaldson, suggested that the Taskforce should go beyond its original brief of considering solutions available within the current legal framework, and consider the idea of shifting to an opt-out system of donation.[11] Here was a classic instance of there being a possible solution to a problem (in this case scarcity of organs)

[11] Department of Health, *2006 Annual Report of the Chief Medical Officer: on the State of Public Health* (London: Department of Health, 2007), pp. 26–33.

which, if effective, would result in an increase in benefit and removal of suffering. However, given the fundamental nature of the change being proposed, even if the empirical evidence suggested that such an increase would follow, the wider costs of moving away from established practice would need to be assessed, as would the integrity of the resulting system. Ethicists clearly needed to be part of this process, and the Taskforce was quick to establish an ethics sub-group.[12]

Historically, we have shown preference for an express consent model within the UK healthcare system, but this is not in itself a reason to reject a change. In the context of organ donation and transplantation, the consent model has been challenged from a number of angles. Some would argue that clicking a computer mouse and thereby joining the NHS Organ Donor Register is not consent as we would define and recognise it in other settings. We have no evidence of the person having informed themselves before making the decision, and we have reason to believe that some of the issues that most trouble those who have a good understanding of transplant processes are invisible or unknown to the average would-be donor. In a sense the person signing up to donation may not know what to worry about beyond the clichéd and discredited concerns about organs being taken in an untimely manner, or personal worries about mutilation or disruption of cultural norms and practices. Few, if any, donors inform themselves of the details of organ donation and therefore some of the ethical issues clinicians debate are invisible to those consenting to become donors.

In common with some other types of medical decision-making, the potential gap between deciding to donate and one's death leads to the standard worries about advance decisions and how to factor in the expression of a wish made perhaps twenty years ago, especially when a family might now be contradicting it, or at least casting doubt over its enduring nature. The law in England, for example, in the form of the Human Tissue Act 2004, does not give the family a legal right to override a person's stated wish to donate, but clinical practice and custom clearly indicate that ultimately a family veto will be upheld. Thus, even where someone has informed themselves, made a conscious decision and acted to ensure it is recorded, they may not be able to do that which they have consented to. So, again, consent does not seem to do the work intended of it.

The ethicist can engage and to some extent facilitate the debate around consent to donation, but the important thing to remember is that the issue

---

[12] Organ Donation Taskforce, *The Potential Impact of an Opt Out System for Organ Donation in the UK: an Independent Report from the Organ Donation Taskforce*, Annex D, Ethics (Working Group Report) (London: Department of Health, 2008), www.dh.gov.uk/prod_consum_dh/groups/dh_digitalassets/@dh/@en/documents/digitalasset/dh_090307.pdf.

at stake is a practical and pressing one, and the goal is public policy change and effective intervention. In rejecting any option put forward, the next step must be to explore and hopefully develop alternative strategies. This is why the work done in the second stage of the Taskforce's project, which led to a rejection of an opt-out system in the short-term,[13] had to be followed up by work to reconsider consent in this setting, concentrating on what could be done to increase donation whilst remaining true to broader moral commitments relating to justice and fairness, choice and individual autonomy.

Consent matters for many different reasons. It is rare, if not completely unknown, for a clinician to be so driven by the imperative to increase organ donation that they can put to one side the need for a meaningful statement of consent or authorisation, be it from a living donor or their family after death. If a donor has consented, then a clinician can feel secure in the belief that what is subsequently done to that person in order to facilitate donation is done with their permission; and in their best interests, as it is done in order to fulfil their wishes. If a donor has consented, their family can similarly understand that what happens on the basis of this consent is something that their loved one wanted and signed up to. Uncertainty is a significant impediment to successful donation, and, as such, an obstacle that the Taskforce sought to remove. However, one also has to acknowledge that certainty regarding the status of consent could require the offer of information that would lead to some individuals deciding that donation is not something they wish to pursue.

Negotiating change

Getting the issue of consent right in the context of deceased organ donation will require an ongoing commitment to creative thinking and negotiation. Having decided that an opt-out system sets the bar too low, we have to be mindful of the risks and attendant costs of setting the bar too high. It is not a heresy to say that given the importance of this issue what we are looking for is a consent system that is 'good enough'. However, we also need to be open to the empirical claim that what counts as consent at present is not consent as we would generally define it in a medical setting. The political philosopher John Plamenatz, when writing about consent in the context of political obligations and voting, stated at the outset:

If then the final definition appears so narrow as to make it appear that no actual government ever acts with the consent of all its subjects, and very seldom with the

---

[13] *Ibid.*

consent of even a majority of them, it is not permissible, for that reason, to conclude that the definition is wrong. For the mere fact that we find ourselves obliged to accept certain unpleasant conclusions is not of itself an indication of the falseness of our premises.[14]

As an ethicist who was part of a group that rejected the opt-out model it was incumbent upon me to keep thinking about and engaging with the issue. As a member of the new UK Donation Ethics Committee[15] and the recently formed NHS Blood and Transplant Working Party on consent, I shall be required to translate these thoughts into proposals for action. I shall also be required to work in a way that makes my ethical concerns and proposals fit with practical reality, and the clinicians I work alongside will need to consider whether or not they can adapt their practices and attitudes to work successfully within whatever consent regime emerges from the process. No-one will forget that the ultimate goal is to do more good and reduce suffering by increasing organ donation rates and facilitating more transplants.

The word 'compromise' does not have a positive ring in the philosophical world in which I grew up, and so I avoid it here. Instead, we need to understand the task as one of negotiation towards an agreed solution. The goal of increasing organ donation has been accepted as ethically sound by those who are working together to achieve it. Those who doubt the virtue of increasing organ donation and transplantation rates are few and far between, and the arguments they would want to have will be substantially different in kind. Those of us who want to see more lives saved may nonetheless continue to debate the best and most ethically acceptable ways of doing this, but the debate should be characterised by flexibility and openness as opposed to rigidity. What has changed in recent times is where those debates will take place and their potential impact upon policy-making and organisational development.

Ethicists have moved out of the philosophy department and have travelled via the hospital and laboratory to the government committee rooms and civil service meetings. Medical and scientific committees and working parties routinely invite an ethics expert into their ranks, and more and more specialised committees are being established within healthcare and biomedical settings. Medical education has developed such that all doctors trained in the UK have some training in ethics, and every generation has its enthusiasts who pursue their study further and incorporate 'ethics work' into their professional careers. At the same

---

[14] J. Plamenatz, *Consent, Freedom and Political Obligation*, 2nd edn (Oxford University Press, 1968), p. 1.
[15] www.aomrc.org.uk/committees/uk-donation-ethics-committee.html.

time as tomorrow's doctors are becoming more ethically aware, tomorrow's patients have become more alert to the ethical components of their care.

Conclusion

In this ethically sensitised world, the role of the ethicist is being brought into the centre of policy-making activity, and this brings with it certain responsibilities. Having decided many years ago that the solutions to moral problems often lie in the close interrogation of the facts of a matter as opposed to protracted arguments over moral principles, it is clear to me that ethicists who claim to have an interest in public policy cannot be lone riders. It is imperative for them to work alongside those who properly understand the facts of the matter. In academic terms, this could mean developing close working relationships with social scientists and statisticians. In the public-policy arena it becomes imperative to work alongside those who will be doing the work that the policy or guidance in question will ultimately affect.

Organ donation and transplantation is an ethically contested field of medicine, and ethical issues will persist and evolve as the landscape changes. Clear guidance on key issues will enable individual clinicians and teams to do their work to best effect. This is why many clinicians have welcomed the formation of the UK Donation Ethics Committee and why bodies such as the British Transplantation Society support the work of active and productive ethics committees. At a local level, there will be the need for occasional advice on particular cases or issues, meaning a role for ethicists on local organ donation committees and the need to develop productive links between hospital clinical ethics committees and clinical leads in organ donation whose task it is to champion donation and make it 'usual rather than unusual', as exhorted by the Taskforce.[16]

Given the almost universal agreement over the importance and value of the goal of increasing organ donation, the emphasis of ongoing ethical work will inevitably be on process, and here there will be room for disagreement. Some disagreements will be profound and fundamental: for example, regarding the moral status of a person after death and the obligations owed to them. Others will arise out of a difference in theoretical approaches to ethics, with the open-ended approach of the consequentialist clashing with the bounded views of the deontologist. Some differences will be essentially political, as reflected in the different societal accounts set out

---

[16] Organ Donation Taskforce, *Organs for Transplants*, p. 36.

during the opt-out debate. The challenge is to accommodate these debates within a process that remains focused upon the shared goal of increasing organ donation by supporting those making the decision to donate and those who translate that donation into a life-saving or life-enhancing transplant. The ethicist should not take centre stage, but rather he or she should work to support those who can make things happen, whilst also protecting the interests of those whose lives and deaths could be affected by how we manage the issue of organ donation and transplantation, both within the UK and beyond.

15 Addressing organ shortage in the European Union: getting the balance right

Anne-Maree Farrell

In recent years, a range of policy and regulatory initiatives have been taken at European Union (EU) level in relation to organ donation and transplantation. The European Commission (Commission) set out its current policy in its *Action Plan on Organ Donation and Transplantation (2009–2015)* (the Action Plan) which was published in December 2008.[1] The plan focuses on the need to improve quality and safety, increase organ availability and make organ transplantation systems more efficient, both within Member States and on an EU-wide basis. It was accompanied by a legislative proposal[2] that has since been adopted at EU level and now establishes an EU-wide regulatory regime for organ donation and transplantation (Organs Directive).[3] The aim of this chapter is to examine such initiatives in detail with a view to assessing whether they are likely to address what is acknowledged to be the main challenge in the field, namely organ shortage.

In using the term 'organ shortage' in this chapter, I take as my starting point the current gap between demand for organs for transplantation and available supply from organ donors. The policy approach taken at EU

This chapter draws in part on research carried out whilst in receipt of the Economic and Social Research Council grant *European Law and New Health Technologies* (RES-451-26-0764). The support of the ESRC is gratefully acknowledged. I would also like to acknowledge the support of the Wellcome Strategic Programme *The Human Body: its Scope, Limits and Future*, conducted under the auspices of the Institute for Science Ethics and Innovation, School of Law, University of Manchester, UK.
[1] Commission of the European Communities, Communication from the Commission: *Action Plan on Organ Donation and Transplantation (2009–2015): Strengthened Cooperation between Member States* (COM (2008) 819/3, Brussels, 8 December 2008).
[2] The legislative proposal takes the form of what is known in the EU legal order as a framework Directive. A framework Directive is a legal instrument which is binding upon each of the EU Member States to which it is addressed as to the result to be achieved. It usually sets out broad minimum standards, but allows a significant amount of discretion to Member States with regard to implementation under national law.
[3] Directive 2010/45/EU of the European Parliament and of the Council of 7 July 2010 on standards of quality and safety of human organs intended for transplantation (OJ L 207, 6 August 2010).

level proceeds from such an understanding and focuses on strategies to address the situation.[4] In adopting this approach, I acknowledge that there are differing views as to how and why organ shortage arose, as well as a division of opinion on whether there is a need to devise strategies to reduce or eliminate the shortage or whether the focus should instead be on how best to allocate existing supply.[5] An examination of such issues, however, is outside the scope of this chapter.

In this chapter, I argue that emerging EU governance in the field of organ donation and transplantation should be viewed as a positive development. The Action Plan for the next six years is ambitious in its scope and there is a need to ensure that the predominant focus remains on implementing effective strategies to address organ shortage in the EU context. To this end, there is a need to prioritise the implementation of efficient and effective organisational structures for achieving the objective of increased organ availability at national level, particularly through deceased organ donation. This needs to be the main priority given the available evidence that achieving this objective offers the best way forward for reducing the current shortage of organs.[6] While the Commission views the establishment of a legally binding EU-wide regulatory regime in the field through the Organs Directive as complementary to the Action Plan, I also argue that there is a need for ongoing evaluation with regard to the likely and actual transaction costs involved in implementing the regime at national level. Such implementation should not result in additional or unexpected administrative and regulatory burdens, to the detriment of focusing on the main challenge of addressing organ shortage. The initial section of the chapter provides a brief overview of the circumstances which have contributed to organ shortage within the EU. The next section examines current EU organ donation and transplantation policy. This is followed by an examination of key aspects of the Organs Directive. The final section of the chapter assesses the extent to which EU governance initiatives in the field are likely to contribute towards addressing the

---

[4] Other commentators have observed that the gap between supply and demand and how best to redress the problem is often the starting point in ethical and political debates about organ donation and transplantation. See S. Schicktanz and M. Schweda, '"One man's trash is another man's treasure": exploring economic and moral subtexts of the "organ shortage" problem in public views on organ donation', *Journal of Medical Ethics*, 35 (2009), 473–6, 473.

[5] For an overview of how the shortage of organs is differentially viewed, see M. Schweda and S. Schicktanz, 'Public moralities concerning donation and disposition of organs: results from a cross-European study', *Cambridge Quarterly of Healthcare Ethics*, 17 (2008), 308–17.

[6] R. Matesanz and B. Domínguez-Gil, 'Strategies to optimize deceased organ donation', *Transplantation Reviews*, 21 (2007), 177–88; Council of Europe, *Meeting Organ Shortage: Current Status and Strategies for Improvement of Organ Donation. A European Consensus Document* (1998), www.coe.int/t/dg3/health/Source/organshortage_en.doc.

problem of organ shortage, both within individual Member States and on an EU-wide basis.

The EU and the problem of organ shortage

The Commission has identified organ shortage as representing the main challenge for those with responsibility for organ donation and transplantation policy in Member States. In 2008, there were over 56,000 patients on waiting lists across Member States, with over 5,500 patients dying annually whilst on these lists.[7] Such statistics do not in any case reflect the true picture in clinical terms. The chronic shortage of organs has meant that transplant clinicians are forced to be extremely selective about the type of patients who are placed on waiting lists in the first place. While this represents a personal tragedy for many individual patients who suffer end-stage organ failure, it also represents a significant financial burden for Member States' health systems. It is currently estimated that 3 per cent of health budgets involve costs associated with patients waiting for organ transplantation.[8] The main economic benefits to be achieved from increasing the rate of organ donation are in the area of kidney transplantation. On a best-case scenario, it has been estimated that Member States could potentially save up to 1.2 billion euros in treatment costs, with productivity gains of up to 2.4 billion euros.[9]

A number of factors have been identified as contributing to this situation. First, there is a limited potential donor pool upon which to draw in terms of available and suitable organs for transplant purposes. Over 90 per cent of current organ donors are patients who were diagnosed with brain stem death whilst in hospital. Yet, less than 3 per cent of deaths in hospital are diagnosed in line with accepted brain stem death criteria.[10] Therefore, the number of potential donors is low. Although the use of donation after

---

[7] Commission of the European Communities (CEC), Commission staff working document accompanying the proposal for a Directive of the European Parliament and of the Council on standards of quality and safety of human organs intended for transplantation and of the Commission action plan on organ donation and transplantation (2009–2015): Strengthened cooperation between Member States: Impact Assessment (SEC (2008) 2956, Brussels, 8 December 2008), p. 9.

[8] Commission of the European Communities (CEC), Commission staff working document accompanying document to the Communication from the Commission to the European Parliament and Council: Organ donation and transplantation: Policy actions at EU Level: Impact Assessment (SEC (2007) 705, Brussels, 30 May 2007), p. 50.

[9] Commission, Impact Assessment 8 December 2008, p. 4.

[10] Commission, Impact Assessment 30 May 2007, p. 22.

controlled and/or uncontrolled cardiac death (DCD) may be ethically and legally acceptable in certain Member States, in others it is not.[11]

Second, there is wide variability between Member States in relation to rates of deceased organ donation, ranging from 34.4 persons per million population (pmp) in Spain, to 14.7 pmp in the United Kingdom (UK), to 8.9 pmp in Greece.[12] Such variability cannot be easily explained in terms of general or specific mortality rates or religious and/or sociocultural differences.[13] Third, there are problems with ensuring compatibility between donors and recipients, as well as ensuring organ viability within specific timeframes for individual organs. The extent to which expanded criteria donors are used in Member States also varies.[14]

Fourth, the current organisational models adopted by many Member States are not as efficient as they could be in facilitating an optimum approach to organ donation and transplantation. The country with the highest rate of deceased organ donation in the EU is Spain, and it has been suggested that its organisational model has been responsible for its spectacular success. The 'Spanish Model' of organ donation and transplantation is focused on achieving optimal efficiency in relation to organ donation, retrieval and transplantation, given that many potential organ donors are often lost either due to lack of evaluation and/or referral, or because the option of donation is not presented to families of (potential) deceased donors.[15]

Fifth, there are differing approaches between Member States with respect to ethically sensitive issues, including the preferred consent regime, diagnosis of brain death and whether, and if so how, DCD should be managed. There has been considerable debate within the academic and policy literature as to whether a legally sanctioned presumed consent regime is likely to contribute in practice to higher rates of deceased

---

[11] For the purposes of this chapter, the term 'donation after cardiac death' (DCD) is used, although it is acknowledged that 'non-heart-beating donation' (NHBD) is also used. M. Snoeijs, L. van Heurn, W. van Mook *et al.*, 'Controlled donation after cardiac death: a European perspective', *Transplantation Reviews*, 21 (2007), 219–29, 221.

[12] Council of Europe, *Transplant Newsletter: International Figures on Organ Donation and Transplantation – 2009*, 15(1) (2010), pp. 26–8.

[13] Commission, Impact Assessment 30 May 2007, p. 22.

[14] R. Metzger, F. Delmonico, S. Feng *et al.*, 'Expanded criteria donors for kidney transplantation', *American Journal of Transplantation*, 3 (Supp. 4) (2003), 114–25; Commission, Impact Assessment 30 May 2007, pp. 22–3; V. Audard, M. Matignon, K. Dahan *et al.*, 'Renal transplantation from extended criteria cadaveric donors: problems and perspectives overview', *Transplant International*, 21 (2008), 11–17. See also Chapter 7.

[15] Matesanz and Domínguez-Gil, 'Strategies to optimize deceased organ donation'. See also Chapter 10.

organ donation.[16] In relation to those Member States which have adopted presumed consent regimes, the preference has been to operate a 'soft' regime in practice whereby the views of families are sought regarding the donation of organs from their deceased relatives.[17] This is certainly the case in Spain, which has nevertheless managed to maintain a very high rate of deceased organ donation.[18] While evidence exists that the adoption of a presumed consent regime may be influential in increasing the rate of deceased organ donation, it is also clear that other factors, such as the organisational model adopted for organ procurement, have also proved to be an effective strategy in countries such as Spain.[19]

In relation to the definition of brain stem death, 86 per cent of Member States have a statutory definition, the diagnosis of which is necessary before organ retrieval is permitted from the deceased person. There is a significant degree of variability regarding the process by which brain stem death is diagnosed, with the number of doctors required to make such a diagnosis ranging between two and four in Member States.[20] This variability with regard to the diagnosis of death is also said to contribute to the failure to make use of DCD, despite the fact that 45 per cent of Member States have legislation and/or guidelines in place with respect to such use.[21] In the UK, the Netherlands and Switzerland, for example, laws permit action to be taken in potential cases of uncontrolled DCD in order to preserve organs post-mortem before consent has been obtained from relatives.[22] Ethical issues about the use of both controlled and uncontrolled DCD, however, remain a matter for concern among healthcare professionals working in intensive care and transplant medicine.[23]

---

[16] R. Gimbel, M. Strosberg, S. Lehrman *et al.*, 'Presumed consent and other predictors of cadaveric organ donation in Europe', *Progress in Transplantation*, 13 (2003), 17–23; A. Abadie and S. Gay, 'The impact of presumed consent legislation on cadaveric organ donation: a cross-country study', *Journal of Health Economics*, 25 (2006), 599–620; A. Rithalia, C. McDaid, S. Suekarran *et al.*, 'Impact of presumed consent for organ donation on donation rates: a systematic review', *British Medical Journal*, 338 (2009), 284–7.

[17] R. Sells, 'What is transplantation law and whom does it serve?', *Transplantation Proceedings*, 35 (2003), 1191–4, 1193.

[18] Matesanz and Domínguez-Gil, 'Strategies to optimize deceased organ donation', 181.

[19] M. Quigley, M. Brazier, R. Chadwick *et al.*, 'The organs crisis and the Spanish model: theoretical versus pragmatic considerations', *Journal of Medical Ethics*, 34 (2008), 223–4; Organ Donation Taskforce, *The Potential Impact of an Opt Out System for Organ Donation in the UK: an Independent Report from the Organ Donation Taskforce* (London: Department of Health, 2008).

[20] Commission, Impact Assessment 30 May 2007, pp. 24, 26.

[21] G. Koffmann and G. Gambaro, 'Renal transplantation from non-heart-beating donors: a review of the European experience', *Journal of Nephrology*, 16 (2003), 334–41.

[22] Snoeijs *et al.*, 'Controlled donation after cardiac death'.

[23] For further discussion of these issues, see Chapter 9 and Chapter 16.

Finally, there are also significant differences between Member States regarding family refusal rates in the case of deceased organ donation. The most recent data available in this regard show that rates vary from low refusal rates in countries such as Portugal (10.6 per cent) and Spain (17.9 per cent) to high refusal rates in countries such as Greece (33.5 per cent) and the UK (38.1 per cent). Data collection on this issue on an EU-wide basis is not yet comprehensive, however, so it is difficult to obtain an overall, reliable picture as to the extent of, and reasons for, such variability.[24] Several reasons have been offered to explain the situation based on available data: wide variation in consent procedures; different practices with regard to the management of donor registers; and differing socio-cultural perceptions about the benefits of organ donation for society in general.[25]

Recently published research derived from interviews conducted with families in the UK who were faced with the prospect of agreeing to the donation of a deceased family member's organs found that a lack of knowledge concerning how brain stem criteria are applied to diagnose death is a key factor influencing families' decisions to donate (or not to donate) organs. In addition, families' desire to protect the body of their deceased family member from being dissected, or otherwise 'cut up', has also been identified as another important factor contributing to family refusals to donate organs. This is so notwithstanding that deceased family members may have held positive views about organ donation during their lifetime. Such research highlights the gap between official organ donation policy and families' levels of knowledge and concerns when confronted with the reality of organ donation.[26]

EU organ donation and transplantation policy

In 1999, the EU was given new legal powers by Member States to adopt minimum harmonisation measures with respect to human material such as blood, human tissue and organs,[27] although such measures were not to affect national provisions on the donation or medical use of organs.[28] Since the creation of these new powers, there have been a number of

---

[24] Council of Europe, *Transplant Newsletter 2010*, p. 38.

[25] Commission, Impact Assessment 30 May 2007, p. 27.

[26] M. Sque, T. Long, S. Payne and D. Allardyce, 'Why relatives do not donate organs for transplants: "sacrifice" or "gift of life"?', *Journal of Advanced Nursing*, 61 (2008), 134–44; see also Chapter 5.

[27] With the Lisbon Treaty having come into force on 1 December 2009, this legal competence is now to be found under Article 168(4)(a) TFEU (ex-Article 152(4)(a) EC).

[28] On this latter point, see Article 168(7) TFEU (ex-Article 152(5) EC).

policy and regulatory initiatives taken at EU level, including the adoption of EU-wide risk-regulation regimes for blood and tissues/cells.[29] EU developments in relation to organ donation and transplantation have taken place over an extended period of time, however, with the Commission acknowledging that a different approach was needed in relation to governance initiatives in the field of organ transplantation from that taken in relation to blood and tissues/cells.[30]

Following extensive consultation with experts, stakeholders and Member State representatives, the Commission published its current Action Plan on organ donation and transplantation in December 2008,[31] together with a legislative proposal for an Organs Directive.[32] The Commission's Action Plan is designed to cover a work programme in the field of organ donation and transplantation for the years 2009 to 2015. Ten Priority Actions were identified to meet the challenges of increasing organ availability, enhancing the efficiency and accessibility of transplantation systems and improving the quality and safety of organs for transplant. For present purposes, the focus of examination will be on Priority Actions that are likely to address the problem of organ shortage in the EU context.

Priority Actions 1 to 5 are focused on strategies to increase organ availability. Under Priority Action 1, the aim is to work towards an increased rate of organ procurement, particularly from deceased organ donors. A key element in achieving this Priority Action is the appointment of a sufficient number of appropriately trained transplant donor co-ordinators in every hospital where the potential for organ donation exists. They are to be provided with ongoing and intensive training in all aspects of organ donation and transplantation, and are to report to the hospitals where they are based, rather than to individual transplant teams. The use of transplant donor co-ordinators in this way has been identified as a key element in

---

[29] The full title of the Blood Directive is Directive 2002/98/EC of the European Parliament and of the Council of 27 January 2003 setting standards of quality and safety for the collection, testing, processing, storage and distribution of human blood and blood components and amending Directive 2001/83/EC (OJ L 33, 8 February 2003). The full title of the Tissues and Cells Directive is Directive 2004/23/EC of the European Parliament and of the Council of 31 March 2004 on setting standards of quality and safety for the donation, procurement, testing, processing, preservation, storage and distribution of human tissues and cells (OJ L 102, 7 April 2004).

[30] For an overview of early EU governance initiatives in the field of organ donation and transplantation, see A. Farrell, 'Adding value? EU governance of organ donation and transplantation', *European Journal of Health Law*, 17 (2010), 51–79, 53–6.

[31] Commission, *Action Plan (2009–2015)*.

[32] Commission of the European Communities (CEC), Proposal for a Directive of the European Parliament and of the Council on standards of quality and safety of human organs intended for transplantation (COM (2008) 818 final, Brussels, 8 December 2008).

the significant increase in the rate of deceased organ donation in Spain, where they are predominantly physicians with specialities in nephrology or intensive care.[33] In order to promote an EU-wide uniform approach to the use of transplant donor co-ordinators, the aim is also to work towards the development of internationally recognised standards and international accreditation in the field.[34]

Priority Action 2 focuses on the development of agreed indicators and best practices for quality improvement programmes at national level, and is seen as key to achieving the objective of increasing organ availability. This is largely a self-evaluative process to be conducted jointly by specialists in intensive care and transplant donor co-ordinators in each hospital setting where there exists the potential for organ donation.[35] Enhancing the capacity for living organ donation, particularly involving kidneys, is to be promoted under Priority Action 3. The Commission has identified that only 17 per cent of organ donation activity on an EU-wide basis involves living organ donation, and the extent to which it is promoted varies widely between Member States. There is a low rate of use in countries such as Spain, but a much higher rate overall within the Nordic region.[36] In strategising the promotion of living organ donation within the EU context, however, the Commission avoids any detailed evaluation of the problematic ethical and human rights issues that have been raised in relation to the performance of a non-therapeutic surgical procedure on individuals, particularly in circumstances where there are recognised risks of serious health consequences resulting from such procedure.[37] This is quite apart from the potential adverse impact on rates of deceased organ donation that could result from focusing more on promoting living organ donation.[38]

The provision of information via the media and other sources, as well as increasing the general level of public education about organ donation and transplantation, is to be promoted under Priority Action 4. Again drawing on the Spanish Model, the Commission has identified that the adoption of

---

[33] Matesanz and Domínguez-Gil, 'Strategies to optimize deceased organ donation', 182.
[34] Commission, *Action Plan (2009–2015)*, pp. 3–4.   [35] *Ibid.*, pp. 5, 9.
[36] Commission, Impact Assessment 8 December 2008, pp. 17–18. For further details on living organ donation in the Nordic region, see Chapter 11.
[37] There are recognised risks of serious complications that could arise for living organ donors, for example in the case of liver lobe donation. For an overview, see P. Clavien, P. Dutkowski and J. Trotter, 'Requiem for a champion? Living donor liver transplantation', *Journal of Hepatology*, 51 (2009), 635–7.
[38] H. Roscam Abbing, 'A Council of Europe Protocol on Transplantation of Organs and Tissue of Human Origin', *European Journal of Health Law*, 9 (2002), 63–76; R. Truog, 'The ethics of organ donation by living donors', *New England Journal of Medicine*, 353 (2005), 444–6; see also Chapter 16.

a systematic approach to media campaigns, as well as being able to provide easily accessible information about key aspects of organ donation and transplantation, has served to create a positive and supportive national environment in countries such as Spain in relation to work done in the field.[39] While the conduct of media and public-education campaigns may indeed have served to create a positive and supportive environment for organ donation and transplantation in Member States such as Spain, the empirical evidence to support the view that this has translated into higher rates of organ procurement is not strong.[40] Further justification is needed in relation to the prioritising of work in this area with respect to addressing issues relating to organ shortage.

Under Priority Actions 6 to 9 the Commission recognises the importance of strategising the development of an efficient organisational model to enhance organ procurement. Although it is clear that the Commission is drawing heavily on key aspects of the Spanish Model for organ procurement, the aim is to identify best practices in relation to the development of such a model, which include:

1. the appointment of transplant donor co-ordinators (as previously discussed);
2. the establishment of a transplant network which operates at local, regional and national levels;
3. ongoing audits of organ donation and transplantation activity;
4. the creation of a central co-ordinating administrative agency;
5. the implementation of a system of financial reimbursement; and
6. the promotion, on a systematic basis, of media and public-education campaigns about the merits of organ donation and transplantation.[41]

Facilitating greater patient mobility in the context of ensuring greater access and efficiency in organ transplant systems is the focus of Priority Action 7. Patient mobility is defined widely to include those seeking treatment who are based both within and outside the EU. General issues relating to patient mobility within the EU have been the subject of considerable legal and political attention in recent years. The Commission has undertaken a significant amount of work in this area and this recently led to the publication of a proposal for an EU-wide regulatory regime

---

[39] Commission, *Action Plan (2009–2015)*, pp. 6, 10.
[40] See Chapter 4, which raises concerns about the design and likely impact of public-education campaigns involving organ donation and transplantation, with regard to increasing the rate of organ donation.
[41] R. Matesanz and B. Miranda, 'A decade of continuous improvement in cadaveric organ donation: the Spanish model', *Journal of Nephrology*, 15 (2002), 22–8; Matesanz and Domínguez-Gil, 'Strategies to optimize deceased organ donation', 181.

dealing with patient mobility;[42] it is therefore understandable that it would wish to be proactive in supporting initiatives that would facilitate greater patient mobility in the context of organ transplantation.

In relation to the issue of organ trafficking both within and outside the EU, the Commission has acknowledged that this remains a matter of ongoing concern. It is an issue that has periodically assumed importance on the EU political agenda in recent years. One of the main problems faced by the Commission, however, has been identifying the nature and extent of the problem in the EU context. As such, it has not specifically identified dealing with organ trafficking as a Priority Action but has emphasised that it will continue to monitor the situation, in addition to supporting the work of the Council of Europe on the issue.[43]

The promotion of greater cross-border exchange of organs is the focus of Priority Action 8. Although the Action Plan acknowledges that there are already several supranational organisations in existence which engage in this activity,[44] the Commission views the added value of EU action in this area as creating an environment in which it would be easier to facilitate organ transplantation in relation to difficult-to-treat and urgent patients, as well as contributing to greater efficiency in the distribution of any surplus organs which become available in Member States.[45] While laudable in its intent given cross-matching difficulties with a range of patients on national organ transplant waiting lists, the Commission needs to be much more explicit as to how it proposes to achieve this Priority Action in an ethically principled manner that promotes justice and fairness for those awaiting organ transplantation. While there is no doubt that allocation criteria are in place at national level, as well as for existing cross-border organ transplantation organisations, it would be beneficial if the Commission led the way in terms of work on this particular Priority Action by ensuring that allocation criteria for organs in the EU context are explicit and transparent, underpinned by principles of fairness and justice.[46]

---

[42] Commission of the European Communities (CEC), Proposal for a Directive of the European Parliament and of the Council on the application of patients' rights in cross-border healthcare (COM (2008) 414 final, 2 July 2008).

[43] European Commission, Health and Consumers Directorate-General, Experts Meeting on Organ Donation and Transplantation Action Plan (11–12 March 2009) Summary Report, http://ec.europa.eu/health/ph_threats/human_substance/oc_organs/docs/ev_20090311_mi_en.pdf.

[44] Farrell, 'Adding value? EU governance of organ donation and transplantation', 62.

[45] Commission, *Action Plan (2009–2015)*, pp. 6, 11–12.

[46] Roscam Abbing, 'A Council of Europe Protocol on Transplantation of Organs and Tissue of Human Origin', 66–7; S. Gevers, 'Editorial: a fair distribution of organs for transplantation purposes: looking to the past and the future', *European Journal of Health Law*, 14 (2007), 215–19, 216–17; Farrell, 'Adding value? EU governance of organ donation and transplantation', 63–4.

An EU-wide regulatory regime for organ donation and transplantation

The publication of a legislative proposal for an Organs Directive followed considerable consultation on the part of the Commission with relevant experts and stakeholders, as well as feedback received from Member State representatives and other national institutional bodies. The Commission initially proposed a regulatory regime which closely followed the format adopted in relation to the earlier Blood and Tissues and Cells Directives: namely, setting quality and safety standards in the context of key links within the donor–recipient chain.[47] Considerable concern was expressed at this proposed approach in the field of organ donation and transplantation, on a number of grounds. First, the risk/benefit ratio was considered to be fundamentally different in this field from that which operates in relation to other types of human material, such as blood and tissue/cells. In the case of organ transplantation, this represents the only lifesaving option for many of those with end-stage failure of organs such as the liver, lung and heart. Therefore, it was argued that a greater margin of discretion was required in relation to the exercise of clinical judgement and patient choice with regard to risk than would otherwise be permitted through the adoption of a narrow approach to standard-setting for quality and safety.[48] Second, reservations were expressed about the potential adverse impact that could result from the 'gold-plating' of EU legislation involving organ donation and transplantation at national level.[49] Finally, concerns were raised about the potential for additional burdens and costs to be imposed at national level as a result of the adoption of the Organs Directive (whether or not the issue of gold-plating arose), given limited existing personnel and administrative resources.[50]

---

[47] Commission, Impact Assessment 30 May 2007, pp. 9–10.

[48] A. Farrell, 'The politics of risk and EU governance of human material', *Maastricht Journal of European and Comparative Law*, 16 (2009), 41–64, 60–2.

[49] The term 'gold-plating' has been used to refer to the way in which Member States implement EU regulation in circumstances that go beyond the minimum requirements set out in such legislation. While still legal, additional requirements may result in unexpected or unwelcome costs and burdens for those affected by the legislation. The potential adverse impact resulting from the gold-plating of EU regulation of organ donation and transplantation in the UK was examined in the House of Lords European Union Committee, 17th Report of Session 2007–08, *Increasing the Supply of Donor Organs within the European Union*, Volume 1: Report, HL Paper 123–I (London: The Stationery Office, 2008), paras 97 and 119.

[50] Commission of the European Communities (CEC), *1st National Expert Meeting on Organ Donation and Transplantation at Community Level: Summary Report* (Brussels, 13 July 2007), http://ec.europa.eu/health/ph_threats/human_substance/events_organs.en.htm.

The Organs Directive has now been adopted at EU level and Member States have until 27 August 2012 in which to transpose it into national law.[51] The Directive is divided into a number of chapters covering:

1. subject matter, scope and definitions;
2. quality and safety standards for organs;
3. donor and recipient protection for donor selection and evaluation;
4. obligations of competent authorities and exchange of information;
5. organ exchange with third countries and European organ exchange organisations; and
6. general and final provisions.

In the following paragraphs, key aspects of the Directive are examined rather than each chapter being covered in detail. In the chapter on quality and safety of organs, it is emphasised that Member States must provide for the adoption and implementation of a set of 'operating procedures' which shall establish a 'framework for quality and safety' in relation to key aspects of organ donation and transplantation.[52] This appears to allow for some degree of flexibility on the part of Member States in meeting their obligations with respect to establishing such a framework, which should include, inter alia, operating procedures for verifying the identity of the donor, as well as the consent of the donor (or the donor's family); the completion of organ and donor characterisation; the traceability of organs; and the reporting of serious adverse events and reactions.[53]

It is also important to note that the requirements regarding quality, safety and traceability set out in the Directive must be met in relation to organ exchange between Member States, as well as between Member States and third countries.[54] While these requirements are aimed at promoting standardisation to facilitate patient mobility, as well as ensuring the health and safety of potential organ recipients, the broader question of the allocation criteria that should be applied in relation to such exchange is not elaborated upon in any detail in the substantive (and therefore legally binding) part of the Directive. As was pointed out earlier in this chapter, it is to be hoped that this aspect will be fleshed out in more detail by the Commission in the future, in the context of implementing the Action Plan.[55]

---

[51] Article 31(1), Organs Directive.
[52] 'Operating procedures' is defined as 'written instructions describing the steps in a specific process, including the materials and methods to be used and the expected end outcome' (see Article 3(p), Organs Directive).
[53] Article 4, Organs Directive.   [54] Articles 20–1, Organs Directive.
[55] See para. 20, Recital, Organs Directive, where it is acknowledged that the allocation of organs should be based on 'transparent, non-discriminatory and scientific criteria' and that such criteria should be taken into account by the Commission in the implementation of the Action Plan.

The Commission's Action Plan emphasises the need to focus on appropriate organisational models to enhance the efficiency of organ procurement, and this is also underlined in the Organs Directive. Member States are required to ensure that organ procurement takes place in, or is carried out by, procurement organisations that comply with the Directive, and to provide information on the national requirements for authorising such organisations.[56] They are also required to ensure that medical activities in procurement organisations, such as donor selection and evaluation, are performed under the advice and guidance of a qualified 'doctor of medicine' and that suitable surgical facilities, materials and equipment are used for organ procurement.[57] Member States will also be required to designate 'one or more competent authorities' to ensure oversight and compliance with these and other legal requirements.[58]

There is a specific chapter in the Organs Directive that sets out the requirements to be met in relation to the protection of donors and recipients, as well as donor selection and evaluation. Key aspects covered in this chapter include those relating to living organ donors, the principles that are to govern organ donation, and the protection of data collected on donors and recipients.[59] In relation to living organ donors, there is a requirement that an appropriate assessment of their health and medical history be conducted by 'suitably qualified or trained and competent professionals', and it is also made clear that potential living donors may be excluded on the grounds that making the donation 'could present unacceptable health risks'.[60] While Member States are required to 'take all necessary measures to ensure the highest possible protection of living donors' in order to ensure the 'quality and safety of organs for transplantation',[61] no detail is provided in the substantive part of the Directive as to the specific protections that are to be afforded to such donors. What detail is provided is to be found in paragraph 23 of the Recital where it is acknowledged that 'physical, psychological and social risk' to the living donor (and the recipient) need to be minimised. Given the problematic ethical and human rights concerns that have been raised about living organ donation,[62] as well as the fact that its use is much more

---

[56] Article 5, Organs Directive.   [57] Article 6, Organs Directive.
[58] Article 17(1); see also generally Articles 17–19, Organs Directive.
[59] Data protection issues will not be considered further in this chapter. For present purposes, it is important to note that the collection of information and data on donors and recipients, particularly in relation to post-transplant results, will need to comply with relevant EU and national data protection legislation (see Article 16, Organs Directive).
[60] Article 15(2), Organs Directive.   [61] Article 15(1), Organs Directive.
[62] Farrell, 'Adding value? EU governance of organ donation and transplantation', 58–9.

narrowly circumscribed in other international legal instruments,[63] the broad-ranging approach adopted in the Directive in this regard is somewhat troubling. It would therefore be useful if more detailed guidelines in relation to the circumstances in which living organ donation should take place, and in particular the protections to be afforded to living donors, are produced by the Commission during the course of implementing the Action Plan.

In relation to the key principles that are to govern organ donation, the Organs Directive makes clear that while the various consent regimes operating at national level shall be respected, organ procurement shall only take place once all necessary requirements have been met under such regimes.[64] Member States are also required to ensure that organ donation is voluntary and unpaid, although this does not prevent living donors receiving compensation representing reimbursement for expenses and loss of income relating to the donation. It will be left to Member States to define the conditions under which such compensation to living donors will be granted, provided that financial incentives or other benefits are avoided. There is a prohibition on advertising the need for, or the availability of, organs for financial gain or comparative advantage, and the procurement of organs should be carried out on a non-profit basis.[65]

While such principles derive normative support from a range of international legal instruments dealing with human material, including organs, what is made clear in the Organs Directive is that EU decision-makers are not prepared to engage in a more wide-ranging discussion of whether such principles should be viewed as policy ends in themselves, or whether they should be evaluated by reference to the extent to which they contribute to addressing the problem of organ shortage. Instead, it is simply asserted (without supporting evidence) in paragraph 19 of the Recital that if the donation is not voluntary or is undertaken with a view to financial gain, then the quality and safety of the donation would be in jeopardy, given that saving the life of the recipient would not be the main objective. There is no acknowledgement of the longstanding academic and policy debate over what alternative methods or incentives for organ donation should be considered by policy-makers and regulators in order to deal with the

---

[63] Article 10 of the Additional Protocol to the Convention on Human Rights and Biomedicine, on Transplantation of Organs and Tissues of Human Origin (Strasbourg, 24 January 2002), states that 'organ removal from a living donor may be carried out for the benefit of a recipient with whom the donor has a close personal relationship as defined by law, or, in the absence of such relationship, only under the conditions defined by law and with the approval of an appropriate independent body'.

[64] Article 14, Organs Directive.   [65] Article 13, Organs Directive.

problem of organ shortage.[66] While it is perhaps understandable that EU decision-makers would be reluctant to engage in a wide-ranging debate on the ethical principles involved in organ donation and transplantation for a range of political and legal reasons,[67] it is to be hoped that this will change over time. An informed public and political debate over the continuing salience of such principles is long overdue, given the adverse consequences resulting from chronic organ shortage within the EU.

The EU and organ shortage: getting the balance right

Having examined recent policy and regulatory initiatives in the field of organ donation and transplantation at EU level, there is a need to consider whether the initiatives are likely to bring about increased organ availability and therefore reduce the shortage of organs at national level. The Commission's Action Plan is ambitious in its scope and comprehensive in its coverage; there is in fact so much to be addressed within the Priority Action framework of the Action Plan that there is a question mark over whether it can realistically be achieved within the stated six-year timeframe. The Commission plans a mid-point assessment on the progress of implementing the plan,[68] so it is likely that necessary adjustments will be made if appropriate.

Those with national responsibility for working on the Priority Actions listed in the Action Plan, and who will most likely be involved in the implementation of the Organs Directive, have expressed concerns about the extent to which additional administrative and other burdens will be imposed upon them and relevant national institutions in order for them to meet their obligations under both the Action Plan and the Directive. The substantive aspects of the ten Priority Actions listed in the Action Plan will require detailed planning, implementation and evaluation over time, and will need to take account of the varying degrees of infrastructural and policy development in relation to organ donation and transplantation at Member State level. As has already been observed at an experts' meeting convened by the Commission to examine the Action Plan, some Priority Actions are already being put on hold while

---

[66] See, for example, Chapter 6. Other examples include L. Cohen, 'A futures market in cadaveric organs: would it work?', *Transplantation Proceedings*, 1 (1993), 60–1; C. Erin and J. Harris, 'An ethical market in human organs', *Journal of Medical Ethics*, 29 (2003), 137–8.

[67] For a further discussion of such reasons, see Farrell, 'Adding value? EU governance of organ donation and transplantation', 73.

[68] Commission, *Action Plan (2009–2015)*, p. 8.

the primary focus remains on developing appropriate organisational models to enhance organ availability.[69] In relation to the work programme set out in the Action Plan, concern has also been expressed by national representatives about the proposed use of what is known as the Open Method of Co-ordination (OMC).[70] The Commission has adopted OMC as the preferred approach for developing (expert) consensus on indicators, benchmarking and best practices in the field.[71] Despite Commission support for the use of OMC, however, it is currently not clear whether it will be a help or a hindrance in relation to implementing the Action Plan.[72] This may become further complicated during the implementation process of the Organs Directive at national level.

The Organs Directive is the first legally binding supranational risk-regulation regime to have been established in the field of organ donation and transplantation. In this respect, it represents an innovative development in governance that is likely to have a significant impact on setting and improving standards in the field. Having said that, the problems of additional administrative burdens and unwanted transaction costs are likely to be a feature of implementation of the Directive at national level, as has already been the case in relation to the national implementation of the earlier Directives dealing with blood, tissue and cells.[73] The Directive will impose legal requirements on Member States that will need to be met within a relatively short space of time. While Member States with more developed national organ donation and transplant systems might not find the process of implementation too onerous, this may not be the case in relation to other Member States, in particular those which have recently joined the EU. In the circumstances, it will be important for the Commission to engage in ongoing monitoring of any problems associated with the implementation of the Directive at national level, and the extent to which this is (or is not) complementary to work being done pursuant to the Action Plan.

---

[69] Commission, Experts Meeting, 11–12 March 2009.
[70] The open method of co-ordination (OMC) refers to a consensus-building decision-making process that has been adopted at EU level and which is aimed at developing co-operation and agreement on achieving common objectives as between the Member States in a given policy sector. It involves: peer-review processes aimed at jointly identifying and defining objectives to be achieved in a given policy sector; the development of jointly agreed measuring instruments (statistics, indicators, guidelines); benchmarking; and the exchange of best practices. Where appropriate, it may also involve the adoption of 'soft law' measures such as recommendations, rather than legally binding 'hard law' measures. For further details concerning the use of OMC in EU organ donation and transplantation policy, see Farrell, 'Adding value? EU governance of organ donation and transplantation', 55–6.
[71] See also Article 168(2), TFEU.
[72] Farrell, 'Adding value? EU governance of organ donation and transplantation', 55–6.
[73] Farrell, 'The politics of risk', 51–4.

The danger of bureaucratic overload, at both national and EU levels, arising from the implementation of recent governance initiatives in the field, is that it may potentially result in a dissipation of focus with respect to addressing the main challenge of organ shortage. The key indicator for increasing organ availability and therefore decreasing organ shortage has been identified by the Commission as the implementation of a suitable organisational model to optimise organ procurement at national level. With the Organs Directive having been adopted at EU level, Member States are now required to ensure that their organisational arrangements for organ procurement meet certain standards, which draw in large part on key aspects of the Spanish Model. Given that Member States will be legally bound to meet such requirements within a specified timeframe, this should incentivise the development of effective organisational models for organ procurement at national level – much more so than under the proposed work programme of the consensus-building, but non-legally binding, Action Plan. In the circumstances, it will be important for both the Commission and Member States to make use of both the Action Plan and the legal impetus provided by the Organs Directive to bring about effective implementation of organisational models that will result in increased rates of organ procurement at national level.

As was discussed in earlier sections of this chapter, there have been lively and ongoing debates within the relevant academic and policy literature about a range of alternative approaches to dealing with the problem of organ shortage. The underlying basis of such debates has been that existing governance arrangements at national and supranational levels have not been effective in addressing this problem. Several suggested alternative approaches challenge, or otherwise raise, ethically problematic issues concerning the circumstances in which organ donation and/or transplantation should take place. While recent EU governance initiatives represent an important development in trying to address some of these problematic issues in organ donation and transplantation, there appears to have been a largely technocratic mindset adopted in respect of resolving such problems. If there is to be a realistic prospect of addressing the problem of organ shortage at national level, as well as on an EU-wide basis, then a more creative and innovative approach is urgently needed in policy-making processes in the field. This would involve being prepared to create receptive political and public environments where alternative approaches may be considered, and in which the ethical challenges that these approaches may create can be evaluated in a way that is both principled and pragmatic.

Conclusion

This chapter has examined emerging EU governance in the field of organ donation and transplantation. Such governance has involved a mix of policy and regulatory initiatives aimed at strengthening Member State co-operation and co-ordination in the field. The expectation at EU level is that this will lead to the development of indicators, benchmarks and, most importantly, best practices in relation to key aspects of organ donation and transplantation. The hope is that this will in turn result in increased accessibility and efficiency of organ transplant systems, as well as improved quality and safety of organ donation and transplantation, at national level. In the short-term, it is clear that the predominant focus needs to be on developing and implementing efficient and effective organisational models at national level in order to increase the rate of organ procurement.

As a result of the need to implement both the Commission's Action Plan and the Organs Directive, the potential exists for the imposition of significant additional administrative and regulatory burdens at national level. The Commission will need to regularly monitor the implementation of the work programme in the field to ensure that it remains manageable for individual Member States, and it would be helpful if EU decision-makers remained open to adopting a principled and pragmatic approach to considering the use of innovative, as well as existing, approaches to increasing organ availability. In the end, the added value of EU governance in the field of organ donation and transplantation will be judged on the extent to which this translates into increased organ availability within Member States, and on an EU-wide basis. For those on lengthening national waiting lists for organ transplant, it is to be hoped that such success is achieved sooner rather than later.

16   Promoting organ donation: challenges for the future

David Price

Data from the Potential Donor Audit (PDA) of all deaths in intensive care units (ICUs) in the United Kingdom (UK) between 1 April 2006 and 31 March 2008 revealed a total of 30,276 audited deaths.[1] In 3,184 patients brain stem death was a likely diagnosis, in 2,475 cases brain stem death tests were carried out and in a further 2,417 cases, death was diagnosed according to such tests (typically patients who suffered traumatic brain injury or intracranial haemorrhage). The possibility of organ donation was then considered in 2,266 cases, leading to the family being approached for permission for donation in 2,125 instances. Consent was given on 1,299 occasions and organ donation occurred in 1,186 cases. Thus, not only are just a small percentage of persons who die in ICUs potential (heart-beating) donors (slightly over 10 per cent), but only a relatively limited percentage of these potential donors become actual donors (the *conversion rate*) – approximately 49 per cent. A process of attrition begins from the moment that brain stem death becomes a possibility. Not only were 22 per cent of these patients not subjected to brain stem death testing at all, but in 12 per cent of instances the family was not approached for consent, nor did any discussion of organ donation take place. The picture presented above replicates that demonstrated by the earlier PDA in the UK between 1 April 2003 and 31 March 2006.[2] This also revealed that 600 patients who die annually in ICUs are determined to be dead by cardiopulmonary criteria, but for whom a diagnosis of brain stem death was likely.[3] Thus, conversion rates are presently very modest. This, coupled with a declining volume of potential heart-beating donors due to a dwindling number of people dying from severe cerebrovascular events, i.e. road

---

[1] UK Transplant, *Potential Donor Audit: Summary Report for the 24 month period 1 April 2006 – 31 March 2008* (2008).

[2] See K. Barber, S. Falvey, C. Hamilton *et al.*, 'Potential for organ donation in the United Kingdom: audit of intensive care records', *British Medical Journal*, 332 (2006), 1124–7.

[3] M. Smith and P. Murphy, 'The Ministerial Taskforce on Organ Donation', *Journal of the Intensive Care Society*, 9 (2008), 72–6, 73.

traffic accidents and intracranial haemorrhage, means that there is a falling percentage of patients who will fulfil the criteria for brain stem death in any event.[4]

It has been observed that there are nine critical 'decision points' for donation. 'Lost opportunities' at these junctures may be minimised by, for example, improved infrastructure, resourcing, identification of donors, retrieval arrangements, co-ordination, communication, and clarity of legal and ethical regulation. These are matters upon which the UK Organ Donation Taskforce (the Taskforce) drew up a comprehensive list of recommendations which have been accepted by government, and set in motion an implementation scheme to give effect to them (co-ordinated by the Organ Donation Taskforce Programme Delivery Board). The key recommendations relate to donor identification and referral, donor co-ordination and retrieval arrangements. It is to be fervently hoped that these measures will indeed bring about a 50 per cent improvement in donation rates over five years (an additional 1,200 transplants per annum), as the Taskforce anticipated. However, demographic changes are significantly increasing demand for organ transplantation over the immediate and longer term. It is estimated that rates of end-stage renal failure will increase at a rate of 2 per cent per annum, and the indications are that the need for liver transplantation will also rise.[5] Indeed, even if 50 per cent more solid organs were transplanted there would still by no means be a surfeit of available organs. The UK currently lags behind many other Western nations in terms of overall deceased organ donor rates. In 2008, the UK figure was 14.7 per million population (pmp), compared with 18.4 in the Republic of Ireland, 20.6 in Austria, 25.3 in France, 25.7 in Belgium, 26.3 in the United States, 26.7 in Portugal and 34.2 in Spain.[6] Consequently, all actual or potential strategies require attention and (re)appraisal, including the examination of all major sources of donor organs.

Although death confirmed by neurological testing will continue to be the source of the majority of organs for heart, lung and liver transplants, other supplemental sources, of kidneys in particular, are likely to be

---

[4] Whilst the numbers of deceased organ donors rose 11 per cent from the financial year 2007–8 to that of 2008–9, these were essentially non-heart-beating donors.

[5] Organ Donation Taskforce, *Organs for Transplants – the Supplement Report* (London: Department of Health, 2008), App. 2, pp. 100, 129. The overall organ transplant waiting list is in any event rising at 8 per cent per annum: see Organ Donation Taskforce, *Organs for Transplants: a Report from the Organ Donation Taskforce* (London: Department of Health, 2008), p. 4.

[6] Council of Europe, *Transplant Newsletter: International Figures on Organ Donation and Transplantation – 2008*, 14(1) (2009), p. 4.

required indefinitely.[7] The most important of these alternative resources are non-heart-beating (asystolic) deceased donors and living donors.[8] Indeed, the volumes of both these types of donation have risen dramatically in the UK since the beginning of the new millennium, driven by dedicated funding and initiatives co-ordinated by the Directorate of Organ Donation and Transplantation of NHS Blood and Transplant (formerly UK Transplant).[9] In the financial year 2008–09, there were 579 non-heart-beating organ donor transplants, a 35 per cent increase over the previous year, compared with only 43 such transplants in the same period 1998–99.[10] In like vein, there were 961 living donor kidney transplants in 2008–09, up from 589 in 2005–06 and 224 in 1997–08. Living donors now constitute more than half of all kidney donors and one-third of all kidney transplants.[11] Moreover, living donation is also expanding in terms of the range of organs and the breadth of the sources of donors used. These strategies have the individual and combined potential to make a very substantial contribution to meeting the necessary supply of organs for transplantation both here and abroad for the foreseeable future.[12] However, both raise their own ethical and legal problems and challenges which are reflected upon in this concluding chapter. Indeed, living organ donation has been viewed with great scepticism during most of its history, and non-heart-beating donation (NHBD) – or 'donation after cardiac death' (DCD) – remains underdeveloped because of lingering ethical and legal concerns.

As has already been seen, the requirement for consent to deceased organ donation is itself presently a substantial source of 'lost' organs. In

---

[7] The use of non-heart-beating liver and lung transplantation is gradually increasing in the UK; however, see Editorial, 'Liver transplantation from non-heart beating donors', *British Medical Journal*, 332 (2006), 376–7.

[8] In those nations, e.g. Japan, where brain death has been problematic for society to accept, transplantation has relied almost exclusively upon living and non-heart-beating deceased donation.

[9] Department of Health, *Saving Lives, Valuing Donors: a Transplant Framework for England* (London: Department of Health, 2003); and Department of Health, *Saving Lives, Valuing Donors – a Transplant Framework for England: One Year On* (London: Department of Health, 2004).

[10] Organ Donation Taskforce, *Working Together to Save Lives – The Organ Donation Taskforce Implementation Programme Annual Report 2008/9* (London: Department of Health, 2009), p. 22.

[11] Royal College of Surgeons of England, *The Report of the Working Party to Review Organ Transplantation* (Royal College of Surgeons, 1999), p. 21. Up until the end of the last decade, they accounted for only around 10 per cent of all renal transplants.

[12] Ironically, the very first solid organ transplants involved non-heart-beating and living organ donation. In many regions, including the UK, living organ donation waned substantially during the 1990s.

the UK, not only is consent not sought at all in many instances, but in others (approximately 39 per cent) consent is refused in any event.[13] This is a figure which has increased significantly since the last reliable statistics were revealed in the early 1990s.[14] It is much higher even amongst certain black and other minority ethnic groups (as high as 70 per cent in some cases), whose populations in the UK are expected to significantly increase.[15] This generates ongoing enquiry regarding what type of consent is and should be required, from whom, and how consent is sought. In the UK, in the context of organ transplantation, explicit consent has always been solicited for donation and this is now a requirement of English law, implicitly embedded in the notion of 'appropriate consent' in the Human Tissue Act 2004 (the 2004 Act) which came into force in England, Wales and Northern Ireland in September 2006.[16] In Scotland there is an analogous requirement for 'authorisation' in the Human Tissue (Scotland) Act 2006 (the 2006 Act). Whilst the respective parliaments rejected presumed consent in the debates leading to the passing of these statutes, and it was not recommended by the Organ Donation Taskforce for adoption at the present time, Wales is currently preparing to explore the possibility of introducing it,[17] and it remains 'waiting in the wings' as a future policy option for the UK as a whole.[18] Presumed consent is the other issue considered in detail in this final contribution.

All the donation sources and policies considered in this chapter have attracted accusations of instrumentalism, i.e. the use of donors as mere means to the ends of others. It was once remarked that 'the irresistible utilitarian appeal of organ transplantation has us hell-bent on increasing the donor pool'.[19] However, the demands of patients needing organ transplants *require* us to push right up to – but not beyond – the ethical margins and to offer ongoing critical analysis. These are debates with global relevance.

---

[13] UK Transplant, *Potential Donor Audit: 36-Month Summary Report 1 April 2003 – 31 March 2006* (2008).

[14] The refusal rates at that time were 30 per cent. See S. Gore, D. Cable and A. Holland, 'Organ donation from intensive care units in England and Wales: two year confidential audit of deaths in intensive care', *British Medical Journal*, 304 (1992), 349–55.

[15] See Chapter 3.

[16] See generally D. Price, 'The Human Tissue Act 2004', *Modern Law Review*, 68 (2005), 798–821.

[17] See http://news.bbc.co.uk/1/hi/wales/8420678.stm.

[18] Organ Donation Taskforce, *The Potential Impact of an Opt Out System for Organ Donation in the UK* (London: Department of Health, 2008).

[19] R. Arnold and S. Youngner, 'The dead donor rule: should we stretch it, bend it, or abandon it?', *Kennedy Institute of Ethics Journal*, 3 (1993), 263–78, 271.

Non-heart-beating donation

The first deceased organ donors in the 1960s and early 1970s were determined as dead by virtue of the absence of cardio-respiratory functioning. These donors were gradually superseded as results using artificially ventilated 'heart-beating' donors significantly improved outcomes, and, effectively, an unofficial global moratorium evolved. The so-called 'non-heart-beating' donors re-emerged over the last two decades, during which programmes have sprung up in, for example, France, Japan, Latvia, the Netherlands, Poland, Spain, Sweden, Switzerland, the United States (USA) and the UK. Results from NHBD are now broadly comparable with those from heart-beating donation and thus such donors are no longer generally considered 'marginal'.[20] Although initially most European centres relied on 'uncontrolled' NHBD where death occurred outside the hospital or in hospital after unsuccessful resuscitation, today the emphasis is typically upon 'controlled' NHBD,[21] including in the UK and USA.[22] These are patients, generally with severe brain injury, who will suffer cardiac arrest (asystole) before brain stem death (Category III in the Maastricht NHBD categories). It is 'controlled' because it is planned, with everything synchronised at the point of death to ensure minimum warm ischaemia (oxygen deprivation) time prior to removal and transplantation (removal must occur very shortly after death). In general, these are patients in ICUs (or occasionally in an accident and emergency department) in respect of whom treatment is deliberately withheld or withdrawn leading to death, either at the request of a competent patient or after further life-sustaining treatment has been adjudged futile and not in an incompetent patient's best interests.

The notion of 'non-heart-beating' donation is, however, associated in the minds of some with an infraction of the dead donor rule, i.e. death which *results* from organ removal rather than preceding it.[23] There are also concerns relating to the administration of pre-mortem medications or

---

[20] A. Barlow, M. Metcalfe, Y. Johari *et al.*, 'Case-matched comparison of long-term results of non-heart beating and heart-beating donor renal transplants', *British Journal of Surgery*, 96 (2009), 685–91. See also Chapter 7.

[21] In Europe, controlled NHBDs now account for 5 per cent of all deceased organ donors: see M. Snoeijs, L. van Heurn, W. van Mook *et al.*, 'Controlled donation after cardiac death: a European perspective', *Transplantation Reviews*, 21 (2007), 219–29, 220. In the Netherlands, NHBDs account for 50 per cent of all deceased donors: *ibid.*, 225.

[22] NHBD is presently confined to uncontrolled NHBDs in France. In the USA, uncontrolled NHBD is hardly practised, although a notable exception is Washington, DC.

[23] R. Truog and F. Miller, 'The dead donor rule and organ transplantation', *New England Journal of Medicine*, 359 (2008), 674–5; and articles on the subject in the (2007) (2) volume of *Philosophy, Ethics and Humanities in Medicine*.

procedures designed entirely to optimise an eventual transplant.[24] Some of the scepticism relating to the former can be attributed to the dichotomous concept of 'death' promoted by many laws and policy instruments themselves. As was observed many years ago:

Another source of confusion has been introduced by the definitions of death that appear in legal dictionaries and the new statutory definitions of death. These do not account for what the layman actually means by death, but merely state the criteria by which physicians legally determine when death has occurred.[25]

In general, death has traditionally been diagnosed on the basis of an absence of cardio-respiratory function. However, in this present context, these 'signs of death' have become inappropriately conflated in the minds of many both inside and outside the transplant community with a *type* of death, i.e. as death itself.

A formulation of death must comprise a definition of what death is, what operational criteria should apply for determining that death has occurred in any specific instance, and tests to be applied to satisfy these relevant criteria. Whilst the concept (definition) of death is essentially a philosophical question, the functional criteria for determining death has occurred are primarily medical, as are the tests to be used to this end. Befuddlement has resulted from the conflation of different aspects of the formulation, e.g. an inflexible fusing of specific (brain death) tests as a part of the realisation of the brain death criterion itself.[26] This may even result in a specific legal barrier to the implementation of NHBD protocols, as has occurred in jurisdictions such as Germany. There is also confusion between the definition or conception of death and the satisfaction of such a standard in any individual instance.

In the UK, the general concept of death is typically articulated as the irreversible loss of capacity for consciousness, combined with irreversible loss of the capacity to breathe.[27] This has been employed to support the

---

[24] Editorial, 'Non-heart-beating organ donation – solution or a step too far?', *Anaesthesia*, 62 (2007), 431–3, 431.

[25] J. Bernat, C. Culver and B. Gert, 'On the definition and criterion of death', *Annals of Internal Medicine*, 94 (1981), 389–94, 389. For example the Uniform Determination of Death Act (UDDA) implemented in most US states has dual (brain plus cardiopulmonary) criteria for the determination of death.

[26] In the UK the satisfaction of brain stem death tests has been regarded by the courts as sufficient for a diagnosis of brain stem death, but this is not necessarily the only means by which such a diagnosis may be reached: see M. Jones, 'Elective ventilation of potential organ donors: the legal background', *British Medical Journal*, 310 (1995), 714–18, 718.

[27] Review by a Working Group convened by the Royal College of Physicians and endorsed by the Conference of Medical Royal Colleges and their Faculties, 'Criteria for the diagnosis of brain stem death', *Journal of the Royal College of Physicians of London*, 29 (1995), 381–2.

irreversible cessation of the functioning of the brain stem as the death of the individual, as a matter of both medicine and (case) law.[28] It raises questions, however, as regards death determined by cardio-respiratory criteria in relation to NHBD. Not only does conceptual confusion here generate perceptions of infractions of the dead donor rule, but it potentially misleads as to the period of cardio-respiratory silence necessary to have elapsed before death can be properly certified.

There are ethical and legal issues which arise here concerning irreversibility, which is a core constituent of the requisite loss of functioning required to enable death to be determined. There is a growing consensus that five minutes of cardio-respiratory silence following the withdrawal of treatment (e.g. artificial ventilation) is a sufficient period to establish confidence that loss of such functions is 'irreversible', although in one recent instance at Denver Children's Hospital only seventy-five seconds elapsed before death was declared following cessation of circulatory function in two paediatric donors.[29] This five-minute interval is supported in medical consensus and policy documents in the USA,[30] Canada[31] and the UK. In the UK, the Intensive Care Society and the British Transplantation Society endorse this period, as do guidelines issued recently by the Academy of Medical Royal Colleges.[32] It is typically defended on the basis that the heart and respiration will not automatically restart of their own initiative (auto-resuscitate) after that time, and that as there is to be no attempt to try to artificially restart the heart, it will never restart thereafter by any means. Snoeijs et al remark that 'consensus within the transplant community defines irreversibility as cessation of function without the capability of spontaneous recovery'.[33] The latter argument appeals to a notion of irreversibility linked to intent rather than capability. Robertson contends that 'a decisional view of irreversibility reflects commonsense views of death, for the person is not now breathing and never will again'.[34] It is nonetheless the

---

[28] See e.g. Re A (A Minor) [1992] 3 Med LR 303 and Airedale NHS Trust v. Bland [1993] AC 789.

[29] M. Boucek, C. Mashburn, S. Dunn et al., 'Pediatric heart transplantation after declaration of cardiocirculatory death', New England Journal of Medicine, 359 (2008), 709–14, 711.

[30] 'Report of a National Conference on Donation after Cardiac Death', American Journal of Transplantation, 6 (2006), 281–91, 282; this recommended that no more than five minutes should elapse; Institute of Medicine, Organ Donation: Opportunities for Action (Washington, DC: National Academies Press, 2006), p. 128.

[31] The Canadian Council for Donation and Transplantation; see S. Shemie, A. Baker, G. Knoll et al., 'Donation after cardiocirculatory death in Canada', Canadian Medical Association Journal, 175 (2006), S1–24.

[32] Academy of Medical Royal Colleges, A Code of Practice for the Diagnosis and Confirmation of Death (Academy of Medical Royal Colleges, 2008), p. 12.

[33] Snoeijs et al., 'Controlled donation', 220.

[34] J. Robertson, 'The dead donor rule', Hastings Center Report, 29 (1999), 6–14, 12.

weakest notion of irreversibility one could employ. Indeed, not only do dictionary definitions of irreversibility allude instead to the relevant state being '*not* reversible' [my emphasis], but Browne argues that such a notion of 'irreversibility', and thus of death, fails to accord with the general perceptions of ordinary people.[35] It does not accord with the views of many clinicians either.[36] Whilst a state may be physiologically or ethically *equivalent* to death, this does not mean that it *is* death. This is an ontological or empirical matter, not an ethical one. In any event, even adoption of a weak notion of irreversibility will not work in the context of the embryonic practice of non-heart-beating *heart* transplantation as the heart *will be* restarted.[37] As Veatch states: 'If a heart is restarted, the person from whom it was taken cannot have been dead according to cardiac criteria.'[38]

Whilst some commentators argue that such practices should be accommodated within, allegedly ethical, exceptions to the dead donor rule,[39] Robertson emphasises the vital role that the rule plays in engendering trust in a voluntary system of organ donation, and asserts that its symbolic importance is such that even the slightest explicit deviation from it confronts a very high presumption of unacceptability.[40] If the patient is not truly dead when organs are removed, an active killing (or euthanasia) has occurred and this is unlikely to garner overwhelming public support, even for such laudable ends.[41]

The conceptual core of the notion of death is also being occluded here. As Tomlinson asserts, these NHBD protocols 'pull apart' heart-orientated and brain-orientated criteria of death.[42] If significant brain function itself had not ceased in such individuals one would clearly have difficulties subscribing to such a notion of the timing of death. The references to a separate 'cardiac death' in official documents/sources[43]

---

[35] A. Browne, 'The Institute of Medicine on non-heart-beating organ transplantation', *Cambridge Quarterly of Healthcare Ethics*, 17 (2008), 75–86, 77.

[36] A. Joffe, N. Anton and A. deCaen, 'Survey of pediatricians' opinions on donation after cardiac death: are the donors dead?', *Pediatrics*, 122 (2008), 967–74.

[37] Although it has been argued that the circulation has however irreversibly ceased: see J. Bernat, A. Capron, T. Bleck *et al.*, 'The circulatory-respiratory determination of death in organ donation', *Critical Care Medicine*, 38 (2010), 972–9.

[38] R. Veatch, 'Donating hearts after cardiac death – reversing the irreversible', *New England Journal of Medicine*, 359 (2008), 672–3, 673.

[39] See Truog and Miller, 'The dead donor rule', 674–5.

[40] Robertson, 'The dead donor rule', 13.

[41] See generally H. Ducharme, 'Thrift euthanasia in theory and practice' in M. Freeman and A. Lewis (eds.), *Law and Medicine: Current Legal Issues*, Vol. 3 (Oxford University Press, 2000), pp. 493–525.

[42] T. Tomlinson, 'The irreversibility of death: reply to Cole', *Kennedy Institute of Ethics Journal*, 3 (1993), 157–65, 164.

[43] 'Report of a National Conference', 281–91.

are unhelpful and misleading.[44] Menikoff rightly criticises the Institute of Medicine for asserting that brain functioning is not relevant where cardiopulmonary criteria are relied upon.[45] It is the fact that after a certain period of time has elapsed, relevant aspects of brain functioning have irreversibly ceased that is central here, not loss of heartbeat and respiration per se. Thus, the *person* may have ceased to exist, even if individual organ systems are maintained. The Code of Practice recently issued in the UK by the Academy of Medical Royal Colleges therefore very properly asserts that diagnosing death following cardio-respiratory arrest (including failed resuscitation) 'requires confirmation that there has been irreversible damage to the vital centres in the brain-stem, due to the length of time in which the circulation to the brain has been absent'.[46] It adds that to establish that *irreversible* cardio-respiratory arrest has occurred the person should be observed for five minutes, after which the patient should be tested for an absence of pupillary responses to light, of the corneal reflexes, and of any motor responses to supra-orbital pressure. Younger, Arnold and DeVita allege that the five-minute rule currently relies upon the weakest version of irreversibility for both cardio-respiratory *and* brain function.[47] However, whether five minutes is a sufficient period to ensure that such (brain) functions are permanently lost by reference to either central concept of reversibility is an empirical, as opposed to ethical or juridical, matter.[48] If instead, a society wishes to rely on a weaker notion of irreversibility, equating to 'permanent cessation', full and transparent debate at all levels is essential.[49]

The other central issue relating to *controlled* non-heart-beating donation links to the decision to no longer administer life-sustaining treatment and the timing of the withdrawal of treatment. There are concerns expressed here that the decision to withdraw life-prolonging care might itself be

---

[44] Menikoff emphasises that the two separate and alternative means of determining death in the UDDA are merely different ways of determining that the same notion of death has been achieved, i.e. irreversible cessation of functioning of the brain as a whole: see J. Menikoff, 'Doubts about death: the silence of the Institute of Medicine', *Journal of Law, Medicine and Ethics*, 26 (1998), 157–65, 160.

[45] See also J. Menikoff, 'The importance of being dead: non-heart-beating organ donation', *Issues in Law and Medicine*, 18 (2002), 3–20, 15.

[46] Academy of Medical Royal Colleges, *A Code of Practice*, para. 2.2.

[47] S. Youngner, R. Arnold and M. De Vita, 'When is "dead"?', *Hastings Center Report*, 29 (1999), 14–21, 18.

[48] DuBois argues that because such brain functions will only be restored if circulation is reinstated by way of ventilatory support, one can uphold such a policy based on inability of autoresuscitation: see J. DuBois, 'Is organ procurement causing the death of patients?', *Issues in Law and Medicine*, 18 (2002), 21–41, 35.

[49] See Bernat *et al.*, 'The circulatory-respiratory determination'.

influenced or dictated by the needs of others, i.e. organ recipients.[50] The House of Lords Select Committee Report stated:

> We understand the potential for a conflict of interests to arise for medical staff when caring for people who are identified as potential organ donors. We are persuaded that it is essential, for the maintenance of trust in health services, that all such people should be dealt with as patients in the first instance. They should be provided with appropriate treatment and care, in line with their best interests, until the point at which it is agreed that withdrawal of treatment is medically justified.[51]

Thus, the decision to withdraw treatment in the first place should be that of the patient himself or herself, where he or she retained decision-making capacity, or that of the intensive or emergency care clinicians (but not transplant personnel) where the patient had lost such capacity. This would be a decision that it was no longer in the best interests of the patient to continue to treat them, i.e. that further treatment would be futile, either because the patient had no prospect of recovery, or the quality of life if treatment were to be continued would not be acceptable to the patient. Whilst the patient and relatives of the patient should be involved as far as is possible in such decisions, to permit relatives to 'decide' this issue in respect of adults would run contrary to English law as stated in the Mental Capacity Act 2005, and might, ironically, generate its own potential conflicts of interest.[52] Thus, it is appropriate to contact transplant co-ordinators and explore the issue of consent, but only once an initial clinical decision has been made to withdraw treatment without regard to issues relating to transplantation or the input of transplant-related staff.

Due to the requirement for synchronicity of treatment withdrawal and organ retrieval, it may however be necessary to *continue* life-sustaining treatment even beyond the point where it has been initially decided that treatment should be withdrawn.[53] Whilst the initial decision to withdraw treatment should not be influenced by transplant professionals or by transplant considerations, the ultimate *timing* of the withdrawal, and hence the timing of death, may quite properly have regard to the potential for subsequent organ donation. Such delayed withdrawal is often perceived as ethically and legally problematic because, once it has been

---

[50] Charges were recently dropped by the Medical Board of California against Dr Hootan Roozrokh, who had been accused of trying to speed up a patient's death in order to recover organs for transplantation; see www.kansascity.com/437/story/1231759.html.

[51] House of Lords European Union Committee, *Increasing the Supply of Donor Organs within the European Union*, 17th Report of Session 2007–08, Volume 1: Report, HL Paper 123–I, (London: The Stationery Office, 2008), para. 439.

[52] See Ducharme, 'Thrift euthanasia', 511.   [53] For further discussion, see Chapter 9.

decided that further treatment is no longer in the best interests of the patient, it is frequently assumed that treatment must be withdrawn at that point in order to avoid a battery to the patient. In England and Wales, many draw attention to the words to this effect of Lord Browne-Wilkinson in the House of Lords in *Airedale NHS Trust* v. *Bland*.[54] However, best interests encompasses all issues relating to the patient's interests,[55] including his or her wishes and values, which would surely include wishes regarding organ donation.[56] They all properly bear on the appropriate end-of-life care of the patient.[57] Nonetheless, insofar as this specific scenario was almost certainly not directly in the contemplation of the person whilst he or she was alive, a degree of caution is appropriate where there is a risk of harm attaching to the chosen strategy. Moreover, we should have explicit evidence of the person's wish to become an organ donor after death, by way of inclusion on the National Health Service (NHS) Organ Donor Register or the signing of a donor card, or at least good evidence (e.g. from relatives) that this is what the deceased would have wanted. Where such evidence exists, there may even be good reason to allow measures to be taken to *increase* cardio-respiratory support where the person deteriorates prior to implementation of the planned withdrawal of life-sustaining treatment (assuming this cannot cause harm to the patient). Moreover, the same legal and ethical analysis applies to the use of specific interventions prior to death designed exclusively to optimise organ viability for transplantation. However, it is necessary in each case to additionally assess whether such measures present any risk of harm or distress to the individual (or others), or might themselves hasten the person's death.

There is a crucial need for a transparent national protocol here, agreed with professionals and representatives of patients and the public, and endorsed by relevant clinical ethics committees at local level. This should be widely published and publicised for the reassurance of the public, patients, relatives and transplant, intensive and emergency care staff.

---

[54] See Lord Browne-Wilkinson's comments in *Airedale NHS Trust* v. *Bland* [1993] AC 789, 883.

[55] *Re A (Medical Treatment: Male Sterilisation)* [2000] 1 FCR 193, 200. This even includes spiritual factors: see *Ahsan* v. *University Hospitals of Leicester NHS Trust* [2007] PIQR P19.

[56] Indeed, the Mental Capacity Act 2005 (section 4(6)) states that such factors must be taken into consideration. See also Department of Health, *Legal Issues Relevant to Non-heart-beating Organ Donation* (London: Department of Health, 2009).

[57] J. Coggon, M. Brazier, P. Murphy *et al.*, 'Best interests and potential organ donors', *British Medical Journal*, 336 (2008), 1346–7. See also General Medical Council, *Treatment and Care Towards the End of Life: Good Practice in Decision-Making* (2010), www.gmc-uk.org/End_of_life.pdf_32486688.pdf.

Living donor transplantation: the parameters of altruism

Living donor organ transplantation (LDT) has always been controversial. Even today there are detractors who maintain that living organ donation is an illegal practice which contravenes the moral and ethical proscription of non-maleficence, or *primum non nocere*.[58] Even living *related* organ donation has been described as an act of 'poaching' rather than a voluntary act of giving.[59] However, LDT has become 'mainstream' in the UK and now even extends to donation between strangers. This marks a distinct transition into a third policy era in the UK following periods of ambivalence and even outright hostility. But the very liberalisation of policy and practice in this sphere itself creates seeds of anxiety and a focus of critical attention. Amongst others, Ross describes herself as 'deeply disturbed by the trend' of extension and liberalisation,[60] one which has already occurred in the USA and is now happening in the UK and various other Western nations. This is an important moment in time to take ethical stock, and to provide a convincing refutation to the accusation that living individuals are being sacrificed in pursuit of a naked utilitarian ethic.

The contemporary era of LDT in the UK is one characterised by explicit endorsement and direct regulation. The 2004 and 2006 Acts are the first pieces of domestic legislation to directly address the legality of LDT.[61] The regime in the 2004 Act can be seen as supportive of LDT, providing oversight of *all* proposed donations and enhanced review of novel procedures.[62] Rather than mere grudging tolerance of it as a 'necessary evil', LDT is now one of the main planks of official transplant policy, supported by discrete funding for dedicated personnel at identified health-provider locations. The UK and many other European nations are actively promoting living organ donation to help boost transplant rates.[63] Moreover, the NHS now funds living non-renal (e.g. liver) donor

---

[58] M. Potts and D. Evans, 'Is solid organ donation by living donors ethical? The case of kidney donation' in W. Weimar, M. Bos and J. Busschbach (eds.), *Organ Transplantation: Ethical, Legal and Psychosocial Aspects* (Lengerich: Pabst Publishing, 2008), pp. 377–8.

[59] N. Scheper-Hughes, 'The tyranny of the gift: sacrificial violence in living donor transplants', *American Journal of Transplantation*, 7 (2007), 507–11, 510.

[60] L. Ross, 'All donations should not be treated equally: a response to Jeffrey Kahn's commentary', *Journal of Law, Medicine and Ethics*, 30 (2002), 448–51, 450.

[61] Whilst the Human Tissue (Scotland) Act 2006 does not contain provisions relating to licensing or the monitoring of living donor transplantation, the HTA carries out such functions on behalf of Scottish Ministers in respect of Scotland.

[62] Although both UK statutes start with a presumption of illegality, making it lawful only subject to the satisfaction of various conditions, this does not signal any negativity in terms of policy. It merely highlights the non-therapeutic character of the procedure for the donor.

[63] BBC News, 'Living organ donor drive launched', 30 May 2005, http://news.bbc.co.uk/2/ hi/health/4586565. Such European nations include Switzerland and the Netherlands. In

transplants and the legal framework and the system as a whole now cater for donations of kidneys between strangers (so-called 'non-directed' donation) and 'swaps' of kidneys between pairs or within groups ('paired' or 'pooled' donation).

What has happened to explain such a radical shift in UK policy? Is today's metamorphosis simply a pragmatic 'needs must' turnabout? There was certainly much hope and expectation during the late 1980s and early 1990s that deceased organ donation would expand to satisfy demand and that good HLA tissue matching and superior immunosuppression would equal or better the outcomes from living donors. But the volume of (heart-beating) deceased donors plateaued and fell during the 1990s and into the new millennium,[64] and outcomes from living donors persisted in showing benefits over deceased donation, even from non-genetically related living donors. This reality partly explains the fundamental general shift of attitude, coupled with an experience now stretching back a considerable length of time highlighting a general lack of major health risks to living renal donors. However we can, I think, additionally attribute these changes to the increasing deference afforded to individual (donor) autonomy, which has contributed to a growing latitude and clinician acceptance. In the light of the above and the shortage of deceased organs, there is presently, contrary to the views of Scheper-Hughes,[65] no ethical or legal reason for reigning back living donation in general to exceptional instances only, assuming the prospective donor is competent and has made a fully informed and voluntary decision.

Safety by procedure

Since the passing of the 2004 Act some degree of scrutiny is now applied – by the Human Tissue Authority (HTA) – to *all* potential living organ donor transplants. An independent assessor must interview the parties and report to the HTA in relation to certain matters. These matters relate to information, communication and inducements, which bear on the voluntariness and the extent to which the alleged consent was informed. This has been dubbed 'safety by procedure',[66] and is safety from an 'ethical', as well as clinical, perspective.

the USA, the number of living donors rose by ten per cent per annum between 1996 and 2001: see H. Nathan, S. Conrad, P. Held *et al.*, 'Organ donation in the United States', *American Journal of Transplantation*, 3 (2003), 29–40, 34.

[64] There was a 9 per cent reduction between 2001 and 2008; see Organ Donation Taskforce, *Organs for Transplants*, p. 21.

[65] Scheper-Hughes, 'The tyranny of the gift'.

[66] Coined by T. Gutmann and W. Land, 'Ethics in living donor organ transplantation', http://trans.klinikum.uni-muenchen.de/ethics.htm.

Living donation is justified principally by way of satisfaction of the autonomous wishes of the prospective donor in conjunction with the anticipated outcome and benefits for the recipient. Greater confidence in the former enhances the ethical legitimacy of the procedure. The engagement of an independent agency here is especially important as transplant clinicians are not necessarily best placed to ascertain or assess such matters. The regulations passed under the 2004 Act require that decisions be made by a panel of at least three HTA members in cases involving novel procedures (e.g. paired, pooled and non-directed donation) and vulnerable individuals (donations by children and adults who lack capacity).[67] Rigour is crucial here as any instances of duress or unwillingness reported later could have greatly deleterious consequences. Moreover, these safeguards will hasten public and clinician acceptance of innovative forms of donation – maybe even allowing for crossovers between the deceased and living donor pools – with the potential to have a real impact on donation rates.[68] There are now an increasing number of consensus documents around the world drawn up by expert groups laying down guidelines for the satisfactory performance of different forms of LDT and containing both baseline health requirements and procedures designed to ensure voluntary and informed consent of donors.[69] They frequently mandate psychological and psychosocial evaluation of donors to ensure both minimum psychological suitability and an absence of ambivalence or pressure to donate. The latter does not presently constitute a legal requirement in the UK, but should be instituted in problematic cases across the board. Whilst supposedly 'routine', even adult kidney donation can generate extreme stress and dissonance in certain situations, e.g. some sibling donations.[70] The relative 'ease' with which living donor rates can be expanded compared with deceased donor rates creates the danger that insufficient effort will be devoted to justifiable strategies to

---

[67] See Human Tissue Act 2004 (Persons who Lack Capacity to Consent and Transplants) Regulations 2006 (SI 2006 No. 1659), although organ donation by minors and adults lacking capacity is not in fact currently practised in the UK.

[68] Although currently ethically contentious, so-called *list exchange* donation is being trialled in the USA and is under review in the Netherlands; see D. Price, *Human Tissue in Transplantation and Research: a Model Legal and Ethical Donation Framework* (Cambridge University Press, 2009), Ch. 7.

[69] 'Consensus statement on the live organ donor', *Journal of the American Medical Association*, 284 (2000), 2919–26, 2922; 'The Ethics Statement of the Vancouver Forum on the live lung, liver, pancreas, and intestine donor', *Transplantation*, 81 (2006), 1386–7; M. Dew, C. Jacobs, S. Jowsey *et al.*, 'Guidelines for the psychosocial evaluation of living unrelated kidney donors in the United States', *American Journal of Transplantation*, 7 (2007), 1047–54.

[70] A. Crombie and P. Franklin, 'Family issues implicit in living donation', *Mortality*, 11 (2006), 196–210, 209.

increase the deceased donor pool, whether pragmatic, legal or ethical in character. There should be no easy *reliance* on living sources of solid organs nor a wilful blindness to the costs involved for living donors in terms of risks to health, livelihood and finances.

In regulatory terms, the UK has shifted from a position of *laissez-faire* clinical discretion, to grudging toleration, to overt and supportive enthusiasm, in half a century. This reflects both the critical need for organs and an uncertainty and ambivalence relating to living organ donation across the board. At the one extreme, living donation is seen merely as a matter of individual donor autonomy in conjunction with clinician willingness to operate (subject to an upper level of permissible risk), as typically seen across the USA, whereas others regard it as an infringement of the duty that a clinician owes to his or her 'patient', and an individual 'sacrifice' which should only be endorsed in exceptional cases.[71] The latter attitude is more prevalent in continental Europe. The cautious, incremental approach in the UK has now matured into a facilitative framework coupled with proper safeguards for donors. This should serve all parties well over the long-term provided there is no over-reliance upon this strategy. Whilst in the UK there is no explicit legal ceiling on the risks to which donors may expose themselves and the types of legitimate LDT, clinicians' sensitivity to the concept of *primum non nocere* and inherent conservatism linked to perceptions of their causal responsibility for outcomes, in addition to regulatory oversight, have proved effective against over-zealousness.[72] Non-renal, paired and non-directed, living donation are growing modestly and cautiously, for example. There are important messages here to be taken away, across the board. In the context of a protective legal framework and modest risks, respecting the autonomous wishes of prospective donors is not to be seen as sacrificing their interests for those of others, nor as adopting a utilitarian philosophy. In the light of this, there is no justification for arbitrary restrictions imposed by legislation upon specific types of donation, e.g. by strangers.[73]

Presumed consent

In the UK, an explicit permission is required for the removal and use of organs for transplantation after death, in the form of either an 'appropriate

---

[71] See generally Price, *Human Tissue for Transplantation and Research*, Ch. 7.
[72] See generally T. Wilkinson, 'Living donor organ transplantation' in R. Ashcroft, A. Dawson, H. Draper and J. McMillan (eds.), *Principles of Health Care Ethics*, 2nd edn (Chichester: John Wiley, 2007), pp. 482–8, p. 486.
[73] As for instance in Germany and Portugal.

consent' in England, Wales and Northern Ireland, or an 'authorisation' in Scotland. This deviates from the official position prior to 2006 when a lack of reason to believe that there was an objection (by the deceased or any surviving relative) would constitute the essential justification for organ donation. In fact, an explicit consent had always been sought in relation to organ transplantation in the UK despite the terms of the 1961 Act, although there was considerably more variability in relation to the retention and use of tissue removed at post-mortem examination for *research*, governed by the same law, which sparked the controversies (resulting from an absence of explicit consent) at the Bristol Royal Infirmary and the Alder Hey Children's Hospital, for example. Thus, whilst *theoretically* there was a prevailing presumed consent law in the UK in connection with organ transplantation, in practice there was none.

No easy correlation can be drawn between types of donation laws and outcomes (i.e. donors or organs per million population), and one cannot simply 'transplant' a solution to organ shortage from one geographical context to another. This notwithstanding, the available empirical evidence which does exist suggests that the existence of a presumed consent law has a generally beneficial and significant effect on organ donation rates, albeit that there may be alternative means of substantially boosting organ donor rates apart from changes to the law relating to donation and that other factors will undoubtedly affect outcomes.[74] Nonetheless, a systematic review conducted for the UK Organ Donation Taskforce (see below) only tentatively endorsed a direct causal association between laws and donation rates, by virtue of the difficulty in controlling for other variables. The most that could ever be established is a 'positive association' between organ donation rates and policies, taking other factors into account. Thus, the evidence suggests a good reason to *consider* the merits of such a change of policy in the UK, where deceased organ donation rates have been extremely modest for some considerable period. This was the extended remit for the Organ Donation Taskforce, which reported to the UK government on presumed consent, negatively for the present time, in the latter part of 2008.[75]

One major obfuscating feature of the notion of 'presumed consent' is its inherent terminological ambiguity and the opaque nature of its legal/ethical basis. There are a variety of justificatory bases for presumed consent with significantly varying credentials and characteristics. By virtue of

---

[74] A. Rithalia, C. McDaid, S. Suekarran *et al.*, 'Impact of presumed consent for organ donation on donation rates: a systematic review', *British Medical Journal*, 338 (2009), a3162–70.

[75] Organ Donation Taskforce, *The Potential Impact of an Opt Out System*.

this, opposing arguments often pass like ships in the night. The first concept is of presumed consent as an expressed 'decision' or choice; this is a *tacit* consent expressed by way of silence. It is not really accurate to dub such a consent 'presumed' at all. It is an actual, *factual* consent, i.e. a decision to donate.[76] Where the circumstances *do* suffice to allow decisions to be expressed in this way, such a scheme is immune from allegations that this is no consent at all or that it is not a 'gift', i.e. that in reality it is a 'taking' by the state. However, such a decision is rarely solicited directly by Western nations at present, and even where it is (e.g. in the Netherlands), silence is instead interpreted as a failure to 'opt in', rather than a failure to object.

A further type of presumed consent system assumes consent from silence in the requisite circumstances, albeit that no observable individual 'decision' or 'choice' can be witnessed. This is the one which best captures the true idea of a 'presumed' or 'imputed' consent, and is the notion to be found in operation in most jurisdictions where presumed consent is the official organ donation policy. However, the notion of a consent divorced from any form of factual consent lies at the heart of the accusations of many critics. For instance, McLachlan remarks:

There might be a good utilitarian case for having an opt-out rather than an opt-in system of organ donation. However, this would mean that there is a case for using our organs even in the absence of our consent. If consent matters in this area, then only the explicit consent of the people concerned can justify the using of their organs after their deaths. If consent does not matter and the use of their organs can be justified without it, then consent does not matter. We should not appeal to the bogus notion of presumed consent.[77]

He alludes to communitarian or utilitarian schemes whose rationale is the need of sufferers requiring organs and the moral obligation of individuals to make their body parts available to them, or perhaps distributive justice. Whilst often (inappropriately) dubbed 'presumed consent', these are centrally rooted in the assumption that a greater number of organs will become available for transplantation, rather than founded upon donor autonomy and consent. Such schemes are of course open to the compelling objection that no real consent has been obtained, for which reason I would dub them 'contracting-out' rather than (presumed) consent schemes. But McLachlan's assertions are too black and white, and ignore the distinctive rationale of many contemporary presumed consent

---

[76] A 'factual' consent refers either to a mental state of acquiescence or to the expression of such a mental state: see P. Westen, *The Logic of Consent* (Aldershot: Ashgate, 2004), p. vii.

[77] H. McLachlan, 'Presumed consent is no consent at all', www.bmj.com/cgi/eltters/336/7638/230#189028.

schemes, founded upon the wishes of the deceased person. In the USA, the Institute of Medicine Report recently observed that: 'Presumed-consent and routine-removal policies are commonly confused or deliberately conflated',[78] but stated that 'routine removal is broadly communitarian, whereas presumed consent – like expressed consent – is largely individualistic, even though it may include a role for the family'.[79] The German National Ethics Council recently opined in similar vein.[80]

The notion that the absence of an individual factual consent is the Achilles heel of presumed consent schemes is frequently based on analogies with the living, where only the explicit consent of the competent individual will typically suffice; *a fortiori* in the case of living organ donation.[81] However, we do not generally, prior to death, allow others to make decisions for competent individuals – assuming they are not minors – as is the case in relation to (explicit) consent to (deceased) organ donation. Although decisions may be made in the medical arena on behalf of individuals lacking decision-making capacity in their best interests, not only are dead people not analogous to living people lacking capacity, but the dead themselves have no physical welfare interests to protect. The only potentially relevant interests are those which may conceivably survive posthumously, i.e. the wishes of the (pre)deceased person. Thus, analogies with the living break down and the notion of 'explicit consent' must be viewed critically here.

It is the explicit consent of *relatives* in the overwhelming preponderance of cases which is determinative in practice in England, Wales and Northern Ireland, if not across the UK as a whole.[82] Whilst relatives typically endorse a positively expressed decision of the deceased to donate, by way of inclusion on the NHS Organ Donor Register or by signing a donor card, the positive or negative views of the deceased repeatedly operate only as a form of *evidence* as to what the deceased would have wanted, which the relatives will take into account in deciding whether to consent to donation or not. Further, in the majority of instances the deceased has made no decision either way prior to death. Thus, any 'decision' is that of the requisite relative(s) or no-one. Admittedly, relatives will sometimes be aware of the unrecorded wish of the deceased to donate organs, but it is nonetheless these 'wishes' which are then the

[78] Institute of Medicine, *Opportunities for Action*, p. 205.   [79] *Ibid.*, p. 206.

[80] German National Ethics Council Opinion, *Increasing the Number of Organ Donations: a Pressing Issue for Transplant Medicine in Germany* (Berlin: German National Ethics Council, 2007), p. 47.

[81] Organ Donation Taskforce, *The Potential Impact of an Opt Out System*, p. 11.

[82] In Scotland, the notion of an 'authorisation' was intended to reinforce still further the fact that it is the views of deceased individuals that are paramount.

crucial aspect, unless one argues that relatives have their *own* independent and autonomous powers of decision-making here. If it is the *decisions* of (pre)deceased persons which are properly the legal and moral driving force, then *all* systems dramatically fail to give effect to this imperative, including explicit consent schemes. Much of the debate surrounding presumed consent can be seen to reduce down to the proper and requisite decision-making roles of deceased persons and their relatives (we are only considering adults here, as parents of children lacking their own decision-making capacity are clearly the appropriate decision-makers in respect of their minor children).

Although the changes wrought by the 2004 Act may not have significantly altered the substantive position in the transplantation sphere, the Act was accompanied by a new emphasis upon the will of the deceased as the primary determinant of a valid donation. The Notes on the Act previously issued by the Human Tissue Authority (HTA), the new statutory regulatory body in this sphere, state that: 'The new Human Tissue Act makes the wishes of the deceased paramount . . . This new permission in the HT Act gives added weight to the wishes of the 13.4m people on the NHS Organ Donor Register, donor card carriers and others who have agreed to donate.'[83] This recent emphasis and policy orientation can also be seen – even more stridently and forcefully – in Scotland (intended to be encapsulated in the discrete notion of 'authorisation') and in various jurisdictions abroad, such as in the USA. The Institute of Medicine Report asserted in 2006 that:

These findings suggest that the US may be in the midst of a paradigm shift from relying on the next-of-kin to make donation decisions for deceased individuals to using donor consent documentation, whenever available, as the official mechanism of consent for organ donation.[84]

However, and unfortunately, most individuals have not explicitly stated their wishes prior to their death and the decision-making largely falls upon relatives in all these explicit consent jurisdictions. Of course, it would be entirely conceivable to construct an explicit consent policy relying exclusively upon the consent of the deceased person for organ donation. This is the stance of, for instance, the Scottish Council on Bioethics. However, such a policy would fail to do justice to the wishes of a very high percentage of the population (of willing donors) who have simply failed to record any decision prior to their deaths (and also inevitably lead to a much lower rate

---

[83] Human Tissue Authority, *Briefing Notes on the Human Tissue Act 2004* (30 August 2006).
[84] Institute of Medicine, *Opportunities for Action*, p. 175. First-person (donor) state registries are being swiftly established to facilitate this policy shift; see state list at www.unos.org.

of donation than even presently prevails). For that reason alone, 'explicit consent' systems have a secondary, 'default' strategy involving relatives incorporated into the applicable legislation.

If it is the wishes of the deceased that highlight the justification for donation, then systems should be compared on this basis. As English and Somerville observe:

> [T]he real choice for society is not between explicit consent and presumed consent. Rather, it is a choice between lack of objection of the relatives and the presumed consent of the individual ... we may ask which of these options is more likely to reflect the deceased's wishes.[85]

We should therefore enquire whether families are generally aware of the wishes of their deceased relatives, and whether their decisions are informed by such wishes where they are. There is presently reason to be dubious in both regards. The wishes of most deceased relatives are not known at death as far as we can ascertain, which ostensibly casts doubt on the rationale for family decision-making across the board, coupled with the fact that a very high percentage of relatives currently refuse permission to donate despite the fact that opinion polls show that the majority of individuals are willing to allow their organs to be used for transplantation after their deaths. The European Commission's recent Eurobarometer survey revealed that across the Member States as a whole only 41 per cent of individuals had even raised the subject of donation with their relatives (43 per cent in the UK).[86]

Thus, the role of relatives cannot be seen as a mere conduit for transmission of the deceased's wishes. Yet it is not clear from where alternative *personal* decision-making powers (ethically or legally) derive. It is sometimes retorted that where relatives know the deceased's wishes by virtue of their inclusion on the NHS Organ Donor Register they do consent to donation, but not only does this concede that in a significant percentage of instances (around 10 per cent, it seems) relatives make a decision that is against the deceased's positive wishes, it draws attention to the fact that only 28 per cent of the population have included their names on the Organ Donor Register.[87] Refusal rates are around 40 per cent in the UK at

---

[85] V. English and A. Sommerville, 'Presumed consent for transplantation: a dead issue after Alder Hey?', *Journal of Medical Ethics*, 29 (2003), 147–52, 149.

[86] *Special Eurobarometer Report* 272D, *Europeans and Organ Donation* (Brussels: European Commission, 2007), ec.europa.eu/public_opinion/archives/ebs/ebs_272d_en.pdf, at pp. 4–5. Figures, however, range from 75 per cent in the Netherlands to 24 per cent in Austria and 16 per cent in Romania. See also http://news.bbc.co.uk/1/health/4165656.stm.

[87] 16,973, 856 as at 9 March 2010: see www.organdonation.nhs.uk/ukt/default.jsp.

present.[88] Lack of knowledge of the deceased's wishes appears to be the primary reason for relatives' refusals. Moreover, because of the trauma which is visited on relatives at the time of such decision-making, very many refuse to consent no matter that the deceased might well have been a willing donor. As has been observed, relatives' decision-making involves a significant form of 'sacrifice'.[89]

Of course, the acceptability of a presumed consent scheme based on an imputed consent partially rests on the cogency of the evidence of the public's general willingness to donate their organs after death, as shown by opinion polls and other general information. However, it may be that it is the general lack of objection to donation which is the proper determinant of the acceptability of a deceased organ donation scheme where it serves a crucial public good. This may be considerably higher than the two-thirds or so of the public who generally say that they wish to donate their organs after death.[90] Moreover, presumed consent systems routinely have reliable means of recording objections to donation (through the use of registers), whereas many explicit consent schemes, including in the UK, do not. Perhaps then, so-called presumed consent schemes rooted in such a rationale are better, and more accurately, dubbed 'presumed non-objection' schemes. Such systems are sometimes condemned for side-lining the views of relatives. However, one can observe that this is not a reasonable criticism of a 'soft' presumed consent scheme where relatives are afforded the last word, i.e. a right of veto. This is the more typical legislative scheme and is operational in Belgium, Latvia and Sweden, and planned for Wales, for example. Not only is this the scheme advocated by the British Medical Association,[91] but the Taskforce considered that there might be potential human rights challenges to a 'hard' presumed consent law which did not cater for approaches to be made to relatives in order to at least ascertain if there was other compelling evidence as to the deceased's wishes.[92]

---

[88] The most recent Potential Donor Audit found a 'true' *relative* refusal rate of 36 per cent, excluding the 3 per cent of cases where the deceased person had informed the relative(s) of their wish not to be an organ donor: see Potential Donor Audit, 2006–8.

[89] M. Sque, S. Payne and J. Macleod Clark, 'Gift of life or sacrifice? Key discourses for understanding decision-making by families of organ donors' in M. Sque and S. Payne (eds.), *Organ and Tissue Donation: an Evidence Base for Practice* (Maidenhead: Open University Press, 2007), pp. 40–58, p. 40.

[90] Human Tissue Authority, *Stakeholder Evaluation*, General Public Qualitative & Quantitative Research (June 2007).

[91] See www.bma.org.uk/ethics/organ_transplantation_donation.

[92] Organ Donation Taskforce, *The Potential Impact of an Opt Out System*, p. 12; although this view has been contested by some commentators, e.g. J. Harris and A. Cronin, 'Authorisation, altruism and compulsion in the organ donation debate', *Journal of Medical Ethics* (in preparation).

Of course, the cogency of any evidence of the deceased's willingness to donate will depend upon the knowledge disseminated regarding the operation of the system, the choices available, and the ease with which objections may be physically recorded. If there is a deficiency in any of these respects then the accusation that the system is one based on a philosophy of communitarianism or utilitarianism, rather than autonomy, becomes distinctly plausible. This is a pragmatic rather than a conceptual question. Indeed, the absence of any mechanism for formally recording objections and the failure to properly communicate with relatives entirely undermines the assertion that the consent of either the deceased or the relatives was obtained for the retention and use of tissue taken post-mortem to be used thereafter for research, e.g. at Alder Hey Hospital and Bristol Royal Infirmary, as mentioned previously. There are echoes here of the practices relating to anatomical dissection carried out under the auspices of the Anatomy Act 1832. They lend credence to the perspective that the state has taken organs from the dead rather than such organs having been donated *to* the state, for the benefit of the sick and needy. These events have led to *conceptual* confusion, however, which has polarised opinion and hindered clear debate.[93] But if pervasive publicity and information were disseminated and an easy and secure opportunity to record one's wishes provided, then it might be considerably more ethically and legally plausible to rely on presumed consent.

For many though, presumed consent could only be an acceptable policy if a true 'decision' could be properly inferred from silence, i.e. a *tacit* consent. It is because a presumed consent is generally not a factual consent that explicit consent is often regarded as being a more satisfactory form of consent, even assuming that a presumed consent is perceived as any kind of consent at all. It may therefore be necessary, if one wishes to depart from a policy of explicit consent, to confront individuals directly with the decision prior to their deaths to enable a tacit consent to be solicited. This could be done by way of a posted letter requesting individuals to record their wishes regarding donation on a multifaceted register. But unless we *mandate* a response by accompanying the request with sanctions, there will be many who will fail to respond to such a request, and even where individuals are compelled to respond there is the likelihood that some will refuse to donate on account of being compelled to decide per se. We should balance the right of individuals to control the use of the parts of their bodies after death with the needs of end-stage organ

[93] R. Richardson, 'Human dissection and organ transplantation in historical context' in M. Sque and S. Payne (eds.), *Organ and Tissue Donation: an Evidence Base for Practice* (Maidenhead: Open University Press, 2007), pp. 4–20.

failure sufferers and their loved ones and carers. We can do so very properly by interpreting any (understandable) inertia as an absence of objection to the use of one's body for such ends after one's death.[94] The letter should contain an express statement that a failure to respond would be treated as a willingness to donate. Individuals would be able to change their minds at any time by an easy and secure method communicated to them.

Alongside the stance of the Organ Donation Taskforce in the UK, the Institute of Medicine in the USA also considered that presumed consent should not be introduced at the present time.[95] In the UK, there is considerable faith being placed in the systemic, resource and infrastructural reforms recommended in the first Taskforce report.[96] If implemented, there is no doubt that these reforms could have a considerable impact upon solid organ donation rates. This has been proved by what has become known as the Spanish Model of organ donation (and indeed also by the Organ Breakthrough Collaboratives in the USA),[97] which has not only yielded remarkable and sustained results in Spain but has been successfully exported to Tuscany in Italy and various South American nations.[98] But not only does the successful *transplantation* of such a model depend upon various prerequisites,[99] individual cultural and societal conditions may also play their part, including perhaps the character of the organ donation law in force. Further, an increased supply of organs may be necessary even in the event of such structural and resourcing issues proving effective. The notion of an 'either/or' approach to reform of organ donation processes and policies is spurious. These all require continuous review and evaluation.

The very ambiguity surrounding presumed consent is its own worst enemy. By virtue of this, were such a policy to be in contemplation, and in order to ensure an adequate future level of public acceptance, reliable and

---

[94] G. den Hartogh, *Farewell to Non-commitment: Decision Systems for Organ Donation from an Ethical Viewpoint* (Monitoring Report Ethics and Health, 2008) (The Hague: Centre for Ethics and Health, 2008) (www.ceg.nl), p. 12.

[95] Organ Donation Taskforce, *The Potential Impact of an Opt Out System*, p. 34. It recommended a review in five years' time. A Committee of Welsh Assembly Ministers also rejected presumed consent in 2008: see www.news.bbc.co.uk/1/hi/wales/7531859.stm. The government in the Netherlands also recently turned its face against presumed consent for the present. Contrast the view of the German National Ethics Council.

[96] M. Brazier and M. Quigley, 'Deceased organ donation: in praise of pragmatism', *Clinical Ethics*, 2 (2007), 164–5.

[97] See Chapter 13.

[98] R. Matesanz and B. Domínguez-Gil, 'Strategies to optimize deceased organ donation', *Transplantation Reviews*, 21 (2007), 177–88.

[99] *Ibid.* For instance, the Spanish Model employs physicians as transplant co-ordinators and has a high number of intensive care beds per million population.

pervasive information and education would constitute essential pre-requisites. False perceptions threaten to undermine the effectiveness of any such strategy. A failing of trust would prove counterproductive to relationships with health professionals as well as to organ donation rates. This was the UK Organ Donation Taskforce's primary and compelling concern. Of course if, during their lives, individuals came to routinely transmit their wishes via either a register or to relatives, there would be no need to consider presumed consent as a means of furthering donor autonomy. If donation rates were then still insufficient, there might be a need to examine communitarian options not founded upon autonomy or consent at all. However, whilst the number of those registered on the NHS Organ Donor Register has grown consistently and impressively over the last few years (and especially in Scotland), the onus of decision-making may arguably need to be shifted even more directly to deceased persons for the immediate future. Thus, although we can both hope for and anticipate that systemic improvements will bring about a marked increase in organ donation rates in the UK in the next few years, it may nonetheless be necessary to continue to appraise the merits of a presumed consent policy both in the UK and in very many other explicit consent jurisdictions, whether based on tacit or imputed consent.

Conclusion

The common thread in this final contribution to the book is the ethical limits of organ donation in the context of deceased and living donors, as well as in terms of consent and donation. All the strategies considered above have the potential to make a major contribution to substantially ameliorating the current organ shortage in countries such as the UK, but at the same time have an enormous capacity to cause significant harm to this same enterprise. To be acceptable such practices and policies must be defensible in terms of general ethical values and consistent with legal principles. The reality, or merely the perception, that individuals are being used purely as means to an end, or their interests sacrificed in favour of others, could have extremely damaging consequences. It is therefore crucial that full debate takes place across the community as a whole in these specific areas, so that society itself has ownership of such policies and a shared commitment to providing an adequate availability of organs for extremely needy individuals. These debates and messages are equally crucial for many other countries as they are for the UK.

Bibliography

Abadie, A. and Gay, S., 'The impact of presumed consent legislation on cadaveric organ donation: a cross-country study', *Journal of Health Economics*, 25 (2006), 599–620.

Abecassis, M., Adams, M., Adams, P., Arnold, R., Atkins, C., Barr, M., Bennett, W., Bia, M., Briscoe, D., Burdick, J., Corry, R., Davis, J., Delmonico, F., Gaston, R., Harmon, W., Jacobs, C., Kahn, J., Leichtman, A., Miller, C., Moss, D., Newmann, J., Rosen, L., Siminoff, L., Spital, A., Starnes, V., Thomas, C., Tyler, L., Williams, L., Wright, F., Youngner, S., Live Organ Donation Consensus Group, 'Consensus statement on the live organ donor', *Journal of the American Medical Association*, 284 (2000), 2919–26.

Academy of Medical Royal Colleges, *A Code of Practice for the Diagnosis and Confirmation of Death* (London: Academy of Medical Royal Colleges, 2008).

Alexandre, G., Squifflet, J., De Bruyere, M., Latinne, D., Moriau, M., Carlier, M., Pirson, Y., Lecomte, C., 'ABO-incompatible related and unrelated living donor renal allografts', *Transplantation Proceedings*, 18 (1986), 452–5.

Alkhawari, F., Stimson, G. and Warrens, A., 'Attitudes towards transplantation in UK Muslim Indo-Asians in West London', *American Journal of Transplantation*, 5 (2005), 1326–31.

American Medical Association, 'Consensus statement on the live organ donor', *Journal of the American Medical Association*, 284 (2000), 2919–26.

Angoitia Gorostiaga, V., 'El régimen reglamentario de la extracción y trasplante de órganos' in Romeo-Casabona, C., *El Nuevo Régimen Jurídico de Los Trasplantes de Órganos y Tejidos* (Granada: Comares, 2005), 137–244.

ANZDATA, *The 32nd Annual Report* (2009), www.anzdata.org.au.

Arnold, R. and Youngner, S., 'The dead donor rule: should we stretch it, bend it, or abandon it?', *Kennedy Institute of Ethics Journal*, 3 (1993), 263–78.

Arnold, R., Bartlett, S., Bernat, J., Colonna, J., Dafoe, D., Dubler, N., Gruber, S., Kahn, J., Luskin, R., Nathan, H., Orloff, S., Prottas, J., Shapiro, R., Ricordi, C., Youngner, S., Delmonico, F., 'Financial incentives for cadaveric organ donation: an ethical reappraisal', *Transplantation*, 73 (2002), 1361–7.

Audard, V., Matignon, M., Dahan, K., Lang, P., Grimbert, P., 'Renal transplantation from extended criteria cadaveric donors: problems and perspectives overview', *Transplant International*, 21 (2008), 11–17.

Bagheri, A., 'Compensated kidney donation: an ethical review of the Iranian Model', *Kennedy Institute of Ethics Journal*, 16 (2006), 269–82.

Baines, L., Joseph, J. and Jindal, R., 'A public forum to promote organ donation amongst Asians: the Scottish initiative', *Transplant International*, 15 (2002), 124–31.

Balpuri, S., Buckley, P., Snowdon, C., Mustafa, M., Sen, B., Griffiths, P., Hannon, M., Manas, D., Kirby, J., Talbot, D., 'The trouble with kidneys derived from the non heart-beating donor: a single centre 10 year experience', *Transplantation*, 69 (2000), 842–6.

Banner, N., Rose, M., Cummins, D., de Silva, M., Pottle, A., Lyster, H., Doyle, P., Carby, M., Khaghani, A., 'Management of an ABO-incompatible lung transplant', *American Journal of Transplantation*, 4 (2004), 1192–6.

Barber, K., Falvey, S., Hamilton, C., Collett, D., Rudge, C., 'Potential for organ donation in the United Kingdom: audit of intensive care records', *British Medical Journal*, 332 (2006), 1124–7.

Barlow, A., Metcalfe, M., Johari, Y., Elwell, R., Veitch, P., Nicholson, M., 'Case-matched comparison of long term results of non-heart beating and heart-beating donor renal transplants', *British Journal of Surgery*, 96 (2009), 685–91.

Bartucci, M. and Seller, M., 'Donor family responses to kidney recipient letters of thanks', *Transplantation Proceedings*, 18 (1986), 401–4.

BBC News, 'Racist organ donation condemned' (24 February 2000), http://news.bbc.co.uk.1.hi.health.652132.stm.

BBC News, 'GMC hears "organs for sale" case' (22 September 2000), http://news.bbc.co.uk/1/hi/health/937204.stm.

BBC News, 'Living organ donor drive launched' (30 May 2005), http://news.bbc.co.uk/2/hi/health/4586565.

BC Transplant, '33 years and still counting', *Transplant Times* (winter 2003), www.transplant.bc.ca/2003_times.htm.

Becker, E., *The Denial of Death* (London: The Free Press, 1973).

Becker, G. and Elías, J., 'Introducing incentives in the market for live and cadaveric organ donations', *Journal of Economic Perspectives*, 21 (2007), 3–24.

Bell, D., 'Non-heart-beating organ donation: old procurement strategy – new ethical problems', *Journal of Medical Ethics*, 29 (2003), 176–81.

Bellali, T. and Papadatou, D., 'Parental grief following the brain death of a child: does consent or refusal to organ donation affect their grief?', *Death Studies*, 30 (2006), 883–917.

Bellali, T. and Papadatou, D., 'The decision-making process of parents regarding organ donation of their brain dead child: a Greek study', *Social Science & Medicine*, 64 (2007), 439–450.

Ben-David, O., *Organ Donation and Transplantation: Body Organs as an Exchangeable Socio-Cultural Resource* (Westport: Praeger, 2005).

Berardinelli, L., Beretta, C., Raiteri, M., Carini, M., 'Early and long term results using older kidneys from cadaver and living donors', *Clinical Transplantation*, (2001), 157–66.

Bernat, J., 'The whole-brain concept of death remains optimum public policy', *Journal of Law, Medicine and Ethics*, 34 (2006), 35–43.

Bernat, J., Culver, C. and Gert, B., 'On the definition and criterion of death', *Annals of Internal Medicine*, 94 (1981), 389–94.

Bernat, J., Capron, A., Bleck, T., Blosser, S., Bratton, S., Childress, J., DeVita, M., Fulda, G., Gries, C., Mathur, M., Nakagawa, T., Rushton, C., Shemie, S., White, D., 'The circulatory-respiratory determination of death in organ donation', *Critical Care Medicine*, 38 (2010), 972–9.

Biotechnology and Biological Sciences Research Council, (BBSRC), *Research Grants: The Guide* (BBSRC Research Innovation and Skills Directorate, October 2009), www.bbsrc.ac.uk/funding/apply/grants_guide.pdf.

Boucek, M., Mashburn, C., Dunn, S., Frizell, R., Edwards, L., Pietra, B., Campbell, D., 'Pediatric heart transplantation after declaration of cardiocirculatory death', *New England Journal of Medicine*, 359 (2008), 709–14.

Boudville, N., Prasad, G., Knoll, G., Muirhead, N., Thiessen-Philbrook, H., Yang, R., Rosas-Arellano, M., Housawi, A., Garg, A., 'Meta-analysis: risk for hypertension in living kidney donors', *Annals of Internal Medicine*, 145 (2006), 185–96.

Bowlby, J., *Attachment and Loss* (Vol. 1: *Attachment*) (London: The Hogarth Press, 1969).

Bowlby, J., *Attachment and Loss* (Vol. 2: *Separation*) (London: The Hogarth Press, 1973).

Bowlby, J., *Attachment and Loss* (Vol. 3: *Loss: Sadness and Depression*) (London: The Hogarth Press, 1980).

Brazier, M., 'Retained organs: ethics and humanity', *Legal Studies*, 22 (2002), 550–69.

Brazier, M., 'Do no harm – do patients have responsibilities too?', *Cambridge Law Journal*, 65 (2006), 397–422.

Brazier, M., 'Human(s) (as) medicine(s)', in MacLean, S. (ed.), *First Do No Harm* (Aldershot: Ashgate, 2006), pp. 187–202.

Brazier, M., 'Exploitation and enrichment: the paradox of medical experimentation', *Journal of Medical Ethics*, 34 (2008), 180–5.

Brazier, M. and Quigley, M., 'Deceased organ donation: in praise of pragmatism', *Clinical Ethics*, 2 (2007), 164–5.

Brenner, B., Cooper, M., de Zeeuw, D., Keane, W., Mitch, W., Parving, H., Remuzzi, G., Snapinn, S., Zhang, Z., Shahinfar, S. (for the RENAAL Study Investigators), 'Effects of Losartan on renal and cardiovascular outcomes in patients with type 2 diabetes and nephropathy', *New England Journal of Medicine*, 345 (2001), 861–9.

Bristol Inquiry, *Learning from Bristol: the Report of the Public Inquiry into Children's Heart Surgery at the Bristol Royal Infirmary 1984–1995* (Command Paper: CM 5207, 2001) (www.bristol-inquiry.org.uk).

British Transplantation Society, *Guidelines Relating to Solid Organ Transplants from Non-heart Beating Donors*, www.bts.org.uk/transplantation/standards-and-guidelines.

Brown, the Rt Hon. Gordon (the former Prime Minister), 'Organs can help us make a difference', *Daily Telegraph*, 14 January 2008.

Browne, A., 'The Institute of Medicine on non-heart-beating organ transplantation', *Cambridge Quarterly of Healthcare Ethics*, 17 (2008), 75–86.

Buell, J., Beebe, T., Trofe, J., Gross, T., Alloway, R., Hanaway, M., Woodle, E., 'Donor transmitted malignancies', *Annals of Transplantation*, 9 (2004), 53–6.

Burden, A., McNally, P., Feehally, J., Walls, J., 'Increased incidence of end-stage renal failure secondary to diabetes mellitus in Asian ethnic groups in the United Kingdom', *Diabetic Medicine*, 9 (1992), 641–5.

Burroughs, T., Hong, B., Kappel, D. and Freedman, B., 'The stability of family decisions to consent or refuse organ donation: would you do it again?', *Psychosomatic Medicine*, 60 (1998), 156–62.

Callender, C., 'The results of transplantation in blacks: just the tip of the iceberg', *Transplantation Proceedings*, 21 (1989), 3407–10.

Canadian Organ Replacement Registry, *E-Statistics Report on Transplant, Wait List and Donor Statistics* (Canadian Institute for Health Information, 2008).

Canadian Organ Replacement Registry, *Organ Donor Activity in Canada, 1999–2008* (Canadian Institute for Health Information, 2009).

Canadian Organ Replacement Registry, *Treatment of End-Stage Organ Failure in Canada 1999–2008 – Report of the Canadian Organ Replacement Register 2010* (Canadian Institute for Health Information, 2010).

Chadwick, R., 'The market for bodily parts: Kant and duties to oneself', *Journal of Applied Philosophy*, 6 (1989), 129–39.

Childress, J., 'Ethics and the allocation of organs for transplantation', *Kennedy Institute of Ethics Journal*, 6 (1996), 397–401.

'The failure to give: reducing barriers to organ donation', *Kennedy Institute of Ethics Journal*, 11 (2001), 1–16.

'Putting patients first in organ allocation', *Cambridge Quarterly of Healthcare Ethics*, 10 (2001), 365–76.

Cinotti, G. and Zucchelli, P., 'Effect of Lisinopril on the progression of renal insufficiency in mild proteinuric non-diabetic nephropathies', *Nephrology Dialysis Transplantation*, 16 (2001), 961–6.

Clancy, M., 'Translating the success of organ breakthrough collaboratives from the USA to the UK', *British Journal of Transplantation*, 2 (2008), 3–7.

Clavien, P., Dutkowski, P. and Trotter, J., 'Requiem for a champion? Living donor liver transplantation', *Journal of Hepatology*, 51 (2009), 635–7.

Coggon, J., 'Best interests, public interest, and the power of the medical profession', *Health Care Analysis*, 16 (2008), 219–32.

'Doing what's best: organ donation and intensive care' in Danbury, C., Newdick, C., Waldmann, C. and Lawson, A. (eds.), *Law and Ethics in Intensive Care* (Oxford University Press, 2010) pp. 213–31.

Coggon, J., Brazier, M., Murphy, P., Price, D., Quigley, M., 'Best interests and potential organ donors', *British Medical Journal*, 336 (2008), 1346–7.

Cohen, L., 'Increasing the supply of transplant organs: the virtues of a futures market', *George Washington Law Review*, 58 (1989), 1–51.

'A futures market in cadaveric organs: would it work?', *Transplantation Proceedings*, 1 (1993), 60–1.

Collini, A., De Bartolomeis, C., Ruggieri, G., Barni, R., Berini, M., Carmellini, M., 'Long-term outcome of renal transplantation from marginal donors', *Transplantation Proceedings*, 38 (2006), 3398–9.

Commission of the European Communities (CEC), Commission staff working document: accompanying document to the Communication from the Commission to the European Parliament and the Council: organ donation and transplantation: policy actions at EU level: Summary of the Impact Assessment (SEC (2007) 705 Brussels, 30 May 2007).

1st National Expert Meeting on Organ Donation and Transplantation at Community Level: Summary Report (Brussels, 13 July 2007), http://ec.europa.eu/health/ph_threats/human_substance/events_organs.en.htm.

Proposal for a Directive of the European Parliament and of the Council on the application of patients' rights in cross-border healthcare (COM (2008) 414 final, 2 July 2008).

Action Plan on Organ Donation and Transplantation (2009–2015): Strengthened Cooperation between Member States (COM (2008) 819/3, Brussels, 8 December 2008).

Commission staff working document accompanying the proposal for a Directive of the European Parliament and of the Council on standards of quality and safety of human organs intended for transplantation and of the Commission action plan on organ donation and transplantation (2009–2015): Strengthened cooperation between Member States: Impact Assessment (SEC (2008) 2956 Brussels, 8 December 2008).

Proposal for a Directive of the European Parliament and of the Council on standards of quality and safety of human organs intended for transplantation (COM (2008) 818 final, Brussels, 8 December 2008).

Experts Meeting on Organ Donation and Transplantation Action Plan 11–12 March 2009: Summary Report, http://ec.europa.eu/health/ph_threats/human_substance/oc_organs/docs/ev_20090311_mi_en.pdf.

Constitutional Law Committee (Finland), Statement Nr. 24 (2010).

Council of Europe, *Meeting Organ Shortage: Current Status and Strategies for Improvement of Organ Donation. A European Consensus Document* (1998), www.coe.int/t/dg3/health/Source/organshortage_en.doc.

Transplant Newsletter: International Figures on Organ Donation and Transplantation – 2004, 10(1) (2005).

Transplant Newsletter: International Figures on Organ Donation and Transplantation – 2007, 13(1) (2008).

Transplant Newsletter: International Figures on Organ Donation and Transplantation – 2008, 14(1) (2009).

Transplant Newsletter: International Figures on Organ Donation and Transplantation – 2009, 15(1) (2010).

Crespi, G., 'Overcoming the legal obstacles to the creation of a futures market in bodily organs', *Ohio State Law Journal*, 55 (1994), 1–77.

Cribb, A., Wainwright, S., Williams, C., Farsides, B., Michael, M., 'Towards the applied: the construction of ethical positions in stem cell translational research', *Medicine, Health Care and Philosophy*, 11 (2008), 351–61.

Crombie, A. and Franklin, P., 'Family issues implicit in living donation', *Mortality*, 11 (2006), 196–210.

Cronin, A. and Price, D., 'Directed organ donation: is the donor the owner?', *Clinical Ethics*, 3 (2008), 127–31.

Daar, A., 'Rewarded gifting', *Transplantation Proceedings*, 24 (1992), 2207–11.

Daniels, N. and Sabin, J., *Setting Limits Fairly* (Oxford University Press, 2002).

Danish Council of Ethics, *Organ Donation – Ethical Deliberations and Recommendations* (2008), Chapter 4.2.2, www.etikoglivet.dk/sw310.asp.

Darr, A. and Randhawa, G., 'Public opinion and perception of organ donation and transplantation among Asian communities: an exploratory study in Luton, UK', *International Journal of Health Promotion and Education*, 37 (1999), 68–74.

Davis, C. and Randhawa, G., 'The influence of religion on organ donation among the Black Caribbean and Black African population – a pilot study in the UK', *Ethnicity & Disease*, 16 (2006), 281–5.

Delmonico, F., 'Exchanging kidneys – advances in living-donor transplantation', *New England Journal of Medicine*, 350 (2004), 1812–14.

Delmonico, F., Arnold, R., Scheper-Hughes, N., Siminoff, L., Kahn, J., Youngner, S., 'Ethical incentives – not payment – for organ donation', *New England Journal of Medicine*, 346 (2002), 2002–5.

Den Hartogh, G., *Farewell to Non-commitment: Decision Systems for Organ Donation from an Ethical Viewpoint* (Monitoring Report Ethics and Health, 2008) (The Hague: Centre for Ethics and Health, 2008), www.ceg.nl.

Department of Health, *An Investigation into Conditional Organ Donation* (London: Department of Health, 2000).

The Report of the Bristol Royal Infirmary Inquiry (London: Department of Health, 2001).

National Service Framework for Diabetes: Standards (London: Department of Health, 2002).

The Isaacs Report: the Investigation of Events that Followed the Death of Cyril Mark Isaacs (London: Department of Health, 2003).

Saving Lives, Valuing Donors: a Transplant Framework for England (London: Department of Health, 2003).

National Service Framework for Renal Services (London: Department of Health, 2004).

Saving Lives, Valuing Donors – a Transplant Framework for England: One Year On (London: Department of Health, 2004).

2006 Annual Report of the Chief Medical Officer: on the State of Public Health (London: Department of Health, 2007).

'Government announces appointment of new national clinical director for transplant' (3 April 2008), http://nds/coi.gov.uk/Content/Detail.asp?ReleaseID=364434&NewsAreaID=2.

Legal Issues Relevant to Non-heart-beating Organ Donation (London: Department of Health, 2009), www.dh.gov.uk/prod_consum_dh/groups/dh_digitalassets/documents/digitalasset/dh_109864.pdf.

Tackling Health Inequalities: 10 Years On (London: Department of Health, 2009).

Requested Allocation of a Deceased Donor Organ (March 2010), www.dh.gov.uk/prod_consum_dh/groups/dh_digitalassets/@dh/@en/@ps/documents/digitalasset/dh_114803.pdf.

Dew, M., Jacobs, C., Jowsey, S., Hanto, R., Miller, C., Delmonico, F., 'Guidelines for the psychosocial evaluation of living unrelated kidney donors in the United States', *American Journal of Transplantation*, 7 (2007), 1047–54.

Diabetes Prevention Program Research Group (DPPRG), 'Reduction in the incidence of type 2 diabetes with lifestyle intervention or Metformin', *New England Journal of Medicine*, 346 (2002), 393–403.

Diario médico (Spain), 30 July 2009.

Dicksen, D., 'Science and its public: the need for a "third way"', *Social Studies of Science*, 30 (2000), 917–23.

Doward, J. and Campbell, D., 'Transplant row over organs for drinkers' (*Observer*, 15 February 2009).

DuBois, J., 'Is organ procurement causing the death of patients?', *Issues in Law and Medicine*, 18 (2002), 21–41.

Ducharme, H., 'Thrift euthanasia in theory and practice' in Freeman, M. and Lewis, A. (eds.), *Law and Medicine: Current Legal Issues*, Vol. 3 (Oxford University Press, 2000), pp. 493–525.

Duxbury, N., 'Do markets degrade?', *Modern Law Review*, 59 (1996), 331–53.

Editorial, 'Liver transplantation from non-heart beating donors', *British Medical Journal*, 332 (2006), 376–7.

'Non-heart-beating organ donation – solution or a step too far?', *Anaesthesia*, 62 (2007), 431–3.

Ellershaw, J. and Wilkinson, S., *Care of the Dying: a Pathway to Excellence* (Oxford University Press, 2003).

Elliot, J., 'Brain death', *Trauma*, 5 (2003), 23–42.

English, V. and Sommerville, A., 'Presumed consent for transplantation: a dead issue after Alder Hey?', *Journal of Medical Ethics*, 29 (2003), 147–52.

Ennis, J., Kocherginsky, M., Schumm, L., Worcester, E., Coe, F., Josephson, M., 'Trends in kidney donation among kidney stone formers: a survey of US centres', *American Journal of Nephrology*, 30 (2009), 12–18.

Epstein, R., 'The human and economic dimensions of altruism: the case of organ transplantation', *Journal of Legal Studies*, 37 (2008), 459–501.

Erin, C. and Harris, J., 'A monopsonistic market – or how to buy and sell human organs, tissues and cells ethically' in Robinson, I. (eds.), *Life and Death under High Technology Medicine* (Manchester University Press in association with the Fullbright Commission, London, 1994), pp. 134–53.

'An ethical market in human organs', *Journal of Medical Ethics*, 29 (2003), 137–8.

'Janet Radcliffe Richards on our modest proposal', *Journal of Medical Ethics*, 29 (2003), 141–2.

Eurobarometer, *Europeans and Organ Donation* (Report: Special Eurobarometer 272D) (Brussels: European Commission, 2007), ec.europa.eu/public_opinion/archives/ebs/ebs_272d_en.pdf.

Europa, *Press Release: Questions & Answers: EU Directive on Organ Donation and Transplantation* (19 May 2010), http://europa.eu/rapid/pressReleasesAction.do?reference=MEMO/10/203&format=HTML&aged=0&language=EN&guiLanguage=en.

Evans, G. and Durant, J., 'The relationship between knowledge and attitudes in the public understanding of science in Britain', *Public Understanding of Science*, 4 (1995), 57–74.

Exley, C., Sim, J., Reid, N., Booth, L., Jackson, S., West, N., 'Attitudes and beliefs within the Sikh community regarding organ donation: a pilot study', *Social Science and Medicine*, 43 (1996), 23–8.

'The admission of Asian patients to intensive therapy units and its implications for kidney donation: a preliminary report from Coventry, UK', *Journal of Epidemiology and Community Health*, 50 (1996), 447–50.

Farrell, A., 'Is the gift still good? Examining the politics and regulation of blood safety in the European Union', *Medical Law Review*, 14 (2006), 155–79.

Transplantation and the Organ Deficit in the UK: Pragmatic Solutions to Ethical Controversy – ESRC Seminar Series Final Report (2008), available at www.esrcsocietytoday.ac.uk.

'The politics of risk and EU governance of human material', *Maastricht Journal of European and Comparative Law*, 16 (2009), 41–64.

'Adding value? EU governance of organ donation and transplantation', *European Journal of Health Law*, 17 (2010), 51–79.

Farsides, B., Alderson, P. and Williams, C., 'Aiming towards "moral equilibrium": health care professionals' views on working within the morally contested field of antenatal screening', *Journal of Medical Ethics*, 30 (2004), 505–9.

Featherstone, M., 'The body in consumer culture' in Featherstone, M., Hepworth, M. and Turner, B. (eds.), *The Body: Social Process and Cultural Theory* (London: Sage Publications, 1991), pp. 170–196.

Feest, T., Dunn, E. and Burton, C., 'Can intensive treatment alter the progress of established diabetic nephropathy to end-stage renal failure?', *QJM*, 92 (1999), 275–82.

Fehrman-Ekholm, I., Duner, F., Brink, B., Tyden, G., Elinder, C., 'No evidence of accelerated loss of kidney function in living kidney donors: results from a cross-sectional follow-up', *Transplantation*, 72 (2001), 444–9.

Fehrman-Ekholm, I., Gabel, H. and Magnusson, G., 'Reasons for not accepting living kidney donors', *Transplantation*, 10 (1996), 695–9.

Feinberg, J., *Harm to Others: the Moral Limits of the Criminal Law* (New York: Oxford University Press, 1984).

Filipponi, F., De Simone, P. and Mosca, F., 'Appraisal of the co-ordinator-based transplant organizational model', *Transplantation Proceedings*, 37 (2005), 2421–2.

Filipponi, F., De Simone, P. and Rossi, E., 'The Tuscany model of a regional transplantation service authority: Organizzazione Toscana Trapianti', *Transplantation Proceedings*, 39 (2007), 2953–60.

Folkman, S., 'Positive psychological states and coping with severe stress', *Social Science & Medicine*, 45 (1997), 1207–21.

Foltyn, J., 'Dead beauty: the preservation, memorialisation and destruction of beauty in death', in Howarth, G. and Jupp, P. (eds.), *Contemporary Issues in the Sociology of Death, Dying and Disposal* (London: Macmillan, 1995), pp. 72–83.

Fortin, M., Roigt, D. and Doucet, H., 'What should we do with patients who buy a kidney overseas?', *Journal of Clinical Ethics*, 18 (2007), 23–4.

Foss, A., Heldal, K., Scott, H., Foss, S., Leivestad, T., Jorgensen, P., Scholz, T., Midtvedt, K., 'Kidneys from deceased donors more than 75 years perform acceptably after transplantation', *Transplantation*, 87 (2009), 1437–41.

Freud, S., *Mourning and Melancholia* (London: The Hogarth Press, 1917).

Frutos, M., 'Percepción social de la donación' in Matesanz, R. (ed.), *El Modelo Español de Coordinación y Trasplantes*, 2nd edn (Madria: Aula Médica Ediciones, 2008), pp. 161–73.

Frutos, M., Blanca, M., Ruiz, P., Mansilla, J., Seller, G., 'Multifactorial snowball effect in the reduction of refusals for organ procurement', *Transplantation Proceedings*, 37 (2005), 3646–8.

Frutos, M., Ruiz, P., Requena, M., Daga, D., 'Family refusal in organ donation: analysis of three patterns', *Transplantation Proceedings*, 34 (2002), 2513–14.

Gardiner, D. and Riley, B., 'Non heart beating donation – solution or a step too far?', *Anaesthesia*, 62 (2007), 431–3.

Garg, A., Muirehead, N., Knoll, G., Yang, R., Prasad, G., Thiessen-Philbrook, H., Rosas-Arellano, M., Housawi, A., Boudville, N., 'Proteinuria and reduced kidney function in living kidney donors: a systematic review, meta-analysis and meta-regression', *Kidney International*, 70 (2006), 1801–10.

Garwood-Gowers, A., *Living Donor Organ Transplantation: Key Legal and Ethical Issues* (Aldershot: Ashgate, 1999).

Geddes, C., Rodger, R., Smith, C., Ganai, A., 'Kidney transplants: more of them, better allocated', *British Medical Journal*, 332 (2006), 1105–06.

General Medical Council, *Treatment and Care Towards the End of Life: Good Practice in Decision-Making* (2010), www.gmc-uk.org/End_of_life.pdf_32486688.pdf.

German National Ethics Council Opinion, *Increasing the Number of Organ Donations: a Pressing Issue for Transplant Medicine in Germany* (Berlin: German National Ethics Council, 2007).

Gervais, K., *Redefining Death* (Yale University Press, 1986).

Gevers, S., 'Editorial: a fair distribution of organs for transplantation purposes: looking to the past and the future', *European Journal of Health Law*, 14 (2007), 215–19.

Ghobrial, R., Freise, C., Trotter, J., Tong, L., Ojo, A., Fair, J., Fisher, R., Emond, J., Koffron, A., Pruett, T., Olthoff, K., A2ALL Study Group, 'Donor morbidity after living donation for liver transplantation', *Gastroenterology*, 135 (2008), 468–76.

Giessing, M., Slowinski, T., Deger, S., Tuerk, I., Schonberger, S., Budde, K., Loening, S., '20 year experience with elderly donors in living renal transplants', *Transplant Proceedings*, 35 (2003), 2855–7.

Giles, S., 'An antidote to the emerging two tier organ donation policy in Canada: the Public Cadaveric Organ Donation Program', *Journal of Medical Ethics*, 31 (2005), 188–91.

Gilks, W., Bradley, B., Gore, S., Klouda, P., 'Substantial benefits of tissue matching in renal transplantation', *Transplantation*, 43 (1987), 669–74.

Gilks, W., Gore, S. and Bradley, B., 'Predicting match grade and waiting time to kidney transplantation', *Transplantation*, 51 (1991), 618–24.

Gill, M. and Sade, R., 'Paying for kidneys: the case against prohibition', *Kennedy Institute of Ethics Journal*, 12 (2002), 17–45.

Gillon, R., 'On giving preference to prior volunteers when allocating organs for transplantation', *Journal of Medical Ethics*, 21 (1995), 199–204.

Gimbel, R., Strosberg, M., Lehrman, S., Gefenas, E., Taft, F., 'Presumed consent and other predictors of cadaveric organ donation in Europe', *Progress in Transplantation*, 13 (2003), 17–23.

Goldfarb, D., Martin, S., Braun, W., Schreiber, M., Mastroianni, B., Papajcik, D., Rolin, H., Flechner, S., Goormastic, M., Novick, A., 'Renal outcome 25 years after donor nephrectomy', *Journal of Urology*, 166 (2001), 2043–7.

Gómez, P. and De Santiago, C., 'La entrevista familiar. Técnica y resultados' in Matesanz, R. (ed.), *El Modelo Español de Coordinación y Trasplantes*, 2nd edn (Madrid: Aula Médica Ediciones, 2008), pp. 105–19.

Gómez, P., De Santiago, C., Getino, A., Moñino, A., Richart, M., Cabrero, J., 'La entrevista familiar: enseñanza de las técnicas de comunicación', *Nefrología*, vol. XXI, Supp. 4 (2001), 57–64.

Gore, S., Cable, D. and Holland, A., 'Organ donation from intensive care units in England and Wales: two year confidential audit of deaths in intensive care', *British Medical Journal*, 304 (1992), 349–55.

Gray, J., *Isaiah Berlin* (Princeton University Press, 1996).

Griffiths, J., Verble, M., Falvey, S., Bell, S., Logan, L., Morgan, K., Wellington, F., 'Culture change initiatives in the procurement of organs in the United Kingdom', *Transplantation Proceedings*, 41 (2009), 1459–62.

Gupta, A., Iveson, V., Varagunam, M., Bodger, S., Sinnott, P., Thuraisingham, R., 'Pre-transplant donor specific antibodies in cytotoxic negative crossmatch kidney transplants: are they relevant?', *Transplantation*, 85 (2008), 1081–2.

Gutmann, T. and Land, W., 'Ethics in living donor organ transplantation', http://trans.klinikum.uni-muenchen.de/ethics.htm.

Haddad, H., Isaac, D., Legare, J., Pflugfelder, P., Hendry, P., Chan, M., Cantin, B., Giannetti, N., Zieroth, S., White, M., Warnica, W., Doucette, K., Rao, V., Dipchand, A., Cantarovich, M., Kostuk, W., Cecere, R., Charbonneau, E., Ross, H., Poirier, N., 'Canadian Cardiovascular Society Consensus Conference update on cardiac transplantation 2008: Executive Summary', *Canadian Journal of Cardiology*, 25 (2009), 197–205.

Hanfling, O., *Life and Meaning: a Reader* (Oxford: Basil Blackwell, 1987).

Harris, J., 'The Marxist conception of violence', *Philosophy and Public Affairs*, 3 (1974), 192–220.

'The survival lottery', *Philosophy*, 50 (1975), 81–8.

The Value of Life (London: Routledge & Kegan Paul, 1985).

'Rights and reproductive choice' in Harris, J. and Holm, S. (eds.), *The Future of Human Reproduction: Choice and Regulation* (Oxford University Press, 1998), pp. 5–37.

'Law and regulation of retained organs: the ethical issues', *Legal Studies*, 22 (2002), 527–49.

'Organ procurement: dead interests, living needs: cadaver organs should be automatically available', *Journal of Medical Ethics*, 29 (2003), 130–4.

On Cloning (London: Routledge, 2004).

'Scientific research is a moral duty', *Journal of Medical Ethics*, 31 (2005), 242–8.

'Sex selection and regulated hatred', *Journal of Medical Ethics*, 31 (2005), 291–5.

Harris, J. and Holm, S., 'Should we presume moral turpitude in our children? Small children and consent to medical research', *Theoretical Medicine and Bioethics*, 24 (2003), 121–9.

Harris, M., 'The donor's tale', *Journal of Medical Ethics*, 34 (2008), 511–12.

Hayward, C. and Madill, A., 'The meanings of organ donation: Muslims of Pakistani origin and white English nationals living in North England', *Social Science and Medicine*, 57 (2003), 389–401.

Health Canada, *Canada's Healthcare System (Medicare)*, www.hc-sc.gc.ca/hcs-sss/medi-assur/index-eng.php.

Heller, R., *GM Nation? The Findings of the Public Debate* (London: Department of Trade and Industry, 2003).

Henderson, A., Landolt, M., McDonald, M., Barrable, W., Soos, J., Gourlay, W., Allison, C., Landsberg, D., 'The living anonymous kidney donor: lunatic or saint?', *American Journal of Transplantation*, 3 (2003), 203–13.

House of Lords, European Union Committee, *Increasing the Supply of Donor Organs within the European Union*, 17th Report of Session 2007–08, Volume 1: Report, HL Paper 123–I (London: The Stationery Office, 2008).

Hsu, C., McCulloch, C., Iribarren, C., Darbinian, J., Go, A., 'Body mass index and risk for end-stage renal disease', *Annals of Internal Medicine*, 144 (2006), 21–8.

Human Tissue Authority, *Briefing Notes on the Human Tissue Act 2004* (30 August 2006).

  Code of Practice: Donation of Organs, Tissue and Cells for Transplantation, Code 2 (2006).

  Stakeholder Evaluation, General Public Qualitative & Quantitative Research (June 2007).

  Written Evidence to the Select Committee on the European Union's Inquiry into the EU Commission's Communication on Organ Donation and Transplantation: Policy Options at EU Level (2007), www.hta.gov.uk.

Hume, D. and Merrill, J., 'Experiences with renal homotransplantation in the human: report of nine cases', *Journal of Clinical Investigation*, 34 (1955), 327–82.

Huxtable, R., 'Whatever you want? Beyond the patient in medical law', *Health Care Analysis*, 16 (2008), 288–301.

Iberoamerican Network/Council of Donation and Transplantation (RCIDT), *Trasplante Iberoamérica Newsletter* (2009), www.ont.es.

Institute for Healthcare Improvement, Improvement Report: *Organ Donation Breakthrough Collaborative* (2006), www.ihi.org.

Institute of Medicine, *Non-Heart-Beating Organ Transplantation: Medical and Ethical Issues in Procurement* (Washington, DC: National Academies Press, 1998).

  Non-Heart-Beating Organ Transplantation: Practice and Protocols (Washington, DC: National Academy Press, 2000).

  Organ Donation: Opportunities for Action (Washington, DC: National Academies Press, 2006).

Irwin, A., 'Beyond the toolkit: bringing engagement into practice' in Turney, J., *Engaging Science: Thoughts, Deeds, Analysis and Action* (London: Wellcome Trust, 2006), 50–5.

Iserson, K., *Death to Dust: What Happens to Dead Bodies?* (Tucson: Galen Press Ltd, 1994).

Jain, N., Farooqi, A. and Feehally, J., 'Raising awareness of chronic kidney disease among South Asians and primary care: the ABLE project', *Journal of Renal Care*, 34 (2008), 173–8.

Jarvis, R., 'Join the club: a modest proposal to increase availability of donor organs', *Journal of Medical Ethics*, 21 (1995), 199–204.

Jasper, J., Nickerson, C., Ubel, P., Asch, D., 'Altruism, incentives, and organ donation: attitudes of the transplant community', *Medical Care*, 42 (2004), 378–86.

Jeffrey, R., Woodrow, G., Mahler, J., Johnson, R., Newstead, C., 'Indo-Asian experience of renal transplantation in Yorkshire: results of a 10 year survey', *Transplantation*, 73 (2002), 1652–7.

Jimenez, M., 'A surgical marathon that spanned the country: unprecedented chain of kidney transplants traded vitally needed organs among three recipients in three different cities all at once', *The Globe and Mail*, Toronto, Canada, 25 June 2009.

Joffe, A., Anton, N. and deCaen, A., 'Survey of pediatricians' opinions on donation after cardiac death: are the donors dead?', *Pediatrics*, 122 (2008), 967–74.

Johnson, E., Remucal, M., Gillingham, K., Dahms, R., Najarian, J., Matas, A., 'Complications and risks of living donor nephrectomy', *Transplantation*, 64 (1997), 1124–8.

Johnson, M., Owen, D. and Blackburn, C., *Black and Minority Ethnic Groups in England: The Second Health and Lifestyles Survey* (London: Health Education Authority, 2000).

Johnson, R., Allen, J., Fuggle, S., Bradley, J., Rudge, C., 'Early experience of paired living kidney donation in the United Kingdom', *Transplantation*, 86 (2008), 1672–7.

Jones, M., 'Elective ventilation of potential organ donors: the legal background', *British Medical Journal*, 310 (1995), 714–18.

Karpinski, M., Knoll, G., Cohn, A., Yang, R., Garg, A., Storsley, L., 'The impact of accepting living kidney donors with mild hypertension or proteinuria on transplantation rates', *American Journal of Kidney Disease*, 47 (2006), 317–23.

Kasiske, B., Ma, J., Louis, T., Swan, S., 'Long-term effects of reduced renal mass in humans', *Kidney International*, 48 (1995), 814–19.

Kauffmann, H., Cherikh, W., McBride, M., Cheng, Y., Hanto, D., 'Deceased donors with a past history of malignancy: an organ procurement and transplantation network/united network for organ sharing update', *Transplantation*, 84 (2007), 272–4.

Kellehear, A., 'Dying as a social relationship: a sociological review of debates on the determination of death', *Social Science & Medicine*, 66 (2008), 1533–44.

Kennedy, I., Sells, R., Daar, A., Guttmann, R., Hoffenberg, R., Lock, M., Radcliffe-Richards, J., Tilney, N., 'The case for "presumed consent" in organ donation', *Lancet*, 351 (1998), 1650–2.

Kent, B., 'Protection behaviour: a phenomenon affecting organ and tissue donation in the 21st century?', *International Journal of Nursing Studies*, 41 (2004), 273–84.

Kesselring, A., Kainz, M. and Kiss, A., 'Traumatic memories of relatives regarding brain death, request for organ donation and interactions with professionals in the ICU', *American Journal of Transplantation*, 7 (2007), 211–17.

Khan, Z. and Randhawa, G., 'Informing the UK's South Asian communities on organ donation and transplantation', *European Dialysis and Transplant Nurses Journal*, 25 (1999), 12–14.

Klass, D., Silverman, P. and Nickman, S., *Continuing Bonds: New Understandings of Grief* (Bristol: Taylor & Francis, 1996).

Klassen, A., Hall, A., Saksvig, B., Curbow, B., Klassne, D., 'Relationship between patients' perceptions of disadvantage and discrimination and listing for kidney transplantation', *American Journal of Public Health*, 92 (2002), 811–17.

Koch, T., 'Normative and prescriptive criteria: the efficacy of organ transplantation allocation protocols', *Theoretical Medicine*, 17 (1996), 75–93.

Koenig, B., 'Dead donors and the "shortage" of human organs: are we missing the point?', *American Journal of Bioethics*, 3 (2003), 26–7.

Koffmann, G. and Gambaro, G., 'Renal transplantation from non-heart-beating donors: a review of the European experience', *Journal of Nephrology*, 16 (2003), 334–41.

Kokkinos, C., Antcliffe, D., Nanidis, T., Darzi, A., Tekkis, P., Papalois, V., 'Outcome of kidney transplantation from non heart-beating versus heart-beating cadaveric donors', *Transplantation*, 83 (2007), 1193–9.

Kondro, W., 'Fragmented organ donation programs hinder progress', *Canadian Medical Association Journal*, 175 (2006), 1043–5.

Kubler-Ross, E., *On Death and Dying* (New York: Macmillan, 1969).

Kuo, P., Lu, A. and Johnson, L., 'Expanded criteria donors/high risk recipients is not always cheaper than haemodialysis', *Transplantation*, 72 (2001), 554–5.

Kyriakides, G., Hadjigavriel, M., Hadjicostas, P., Nicolaides, A., Kyriakides, M., 'Public awareness and attitudes toward transplantation in Cyprus', *Transplantation Proceedings*, 25 (1993), 2279.

La Spina, F., Sedda, L., Pizzi, C., Verlato, R., Boselli, L., Candiani, A., Chiaranda, M., Frova, G., Gorgerino, F., Gravame, V., 'Donor families' attitudes toward organ donation: the North Italy transplant program', *Transplantation Proceedings*, 25 (1993), 1699–1701.

Lamb, D., *Death, Brain Death and Ethics* (London: Croom Helm, 1985).

Landry, D., 'Voluntary reciprocal altruism: a novel strategy to encourage deceased donation', *Kidney International*, 69 (2006), 957–9.

Langley, G., Moen, R., Nolan, K., Nolan, T., Norman, C., Provost, L. (eds.), *The Improvement Guide: A Practical Approach to Enhancing Organizational Performance* (New York: Jossey-Bass, 1996).

Lavee, J., Ashkenazi, T. and Steinberg, D., 'A new law for allocation of donor organs in Israel', *Lancet*, 375 (2010), 1131–3.

Lazarus, R. and Folkman, S., *Stress, Appraisal and Coping* (New York: Springer-Verlag, 1984).

Lederer, S., *Flesh and Blood: Organ Transplantation and Blood Transfusion in Twentieth-Century America* (Oxford University Press, 2008).

Lee, C., Scandling, J., Shen, G., Salvatierra, O., Dafoe, D., Alfrey, E., 'The kidneys that nobody wanted: support for the utilisation of expanded criteria donors', *Transplantation*, 62 (1996), 1832–41.

Lee, R. and Morgan, D. (eds.), *Death Rites: Law and Ethics at the End of Life* (London: Routledge, 1996).

Lewis, E., Hunsicker, L., Clarke, W., Berl, T., Pohl, M., Lewis, J., Ritz, E., Atkins, R., Rohde, R., Raz, I. (for the Collaborative Study Group), 'Renoprotective effect of the angiotensin-receptor antagonist irbesartan in patients with nephropathy due to type 2 diabetes', *New England Journal of Medicine*, 345 (2001), 851–60.

Li, S., Chan, C. and Lee, D., 'Helpfulness of nursing actions to suddenly bereaved family members in an accident and emergency setting in Hong Kong', *Journal of Advanced Nursing*, 40 (2002), 170–80.

Lightstone, L., *Preventing Kidney Disease: The Ethnic Challenge* (Peterborough: National Kidney Research Fund, 2001).

Lindsay, B., 'Translation of the Spanish model to Australia: pros and cons', *Nefrología*, vol. XXI, Supp. 4 (2001), 130–3.

Lo, C., Fan, S., Liu, C., Yong, B., Wong, Y., Ng, I., Wong, J., 'Safety and outcome of hepatitis B core antibody-positive donors in right-lobe living donor liver transplantation', *Liver Transplantation*, 9 (2003), 827–32.

Long, T. and Sque, M., 'An update on initiatives to increase organ donation: a UK perspective', *British Journal of Transplantation*, 2 (2007), 10–15.

Long, T., Sque, M. and Addington-Hall, J., 'Conflict rationalisation: how family members cope with a diagnosis of brain stem death', *Social Science & Medicine*, 67 (2008), 253–61.

'What does the diagnosis of brain death mean to families approached about organ donation: a review of the literature', *Progress in Transplantation*, 18 (2008), 118–25.

Long, T., Sque, M. and Payne, S., 'Information sharing: its impact on donor and nondonor families' experience in the hospital', *Progress in Transplantation*, 16 (2006), 144–9.

Machado, C., 'A definition of human death should not be related to organ transplants', *Journal of Medical Ethics*, 29 (2003), 201–2.

Machado, C. and Shewmon, D. (eds.), *Brain Death and Disorders of Consciousness* (New York: Kluwer Academic, 2004).

Maloney, G. and Walker, I., 'Talking about transplants: social representations and the dialectical, dilemmatic nature of organ donation and transplantation', *British Journal of Social Psychology*, 41 (2002), 299–320.

Manyalich, M., Paredes, D. and Vilardell, J., 'La donación de vivo para trasplantes' in Matesanz, R. (ed.), *El Modelo Español de Coordinación y Trasplantes*, 2nd edn (Madrid: Aula Médica Ediciones, 2008), 181–5.

Marco Molina, J., 'El régimen jurídico de la extracción y trasplante de órganos', *Diario la Ley*, 5 (2001), 1714–20.

Martin, S., 'Letter', *Canadian Medical Association Journal*, 176 (2007), 1128.

Martínez, J., López, J., Martín, A., Martín, M., Martín, J., 'Organ donation and family decision-making within the Spanish donation system', *Social Science & Medicine*, 53 (2001), 405–21.

Marx, K. *Critique of the Gotha Program* (Rockville: Wildside Press, 2008).

Mason, J. and Laurie, G., *Law and Medical Ethics*, 7th edn (Oxford University Press, 2005).

Matas, A., 'Design of a regulated system of compensation for living kidney donors', *Clinical Transplant*, 22 (2008), 378–84.

Matesanz, R., 'La insólita traslación del "modelo español" de donación de órganos al Reino Unido', *Nefrología*, 21 (2001), 99–103.

'Factors influencing the adaptation of the Spanish Model of organ donation', *Transplant International*, 16 (2003), 736–41.

'El modelo español de donación y trasplante de órganos: la ONT' in Matesanz, R. (ed.), *El Modelo Español de Coordinación y Trasplantes*, 2nd edn (Madrid: Aula Médica Ediciones, 2008), pp. 11–26.

'El diagnóstico de la muerte encefálica en Latinoamérica', *Medicina Intensiva*, 33 (2009), 423–4.

Matesanz, R. and Domínguez-Gil, B., 'Strategies to optimize deceased organ donation', *Transplantation Reviews*, 21 (2007), 177–88.

Matesanz, R., Domínguez-Gil, B., Martín Escobar, E., Mahillo, B., Carmona, M., Luengo, A., Álvarez, M., 'La traslación del modelo español a otros países. Cooperación internacional' in *El Modelo Español de Coordinación y Trasplantes* (Madrid: Aula Médica Ediciones, 2008), 271–308.

Matesanz, R. and Miranda, B., 'Organ donation – the role of the media and of public opinion', *Nephrology Dialysis Transplantation*, 11 (1996), 2127–8.

'A decade of continuous improvement in cadaveric organ donation: the Spanish model', *Journal of Nephrology*, 15 (2002), 22–8.

Mauss, M., *The Gift: The Form and Reason for Exchange in Archaic Societies* (London: Routledge, 1990).

McAlister, V. and Badovinac, K., 'Transplantation in Canada: report of the Canadian Organ Replacement Register', *Transplantation Proceedings*, 35 (2003), 2428–30.

McDermott, M., 'Obtaining consent for autopsy', *British Medical Journal*, 327 (2003), 804–6.

McGuinness, S. and Brazier, M., 'Respecting the living means respecting the dead too', *Oxford Journal of Legal Studies*, 28 (2008), 297–316.

McHale, J., 'Effective ventilation – pragmatic solution or ethical minefield', *Professional Negligence*, 11 (1995), 23–7.

McLachlan, H., 'Presumed consent is no consent at all', www.bmj.com/cgi/eltters/336/7638/230#189028.

McMahan, J., *The Ethics of Killing – Problems at the Margins of Life* (Oxford University Press, 2002).

Medical Research Council, *Applicant Handbook 2008–2009*, www.mrc.ac.uk/Utilities/Documentrecord/index/htm.

Menikoff, J., 'Doubts about death: the silence of the Institute of Medicine', *Journal of Law, Medicine and Ethics*, 26 (1998), 157–65.

'The importance of being dead: non-heart-beating organ donation', *Issues in Law and Medicine*, 18 (2002), 3–20.

Metzger, R., Delmonico, F., Feng, S., Port, F., Wynn, J., Merion, R., 'Expanded criteria donors for kidney transplantation', *American Journal of Transplantation*, 3 (Supp. 4) (2003), 114–25.

Mill, J., *On Liberty* (London: Penguin Books, 1985).

Ministry of Health and Consumer Affairs (Spain), Press Release: *Symposium: Trasplante renal de donante vivo: nuevos retos*, 23 June 2008.

Miranda, B., Cañón, J. and Cuende, N., 'The Spanish organizational structure for organ donation – up to date', *Chirurgische Gastroenterologie*, 18, 7–16.

Mittler, J., Pascher, A., Neuhaus, P., Pratschke, J., 'The utility of extended criteria donor organs in severely ill liver transplant recipients', *Transplantation*, 86 (2008), 895–6.

Mizraji, R., Alvarez, I., Palacios, R., Fajardo, C., Berrios, C., Morales, F., Luna, E., Milanés, C., Andrade, M., Duque, E., Giron, F., Alfonso J., Herra, S., Soratti, C., Ibar, R., Garcia, V., for the Punta Cana Group of Latin American Transplant Coordinators, 'Organ Donation in Latin America', *Transplantation Proceedings*, 39 (2007), 333–5.

Mizraji, R., Pérez, S. and Alvarez, I., 'Activity of transplant coordination in Uruguay', *Transplantation Proceedings*, 39 (2007), 339–40.

Moers, C., Leuvenink, H. and Ploeg, R., 'Non-heart-beating organ donation: overview and future perspectives', *Transplant International*, 20 (2007), 567–75.

Mollaret, P. and Goulon, M., 'Le coma depasse', *Revue Neurologique*, 101 (1959), 3–15.

Mongoven, A., 'Sharing our body and blood: organ donation and feminist critiques of sacrifice', *Journal of Medicine and Philosophy*, 28 (2003), 89–114.

Montgomery, R., Zachary, A., Ratner, L., Segev, D., Hiller, J., Cooper, M., Kavoussi, L., Jarrett, T., Burdick, J., Maley, W., Melancon, J., Kozlowski, T., Simpkins, C., Phillips, M., Desai, A., Collins, V., Reeb, B., Kraus, E., Rabb, H., Leffell, M., Warren, D., 'Clinical results from transplanting incompatible live kidney donor/recipient pairs using kidney paired donation', *Journal of the American Medical Association*, 294 (2005), 1691–3.

Morgan, M., Hooper, R., Mayblin, M., Jones, R., 'Attitudes to kidney donation and registering as a donor among ethnic groups in the UK', *Journal of Public Health*, 28 (2006), 226–34.

Mullen, M., Kohut, N., Sam, M., Blendis, L., Singer, P., 'Access to adult liver transplantation in Canada: a survey and ethical analysis', *Canadian Medical Assocation Journal*, 154 (1996), 337–42.

Munoz, S., 'Use of hepatitis B core antibody-positive donors for liver transplantation', *Liver Transplantation*, 8 (2002), S82–7.

Murphy, P., Manara, A., Bell, D., Smith, M., 'Controlled non-heart beating organ donation: neither the whole solution nor a step too far', *Anaesthesia*, 63 (2008), 526–30.

Murray, J., Merrill, J., Dammin, G., Dealy, J., Walter, C., Brooke, M., Wilson, R., 'Study on transplantation immunity after total body irradiation, clinical and experimental investigation', *Surgery*, 48 (1960), 272–84.

Najarian, J., Chavers, B., McHugh, L., Matas, A., 'Twenty years or more of follow-up of living kidney donors', *Lancet*, 340 (1992), 807–10.

Narkun-Burgess, D., Nolan, C., Norman, J., Page, W., Miller, P., Meyer, T., 'Forty-five year follow-up after uninephrectomy', *Kidney International*, 43 (1993), 1110–15.

Nathan, H., Conrad, S., Held, P., McCullough, K., Pietroski, R., Siminoff, L., Ojo, A., 'Organ donation in the United States', 3 (2003), *American Journal of Transplantation*, 29–40.

National Assembly for Wales, *Inquiry into Presumed Consent for Organ Donation* (Health, Wellbeing and Local Government Committee, July 2008), www.assemblywales.org/cr-ld7192-e.pdf.

National Healthcare Service (Spain), Circular 3/1997, issued by the *Dirección General de Atención Primariay Especializada*, 10 April 1997.

Navarro-Michel, M., 'Los derechos a la intimidad y propia imagen del menor de edad. Algunos supuestos conflictivos', *Revista de Derecho Privado*, 2 (2009), 47–74.

Nazroo, J., *The Health of Britain's Ethnic Minorities* (London: Policy Studies Institute, 1997).

Neades, B., 'Healthcare professionals' experiences in applying presumed consent legislation in organ donation in three European countries: a phenomenological study' in Weimar, W., Bos, M. and Busschbach, J., *Organ Transplantation: Ethical, Legal and Psychosocial Aspects* (Lengerich: Pabst Science Publishers, 2008), pp. 150–4.

Neipp, M., Jackobs, S., Jaeger, M., Schwarz, A., Lueck, R., Gwinner, W., Becker, T., Klempnauer, J., 'Living kidney donors >60 years of age: is it acceptable for the donor and the recipient?', *Transplant International*, 19 (2006), 213–7.

NHS Blood and Transplant, *Give and Let Live*, www.giveandletlive.co.uk/en.

NHS Blood and Transplant, *Transplant Activity in the UK 2006–2007* (2007), available at www.organdonation.nhs.uk.

NHS Blood and Transplant, *Transplant Activity in the UK 2008–2009* (2009), available at www.organdonation.nhs.uk.

Nowenstein, G., 'Organ procurement rates: does presumed consent legislation really make a difference?', *Law, Social Justice & Global Development Journal*, 1 (2004), 1–17.

Ojo, A., 'Expanded criteria donors: process and outcomes', *Seminars in Dialysis*, 18 (2005), 463–8.

Ojo, A., Luan, F., Sung, R., Merion, R., 'The use of expanded criteria donor organs for transplantation', *Transplantation Reviews*, 20 (2006), 41–8.

Organ Donation Taskforce, *Organs for Transplants: a Report from the Organ Donation Taskforce* (London: Department of Health, 2008).

Organs for Transplants – The Supplement Report (London: Department of Health, 2008).

The Potential Impact of an Opt Out System for Organ Donation in the UK: an Independent Report from the Organ Donation Taskforce (London: Department of Health, 2008), www.dh.gov.uk/en/Publicationsandstatistics.Publications/PublicationsPolicyAndGuidance.DH_090312.

Working Together to Save Lives – The Organ Donation Taskforce Implementation Programme Annual Report 2008/9 (London: Department of Health, 2009).

Organización Nacional de Trasplantes (ONT), *Consensus Document on Organ Retrieval after Cardiac Arrest* (1995).

Organ Shortage for Transplantation: Increasing Deceased Donation Activity Through the Spanish Model of Organization (18 June 2007), www.ont.es.

Memoria de Actividad de Donación (2008), www.ont.es.

Evolución de la Actividad de Donación y Trasplante en España (2010), www.ont.es.

Organizzazione Toscana Trapianti (OTT), *Attività* 2008, www.sanita.toscana.it.

Panorama (BBC), 'Transplants: are donors really dead?', BBC2, 13 October 1980.

Parker, F., Winslade, W. and Paine, C., 'Organ procurement and tax policy', *Houston Journal of Health Law & Policy*, 2 (2002), 173–85.

Pascual, J., Zamora, J. and Pirsch, J., 'A systematic review of kidney transplantation from expanded criteria donors', *American Journal of Kidney Disease*, 52 (2008), 553–8.

Payne, S., 'Contemporary views of bereavement and the experience of grief' in Sque, M. and Payne, S. (eds.), *Organ and Tissue Donation: an Evidence Base for Practice* (Maidenhead: Open University Press, 2007), 21–39.

Plamenatz, J., *Consent, Freedom and Political Obligation*, 2nd edn, (Oxford University Press, 1968).

Potts, M. and Evans, D., 'Does it matter that organ donors are not dead? Ethical and policy implications', *Journal of Medical Ethics*, 31 (2005), 406–9.

'Is solid organ donation by living donors ethical? The case of kidney donation' in Weimar, W., Bos, M. and Busschbach, J. (eds.), *Organ Transplantation: Ethical, Legal and Psychosocial Aspects* (Lengerich: Pabst Publishing, 2008), pp. 377–8.

Powers, M. and Faden, R., 'Inequalities in health, inequalities in health care: four generations of discussion about justice and cost-effectiveness analysis', *Kennedy Institute of Ethics Journal*, 10 (2000), 109–27.

President's Council on Bioethics, *Controversies in the Determination of Death* (Washington, DC, 2008), www.bioethics.gov.

Pretagostini, R., De Simona, P., Peritote, D., Cortesini, R., 'The organizational model of interregional transplant agency – Organizzazione Centro-Sud Trapianti', *Transplantation Proceedings*, 37 (2005), 2417–8.

Price, D., *Legal and Ethical Aspects of Organ Transplantation* (Cambridge University Press, 2000).

'The Human Tissue Act 2004', *Modern Law Review*, 68 (2005), 798–821.

Human Tissue in Transplantation and Research: a Model Legal and Ethical Donation Framework (Cambridge University Press, 2009).

Prottas, J., 'Encouraging altruism: public attitudes and the marketing of organ donation', *Milbank Quarterly*, 61 (1983), 278–306.

Punnett, A., McCarthy, L., Dirks, P., Hawkins, C., Bouffet, E., 'Patients with primary brain tumours as organ donors: case report and review of the literature', *Paediatric Blood Cancer*, 43 (2004), 73–7.

Quigley, M., 'Directed deceased organ donation: the problem with algorithmic ethics', www.ccels.cf.ac.uk/archives/issues/2008/quigley.pdf (2008).

Quigley, M., Brazier, M., Chadwick, R., Navarro-Michel, M., Paredes, D., 'The organs crisis and the Spanish model: theoretical versus pragmatic considerations', *Journal of Medical Ethics*, 34 (2008), 223–4.

Radcliffe-Richards, J., Daar, A., Guttmann, R., Kennedy, I., Lock, M., Sells, R., Tilney, N., 'The case for allowing kidney sales', *Lancet*, 351 (1998), 1950–2.

Radin, M., 'Market-inalienability', *Harvard Law Review*, 100 (1987), 1849–937.

Raleigh, V., 'Diabetes and hypertension in Britain's ethnic minorities: implications for the future of renal services', *British Medical Journal*, 314 (1997), 209–12.

Randhawa, G., 'Enhancing the health professional's role in requesting transplant organs', *British Journal of Nursing*, 6 (1997), 429–34.

'An exploratory study examining the influence of religion on attitudes towards organ donation among the Asian population in Luton, UK', *Nephrology Dialysis Transplantation*, 13 (1998), 1949–54.

'The impending kidney transplant crisis for the Asian population in the UK', *Public Health*, 112 (1998), 265–8.

'Increasing the donor supply from the UK's Asian population: the need for further research', *Transplantation Proceedings*, 32 (2000), 1561–2.

'Developing culturally competent renal services in the United Kingdom: tackling inequalities in health', *Transplantation Proceedings*, 35 (2003), 21–3.

Randhawa, G., Jetha, C., Gill, B., Paramasivan, S., Lightstone, E., Waqar, M., 'Understanding kidney disease and perceptions of kidney services among South Asians in West London: focus group study', *British Journal of Renal Medicine*, 15 (2010), 23–7.

Rapaport, F., 'Progress in organ procurement: the non-heart-beating cadaver donor and other issues in transplantation', *Transplantation Proceedings*, 23 (1991), 2699–701.

Raphael, B., *The Anatomy of Bereavement* (London: Routledge, 1985).

Redfern, M., *The Royal Liverpool Children's Inquiry Report* (London: The Stationery Office, 2001).

Reisaeter, A., 'Kidney transplantation in Norway – an historical perspective', *Tidskrift for den Norske lægeforening*, 119 (1999), 3163–6.

Rela, M. and Jassem, W., 'Transplantation from non-heart-beating donors', *Transplantation Proceedings*, 39 (2007), 726–7.

'Report of a National Conference on Donation after Cardiac Death', *American Journal of Transplantation*, 6 (2006), 281–91.

Resende, L., Guerra, J., Santana, A., Mil-Homens, C., Abreu, F., da Costa, A., 'Impact of donor age on renal allograft function and survival', *Transplantation Proceedings*, 41 (2009), 794–6.

Review by a Working Group convened by the Royal College of Physicians and endorsed by the Conference of Medical Royal Colleges and their Faculties, 'Criteria for the diagnosis of brain stem death', *Journal of the Royal College of Physicians of London*, 29 (1995), 381–2.

Richardson, R., *Death, Dissection and the Destitute*, 2nd edn (University of Chicago Press, 2000).

'Human dissection and organ transplantation in historical context' in Sque, M. and Payne, S. (eds.), *Organ and Tissue Donation: an Evidence Base for Practice* (Maidenhead: Open University Press, 2007), pp. 4–20.

Ridley, S., Bonner, S., Bray, K., Falvey, S., Mackay, J., Manara, A., 'Intensive Care Society's Working Group on Organ and Tissue Donation, UK guidance for non-heart-beating donation', *British Journal of Anaesthesia*, 95 (2005), 592–5.

Río-Gallegos, F., Escalante-Cobo, J., Núñez-Peña, J., Calvo-Manuel, E., 'Donación tras la muerte encefálica. Parada cardíaca en el mantenimiento del donante en muerte encefálica', *Medicina Intensiva*, 33 (2009), 327–35.

Rithalia, A., McDaid, C., Suekarran, S., Myers, L., Sowden, A., 'Impact of presumed consent for organ donation on donation rates: a systematic review', *British Medical Journal*, 338 (2009), a3162–70.

Robertson, J., 'The dead donor rule', *Hastings Center Report*, 29 (1999), 6–14.

Roderick, P., Raleigh, V., Hallam, L., Mallick, N., 'The need and demand for renal replacement therapy amongst ethnic minorities in England', *Journal of Epidemiology and Community Health*, 50 (1996), 334–9.

Rodríguez Lainz, J., 'Juzgado de guardia y trasplante de órganos', *Diario La Ley*, 6809 (2007), 1–20.

Romeo-Casabona, C., 'Los principios jurídicos aplicables a los trasplantes de órganos y tejidos' in Romeo-Casabona, C. (ed.), *El Nuevo Régimen Jurídico de Los Trasplantes de Órganos y Tejidos* (Granada: Comares, 2005), pp. 1–81.

Roscam Abbing, H., 'A Council of Europe Protocol on Transplantation of Organs and Tissue of Human Origin', *European Journal of Health Law*, 9 (2002), 63–76.

Ross, L., 'All donations should not be treated equally: a response to Jeffrey Kahn's commentary', *Journal of Law, Medicine and Ethics*, 30 (2002), 448–51.

Rothman, S. and Rothman, D., 'The hidden cost of organ sale', *American Journal of Transplantation*, 6 (2006), 1524–8.

Royal College of Surgeons of England, *The Report of the Working Party to Review Organ Transplantation* (Royal College of Surgeons, 1999).

Ruiz Jiménez, J. and Tejedor Muñoz, L., 'Notas sobre la responsabilidad en torno a las donaciones de órganos cuando el donante es un menor', *Revista Crítica Derecho Inmobiliario*, 705 (2008), 427–40.

Sanner, M., 'A comparison of public attitudes toward autopsy, organ donation and anatomic dissection', *Journal of the American Medical Association*, 271 (1994), 284–8.

'People's attitudes and reactions to organ donation', *Mortality*, 11 (2006), 133–50.

Sarnesto, S., Uusin tutkimus: suomalaisilla on myönteinen asenne elinluovutukseen (12 October 2006), www.musili.fi/fin/ajankohtaista/?nid=20&fs=m.

Sasso-Mendes, K., Curvo, P., Silveira, R., Galvao, C., 'Organ donation: acceptance and refusal among users of the public health system from Brasil', *Transplantation Proceedings*, 40 (2008), 660–2.

Satz, D., 'Why should some things not be for sale?' in Cullenberg, S. and Pattanaik, P. (eds.), *Globalization, Culture, and the Limits of the Market* (Oxford University Press, 2004), pp. 10–37.

Scandiatransplant, *Waiting List and Transplantation Figures According to European Standard* (2007), www.scandiatransplant.org/tx_newsletter2007.htm.

Diashow for Scandiatransplant (2008), www.scandiatransplant.org/aar08_04/dias2008.html.

Transplantation and Waiting List Figures Quarterly (2006–2009), www.scandiatransplant.org.

Schauenburg, H. and Hildebrandt, A., 'Public knowledge and attitudes on organ donation do not differ in Germany and Spain', *Transplantation Proceedings*, 38 (2006), 1218–20.

Scheper-Hughes, N., 'The tyranny of the gift: sacrificial violence in living donor transplants', *American Journal of Transplantation*, 7 (2007), 507–11.

Scheufele, D., 'Messages and heuristics: how audiences form attitudes about emerging technologies' in Turney, J. (ed.), *Engaging Science: Thoughts, Deeds, Analysis and Action* (London: Wellcome Trust, 2006), pp. 20–5.

Schicktanz, S. and Schweda, M., '"One man's trash is another man's treasure": exploring economic and moral subtexts of the "organ shortage" problem in public views on organ donation', *Journal of Medical Ethics*, 35 (2009), 473–6.

Schol, J., Srinivas, T., Sehgal, A., Meier-Kriesche, H., 'Half of kidney transplant candidates who are older than 60 years now placed on the waiting list will die before receiving a deceased-donor transplant', *Clinical Journal of the American Society of Nephrology*, 4 (2009), 1239–45.

Schweda, M. and Schicktanz, S., 'Public moralities concerning donation and disposition of organs: results from a cross-European study', *Cambridge Quarterly of Healthcare Ethics*, 17 (2008), 308–17.

'Public ideas and values concerning the commercialization of organ donation in four European countries', *Social Science & Medicine*, 68 (2009), 1129–36.

Scottish Transplant Group, *An Organ Donation Strategy for Scotland: Scottish Transplant Group Report* (June 2002), (www.sedh.scot.nhs.uk/publications/odss/odss.pdf).

Seale, C., 'Heroic death', *Sociology*, 29 (1995), 597–613.

Constructing Death: the Sociology of Dying and Bereavement (Cambridge University Press, 1998).

Sells, R., 'Voluntarism and coercion in living organ donation' in Collins, G., Dubernard, J., Land, W., Persijn, G. (eds.), *Procurement, Preservation and Allocation of Vascularized Organs* (Dordrecht: Kluwer Academic Publishers, 1997), pp. 295–300.

'What is transplantation law and whom does it serve?', *Transplantation Proceedings*, 35 (2003), 1191–4.

Shafer, T., Wagner, D., Chessare, J., Zampiello, F., McBride, V., Perdue, J., 'Increasing organ donation through system redesign', *Critical Care Nursing Quarterly*, 26 (2006), 33–48.

'Organ Donation Breakthrough Collaborative: increasing organ donation through system redesign', *Critical Care Nurse*, 26 (2006), 23–49.

Shafer, T., Wagner, D., Chessare, J., Schall, M., McBride, V., Zampiello, F., Perdue, J., O'Connor, K., Lin, M., Burdick, J., 'US Organ Donation Breakthrough Collaborative increases organ donation', *Critical Care Nursing Quarterly*, 31 (2008), 190–210.

Sharpe, L., *Strange Harvest: Organ Transplants, Denatured Bodies, and the Transformed Self* (Berkeley: University of California Press, 2006).

Shemie, S., Baker, A., Knoll, G., Wall, W., Rocker, G., Howes, D., Davidson, J., Pagliarello, J., Chambers-Evans, J., Cockfield, S., Farrell, C., Glannon, W., Gourlay, W., Grant, D., Langevin, S., Wheelock, B., Young, K., Dossetor, J., 'Donation after cardiocirculatory death in Canada', *Canadian Medical Association Journal*, 175 (2006), S1–24.

Shewmon, D., 'The brain and somatic integration: insights into the standard biological rationale for equating "brain death" with death', *Journal of Medicine and Philosophy*, 26 (2001), 457–78.

Shipman Inquiry, The (2005), www.the-shipman-inquiry.org.uk.

Siminoff, L. and Chillag, K., 'The fallacy of the "Gift of Life"', *The Hastings Center Report*, 29 (1999), 34–41.

Smith, M. and Murphy, P., 'The Ministerial Taskforce on Organ Donation', *Journal of the Intensive Care Society*, 9 (2008), 72–6.

Snoeijs, M., van Heurn, L., van Mook, W., Christiaans, M., van Hooff, J., 'Controlled donation after cardiac death: a European perspective', *Transplantation Reviews*, 21 (2007), 219–29.

Soukup, M., 'Organ donation from the family of a totally brain-dead donor: professional responsiveness', *Critical Care Nursing*, 13 (1991), 8–18.

Sque, M., *'A Story to Tell': Post Bereavement Correspondence between Organ Donor Families, Recipients, their OPOs and the National Donor Family Council – An American Investigation* (a report of a study funded by The General Nursing Council of England and Wales Trust) (University of Surrey, 2000).

Sque, M., Long, T. and Payne, S., *Organ and Tissue Donation: Exploring the Needs of Families* (final report of a three-year study commissioned by the British Organ Donor Society, funded by the Community Fund) (University of Southampton, 2003).

From Understanding to Implementation: Meeting the Needs of Families and Individuals Affected by Post-Mortem Organ Retention (final report of a study funded by the Department of Health and The Retained Organs Commission) (University of Southampton, 2004).

Sque, M., Long, T., Payne, S., Allardyce, D., *Exploring the end of life decision-making and hospital experiences of families who did not donate organs for transplant operations. Final Report for UK Transplant* (University of Southampton, 2006).

'Why relatives do not donate organs for transplants: "sacrifice" or "gift of life"?', *Journal of Advanced Nursing*, 61 (2008), 134–44.

Sque, M., Long, T., Payne, S., Roche, W., Speck, P., 'The UK post mortem organ retention crisis: a qualitative study of its impact on parents', *Journal of the Royal Society of Medicine*, 101 (2008), 71–7.

Sque, M. and Payne, S., 'Gift exchange theory: a critique in relation to organ transplantation', *Journal of Advanced Nursing*, 19 (1994), 45–51.

'Dissonant loss: the experience of donor relatives', *Social Science & Medicine*, 43 (1996), 1359–70.

Sque, M., Payne, S. and Macleod Clark, J., 'Gift of life or sacrifice? Key discourses to understanding organ donor families' decision-making', *Mortality*, 11 (2006), 117–32.

'Gift of life or sacrifice? Key discourses for understanding decision-making by families of organ donors' in Sque, M. and Payne, S. (eds.), *Organ and Tissue Donation: an Evidence Base for Practice* (Maidenhead: Open University Press, 2007), pp. 40–58.

Sque, M., Payne, S. and Vlachonikolis, I., 'Cadaveric donor transplantation: nurses' attitudes, knowledge and behaviour', *Social Science & Medicine*, 50 (2000), 541–52.

Starzl, T., Marchioro, T., Holmes, J., Hermann, G., Brittain, R., Stonington, O., Talmage, D., Waddell, W., 'Renal homografts in patients with major donor-recipient blood group incompatibilities', *Surgery*, 55 (1964), 195–200.

Stein, R., 'States revising organ-donation law: critics fear measure may not go far enough to protect donors', *Washington Post*, 4 April 2007, A01.

Steinbrook, R., 'Organ donation after cardiac death', *Journal of the American Medical Association*, 357 (2007), 209–13.

Stewart, J., 'First Canadian live-donor lung transplants performed in Winnipeg', *Canadian Medical Association Journal*, 162 (2000), 1339.

Stroebe, M. and Schut, H., 'The dual process model of coping with bereavement: rationale and description', *Death Studies*, 23 (1999), 197–224.

'To continue or relinquish bonds: a review of consequences for the bereaved', *Death Studies*, 29 (2005), 477–94.

Tanabe, K., Takahashi, K., Sonda, K., Tokumoto, T., Ishikawa, N., Kawai, T., Fuchinoue, S., Oshima, T., Yagisawa, T., Nakazawa, H., Goya, N., Koga, S., Kawaguchi, H., Ito, K., Toma, H., Agishi, T., Ota, K., 'Long-term results of ABO-incompatible living kidney transplantation: a single-center experience', *Transplantation*, 65 (1998), 224–8.

Tanabe, K., Tokumoto, T., Ishida, H., Ishikawa, N., Miyamoto, N., Kondo, T., Shimmura, H., Setogucji, K., Toma, H., 'Excellent outcome of ABO-incompatible living kidney transplantation under pretransplantation immunosuppression with tacrolimus, mycophenolate mofetil, and steroid', *Transplantation Proceedings*, 36 (2004), 2175–7.

Tavakol, M., Vincenti, F., Assadi, H., Frederick, M., Tomlanovich, S., Roberts, J., Posselt, A., 'Long-term renal function and cardiovascular disease in obese kidney donors', *Clinical Journal of the American Society of Nephrology*, 4 (2009), 1230–8.

Taylor, J., *Stakes and Kidneys: why Markets in Human Body Parts are Morally Imperative* (Burlington: Ashgate Press, 2005).

Terés, J., 'Transplantament hepàtic de donant viu a l'adult. Elements per una anàlisi ètica', *Annals de Medicina*, 87 (2004), 1–10.

Textor, S., Taler, S., Driscoll, N., Larson, T., Gloor, J., Griffin, M., Cosio, F., Schwab, T., Prieto, M., Nyberg, S., Ishitani, M., Stegall, M., 'Blood pressure and renal function after kidney donation from hypertensive living donors', *Transplantation*, 78 (2004), 276–82.

Textor, S., Taler, S., Larson, T., Prieto, M., Griffin, M., Gloor, J., Nyberg, S., Velosa, J., Schwab, T., Stegall, M., 'Blood pressure evaluation among older living kidney donors', *Journal of the American Society of Nephrology*, 14 (2003), 2159–67.

The Concise Oxford Dictionary, 10th edn (Oxford University Press, 2001).

The Gallup Organization, *2005 National Survey of Organ and Tissue Donation Attitudes and Behavior*, www.organdonor.gov.

The Retained Organs Commission, *External Review of Birmingham Children's Hospital NHS Trust: Report on Organ Retention* (London: Department of Health, 2002).

Investigation into Organ Retention at Central Manchester and Manchester Children's University Hospitals (London: Department of Health, 2002).

Titmuss, R., *The Gift Relationship: from Human Blood to Social Policy* (London: Allen & Unwin, 1970).

Tomlinson, T., 'The irreversibility of death: reply to Cole', *Kennedy Institute of Ethics Journal*, 3 (1993), 157–65.

Tonelli, M., Klarenbach, S., Manns, B., Culleton, B., Hemmelgarn, B., Bertazzon, S., Wiebe, N., Gill, J., for the Alberta Kidney Disease Network, 'Residence location and likelihood of kidney transplantation', *Canadian Medical Assocation Journal*, 175 (2006), 478–82.

Tong, A., Howard, K., Jan, S., Cass, A., Rose, J., Chadban, S., Allen, R., Craig, J., 'Community preferences for allocation of solid organs for transplantation: a systematic review', *Transplantation*, 89 (2010), 796–805.

Truog, R., 'The ethics of organ donation by living donors', *New England Journal of Medicine*, 353 (2005), 444–6.

Truog, R. and Miller, F., 'The dead donor rule and organ transplantation', *New England Journal of Medicine*, 359 (2008), 674–5.

Tuomilehto, J., Lindstrom, J., Eriksson, J., Valle, T., Hamalainen, H., Ilanne-Parikka, P., Keinanen-Kiukaanniemi, S., Laakso, M., Louheranta, A., Rastas, M., Salminen, V., Aunola, S., Cepaitis, Z., Moltchanov, V., Hakumaki, M., Mannelin, M., Martikkala, V., Sundvall, J., Uusitupa, M. and Group, for the Finnish Diabetes Prevention Study Group, 'Prevention of type 2 diabetes mellitus by changes in lifestyle among subjects with impaired glucose tolerance', *New England Journal of Medicine*, 344 (2001), 1343–50.

Ubel, P., 'How stable are people's preferences for giving priority to severely ill patients?', *Social Science & Medicine*, 49 (1999), 895–903.

Ubel, P. and Loewenstein, G., 'Distributing scarce livers: the moral reasoning of the general public', *Social Science & Medicine*, 42 (1996), 1049–55.

UK Prospective Diabetes Study (UKPDS) Group, 'Intensive blood-glucose control with sulphonylureas or insulin compared with conventional treatment and risk of complications in patients with type 2 diabetes (UKPDS 33)', *Lancet*, 352 (1998), 837–53.

UK Registry of Antibody Incompatible Renal Transplantation (2001–2009).

UK Transplant, Guidelines 3.2, *Donor Organ Sharing Scheme: Operating Principles for Cardiothoracic Transplant Units in the UK and the Republic of Ireland*, www. organdonation.nhs.uk.

Potential Donor Audit: Summary Report for the 24 month period 1 April 2006 – 31 March 2008 (2008).

Potential Donor Audit: 36-Month Summary Report 1 April 2003 – 31 March 2006 (2008).

United Network for Organ Sharing (UNOS), *Policy 6.0, Transplantation of Non-Resident Aliens* (2005).

Position Statement: Intended Recipient Donations, Paired Donations and NOTA 301 (2005), www.unos.org/publications.

Resource Document for Informed Consent of Living Donors (18 September 2007), www.unos.org.

United States Attorney General's Office, *Memorandum for General Counsel, Department of Health and Human Services: Legality of Alternative Organ Donation Practices Under 42 USC § 274e* (28 March 2007).

United States Renal Data System, '2006 Annual Data Report', *American Journal of Kidney Disease*, 114 (2007), 2806–2814.

van Dijk, G., Hilhorst, M., *Financial Incentives for Organ Donation: an Investigation of the Ethical Issues* (Ethics and Health Monitoring Report 2007/3) (The

Hague: Centre for Ethics and Health, 2007) (www.ceg.nl/data/download/
Orgaandonatie_huisstijl_eng_def.pdf).

Vancouver Forum, 'The Ethics Statement of the Vancouver Forum on the live
long, liver, pancreas, and intestine donor', *Transplantation*, 81 (2006),
1386–7.

Veatch, R., *Death, Dying and the Biological Revolution – Our Last Quest for
Responsibility* (Yale University Press, 1976).

Transplantation Ethics (Washington, DC: Georgetown University Press, 2000).

'Why liberals should accept financial incentives for organ procurement',
Kennedy Institute of Ethics Journal, 13 (2003), 19–36.

'Donating hearts after cardiac death – reversing the irreversible', *New England
Journal of Medicine*, 359 (2008), 672–3.

Volk, M., Lok, A., Pelletier, S., Ubel, P., Hayward, R., 'Impact of the model for
end-stage liver disease allocation policy on the use of high-risk organs for liver
transplantation', *Gastroenterology*, 135 (2008), 1568–74.

Waite, S. and Nolte, E., 'Public involvement policies in health: exploring their
conceptual basis', *Health Economics, Policy and Law*, 1 (2006), 149–62.

Walter, T., *The Revival of Death* (London: Routledge, 1994).

'A new model of grief: bereavement and biography', *Mortality*, 1 (1996), 1–29.

Waterman, A., Schenk, E., Barrett, A., Waterman, B., Rodrigue, J., Woodle, E.,
Shenoy, S., Jendrisak, M., Schnitzler, M., 'Incompatible kidney donor candidates' willingness to participate in donor-exchange and non-directed donation', *American Journal of Transplantation*, 6 (2006), 1631–8.

Wellcome Trust, *Public Perspectives on Human Cloning* (London: Wellcome Trust,
1998).

Wertheimer, A., *Coercion* (Princeton University Press, 1987).

Exploitation (Princeton University Press, 1999).

West, S., Pollock-Barziv, A., Dipchand A., Lee, K., Cardella, C., Benson, L.,
Rebeyka, I., Coles, J., 'ABO incompatible heart transplantation in infants',
New England Journal of Medicine, 344 (2001), 793–800.

Westen, P., *The Logic of Consent* (Aldershot: Ashgate, 2004).

Wilkinson, S., *Bodies for Sale: Ethics and Exploitation in the Human Body Trade*
(London: Routledge, 2003).

Wilkinson, T., 'Living donor organ transplantation' in Ashcroft, R., Dawson, A.,
Draper, H. and McMillan, J. (eds.), *Principles of Health Care Ethics*, 2nd edn
(Chichester: John Wiley, 2007), pp. 482–8.

Williams, C., Alderson, P. and Farsides, B., 'Dilemmas encountered by health
care practitioners offering nuchal translucency screening: a qualitative case
study', *Prenatal Diagnosis*, 22 (2002), 216–20.

Wilsden, J. and Willis, R., *See-Through Science: Why Public Engagement Needs to
Move Upstream* (London: Demos, 2004).

Worden, J., *Grief Counselling and Grief Therapy: a Handbook for the Mental Health
Practitioner*, 3rd edn (New York: Springer Publishing, 2002).

Worthington, J., McEwen, A., McWilliam, L., Picton, M., Martin, S.,
'Association between C4d staining in renal transplant biopsies, production
of donor-specific HLA antibodies, and graft outcome', *Transplantation*, 83
(2007), 398–403.

Wright, B., *Sudden Death: a Research Base for Practice*, 2nd edn (New York: Churchill Livingstone, 1996).

Wright, L., Faith, K., Richardson, R., Grant, D., 'Ethical guidelines for the evaluation of living organ donors', *Canadian Journal of Surgery*, 47 (2004), 408–14.

Yates, D., Ellison, G. and McGuiness, S., 'Care of the suddenly bereaved', *British Medical Journal*, 301 (1990), 29–31.

Young, A., Storsley, L., Garg, A., Treleaven, D., Nquan, C., Cuerden, M., Karpinski, M., 'Health outcomes for living kidney donors with isolated medical abnormalities: a systematic review', *American Journal of Transplantation*, 8 (2008), 1878–90.

Youngner, S., Arnold, R. and De Vita, M., 'When is "dead"?', *Hastings Center Report*, 29 (1999), 14–21.

Youngner, S., Arnold, R. and Shapiro, R. (eds.), *The Definition of Death: Contemporary Controversies* (Baltimore: Johns Hopkins University Press, 1999).

Zaltzman, Z., 'Kidney transplantation in Canada: unequal access', *Canadian Medical Association Journal*, 175 (2006), 489–90.

Websites

Canada

BC Transplant – www.transplant.bc.ca
Canadian Council for Donation and Transplantation – www.ccdt.ca/collaborative/index.html
Quebec Transplant – www.quebec-transplant.qc.ca
Trillium Gift of Life – www.giftoflife.on.ca

Nordic countries

Scandiatransplant – www.scandiatransplant.org

United Kingdom

Give and Let Live – www.giveandletlive.co.uk
How to Become a Donor – www.uktransplant.org.uk
National Institute for Health and Clinical Excellence (NICE) – www.nice.org.uk
NHS Blood and Transplant – www.nhsbt.nhs.uk
NHS Blood and Transplant (NHSBT), Organ Donation and Transplantation Directorate – www.organdonation.nhs.uk
Organ and Tissue Donation: Your Questions Answered – www.uktransplant.org.uk

Personal Social Health and Economic Education Association – www.pshe-association.org.uk
Your health, your choices – www.nhs.uk

United States

Uniform Law Commission – www.nccusl.org
United Network of Organ Sharing (UNOS) – www.unos.org

Index